SUSTAINABLE LONDON?

The future of a global city

Edited by Rob Imrie and Loretta Lees

First published in Great Britain in 2014 by

Policy Press
University of Bristol
6th Floor
Howard House
Queen's Avenue
Clifton
Bristol BS8 1SD
UK
t: +44 (0)117 331 5020
pp-info@bristol.ac.uk
www.policypress.co.uk

North America office:
Policy Press
c/o The University of Chicago Press
1427 East 60th Street
Chicago, IL 60637, USA
t: +1 773 702 7700
f: +1 773 702 9756
sales@press.uchicago.edu
www.press.uchicago.edu

British Library Cataloguing in Publication Data
A catalogue record for this book is available from the British Library.

Library of Congress Cataloging-in-Publication Data
A catalog record for this book has been requested.

ISBN: 978 1 44731 059 4 hardcover
ISBN: 978 1 44731 060 0 paperback

The rights of Rob Imrie and Loretta Lees to be identified as editors of this work has been asserted by them in accordance with the Copyright, Designs and Patents Act 1988.

Cover design by Qube, Bristol.
Front cover: image kindly supplied by Rob Imrie.
Printed and bound in Great Britain by Short Run Press, Exeter.
Policy Press uses environmentally responsible print partners.

FSC
www.fsc.org
MIX
Paper from
responsible sources
FSC® C014540

In memory of Sir Peter Hall,
a wonderful colleague and one of the best urbanists
and commentators on London

Contents

List of tables, figures and boxes

Tables

Figures

Boxes

Acknowledgements

We would like to thank Sarah Fielder who helped to copyedit the draft chapters prior to the submission of the typescript to Policy Press. Her assistance was invaluable. Our thanks to a team of referees who read draft chapters and provided feedback to the book's contributors. We are grateful to Emily Watt, Laura Vickers, Rebecca Tomlinson and Laura Greaves at Policy Press for their guidance and advice in the preparation and delivery of the book.

Notes on the editors and contributors

Editors

Rob Imrie is Professor of Sociology at Goldsmiths, University of London, UK. He has international expertise in urban governance, architecture and community development in cities, the impact and implications of urban policy in British and international cities, the geographies of disability and the built environment, and the body, embodiment and urban design. He is the co-editor of *Regenerating London: governance, sustainability and community in a global city* (with Loretta Lees and Mike Raco, 2009, Routledge); *Urban renaissance? New Labour, community and urban policy* (with Mike Raco, 2003, Policy Press); and *British urban policy* (1993, Paul Chapman Publishing; second edition 1999, Sage). His most recent book is *Architectural design and regulation* (with Emma Street, 2011, Wiley-Blackwell). He was formerly Professor of Geography at King's College London.

Loretta Lees is Professor of Human Geography at the University of Leicester, UK. She is an international expert on gentrification and urban regeneration. Her 2012 Antipode Activist Scholar Award researched the state-led gentrification of council estates in inner London from which she recently published *Staying Put: an anti-gentrification handbook for council estates in London* (authored with the London Tenants Federation, Just Space and Southwark Notes Archive Group, 2014). Her recent books include *Mixed communities: gentrification by stealth?* (with Gary Bridge and Tim Butler, 2011, Policy Press); *Regenerating London: governance, sustainability and community in a global city* (with Rob Imrie and Mike Raco, 2009, Routledge); and *Gentrification* (with Tom Slater and Elvin Wyly, 2008, Routledge). She lives in inner London and is co-organiser of the Urban Salon, a London forum for architecture, cities and international urbanism (www.theurbansalon.org), and a member of the London Action and Research on Regeneration Group. In 2013 she was an expert witness for the Greater London Authority's new Regeneration Committee. She was formerly Professor of Human Geography at King's College London.

Contributors

Robin Brown is a chartered town planner and a Londoner, born and bred. Having moved on from planning in local government, he is supporting a wide range of voluntary activities in and around Hayes, West London. In seeking wider alliances to progress local community development, he became involved in the origins of Just Space, and is now its treasurer.

Tim Butler is Professor of Geography at King's College London, UK, and his main interests focus around London's changing class structure. He has written on the gentrification of London and the implications of this for education and school choice. He is completing a book on social mixing in London and Paris with colleagues from the UK and France. His most recent books include *Mixed communities: gentrification by stealth?* (with Gary Bridge and Loretta Lees, 2012, Policy Press) and *Ethnicity, class and aspiration: understanding London's new East End* (with Chris Hamnett, 2011, Policy Press).

Kavita Datta is Reader in Geography at Queen Mary, University of London, UK. Her main research interests are in transnational migration, finance and exclusion. She has conducted research in both the Global North and South. Her most recent publications are *Migrants and their money: surviving financial exclusion in London* (2012, Policy Press) and *Global cities at work: new migrant divisions of labour* (with Jane Wills, Yara Evans, Joanna Herbert, Jon May and Cathy McIlwaine, 2010, Pluto Press).

Mike Dolton teaches sustainability in the Department of Geography, Royal Holloway, University of London, UK. His background is in urban studies and sustainability, and his research interests are the politics of urban regeneration, democracy and local governance, privatisation of the public sphere and urban sustainability.

Michael Edwards has lectured in the Economics of Planning at the Bartlett School, University College London, since 1969, and is now semi-retired. He was involved with community struggles at Covent Garden, Tolmers Square and King's Cross before becoming involved in Just Space and the International Network for Urban Research and Action (www.inura.org). He blogs at michaeledwards.org. uk and is active on Twitter.

James Fournière is a doctoral candidate at King's College London, UK, and Humboldt-Universität, Berlin. He is currently undertaking research into the development of public space in large-scale urban development projects in London and Berlin, with a specific focus on the production of legal geographies, affectivity and the built environment, diversity and the public realm, and the securitisation of public space.

Robert A. Francis is Senior Lecturer in Ecology at King's College London, UK. His main research interests are ecological patterns and processes within urban ecosystems, the practice of ecological engineering and reconciliation ecology for urban conservation and management, and the ecology of urban rivers. His most recent book is *Urban ecosystems: understanding the human environment* (with Michael Chadwick, 2013, Routledge).

Franklin Ginn is Lecturer in Human Geography at the University of Edinburgh, UK. His research focuses on geographies of nature, in particular on memory and gardening. Previous work has included botanical and suburban garden naturecultures. His current interests concern geo-engineering, cultures of environmental apocalypse and faith-based activism.

Chris Hamnett is Professor of Geography at King's College London, UK. He has written on social inequality, education, gentrification and the global city in London. His most recent book is *Ethnicity, class and aspiration: understanding London's new East End* (with Tim Butler, 2011, Policy Press).

Clare Herrick is Senior Lecturer in Human Geography at King's College London, UK. Her research is concerned with the ways in which health and wellbeing are governed in urban settings and the influence of the global 'unhealthy industries' on these processes. She has written about the regulation of obesity and alcohol, and is author of *Governing health and consumption: sensible citizens, behaviour and the city* (2011, Policy Press).

Robin Hickman is Senior Lecturer at the Bartlett School of Planning, University College London, UK. He has research interests in transport and climate change, urban structure and travel, integrated transport and urban planning strategies, the affective dimensions of travel, and sustainable transport strategies in the UK, Europe and Asia. His most recent book is *Transport, climate change and the city* (2013, Routledge).

Richard Lee is coordinator of Just Space, a community-led network influencing planning policy in London. He is a community activist at the Elephant & Castle, South London, where he lives. He has had a long involvement with council tenants' campaigns in many different parts of England.

Cathy McIlwaine is Professor of Geography at Queen Mary, University of London, UK. Her early research focused on gender, civil society and urban violence in the Global South, but more recent work has examined low-paid migrant labour and transnational migration in the UK, with a specific focus on Latin Americans from the perspective of livelihoods and transnational voting. Cathy's most recent books include *Cross-border migration among Latin Americans* (2011, Palgrave Macmillan) and *Global cities at work: new migrant divisions of labour* (with Jane Wills, Kavita Datta, Yara Evans, Joanna Herbert and Jon May, 2010, Pluto Press).

Anna Minton is a writer and journalist and the author of *Ground control: fear and happiness in the 21st century city* (2012, Penguin). She is Visiting Professor in Architecture at the University of East London and is currently the 1851 Royal Commission Fellow in the Built Environment. She is a regular contributor to *The Guardian* and a frequent broadcaster.

Mike Raco is Professor of Urban Governance and Development at the Bartlett School, University College London, UK. His background is in planning, geography and urban studies. He has published widely on the topics of urban governance and regeneration, urban sustainability, urban communities and the politics of urban and regional economic development. Recent books include *State-led privatisation and the demise of the democratic state: welfare reform and localism in an era of regulatory capitalism* (2013, Ashgate); *The future of sustainable cities: critical reflections* (with John Flint, 2012, Policy Press); and *Regenerating London: governance, sustainability and community in a global city* (with Rob Imrie and Loretta Lees, 2009, Routledge). He was formerly Reader in Human Geography at King's College London.

Emma Street is Lecturer in Real Estate and Planning at the University of Reading, UK. She has cross-cutting research interests in urban governance, business and politics; sustainable community building, urban policy and planning; and architecture, urban design and the built environment. Her most recent book is *Architectural design and regulation* (with Rob Imrie, 2011, Blackwell-Wiley).

Preface

Sustainable London? explores the rise of sustainable development policies as they relate to London, and evaluates their relevance and role in sustaining people and the places and environments in which they live. The contributors to this book show how sustainable development discourse has permeated different policy fields in London, including transport, housing, property development and education, and highlights the uneven impacts and effects, including the creation of new social inequalities and extending and deepening existing ones. The book is not a conventional textbook in that it does not seek to review, in any exhaustive sense, the spectrum of debates about sustainable development, planning, or the global city. This is a task beyond its scope, and such topics are already well covered in other texts in relation to London and other cities. Rather, our focus is the contradictory, and tension-laden, nature of sustainable development discourse, and the ways in which the term has filtrated into, and is shaping, aspects of London's socio-spatial futures. Such futures are, more often than not, presented as 'good news' stories, in which the rise in property values, and the appropriation of low-income housing areas by wealthy investors, is heralded as part of a city on the move, creating the basis for social and economic wellbeing.

This may be so for some, but the notion of sustainable development in London is closely aligned with a 'growth first' agenda, and the propagation of the market as the purveyor of London's infrastructure, ranging from the privatisation of its housing stock, to the supply of new public hospitals and educational facilities by private sector corporations. There is an elision between privatisation and sustainability, where one is more or less indistinguishable from the other, and the promotion of political rhetoric that Londoners' wellbeing depends on people's activation as self-making individuals. The understanding is that whatever a person's status in London, with regards to access to a job, income and housing, it depends, in large part, on their individual characters and personal attributes, reflecting a roll back to social pathology. In contrast, the contributors to the book seek to challenge some of the, individualising, trajectories of sustainable development discourse in London, and to contest the sorts of futures implied by it. Here, the collection is concerned with documenting the interrelationships between sustainability and social justice, and developing a critique of the different ways in which sustainable development discourse seeks to present itself as post-political when it is anything but.

In the shaping of the book, we invited a mix of well-known authors to contribute chapters, and new and emerging writers, some still at the early stages of their academic careers. We were mindful of not only engaging in theoretical exploration, and conceptual evaluation, but also embedding the book into policy and practice. We sourced contributions from people and organisations involved directly in London's politics around social justice and sustainable development issues, including the journalist Anna Minton, and a pan-London campaign group for social justice, Just Space. Their concerns, shared by the editors, resonate with Henri Lefebvre's (1991) call to the 'right to the city', and the development of radical politics based, in part, on a collective sense of self, and on an ethics of care. In distinction to the shaping of sustainable development discourses by policies to recapitalise land and property, the contributors to the book recognise the multiple ways in which people are dependent on others, and their actions, for their wellbeing and sustenance, and that sustainable living requires the mutuality of life to be centrally placed as part of programmes of social and political change.

Rob Imrie and Loretta Lees
June 2014

Foreword

Ben Rogers, Director, Centre for London

The world is urbanising at a breath-taking pace – The World Bank estimates that around 180,000 people move into cities every day. Against this background, London is something of a veteran. One of the oldest 'world cities', many of its streets, public places and buildings – and some of its institutions – date back centuries.

Yet the city remains extraordinarily vital. Only 20 years ago, in 1994, the historian Roy Porter introduced his best-selling *London: a social history* by predicting that the capital's days as a pioneering, global city were coming to an end. How wrong he was. London's economy has boomed over the last two decades. Although the city was deeply implicated in the banking crisis that began in 2007, it has weathered the ensuing economic storm better than the rest of the United Kingdom – more cranes have been erected in London over the last three years than across the remainder of the country as a whole. The city has attracted a large number of migrants from all over the world, including poor people and billionaires, and absorbed them seemingly successfully. Much to everyone's surprise, the 2010 Census revealed that Londoners describing themselves as 'White-British' are now in a minority, yet a large majority of residents say that people of different backgrounds in their local area get on well together.

There are many things that anyone transported from the London of 1994 to the London of 2014 would find surprising. But several in particular would likely stand out. First, the time-traveller would be impressed by the level of investment in transport infrastructure, after decades when the Underground, in particular, had remained neglected. Second, he or she would surely be surprised by the creation of a popular new pan-London government, centred on the very un-British novelty of a mayor – only one in 20 Londoners support the abolition of the mayoralty. The 2012 Olympics showed what was to many people around the world – and to many people at home – an unfamiliar city, apparently safe (or at least safer than it was), efficient, democratic, creative and confident in its diversity. The capital's universities, and cultural institutions – the Tate Galleries, National Theatre, Globe, the British Museum, to name a few – are enjoying relatively good times and have an increasingly international reach.

The example of Roy Porter should teach us to be careful about making predictions. But looking forward it is hard to believe that the developments of the last few decades won't continue apace. Ongoing processes of urbanisation and economic development will generate new markets for the British capital, which is expected to grow by nearly two million people by 2030. As the urban policy commentators Bruce Katz and Richard Florida, among others, have suggested, large globally integrated cities like London are likely to play an ever more important role in the economies of developed nations. There is every sign that devolution of power from central government to London will continue, with the city becoming perhaps more civically self-aware in the process. Will 'I love London', or a similar phrase, become as well known as 'I love New York'?

Yet, as this collection reminds us, these developments have had dark sides to them. The capital has grown more dominant vis-à-vis the rest of the country. Globalisation has brought ever-greater inequality. Housing is in desperately short supply and, on present trends, will only become more expensive. Homelessness and over-crowding are on the rise. Increased wealth has not led to a diminution of poverty (contra fashionable trickle-down theories), although the character of poverty has changed, with poor Londoners increasingly likely to be in work, rather than out of it, living in outer London, rather than near the centre, and in insecure private rented accommodation, rather than in social housing. The squeeze on public spending being pursued by the present government – and likely to be pursued by the next, regardless of its political complexion – is inevitably hitting more vulnerable Londoners hardest. Things look particularly tough for low to middle-income young Londoners. They are more likely to have debts and less likely to have a home than their counterparts of 25 years ago. One in four of London's young people are unemployed.

Despite the impressive investment in public transport infrastructure, the city remains a congested and polluting place. Developments in technology appear to be fuelling long distance travel, not lessening it, as might have been predicted, and all the main political parties are committed to expanding London's airport capacity. At the same time, businesses appear to place an increasing value on a city centre location, sucking the life out of outer town centres and increasing longer 'radial' journeys, in and out of Zone 1.

As the chapters in this volume set out, recent developments in London pose big challenges for the hallowed goals of equity, social inclusion, and in particular, sustainability. Many people seem to feel an increasing wariness of the latter concept, perhaps because it has become so vague, perhaps, not unrelatedly, because as it has become part of official discourse it has lost some of its critical edge. Ironically those wary of it include some of the contributors to this collection and, from a rather different point of view, the Mayor of London, Boris Johnson, who, while paying lip-service to the concept, is more at home writing and talking about London as a global, enterprising, business centre than as a pioneer of sustainable living.

But while we can argue about what the concept of sustainability entails, it is hard to deny that ever since the financial crisis and recession, talk of sustainability has given way to a focus on 'jobs and growth', with little reference to the sorts of jobs and growth we want. The contributors to this collection both describe this process and rightly regret this. London needs to aim higher. It should set out to become a globally acknowledged leader in green and socially inclusive growth.

The chapters in *Sustainable London?* explore some of the big questions raised by the latest chapter in London's economic development, and help point the way towards more sustainable models of development. They won't be the last word on the subject, but they are a very welcome contribution to the discussion.

Part 1

SUSTAINING LONDON:
THE KEY CHALLENGES

ONE

London's future and sustainable city building

Rob Imrie and Loretta Lees

Introduction

> The Mayor wants London to be the best big city in the world. The London Sustainable Development Commission supports this aspiration and believes that as part of being "best" we should work to make London the benchmark for sustainable cities by 2020. (Plowman, 2012, p 4)

The notion of sustainable development has rapidly become centre place in the governance of cities, and there are few policy makers who do not refer to it or use it as part of strategic policy making and implementation. In cities stretching from Beijing in China to São Paulo in Brazil and London in the UK, principles of sustainable development are seen as the saviour of cities, by providing the steer to crafting and creating liveable and habitable places. This is reflected in the place marketing of cities, and the various promotional activities by developers, designers and politicians extolling the virtues of space-shaping strategies allegedly assuring the development of sustainable urban environments. In London, the first explicit political overtures towards sustainable development were inbuilt into the Greater London Authority (GLA) Plan in 2004, with the then Mayor, Ken Livingstone (2004, p xii), noting that London's future depended on enhancing 'its economic and business efficiency ... accompanied by strong improvements in the quality of life and environment and greater social and economic inclusion.'

His vision tallied with those of previous British governments, particularly New Labour's national policy discourse of economic growth and competitiveness combined with the building of responsible and balanced communities capable of sustaining that growth. New Labour's model of sustainable development meant, primarily, a focus on economic and environmental relations, but Livingstone also pushed other, more social, dimensions of sustainability as far as he could (Cochrane, 2006). His pronouncements for London reflected not only a broader global consciousness of the ecological and environmental harm wrought by urban lifestyles, but also the understanding that sustainable development ought to encompass, and respond to, social and economic, as well as environmental, dimensions of urban living (see Imrie et al, 2009, pp 10-12). Some examples of this were policies to increase affordable housing to 40 per cent on new developments, and requiring builders to provide Lifetime Homes to meet the needs of people ageing through the life course.

For Livingstone (2004), London's sustainable future was more than the pursuit of a one-dimensional approach to development, based on the promotion of economic growth and the mitigation of harm to ecological and natural resources. His was also a moral discourse about the social and human dimensions of urban habitation, in which he sought to reduce social inequalities and create opportunities for social enhancement and wellbeing. Here, sustainable development was as much about the creation of new social relations, characterised by inclusive, open and tolerant places, respecting ethnic and sexual differences, redressing social inequality and enabling people to live healthy lives, as it was about securing socio-ecological resources. As Livingstone (2004, p ix) outlined, 'My vision … is to develop London as an exemplary, sustainable world city [and] to give all Londoners the opportunity to share in London's future success.'

The reality, for Livingstone, was that much of his vision, and the social dimensions of sustainable development, were never likely to be achievable in a context whereby the pursuit of an economic, 'growth first', agenda was shaping much of the policy and political discourse. Responding to the economic crash of 2008, there was renewed emphasis by policy makers on pursuing economic development and private sector-led regeneration to create the conditions for global investment in jobs and wealth creation in London. The contemporary politics of sustainable development in London (and indeed nationally) reflect the understanding that social and welfare benefits, including access to jobs, income and good housing, depend on liberalising markets. Facilitating investment opportunities for private investors in land, property and other sectors of London's economy is presented as a *fait accompli*. Here, the logic is eco-modernisation in which, so it is argued, practical management and operational interventions will mitigate the environmental and social costs of economic growth.

This view has, if anything, sharpened since the Coalition government came to power in 2010. Austerity has become the clarion call to politicians to pursue urban development strategies that do not deflect potential inward investment, or place financial burdens on public sector debt and its management. The pursuit of sustainable development has to occur within fiscal constraint, and the supply and management of public sector goods and services, such as parks, lighting and transport, is no longer guaranteed or underwritten by public finance. Rather, the necessary components of social reproduction, including the air that Londoners breathe and the water that they drink, are subject to a diminution of public controls and regulation, and instead, various quasi-public and privatised formations preside over what some detect as a deterioration in the socio-environmental quality of London life (Higgins et al, 2012). Thus, despite recognition of London's poor air quality, it has deteriorated since 2008, and the government's own estimates indicate that illegal levels of nitrogen dioxide will affect 16 British regions and cities, including London, until 2020-25.

It is our argument in this book that such scenarios, and others like them, are unsustainable, and that it is not the future that London and Londoners deserve. The sustainable development agenda no longer fosters policies with Keynesian echoes (that is, the state investing in London's hospitals, schools, infrastructure, and so on), as it aspired to do under Livingstone; rather, it extends a weak state entrepreneurialism, already evident during Livingstone's tenure, led by the private sector and its interests.[1] This is a recipe for what Tony Fry (2011) calls 'defuturing', that is, a way to name the unsustainable or those values and practices that undermine the future or people's capacities to (self-)reproduce in ways whereby life itself is not undermined or threatened. To defuture is, for Fry (2011), part of a totalitarian culture embedded into the modernist project of human fulfilment through consumption. To critique defuturing is to describe the spatial-temporal patterns and processes of unsustainability, and to direct attention to the historically constituted nature of sustainable development discourse as not natural, inevitable or unchallengeable.

In London, defuturing, as the basis of sustainable development discourse, is the perpetuation of socio-economic and political practices that naturalise resource exploitation, fail to place limits on consumption, and rely on market allocative and distributional systems, shaped by a 'development logic', to provide people with access to life's necessities.[2] This logic is anathema to sustaining and supporting many people as it exposes them to vulnerabilities. These relate to reduced state welfare and support, the privatised control of land and key resources, including propensity for price fixing by corporate cartels, and market exchange that requires, for its functioning, people to be in work, and living off a decent and fair wage. This is not so for many people in London, and in 2012, just under 600,000 jobs were paid below the London Living Wage (£8.55 per hour) (see Aldridge et al, 2012). It is also estimated that from 2009 to 2012, 2.1 million people in London were living in poverty, and that income inequalities were greater than anywhere else in the UK (Aldridge et al, 2012).

Such data are symptomatic of a broader, structural crisis in relation to London's policy approaches to sustaining people and the places and environments that they live in. As contributors to this book show, there is nothing radical or far-reaching about how London's politicians engage with issues of sustainable development. Rather, as is argued throughout the book, sustainable development discourse is entwined with the perpetuation of market-based processes by, for example, (re)creating the basis for new rounds of investment in land and property. While London's spatial development is premised on sustainable development as a key principle, it is difficult to find much evidence of such principles in practice. Indeed, far from sustainable development policy in London delivering the basis of the Brundtland Commission's proclamation in 1987 (WCED, 1987), that is, intergenerational equity, sustainable development regeneration policies and programmes appear to be creating new social inequalities and extending and deepening existing ones in ways whereby the future is more likely to be characterised by intergenerational inequity.

We divide the rest of this introductory chapter into three parts. In the next section, we outline the different dimensions of sustainable development discourse in London, situating it within its historical context and, in particular, focusing on the period of economic austerity since 2008. We develop the argument that sustainable development discourse is neither new nor novel but is embedded in historically rooted debates about London's future, in both the national economy and the world of cities. We then evaluate contemporary sustainable development discourse in London, and subject its elements to critique. There is an urgent need for sustainable development discourse in London to (re)engage with debates about social justice and 'the rights to the city', and to consider recent proclamations by UN Habitat (2010), that sustainable development is, first and foremost, a matter of human rights. What is required is no less than the development of redirectional practice, including the restructuring of socio-cultural and political relations, and the reanimation of what Fry (2011, p 8) refers to as 'the common good'. We conclude by outlining the content, structure and key arguments of the book.

London and sustainable development discourse

There is heightened awareness of the deleterious effects of social and economic processes on socio-ecological relations, including constraints on capacities for economic growth. There is, however, nothing new about this, and London's histories are embedded in social and political struggles over people's access to land, property and public space, means of livelihood, or creating possibilities for socially sustainable ways of living. For instance, in Georgian and Victorian London, a perennial issue was social inequality relating to access to privatised water supplies in which, as Bynum and Porter (1991, p xv) observe, 'consumers got the water supply they were prepared, or able, to pay for.' Access to good quality housing was also an issue for many poorer Londoners, and Charles Dickens' (1839, p 196) observation of St Giles Rookery was typical of social commentary at that time: 'Wretched houses with broken windows patched with rags and paper; every room let out to a different family, and in many instances to two or even three.'

Many of the socio-spatial inequalities of 18th and 19th-century London have barely disappeared, and questions raised then by social commentators, about people's health, welfare and longevity, are still being raised today. Thus, in the mid-19th century, one of the major issues was water and air-borne pollution, highlighted most evocatively in an edition of the popular, widely read, publication *Punch*, in 1858. Here, a cartoon (see Figure 1.1) depicted the grim reaper ('the silent highwayman') scouring the River Thames, populated by sewage, carcasses and other rotting matter. The burning of fossil fuels during the winter was also a significant threat to health and wellbeing, and by the end of the 19th century, London had 60 smog-bound days a year. While various public health measures reduced the nature of both water and air-borne pollution, London is still beset by the problem of poor air quality and, according to Clear Air in London (2013,

Figure 1.1: The silent highwayman

Source: Cartoon from *Punch* magazine (1858), volume 35, page 37

p 1), it 'has the highest levels of nitrogen dioxide, a toxic gas, of any capital city in Europe.'

The continuing socio-ecological crisis relating to London's air quality is reflective, in part, of the postwar modernist trajectory of London's socio-spatial development. This was sketched out in the formative County of London Plan of 1943, drawn up by Forshaw and Abercrombie (1943). Campkin (2013, p 5) describes it as 'an ambitious collective vision for post war London' that, in Forshaw and Abercrombie's (1943, p 12) words, 'sought a comprehensive renewal [and] order and efficiency and beauty and spaciousness'. Forshaw and Abercrombie's plan outlined far-reaching ideas to reshape London's people and places, including the containment of suburban building, decanting inner area populations to satellite new towns, and limiting London's population density to 136 people per acre. Ambitious schemes to cater for the private motorcar were also proposed. A new ring road was outlined in the 1943 Plan and later amplified in the Greater London Plan of 1944, including the proposed construction of concentric roads to encircle London, and arterial routes to radiate from its centre.

The plans for a mobile London were already set in place by a series of interwar reports, with the Minister for Transport, Herbert Tripp (1938, p 1), noting in 1938 that London's wellbeing depended, in part, on developing 'a rapid free flow of traffic'. For Forshaw and Abercrombie, while their traffic plans were not wholly implemented, they were emblematic of modern, anthropocentric values, or the crafting of places to satiate the liberal, modern subject. Rajan (2006, p 113) describes this as facilitating 'the ideal of a free person whose actions are her own.' Forshaw and Abercrombie's plans for traffic were no less than the purveyors of automobility, or those values seeking to shape a modern society premised on facilitating mobility and movement. Throughout the 1950s and 1960s, much of London's spatial (re)development featured major road building projects that became symbolic of the contradictions of modern urbanism, including the despoliation of large tracts of land, escalating air pollution, but also the promise of unfettered mass mobility.

The modernist project of postwar redevelopment was shaped by politicians seeking to retain London's international and cosmopolitan status, its formative role as an imperial capital and, later on, as the world's major financial and metropolitan centre. This reflected the dominance of globalisation as the pre-eminent political discourse shaping London's postwar socio-spatial development. From the earliest periods of its history, London's politicians have sought to enhance its global status, and, as Abercrombie (1945) pronounced, in the Greater London Plan of 1944, 'the central idea [is] London, the capital of the Empire.' This theme has continued to shape development discourse in London, and the previous Mayor, Ken Livingstone (2004, p xi), suggested that London's future depended on building 'globalisation into the very foundation of the city and our thinking'. Likewise, the present Mayor, Boris Johnson, is an ardent advocate of expanding London's economy and global reach, noting, in the 2011 London Plan, that 'London must retain and build upon its world city status ... of global reach' (Johnson, 2011, p 5).

Globalisation, as the driving force of London's development, was particularly to the fore in the property booms of the late 1950s and late 1960s, and again was shaping major rebuilding programmes in the wake of deindustrialisation in the 1970s and 1980s. Peter Ackroyd (2001, p 777) describes London's post-1980s experiences as *resurgem*, or its revitalisation as a place characterised by 'the renovation or rejuvenation of the inner core'. Insofar that the term 'sustainable development' had any resonance in the early 1980s, it was defined by 'development' or the encouragement of private sector investment in land and property to create new economic and employment opportunities. The state's dispersal of large tracts of land to private investors heralded the rise of property-led regeneration (PLR), or a model of development that has since become centre stage in shaping sustainable development discourse. The 1980s version of PLR operated with little regard for creating community cohesion or assuring residential stability, and instead, encouraged labour and residential mobility as a pre-requisite for people to secure jobs and livelihoods.

A growing critique of the PLR approach, and its physical manifestation as 'islands of development', more or less detached from the often poorer neighbourhoods that they were located within, was part of policy reappraisal in the mid-1990s (Imrie and Thomas, 1999; McGuirk, 2000). For some, PLR, while creating wealth and new jobs, was implicated in inflating local land values, particularly residential property prices, offering limited job opportunities for people living in established communities, and failing to respond to community-based needs in relation to skills, education and housing (Brownill, 1999). A response by New Labour governments of the late 1990s and 2000s, and Ken Livingstone's reign as London's Mayor, included a raft of community and neighbourhood renewal programmes, seeking to reduce worklessness and social exclusion and to create places that worked well for all. While much of the PLR approach was still in evidence, Ruth Lupton (2013, p 1), in looking back over the period, suggests that the policy emphasis was about securing 'greater equity in the distribution of services, opportunities, and economic and social goods.'

This formative emphasis on the social context of sustainable development was, however, subsumed by a focus on the ecological and environmental dimensions of sustainability, certainly in the 1990s. It is difficult to be precise about when consciousness about sustainable development entered into the mainstream of London's planning and politics, although some documentary evidence suggests that, like other cities, it followed on from the proclamations of the Brundtland Commission in 1987 and the Rio Earth Summit in 1992. By the early to mid-1990s, the notion of sustainable development was circulating around London's boroughs, but the development of governance in relation to the promotion of sustainable development was signalled in 2002 by the establishment of the London Sustainable Development Commission (LSDC) to advise the Mayor of London on making London an exemplary sustainable world city. It described its objective as developing 'a coherent approach to sustainable development throughout London, not only to improve the quality of life for people living, working and visiting London today and for generations to come but also to reduce London's footprint on the rest of the UK and the world' (LSDC, 2003, p 4).

The LSDC, complemented by other organisations, has been at the vanguard of promoting a variety of initiatives relating to sustainable development that may be described as eco-modernism, or what Fry (2011) suggests is a perspective that misses the point by not challenging the central ethos of what sustainability is or ought to be, that is, rolling back consumerism and modernist, anthropogenic mentalities. While the institutionalisation of sustainable development, as evidenced in Table 1.1, appears to signal serious intent by policy makers, we wish to argue that much of sustainable development discourse in London, as embedded in such initiatives, is characterised by a symbolic politics or the priority of style and presentation over substance and action that does no more than 'sustain what is known to be unsustainable' (Blühdorn, 2007, p 251). Blühdorn (2007) also suggests that sustainable development is subject to symbolic politics because of the complexity of the subject matter, and the need for policy makers to engage in 'complexity reduction' in ways whereby identifiable objects, amenable to management, can be identified.

One measure of the heightened emphasis, by London's politicians, on sustainable development, is how far it features in policy documents. In the 2004 London

Table 1.1: Governance and sustainable development in London: the key initiatives

Organisation/initiative	Terms of reference
London Sustainable Development Commission (LSDC), 2002	Set up in 2002 and continues to advise the London Mayor on his approach to sustainable development, promoting sustainability, and ensuring sustainability is included in London's strategies.
Making your plans sustainable: a London guide, 2004	A guide by the LSDC for business, voluntary and public sector organisations on how to make their plans more sustainable.
Greater London Plan, 2004	Statutory planning strategy for Greater London, first produced by the Mayor of London in 2004, and replacing regional planning guidance. Supplementary Planning Guidance on sustainable design and construction was published in 2006 to help implement the London Plan.
A Sustainable Development Framework for London, 2006	Produced by the LSDC, sets out their vision for achieving sustainable (environmental, social and economic) development in London.
London Leaders Initiative, 2008	An annual programme commencing in 2008 and run by the LSDC to identify and support groups and volunteers in London undertaking projects that encompass sustainability.
London Fire Brigade, Sustainable Development Strategy, 2009-12	The Strategy by London's fire and rescue services, under the auspices of the Mayor and GLA, focuses on their contribution to environmental sustainability, and managing the impact of their activities. (Updated by the 2013-16 Strategy.)
Mayor's Transport Strategy, 2010	A statutory document, alongside the London Plan and Economic Development Strategy, which sets out a 'vision' for London's transport infrastructure and how Transport for London will implement this.
Greater London Plan (Revised), 2011	The current statutory planning strategy for Greater London, substantially revised from the 2004 version (above). Objectives encompass sustainability.
The Commission for a Sustainable London 2012	The Commission was set up to monitor and ensure that the sustainability commitments for the London Olympics were achieved.
London 2012 Sustainability Plan: towards a one planet Olympics	Part of the bid for the London Olympics and Paralympics, a sustainability strategy to make London 2012 the greenest ever Games.
2020 vision, GLA, 2013	The Mayor of London's vision for London's growth and position in the UK economy, following the Olympics. Covers development, regeneration and infrastructure projects and opportunities.

Plan the word 'sustainable' is mentioned 100 times, and in the 2011 version there are 178 references to the term. The quantitative increase in references to sustainable development may indicate its increasing significance in shaping policy, yet Holman (2010, p 32) detects a retreat from sustainable development in the 2011 London Plan characterised by vague statements such as London becoming 'a city that delights the senses'. It is unclear what such a statement means or entails for planning policy or how it is even achievable. Holman (2010, p 35) contrasts the 2011 London Plan with the 2004 version in which sustainable development directives were much more specific, such as requiring local planning authorities to strengthen 'local communities and economies including opportunities for local businesses and for the training of local people'. The contrast between 2004 and 2011 reflects political regime change, with Boris Johnson's predilection for minimal government and diminution in strategic steering, and an approach 'more on agreed and shared objectives and less on process and structure' (GLA, 2011: para 1.45).

This reflects the antipathy, of the Johnson administration, to anything resembling prescriptive directives or setting in place government that, in Conservative Party (2010, p 1) terms, is likely to inhibit economic growth by creating 'bureaucratic burdens'. For Johnson, sustainable development is fine as long as economic growth is the priority or, as he said about the 2011 London Plan, 'this is a Plan for growth and opportunity. In London that means welcoming development ...' (Johnson, 2011, p 6). The 'growth agenda', as the basis of a revitalised, sustainable London, has become increasingly important in the wake of the global economic crisis since 2008. The onset of austerity has changed the policy and planning context and, in Peck's (2012, p 630) terms, has led to 'fiscal purging' characterised by a reduction in state activity, including the dismantling of programmes related to social, ecological and environmental sustainability. Instead, the predominant ethos is removing obstacles to economic growth, and promoting initiatives to encourage international investment and wealth creation.

These include, primarily, measures to reduce environmental regulation and exhortations by policy makers encouraging people to change their behaviour. The latter has been increasingly to the fore since Boris Johnson became London's Mayor, developing strategy that is individualising or couched as requiring less control of corporate organisation, or environmental regulation, and much more control of individuals' actions, or what Brand (2007, p 624) describes as 'sanction, inducement, exhortation, and cajolery'. The key message propagated by GLA politicians is that sustainable development is the responsibility of citizens, and that individual behaviour patterns need to change to assure London's future. A typical view is expounded by the Economist Intelligence Unit (EIU) (2008, p 10) that, in analysing London's sustainable development challenges, suggest that 'most of the choices are in the hands of individuals'. The EIU (2008, p 10) notes that carbon emissions, and other harmful effects of production and consumption in London, can be curtailed by 'changes in regulation, taxes ... and marketing and campaigning to raise the awareness and encourage consumers.'

Here, the problem of and for sustainable development rests with individuals and their lifestyles. In London, as elsewhere, this translates into sustainable development discourse that fails to identify, and seeks to control, the major sources of environmental pollution and harm, that is, corporate practice. Instead, it results in what Brand (2007, p 625) regards as 'a field of social regulation which intrudes on personal/private life'. Sustainable development practice thus entails highly fragmented, individualising, policy programmes, and the emphasis on the individual to self-care by judicious control of lifestyle, including stress management, exercise, diet and management of consumption and waste commensurate with what sustainable development is defined, by government and corporate organisations, to be. This is no more than the politically constructed nature of sustainable development discourse, and it brings into question its relevance in seeking to redress many of the social and economic issues facing London's citizens. For many people living in London, sustainable development discourse is implicated in reinforcing their disadvantaged status, and contributing to the inflation of land markets, the privatisation of significant swathes of London's public spaces and diminution in people's abilities to gain access to decision makers and centres of power. Sustainable development discourse is neither neutral nor independent of political power wielded by the state and corporate interest.

London's un-sustainment and the significance of re-directive practice

London's spatial development is archetypically modern in perpetuating socio-economic and ecological processes that are de-sensitised to their material and human consequences. In the opening to this chapter we described such processes as 'defuturing' (Fry, 2011). Defuturing is, in its most general sense, the operational mentalities of social and economic systems that perpetuate structural unsustainability, characterised by the rationality of economic growth as a quantitative outcome rather than 'a qualitative mode of being' (Fry, 2011). To defuture is to retain, centre stage, the exploitation of people and the denudation of material resources, or what Fry (2011, p 3) describes as 'a reflection and projection of a globalizing world of manufacturing desires'. A defutured scenario is one whereby the future is taken away by structurally embedded values and practices that regard unsustainable practices as intrinsic to the 'modernised human being' (Fry, 2011, p 23).

A defutured future is reflected in much of London's spatial development that is anthropocentric and reflects the exploitation of the environment (see Brand, 2007; Thornley and Newman, 2011). This includes constant (re)building programmes in London that consume space and energy, and new waves of gentrification that create new social inequalities, and embrace and extend the reach of consumption and material culture. The model of unsustainable practices is, primarily, PLR, in which land and buildings are recycled as commodities to be sold to the highest bidders. The emergent 'spaces of excess' contrast with those of poverty, and are consistent with a defutured future that regards unsustainable practice as natural and 'a price worth paying'. Thus, from the lavish apartments at One Hyde Park in Kensington to the penthouse suites located on the top floors of the Shard, slippery terms such as 'sustainable' may be regarded as little more than a tool or means to legitimise 'excessive urbanism' (see Figure 1.2).

Sustainable development discourse, premised on defuturing, reflects an instrumental logic that conceives of the problems of cities as resolvable through the development and use of technology, technique and the deployment of managerial and administrative systems. Sustainable development, so some argue, is not a matter of contestation, or achievable by conflict, or resolvable by politics. Rather, it is more likely to be attainable as part of a consensus politics, including the management and containment of dissent. In London, like elsewhere, sustainable development discourse, politically packaged by elite groups, is part of a post-political framing of the problems of urbanisation that offers people little or no option other than to follow the prognosis of what a sustainable place is or ought to be. Such prognosis is handed down by national and local governments who, allied to key stakeholders, such as major corporate organisations, seek to persuade Londoners of the relevance of regeneration initiatives that, at face value, appear to be doing no more than expanding the scope and capabilities of private investors to shape spatial development processes and outcomes.

Figure 1.2: One Hyde Park, Knightsbridge, London

© Rob Imrie

Such processes, and the governance underpinning them, are characterised by the primacy of the market in shaping spatial development, and there is much evidence of post-political rationalities in play. This is particularly so with sustainable development discourse, which has, at its fulcrum, the promotion of markets and the commercialisation and commodification of London's land and property. Sustainable development discourse *appears* to be post-political by foreclosing debate on spatial development that is not commensurate with promoting economic growth. In doing so, this opens up the way to promote property-led investment, including gentrification, as consensually derived objectives that provide the best way to revitalise declining neighbourhoods and places. For post-politics, pursuing PLR is a (pre-)given, and there is little recognition that dissent might exist. How could anyone possibly object to regenerating land and property as a pre-requisite to securing London's economic future and promoting social and welfare benefits?

As an example, Lees (2013) documents London's approach to mixed communities that was constructed, by politicians and policy makers, as a good thing that would benefit all by revitalising sink estates and giving the people living in them a better future. For Lees (2013), the discursive construction of such environs, as places unfit for habitation, has been spun around a rhetoric of mixed community building that is, effectively, state-led gentrification or displacement of original occupiers of council estates and replacement by wealthier, middle-class people. That such programmes have occurred, and continue to be part of London's spatial development, is, so some claim, evidence of a post-politics or the dissipation of conflict and antagonism in which urban politics is no longer evident or necessary. Instead, GLA politicians are in the vanguard of presenting programmes, such as mixed communities, as beneficial to all, and the only way to eradicate concentrations of poverty and poor housing is by utilising market mechanisms.

For politicians to present sustainable development in this way is overtly political, and it undermines any creditable claim to a post-politics in shaping the substance of London's socio-spatial development. In Vanolo's (2013) terms, the notion of sustainable development is contested and part of a political struggle, between vested interests, to define what the good city is. Part of its contestation is for elite groups, including major corporate actors, to deny the contested, hence political, nature of the term, and for politicians to present sustainable development as 'for the good of all'. To claim sustainable development in this way is to be, in presentation terms, post-political, yet the actions of those seeking to create (post-)political consensus, about the 'goodness' of sustainable development, are no less than political in form and content. How could it be otherwise when what is offered is the allocative and distributional logic of the market as the basis for securing London's socio-economic and ecological future? To claim that sustainable development is post-political is to attempt to disarm dissent or, in the name of sustainability, to wield disciplinary power to create docile citizens as part of a process of *political* legitimation.

This interpretation, of the political nature of sustainable development discourse, has relevance in relation to the appropriation of policing as a means to manage urban space. One of the themes of sustainable development discourse in London, evident in mixed communities policy, is creating places free of crime, disorder and behaviour labelled as dysfunctional and anti-social. The 'law and (dis)order' agenda is a significant part of sustainable city politics. A major feature of London's economic development relates to security and surveillance, and the interlocking of sustainable development discourse with forms of spatial regulation that seek to secure land and property for investment opportunity. Policing has always been at the fulcrum of urban policy, and a perennial theme is securing places from threat to property and individual wellbeing. This emphasis has been heightened in recent years due to perceived and actual threats and incidents relating to terrorism, and in the wake of the post-2008 economic crisis that is exacerbating social inequalities and tensions between different segments of London's communities (see Fussey et al, 2011).

The focus is re-balancing people and places regarded as out of sync with mainstream values, and creating environs that are, in popular jargon, 'resilient' (see MacKinnon and Driscoll Derickson, 2012). The notion of resilience is supplanting sustainable development in framing development politics, with the emphasis on private sector-led recovery bolstered by a supportive, pro-market planning system (see also Chapter Fifteen, this volume). As suggested in the Economic Development Plan (GLA, 2010, p 12) for London, the point of the planning system is to address the cause of market failure rather 'than supplanting the market', an understanding that does not see the market as the cause of failure itself. Rather, the model to 'secure' and make resilient London's social, economic and ecological future revolves round the privatisation of its infrastructure, including the supply of necessary services such as water, energy and, increasingly, education and transportation. The governance of London's resource base is fragmented between many different providers and based, primarily, on securing stakeholder value and only then, serving the needs of communities.

The resilient city discourse does not sit easily with the version of sustainable development that identifies social equity as a paramount concern. This is because the concept of resilience is premised on systems stability or the foreclosure of threats or challenges to the (pre-)existing social order. As MacKinnon and Driscoll Derickson (2012, p 254) suggest, a focus on resilience by policy makers 'closes off wider questions of progressive social change which require interference with, and transformations of, established systems.' In London, as elsewhere, the resilient cities agenda is orchestrated by large-scale, state and corporate institutions, and revolves around securing the city from threats to its socio-economic and ecological integrity by primarily placing the onus on individuals and communities to adapt to external threats, such as global fluctuations in energy prices. Here, resilience is not to challenge the global and corporate sources of such fluctuations, but, in MacKinnon and Driscoll Derickson's (2012) terms, to accept them, passively, as part of the natural workings of globalisation.

How might such discourse be challenged and transformed and be made to influence London's socio-spatial development in ways whereby urban injustices are reduced, if not eradicated? Part of the challenge is to dispel the myth of the post-democratic city characterised by post-political formations in which what dominates is consensus about London's spatial development. Sustainable development discourse is entwined with ideological constructions of this type that serve to neuter debate about alternative models or ways of organising London's society, economy and environment. The reality is that sustainable development discourse, riven with contradictions and tensions, cannot suppress or contain dissent or alternative views of what London is or ought to be. The evidence of counter-views, and points of resistance to the dominance of sustainable development as a pro-development model, is scattered across London. The Occupy movement, and its occupation of Paternoster Square, is illustrative of such tensions, and, in this instance, asking awkward questions about the financial system and social inequities.

What might the alternative views be to counter sustainable development discourse, and how might the many political subventions across London be given a platform to challenge the de-democratising nature of London's formal political structures? These questions are core to a social justice agenda, and highlight Lefebvre's (1991) notion of the 'right to the city', that is, for all citizens, irrespective of income or social status, to participate in shaping urban life for the benefit of all. It is difficult to imagine this occurring in London because the means to participate are weakly developed or absent, and too many strategic decisions occur behind closed doors with the public unable to access, with any ease, relevant data and information. An example of this is public infrastructure provision that occurs, primarily, through major, state-sponsored private finance initiative (PFI) contracts, many of the details of which are deemed to be commercially confidential and not available to individuals to scrutinise.

To challenge, and transform, the defuturing nature of sustainable development discourse is, in Fry's (2011) terms, to engage in re-directive practice. This is to (re)position sustainability as a political object and to develop it as part of political, and politicised, practices. The task includes the de-objectification of terms such as 'sustainable development' that presents the development logic of capitalism as natural, inevitable, and as though there are no realistic alternative modes of being. For Fry (2011), the dismantling of the objective guise of sustainable development discourse is a pre-requisite for transformations in socio-political consciousness, and part of an agenda for 'futuring'. This is to create the possibilities for undermining the structurally unsustainable nature of corporate activity, and, as Fry (2011, p 79) suggests, affirming 'a commitment to the value of that which has to be sustained'. This cannot be the 'growth agenda' or the inexorable (re)production of social inequalities that underpin contemporary sustainable development discourse.

The collection

Sustainable development discourse is part of a political struggle to assert values and, in ideological and practical terms, pro-market views, promoting privatisation and property investment, have gained centre place in shaping spatial development strategies. Advocates of the market model are engaged in the purposive construction of a post-politics to legitimise what various authors, such as Fry (2011) and Flint and Raco (2012), regard as a flawed model of, and approach to, sustainable development. Some of this reflects Vallance et al's (2012, p 1695) observations that sustainable development discourse 'may actually be working against the city and its residents'. They note that the operationality of sustainability is shaped by a biophysical environmental focus with a consequence of policy makers 'ignoring the social world in favour of manipulating the built form of the city' (Vallance et al, 2012, p 1705). London's politicians appear to approach sustainable development in a similar way, with the focus on technical and instrumental means to resolve problems defined, primarily, as biophysical, such as air and water pollution.

The difficulty here is the narrow definition of sustainable development, and a focus that, in conceptual terms, is unlikely to draw attention to what we regard as the fulcrum of what development is or ought to be about. This is social injustice in London, and the ways in which sustainable development discourse is part of the problem in perpetuating socio-economic inequalities in the city. We suggest that the notion of sustainable development has been put to work by political and corporate interests to shape London's socio-spatial development commensurate with extracting maximum profits from the commodification of everyday life. This is not to assert a capital logic, but to highlight how life opportunities in London, from healthcare to education and job opportunities, are co-constituted by de-democratising governance, a withdrawal of the state as guarantor of life, and people's exposure to the vagaries of the market. While the precise nature of the political agenda shaping sustainable development discourse is not easy to disentangle, some of its main features include:

- The heightening of technical and managerial modes of governance, in which, so some allege, the real politics of social (in)justice are supplanted, increasingly, by (post-)political rhetoric and practices (see Swyngedouw, 2011). In this book we adopt a critical stance towards the understanding of sustainable development as post-political, or something that is alleged to be above and beyond dispute in relation to its values and objectives. Rather, we suggest that sustainable development is highly charged, politically, and part of neoliberalising strategies in London to extend the commodification and commercialisation of the built and natural environment.
- In London, sustainable development discourse is committed to a 'growth first' logic premised on market expansion and encouragement of investment in land and property markets. To sustain London's economy, and to enhance

social wellbeing, it is argued that economic growth, including the stimulation of consumption, is required (GLA, 2010). Insofar that negative social and environmental externalities may ensue, these can be dealt with by appropriate planning and management. Such mentalities reflect the political framing of socio-environmental discourses around a scientific technocracy and the values of ecological modernism, with corporate organisation and governance at the vanguard of delivering sustainable futures.

• The privatisation of spatial development and a diminution of local states' capacities to intervene in, and shape, the changing socio-ecological, economic and environmental geographies of places like London. This is likely to exacerbate a state of unsustainability by virtue of, for example, a reduction in housing benefits and other welfare benefits to poorer people, and greater income inequalities in London. This has the potential to undermine community cohesion, to fragment neighbourhoods and to create unsustainable places unable to provide the support mechanisms, such as affordable housing, to enhance habitability and social and economic opportunities.

The chapters in this book develop one or more of the above themes to highlight the contradictions in the development and deployment of sustainable development discourse in one of the world's significant cities – London. As the dominant metropolitan centre, not just in the UK but also, arguably, worldwide, London is a place where the diverse dimensions of contemporary urban challenges are evident. The sheer size of London provides a much larger laboratory through which to explore the key concepts driving sustainable development, and the different ways in which these are shaping the city's urban fabric and future. The book deals with different themes and debates about London's sustainable development in five parts and 14 further chapters.

Chapter Two is a conversation between the editors and Anna Minton, author of *Ground control*. This is an important book that has brought to popular attention the implications of the privatisation of public space in cities such as London, and the effects of private corporate control over the socio-spatial development of cities. Minton notes that the term 'sustainable' is more or less meaningless, and that what has been happening in London, particularly with the mixed communities policy, is anything but sustaining people's livelihoods and habitation. Instead of purposive planning for the market, driven by corporate speculation, Minton argues the case for unplanned urbanism in London, in which some spaces need to be free spaces for all people to access, and in particular, environs free from corporate property investment interests and speculation. For Minton, a sustainable London must permit politicians and planners to be open-minded about alternative community uses, different ways of doing things, and to approach alternatives with a 'yes' rather than a 'no'.

In Chapter Three, Robin Brown, Michael Edwards and Richard Lee, members of the London-based organisation Just Space, outline how it emerged in 2007 to combat issues of social injustice, and to challenge London-wide policies about urban regeneration and economic and environmental sustainability. They open their chapter with the cautionary note, that the word 'sustainability' is a problem because 'we often find it being emptied of meaning'. For Brown, Edwards and Lee, there is a need to re-balance both debate and policy about London's future in ways whereby politicians' focus should be on those who are poor, exploited or in some ways excluded from access to decent housing, employment and good quality public services and spaces. The remit of Just Space is, therefore, to provide a community voice or forum to articulate ideas about realistic alternatives to neoliberalism, and to develop ways of organising London's society to avoid pricing people out of housing and other facilities in low-income communities.

Part 2, 'Sustaining London in an era of austerity', notes that the overarching influence on London's sustainable development is austerity politics and policies. The onset of global recession is intertwined with a changing political economy of urbanism and the rise of new challenges in seeking to govern the city. The major challenge relates to creating a context for economic growth, while ensuring that social and economic inequalities, relating to the restructuring of welfare, housing and labour markets, do not lead to patterns of living that undermine, and dismantle, people's livelihoods and capacities to reproduce themselves. Much evidence suggests that there is a crisis in relation to some of the basic everyday means of sustenance. London's housing is far too expensive for many people, and health and income inequalities have increased. Child poverty remains endemic and above the national average, and life expectancy between the rich and poor is more pronounced in London than in other parts of the UK. Contributors in this part develop these themes, and consider how sustainability in London is being reframed in the transition from a background politics of Big State to Big Society and in a period of austerity and an uncertain (economic) future.

In Chapter Four, Emma Street notes that the political and policy discourse shaping urban planning and governance is characterised by a neoliberal conception of sustainable development. This conceives of sustainability as the pursuit of economic growth while simultaneously ensuring that specified social equity and ecological objectives are attained. For Street, New Labour's (2003) Sustainable Communities Plan encapsulated development goals with economic growth agendas. The Plan sought to achieve social equity and sustained economic growth alongside enhanced democratic accountability delivered through devolved governance arrangements such as business improvement districts and constitutional and planning system reforms. In London, urban sustainability has primarily been framed as a way to support the city's 'global status', with the property development industry called on to deliver buildings supporting an enhanced quality of life and sustainability targets while also contributing to the city's economic growth. The chapter highlights the parallels between contemporary iterations of sustainable governance aligned to the Big Society, and past approaches. In so doing, it considers the ways in which, following the global credit crisis of 2008 and the emergence of the 'austerity agenda', the understanding of sustainable development has become more closely aligned to a politics of economic development.

Mike Raco, in Chapter Five, explores the relationships between governance capacities in London and future planning practices in the wake of economic austerity agendas. He focuses on the complex public–private sector *entanglements* that now exist in the city and the legacies left by earlier rounds of reform that have seen the wide-scale privatisation of welfare assets and services. The discussion assesses the structural limitations that privatisation and private financing have placed on state capacities, and the broader implications of change for the future governance and management of London. He notes that London's governance is fragmented, with a disproportionate amount of its public infrastructure constructed through inflexible, expensive and long-term PFIs and development partnerships. Implementing policies in a context of austerity in which state resources are likely to be reduced further will be particularly challenging. Indeed, for Raco, the longer-term viability of the city's existing planning system may be called into question. By drawing on the case of London, the chapter directly engages with contemporary debates over welfare state reform. It concludes with some reflections on wider understandings of localism, and the importance of asset ownership and management to the future of London's sustainability.

In Chapter Six, Cathy McIlwaine and Kavita Datta explore the roles of migrant workers in London's labour market and in sustaining its wealth and economic status. Over the past two decades, a restructuring of the London economy, deregulation of the labour market, processes of sub-contraction, limited access to welfare and the imposition of an increasingly restrictive immigration regime have combined to produce a distinctive migrant division of labour at the bottom end of the London labour market. Even while researchers have documented the multiple vulnerabilities that low-paid migrant workers endure, research suggests that these vulnerabilities may have intensified since 2008, as job insecurity has worsened and anti-immigration sentiments have escalated. Differences between migrant workers have also intensified, partly due to an immigration regime that has increasingly distinguished between migrants originating from an expanded European Union (EU), and those from the Global South, thus creating a distinct hierarchy of labour market rights. Based on research with migrants employed in London's low wage economy, the chapter documents the changing nature of London's labour market and immigration regime during the economic downturn, the implications of this on different migrant groups and the strategies adopted by them to cope with the crisis in London. The chapter concludes by assessing the broader implications of the migrant division of labour in sustaining a global city at work.

Chris Hamnett's concern, in Chapter Seven, is changes in government welfare expenditure and the impact on social sustainability or the destabilisation of communities. As Hamnett outlines, welfare spending is as important in London as any other region of Britain, although London and the South East do have a slightly lower percentage of households in receipt of welfare support than the poorer, ex-industrial northern regions. While some areas of welfare expenditure, such as pensions and child allowances, apply to all eligible groups, wherever they live in Britain, there are aspects of welfare spending that are strongly regionally specific. Thus the incidence of Incapacity Benefit is much higher in South Wales and the North East than in southern Britain as a result of the legacy of mining. But because of the generally high cost of housing in London, and the above average number of households in poverty, London has a disproportionate volume of Housing Benefit expenditure. Government cuts in welfare spending, particularly the cap on Housing Benefit payments and the overall £500 per week cap on benefits per household, will hit London hard. One effect is that a significant number of low-income Londoners will be forced out of inner London when their welfare benefit payments are cut, as they will no longer be able to afford to pay high rents.

In Part 3, 'The challenges for a socially sustainable London', contributors explore the exacerbation of socio-spatial inequalities related to a development discourse that revolves around the supply of privatised infrastructure provision, the privatisation of the public realm and the encouragement of new rounds of property-led investment. The question of 'whose city' is broached in relation to the widening of social and economic inequalities in London, and evidence of a worsening crisis in relation to many of the basic everyday essentials of life. These include the failing of the schooling system in London in which many children are denied access to the best schools, and the development of affordable housing schemes by recourse to planning agreement with house builders and developers. The latter is never likely to provide on the scale required, and aspirations for a socially sustainable London, affordable to the many and not just the few, seem to be further away than 10 years ago. The chapters in this part of the book suggest that sustainable development is closely interrelated with the privatisation of land and resources, and brings to the fore a class politics, or at least the restructuring of socio-spatial relations, in which a socially exclusive society appears to be in the making.

In Chapter Eight, Loretta Lees argues that there needs to be much better debate around social sustainability and what it might offer London. Focusing on mixed communities policy and how it has been/is being used to gentrify large council estates in inner London, and drawing on the case of the Heygate Estate in Elephant & Castle, she shows that the deconcentration of poverty (one of the main aims of mixed communities policy) plays itself out as working-class/low-income population displacement and community destruction. The result is social *exclusion* and new forms of social segregation, rather than social *inclusion*. Sustaining *people* is dependent, so government suggests, on the activities of individuals and local communities. Prime Minister David Cameron (2009) describes this as 'galvanising, catalysing, prompting, encouraging and agitating for community engagement and social renewal'. Loretta Lees investigates one community group – the Southwark Notes Archive Group (SNAG) – who have done this, and in so doing she critiques 'post-political correctness' and suggests bottom-up social sustainability as the way forward for London.

In Chapter Nine, Rob Imrie and Mike Dolton argue that in a context of fiscal austerity and public expenditure cutbacks in the UK, the private sector's role in the development and delivery of sustainable places is likely to be extended. This chapter seeks to describe and evaluate one example of private sector involvement in the shaping of spatial development, and to highlight the implications for place-making, particularly civic engagement, including the organisation and effects of community-based participation. The empirical focus is Tesco PLC and its involvement in the planned regeneration of one part of Bromley-by-Bow, in the London Borough of Tower Hamlets, an area characterised by high levels of multiple deprivation situated in the footprint of the London 2012 Olympics. The development of what has been coined 'Tesco Town' represents more than an example of retail-led regeneration; it highlights the potential for corporate control of spatial development, and the emasculation of public spaces by private interests. The authors draw out implications from the case for thinking about the politics of sustainable place-making, rights and citizenship, and the shaping of urban space.

Tim Butler, in Chapter Ten, notes that education has joined housing and transport as one of the crunch issues for London's ability to sustain itself as a world-leading city. London has inherited an education system from a past era when its largely working-class population left school to labour in its semi-skilled industries. With de-industrialisation and widespread gentrification, London's middle class and those aspiring to join them now form the largest population group in the city, and are competing for places in its comparatively few high-performing schools. At the same time, there is a premium, as never before, on educational skills in London's labour markets – in the changed environment of neoliberal governance, the responsibility is on parents to garner what educational assets are on offer to their children. In this situation, the ability to live near a high-performing school ranks as the single most important determinant of a child's success and, in turn, this means that London's education system increasingly reflects rather than overturns existing privilege. For Butler, London's schooling system is socially regressive and is likely to contribute to, rather than mitigate, London's failure to build itself a sustainable future.

In Chapter Eleven, James Fournière considers the changing nature of public space in London and what appears to be a growing trend towards its privatisation. He comments on how far privatised public spaces, such as Canary Wharf and Granary Square, King's Cross, are able to contribute to a key part of social sustainability, that is, the production of places that encourage social mixing, mingling and encounters between diverse groups. He suggests that one reading of such spaces is that the mix of commercial and leisure uses that comprise privatised public places may attract diverse publics and create the possibilities for 'encounters with difference'. Here, there is potential for the production of culturally diverse spaces where people of different backgrounds can *be* part of a public alongside one another, reducing insularity and creating place, the key factors to socially sustainable public space. All of this is a stated aspiration of the Mayor of London.

However, Fournière's observations, based on a study of a range of private-public spaces in London, suggest that this aspiration is yet to materialise, and that the prospects for socially sustainable, socially just, public space in London remain weak.

In Part 4, 'Sustaining London's environmental future', the chapters discuss how far an environmentally sustainable London is emerging, in relation to creating a less than polluting transport system that provides for all, a healthy London in which, wherever one lives, exposure to environmental harm and risk is minimised, and a place where ecology and environment are maintained in ways whereby their richness is passed on to future generations. The London Plan states that you cannot plan for London's economic and social sustainability without creating a sustainable environmental future for its populations, both human and non-human. However, one of the effects of austerity appears to be a shift towards deregulated government, and a loosening of controls on activities that may be harmful to ecological and environmental goals. The crisis of the economic model appears to be intertwined with the possibilities of a crisis of ecological reproduction and sustenance. Given that London's sustainability is under threat from climate change, in terms of an increased risk of flooding, drought and high temperatures, how can economy and ecology be reconciled in ways whereby London's resilience to environmental threats is enhanced, while its population is provided with the safeguards from the deleterious effects of environmental change?

Robin Hickman's focus in Chapter Twelve is the underestimated challenges in moving towards greater sustainability in travel in London. He considers the likely policy measures and interventions available in infrastructural, vehicle technology and built environmental terms, the deeper socio-cultural 'embeddedness' (and hence potentially fixed nature) of travel within everyday life, and the many complexities and inconsistencies involved in transitioning towards sustainable travel behaviours. Included here, for example, are the definitions of 'success': whether progress is judged against environmental, social and economic objectives, often where these aspirations will compete in direction; whether the transport sector plays its 'fair share' in reducing transport carbon dioxide emissions relative to other sectors; whether London, particularly inner London as a relatively low per capita transport emitter, should aim for a similar environmental aspiration as other parts of the UK; and whether international air emissions are included in the target calculations. The argument is that there is a large gap between policy aspirations and the likely achievements, particularly given funding constraints for infrastructure investment and the 'governance at a distance' nature of contemporary government.

Clare Herrick, in Chapter Thirteen, examines the future of London's Healthy City aspirations at a time when the need to address environmental risk factors grows ever stronger, but the political will and capacity to do so is limited by economic retrenchment and policies highlighting the need for 'personal responsibility'. The entwinement of the built environment with health outcomes and opportunities has a long history in urban planning and public health in the UK. However, the express incorporation of public health sensibilities within urban planning's logic has been hailed a recent and welcome advancement in the 'Healthy Cities' agenda. Emerging from the realisation that chronic health challenges (that is, obesity, diabetes, and so on) require the same attention to environmental risk factors as infectious diseases have, in the past, courted, has produced a wealth of research investigating the environmental determinants of health. However, the flow of knowledge has been largely unidirectional and, consequentially, policy to build healthier environments has been limited in scale and scope. Given that political attention is trained on modifiable risk factors (for example, diet, exercise, alcohol consumption), through the formation of 'Responsibility Deals' between public health bodies and industry, the long-term sustainability of London as a 'Healthy City' seems in doubt.

In Chapter Fourteen, Franklin Ginn and Robert A. Francis examine the political ecologies of wildlife conservation in London. Long-standing concerns with setting aside places for nature in the city are being supplanted by a desire to integrate ecological forms and processes as components of a connected urban 'green infrastructure'. This includes novel forms of ecological engineering such as living walls and roofs, alongside the restoration of post-industrial brownfield land to create 'green grids'. There has also been a growing appreciation of the physical and mental health benefits of urban green space for citizens, and ongoing efforts to map and address long-standing inequalities in access. However, the public discourse of social and ecological reconnection must be reconciled with changes in urban ecological governance. These include a decline in public control over planning and spending on restoration, and growing enthusiasm for both voluntary citizenship and public–private partnership. Important gains in urban green space have been achieved through persuading and compelling developers to mitigate for ecological damage. But critical urban ecologists are concerned about the political processes through which this is occurring, and dispute the ecological merits of some of the spaces created when vernacular and unofficial brownfield ecologies are tidied up under public–private partnership developments.

In Part 5 of the book, 'Postscript', the editors note how sustainable development discourse is shifting towards the notion of resilience that, if anything, is more conservative than the concept of sustainability, and less likely, in the way it is being deployed by politicians, to offer a way to challenge the inequities of socio-spatial development pursued in the name of sustainable development. In evaluating the potential effects of the shift in emphasis, the editors suggest that there is need to move debates, plans and policies away from the current sustainable cities agenda, which is concerned primarily with pursuing 'sustainable cities that balance environmental concerns, the needs of future populations and economic growth' (Beauregard, 2005, p 204). Instead, what ought to be encouraged is a (re)consideration of interpretations of sustainability concerned with what may seem to be traditional notions of social justice which, at the very least, seek to balance market and social interests in the public good. Here, the objective is to refocus sustainability around issues of equity and social justice, in which London's sustainable development ought to be conceived as a moral response to what Davoudi (2001, p 88) describes as the 'pernicious factors of capitalism and scientific rationality.'

Notes

[1] Ken Livingstone's aspirations were curtailed by having no investment powers and little influence over central government spending. His aspiration for London to develop its world city status recognised that this was only likely to occur by facilitating, and supporting, the financial service sector, and providing a political context for private sector-led growth (see Gordon, 2010).

[2] However, one should note that their were components in the 2004 and 2008 London Plans that sought to put a limit on the consumption of natural resources, while nevertheless relying on market-led distribution.

Acknowledgement

Our thanks to Sarah Fielder who read a draft of the chapter and made a number of important comments about both substance and style. We are indebted to her.

References

Abercrombie, P. (1945) *Greater London Plan 1944: a report prepared on behalf of the Standing Conference on London Regional Planning*, London: HMSO.

Ackroyd, P. (2001) *London: the biography*, London: Vintage.

Aldridge, H., Kenway, P., MacInnes, T. and Parekh, A. (2012) *Monitoring poverty and social exclusion 2012*, York: Joseph Rowntree Foundation.

Beauregard, R. (2005) 'Introduction: institutional transformations', *Planning Theory*, vol 4, no 3, pp 203-7.

Blühdorn, I. (2007) 'Sustaining the unsustainable: symbolic politics and the politics of simulation', *Environmental Politics*, vol 16, no 2, pp 251-75.

Brand, P. (2007) 'Green subjection: the politics of neoliberal urban environmental management', *International Journal of Urban and Regional Research*, vol 31, no 3, pp 616-32.

Brownill, S. (1999) 'Turning the East End into the West End: the lessons and legacies of the London Docklands Development Corporation', in R. Imrie and H. Thomas (eds) *British urban policy*, London: Sage, pp 43-63.

Bynum, W.F. and Porter, R. (eds) (1991) *Living and dying in London*, London: Wellcome Institute for the History of Medicine.

Cameron, D. (2009) *The Big Society*, Hugo Young Memorial Lecture, November 10th, London.

Campkin, B. (2013) *Remaking London: decline and regeneration in urban culture*, London: I.B. Tauris.

Clear Air in London (2013) 'Quick guide to air pollution and the "Year of Air" in 2013' (http://cleanairinlondon.org/news/quick-guide-to-air-pollution).

Cochrane, A. (2006) 'Devolving the heartland: making up a new social policy for the "South East"', *Critical Social Policy*, vol 26, no 3, pp 685-96.

Conservative Party (2010) *Modern conservatism: the Conservative quality of life manifesto*, London: Conservative Party.

Davoudi, S. (2001) 'Planning and the twin discourses of sustainability', in A. Layard, S. Davoudi and S. Batty (eds) *Planning for a sustainable future*, London, Spon, pp 81-99.

Dickens, C. (1839) *Sketches by 'Boz', illustrative of every-day life and every-day people*, London: John Macrone.

EIU (Economist Intelligence Unit) (2008) *Doing good: business and the sustainability challenge*, Briefing paper, London: EIU.

Flint, J. and Raco, M. (eds) (2012) *The future of sustainable cities: critical reflections*, Bristol: Policy Press.

Forshaw, J. and Abercrombie, P. (1943) *County of London Plan*, London: Macmillan and Co Ltd, London County Council.

Fry, T. (2011) *Design as politics*, Oxford: Berg.

Fussey, P., Coafee, J., Armstrong, G. and Hobbs, D. (2011) *Securing and sustaining the Olympic City: reconfiguring London for 2012 and beyond*, Aldershot: Ashgate.

Gordon, I. (2010) 'Scenarios and planning for alternative London futures – or making a drama out of a strategy', in B. Kochan and K. Scanlon (eds) *London: coping with austerity*, London: London School of Economics and Political Science, pp 49-56.

GLA (Greater London Authority) (2010) *The Mayor's Economic Development Strategy for London*, London: GLA.

GLA (Greater London Authority) (2011) *The London Plan*, London: GLA.

Higgins, P., Campanera, J. and Nobajas, A. (2012) 'Quality of life and spatial inequality in London', *European Urban and Regional Studies*, 5 April.

Holman, N. (2010) 'The changing nature of the London Plan', in K. Scanlon and B. Kochan (eds) *London: coping with austerity*, London: London School of Economics and Political Science, pp 29-40.

Imrie, R. and Thomas, H. (eds) (1999) *British urban policy*, London: Sage.

Imrie, R., Lees, L. and Raco, M. (eds) (2009) *Regenerating London: governance, sustainability and community in a global city*, London: Routledge.

Johnson, B. (2011) 'Foreword', in Greater London Authority (GLA), *The London Plan: Spatial Development Strategy for Greater London*, London: GLA.

Lees, L. (2013) 'The urban injustices of New Labour's "new urban renewal": the case of the Aylesbury Estate in London', *Antipode*.

Lefebvre, H. (1991) *The production of space*, Oxford: Blackwell.

Livingstone, K. (2004) 'Foreword', in Greater London Authority (GLA), *The London Plan: Spatial Development Strategy for Greater London*, London: GLA.

LSDC (London Sustainable Development Commission) (2003) *First annual report*, London: LSDC.

Lupton, R., with Hills, J., Stewart, K. and Vizard, P. (2013) *Labour's social policy record: policy, spending and outcomes 1997-2010*, Summary Research Report 1, Social Policy in a Cold Climate, London: Centre for Analysis of Social Exclusion, London School of Economics and Political Science.

MacKinnon, D. and Driscoll Derickson, K. (2012) 'From resilience to resourcefulness: a critique of resilience policy and activism', *Progress in Human Geography*, 8 August.

McGuirk, P. (2000) 'Power and policy networks in urban governance: local government and property-led regeneration in Dublin', *Urban Studies*, vol 37, no 4, pp 651-72.

Peck, J. (2012) 'Austerity urbanism: American cities under extreme economy', *City*, vol 16, no 6, pp 626-55.

Plowman, J. (2012) 'Foreword', in London Sustainable Development Commission, *London's Quality of Life indicators 2012 report*, London: Greater London Authority.

Rajan, A. (2006) 'Automobility and the liberal disposition', *The Sociological Review*, vol 54, no 1, pp 113-29.

Swyngedouw, E. (2011) 'Interrogating post-democratization: reclaiming egalitarian political spaces', *Political Geography*, vol 30, no 7, pp 370-80.

Thornley, A. and Newman, P. (2011) *Planning world cities: globalization and urban politics*, Planning, Environment, Cities series, London: Palgrave Macmillan.

Tripp, H. (1938) *Road traffic and its control*, London: Edward Arnold.

UN Habitat, (2010) *The right to the city: bridging the urban divide*, Rio de Janeiro: World Urban Forum.

Vallance, S., Perkins, H., Bowring, J. and Dixon, J., (2013) 'Almost invisible: glimpsing the city and its residents in the urban sustainability discourse', *Urban Studies*, vol 49, no 8, pp 1695-710.

Vanolo, A. (2013) 'Smartmentality: the smart city as disciplinary strategy', *Urban Studies*, 11 July.

WCED (World Commission on Environment and Development) (1987) *Our Common Future*, Geneva, United Nations.

TWO

Privatising London

A conversation with Anna Minton

Introduction

This chapter is a conversation between the editors and Anna Minton, a writer and journalist who has written extensively about urban regeneration, with a focus on the privatisation of public space. The conversation occurred in December 2012 and it provides an important reference for understanding sustainable development in London that is part of an anti-democratic, pro-market politics, encouraging the recapitalising of land for profit. There is nothing new about the pro-growth agenda of London's politics, but, for Minton, it is disingenuous for politicians to use the term 'sustainable development' to describe processes and outcomes that do not seem to be promoting much beyond social inequality, social polarisation and increasing consumption of environmental resources. As Minton suggests, the notion of sustainable development appears to be no more than a euphemism for property-led regeneration, and a smokescreen for politicians' pursuit of an economic growth agenda with limited regard for the social and distributive consequences. Such consequences, for Minton, require much more scrutiny, and include the privatisation of places that are ostensibly about creating socially mixed communities that are, on closer inspection, far from mixed and far from inclusive. Instead, housing and planning policies in London are failing to provide sufficient low-cost dwellings, or places that enable people on a mix of incomes to be part of stable, affordable communities.

EDITORS: In your 2009 book, *Ground control*, you said that the London Docklands model of regeneration is deeply flawed and ineffective. Can you reflect on your arguments in light of current plans for Docklands that would double Canary Wharf's working population by 2025?

ANNA MINTON: When I was in the early stages of researching *Ground control* and the Docklands part of the book I remember reading about the etymology of the word 'regeneration' and how it really came into vogue from the late 1980s (before that 'redevelopment' was the term). It was seen to be a new way of doing things, the phoenix rising from the ashes. But at an event recently a very senior regeneration figure at Newham Council was talking about how all the plans that Newham had put in place for swathes of private housing, you know – totally developer-led schemes – had all been abandoned in the new regeneration plan for Docklands, and how absolutely thrilled she was by this because it gave them an opportunity to really look at things again and to do things differently, and how actually the financial crisis was paving the way to look at alternative models. I was very surprised to hear this, as Newham's whole approach to regeneration certainly seems to be very much the pre-crash approach. For example, I have seen a promotional film that Newham showed at the Shanghai Expo in 2010; it is accompanied by a brochure that you can get online. The film is only available through a freedom of information request. The topic is the 'regeneration supernova', which is spreading throughout the wider Docklands area. The 'supernova' is creating world-class opportunities: you've got an airport on your doorstep, you've got one of the most fantastic shopping centres in Western Europe – this is obviously an 'arc of opportunity', to use their terminology. It's quite astonishing promotional material aimed at an international investor audience. I find the term 'supernova' quite crass, unbridled, a sort of rocket shooting through the stratosphere-type terminology. My perception is that this 'supernova approach' is not signalling anything different at all from what's already gone ahead. But my other point on this is that we're just not really in a position to be speculating about any kind of sizable transformation of Docklands or any other area in the current economic climate.

EDITORS: It strikes us that this regeneration agent thinks that there might be alternatives now that they can step back and do things differently. You're very sceptical of that?

ANNA MINTON: They are saying this because the economic reality means that much of this masterplan stuff is not going to happen. So they have to do things differently rather than not doing anything at all. It's economically driven. But in my experience, over the last couple of years, local authorities have, almost without exception, been very, very unwilling to look at different ways of doing things. Different ways of doing things have been proposed by various coalitions and community groups, but they have been met with resistance from local authorities. It's the 'head in the sand' approach, waiting for return to business as usual.

EDITORS: In the meantime, business as usual is the London Plan, which sees mixed developments as essential in terms of mixing our communities, and they link this to a broader, if incredibly vague, discourse about sustainability.

ANNA MINTON: I think mixed communities and sustainability are incredibly problematic terms that have become increasingly problematic over the last decade, and actually both of them have been smokescreens for a whole host of other issues. I used to do a lot of work on mixed communities, about 10 years ago, partly as a consultant and partly as a journalist. Initially, I was a big supporter of the whole idea of mixed communities, but I came to see, unfortunately, that lying behind the mixed communities mantra is very often the replacement of predominantly affordable housing by predominantly private and unaffordable housing. I think there's a general acceptance that the residualisation of social housing has been a really terrible thing, and concentrations of low-income housing, concentrations of deprivation, are a bad thing. But if you unpack what is happening in the name of mixed communities, it's not at all about mixing up low income with key worker with owner-occupation housing. It is privatisation. Indeed, the developers are currently on holiday from affordable housing requirements thanks to the Chancellor's most recent intervention.[1] I think mixed communities has been a smokescreen for far more powerful economic-led, property-led regeneration agendas.

EDITORS: And sustainability?

ANNA MINTON: Sustainability is at least as problematic a word. I mean it just seems such a vague term. It's hard to say what it is. The government are pro-development so does that mean that development is sustainable? What does it mean to be sustainable? It has to meet various economic, social and environmental needs. But pretty much any developer is going to be able to give a nod to some of that. In 2004 there were changes to the Planning and Compulsory Purchase Act, which basically meant that sustainability has come to mean economic benefit to areas, which is quite the opposite from what it's supposed to mean and what its original meaning was. So I think it's a catch-all term. It's far too loose. It has no definition. It means all things to all people. But it's still got this kind of fluffy feel to it. So I don't see how it can be co-opted or brought back. I just think it should be bent, or seen for what it really is.

EDITORS: The problem, of course, is that companies or private organisations actually find it useful the way it is. It can be used to support and reinforce their particular reputations.

ANNA MINTON: Oh absolutely. It's positive, it has a moral persuasion and it's quite surprising to me that it has retained that. I think the positive rhetoric of sustainability is still in most people's minds connected with the environment. But the reality of it is that actually it pays the way for property development schemes, which are fundamentally given the go-ahead on the basis of economic benefit. They come to mean the opposite of what they're supposed to do. But that's the case with so much of the language in these fields.

EDITORS: An interesting issue relates to the Coalition and its politics in contrast to New Labour. Has there been a real meaningful shift or change in broader national politics in relation to planning, spatial development, and in particular, some of the development issues that we're seeing now?

ANNA MINTON: I can't see any. The rhetoric was brilliant before the 2010 election. The *Open source planning* document was great.[2] You look at it and think well, this is all really, really good stuff. But you could tell from day one that there was going to be a big contradiction/schism in Tory thinking because the Conservative manifesto said right up front that economic benefit, economic concerns, were going to be at the forefront of the planning system. What seems to have been the case since they came to power is that we've seen the loosening of planning regulations one after another, the holidays from affordable housing, etc. Sadly, all the great promises of open source planning are not bearing fruit at all. Despite all of this stuff about neighbourhood planning and localism, ultimately it's overridden. So I think it's a great shame. I think the thinking went in there and the thinking was really good. And it's still there and it could still be revived.

EDITORS: We've been talking about mixed communities policy now for the last 10 years, but actually mixed communities policy may yet just disappear, and because of the rollbacks that are going on under the Coalition government, developers are basically going to get away with redeveloping neighbourhoods without mixed communities.

ANNA MINTON: I know. Having spent so much time criticising the failings of mixed communities policy, it's possible there will come a time in the not too distant future when we'll look back and think, well, at least we had something of a mixed communities policy. I think you're right. It did build some affordable housing; it just didn't build enough. We might just see the end of that and one of the main catalysts will be the financial/economic crisis. Developers never really wanted to do it anyway. Where will that leave us? No state subsidy for housing. Just a burgeoning private rented sector. That's certainly a possibility.

EDITORS: But it isn't just speculating on what the alternatives will be in terms of providing social housing or housing people with low incomes; of course, the big issue is the burgeoning private rented market.

ANNA MINTON: I have covered this in quite a lot of detail in the new chapter I wrote updating *Ground control*, which was published in 2012. It looked at the true legacy of the Olympics. I spent quite a lot of time looking at housing in Newham to show what's really going on on the ground for the local community there. I was taken around Newham by a council housing officer off the record, so I won't mention their name. The officer was absolutely great, taking me around and telling me just what their daily working life was like. The stories I detailed in there are hair-raising. You know, 38 people living in a two-up, two-down, house, 10 to a room, sheds everywhere. I was told that one of their clients in Newham was even sleeping in a commercial fridge and paying rent for it! The officer said I wonder if they dreamt that. That was the most unbelievable story. But it's completely out of control. What I hope is that the Left and ordinary people will start to be galvanised about the housing situation and a few links will start to be made in people's minds, so that we can shift back the parameters of the debate, but perhaps that's just naïve.

EDITORS: Not necessarily.

ANNA MINTON: I think one of the other things is that it has to go wider than affected council estate tenants. It's about the sort of city that you want to live in. That affects everybody who lives there. I think this may be one of the problems in getting political will off the ground in that the stories told are very localised and they are always bound to individual battles, individual personalities, individual circumstances. Somehow that has to be knitted into a bigger debate about what sort of neighbourhood, city, Londoners want to live in. I'm very reluctant to say anything positive about Boris Johnson given the sorts of changes he's presiding over. But that Kosovo comment about 'social cleansing' has been invaluable, and it's a starting point for the debate.[3] He probably recognised that. So I think it's a debate that has got some hope. Some of the stories have really galvanised people. The story of Newham saying that they wanted to export council tenants to Stoke-on-Trent and a housing association in Stoke complaining on receipt of the letter. I mean, what possessed them to want to actually publicise this, or did it come out by mistake? But these are issues for everybody to get really involved in. I suppose it's the organisations and the institutions that are going to drive forward that change. That's the difficulty and the problem. I mean I'm involved in trying to set up this 'right to the city' campaign in London at the moment, and that's difficult.

EDITORS: In *Ground control* you talk about a blinkered view of public space, a playground that marginalises the poor. The role of the private sector appears to be increasing in regeneration schemes, as witnessed by the redevelopment in King's Cross, the Westfield scheme in Stratford, and the new IKEA-led development near the Olympic Park. What do you think of what appears to be a privatisation of regeneration in London, particularly around public space?

ANNA MINTON: Obviously I take a fairly critical view on the privatisation of public space, the proliferation of privately owned, privately controlled security guard-manned estates. So let's talk about the problems with the model itself. One of the main themes of *Ground control* is that we build, create places that reflect where we are politically, economically and socially. We've been building undemocratic spaces now for the last 10 years plus. I think it's been an indication of where we are politically. But we're beginning to live in increasingly undemocratic times, because we're building large parts of the city that are not democratic at all. The Occupy protest at St Paul's Cathedral (from December 2011 to June 2012) is the best possible illustration of this that you could hope to find. It is a perfect illustration of what's happened in the City of London since the Big Bang in 1986.

The reason that Occupy was outside the steps of St Paul's Cathedral was because they couldn't put that protest in Paternoster Square, which is actually where the Stock Exchange is. They were called Occupy London Stock Exchange. But Paternoster Square is a privately owned estate and they were immediately ejected from there. In fact, the City of London today is a series of privately owned estates. It wasn't at all before Big Bang. The small space outside St Paul's Cathedral is actually pretty much the only sizable publicly owned land that's left under the Corporation of London's jurisdiction. The Church owns some of it and some of it is owned by the Corporation. But that's the only effectively public space. So that's why they were there.

To continue on my theme about the impact of the Big Bang and the deregulation of finance – that was the spur for the creation of Canary Wharf and the Broadgate Centre, because suddenly you needed huge trading floors to manage a new kind of financial industry – the city with its little maze of tiny streets and nooks and crannies wasn't suitable for that. So they went out to Broadgate and Canary Wharf and pioneered the regeneration of East London. But actually you saw this process come back into the City of London and now the City of London is a collection of privately owned estates. It's just the perfect reflection of the failures of democratic governance in the Corporation itself.

EDITORS: You've mentioned in your work that such privatisation dates back to the 18th century, when many London environs were private. So the question becomes, what has changed?

ANNA MINTON: Georgian squares, such as Bedford Square, were entirely closed off to the public during the 18th century and the early 19th century, barricaded with fences and gates and security guards and sentry boxes. But as local government took hold and grew in power, paralleled with the rise in democracy in parliamentary and central government, you started to see huge public protests against the gating of these very large parts of the city. It resulted in two massive parliamentary enquiries in the mid-19th century. Of course the aristocratic landlords, the dukes and the earls very much wanted to maintain the status quo, so a real battle went on. But as a result of the two parliamentary enquiries, it was decided that it was completely unacceptable to close off these large areas of London. It was decided that henceforth all local authorities would adopt streets and public places in the city. That's why we had/have this assumption that the streets are public and that they always have been so. They haven't always been so. They've been so for the last 150 years since our grandparents and our great grandparents' time. This was a huge democratic achievement. What we're seeing now is this democratic achievement going into reverse.

EDITORS: It's almost like we're reverting back to the early Victorian city: low-income people in private rented property, multiple occupation, severe pressure on housing, very little social housing, social polarisation between low income and high/very high income and privatisation. What does this mean for the future of London, if we're going back to what we were 200 years ago?

ANNA MINTON: I wouldn't say we've gone back to the 1820s yet. But we're sort of heading back in that direction, with really dire economic consequences.

EDITORS: What is the evidence in terms of the privatisation of London? How are public interactions shifting or changing?

ANNA MINTON: My negative view stems from the sharp, visible polarisation. Take the Westfield shopping centre in Stratford City – you don't even need to know you're in Stratford. You've come by tube or you've come straight in on the motorway, which has taken you into the car park. You can go shopping. But if you make the effort to look across the road from the top of the entrance staircase, and you look down over the gyratory system, you've got this run-down 1970s mall, which is where local people go. I think that really sharp social segregation in the city is unhealthy.

EDITORS: What kind of social mixing/interaction would you like to see in London?

ANNA MINTON: I think people rubbing up against each other, but not really interacting, is okay. That's how we all live in the city. We don't talk to each other when we pass each other on a crowded street, but we're just aware of each other's presence. This becomes problematic when there are barriers to it. Barriers are created when the visible difference becomes too great to ignore, and this impinges on our unconsciousness as we walk through the streets of the city. When the visible barriers are massive, that unconsciousness is punctured. You're like, oh, look at that, that's odd, that makes me feel frightened, I can't quite deal with that. I think that's really amplified by the physical characteristics of these new private estates, which make concerted efforts to separate themselves off from the rest of the city, to delineate themselves they use different materials. One of my favourite examples is Paddington Basin. Go into Paddington Basin, if you can find the entrance, it's very difficult to actually know how to enter this place. But when you do you enter this huge enclave, which is the size of Soho, it's almost entirely empty. There's this pristine privatised estate of glass apartment boxes, office premises and the metro, but it's almost empty. If you see a stranger walking along across the plaza, you notice them. It's a world away from the busy street outside where you won't notice strangers, you won't notice difference. They are starkly different environments.

EDITORS: What's interesting of course is that the usual suspects are involved in this. So there's an institutionalisation of property development and regeneration. Probably nothing new about it. But to what extent has it been heightened?

ANNA MINTON: It is the same players, but the process has become much more transnational over recent years. The private sector has always been involved in regeneration, and I am not arguing to get them out of regeneration. My take on it is that it's actually policy which has made this a really, really big issue. I mean private developers are not the ones who insisted on having private estates. It's central and local government who have absolved their democratic responsibilities and handed them over to the private sector, because they don't want to pay for property development. We've sleepwalked into it. But I don't think it's led by the developers. The local authority mindset is lamentable; after 25-30 years of areas being run into the ground, it's not really surprising that they need to be redeveloped. The local authorities and developers are hand in glove. Local authorities are basically falling over themselves to attract developers to come and do these schemes. They are desperate for it. That's the problem.

EDITORS: And transnational money that still sees London as a safe place to invest has totally distorted the property market. A one-bedroom flat in Hyde Park costs £6.5 million!

ANNA MINTON: It's absolutely ludicrous!

EDITORS: In your recent 2013-report *Fortress Britain* for the New Economics Foundation, you reflect on the impact of 'security'. Parts of the sustainability agenda identified in the London Plan aim to create safe and secured spaces. What do you think about this agenda, and what are its implications for London's residential neighbourhoods and public space environment?

ANNA MINTON: What I found really interesting in my *Fortress Britain* report was that I encountered 'secure by design' for schools and public buildings, but not for housing.[4] For schools and public buildings there are 'Secured by Design' standards directly linked to an audit of local crime risk. But housing is a question of negotiation between individual police officers, developers, architects and the council. This has led to some unbelievably militarised buildings, especially in deprived areas, where crime tends to be higher. Gating is a reflection of the very sharp social inequalities in London, with very, very wealthy areas and very poor areas being the most heavily securitised. My take on it is that it is not down to consumer preference at all. It's much more because developers feel, justifiably, that they can market these places with the added security seen as a bonus. Most people are not looking for a gated development, but when offered a house with lots of extra security, very often they'll see it as a bonus. Also the insurance industry offers lower premiums for homes with 'Secured by Design'.

EDITORS: So in terms of creating a sustainable London, this might revolve around opening up places and people to each other?

ANNA MINTON: I think there's recognition, even among policy makers, nowadays, that gated developments with really visible gating are something to be wary of. But it's not something that seems to have filtered through that much to social housing. This isn't a 'sustainable', to use the awful word, way to live. 'Safe and secure' is just as problematic a term as 'mixed communities' and 'sustainability', which can mean all things to all people. What sort of safety are you talking about? Are you talking about physical safety or emotional safety or actual crime or fear of crime? All of these things are really different. The phrase is a smokescreen for the increasing securitisation of city space, and that has a serious impact on fear of crime and lack of trust.

EDITORS: How has education in London been impacted?

ANNA MINTON: Education has followed behind, hot on the heels of housing. The changes in the housing market have filtered through and transformed schools. I went to my local state primary school in Barnes in London, now a very exclusive part of London. In the 1970s it was a really average part of London because there were lots of council estates nearby. My primary school was basically 50 per cent kids from council estates and 50 per cent kids, like me, who had professional parents. That is exactly the way it should be. It was great. It's a model that actually has completely influenced my life and the things I do and the work I do. But Barnes is now a completely different place. Most of the council housing has been sold off. The demographic is completely different. So the sort of primary school I went to is now predominantly middle-class or has become private, joining the growing number of other private schools opening in the area. What happened (and is still happening) to council housing has had an enormous impact on education too. We're going to send our little boy to the school around the corner. It will be quite dissimilar from the school I went to; it's going to be much more of a middle-class environment. He won't grow up knowing the sort of people I knew growing up. He won't. What am I saying here? It's just that the issue of social mixing in the city, in London, is so important.

EDITORS: What we'd like to ask now is about alternatives. You've advocated 'flexible urbanism' as a way to create better places – what do you mean by this?

ANNA MINTON: By 'flexible urbanism' I mean much greater open-mindedness, but not a loosening of planning regulations that have built really important protections for the urban environment. All the developments being built in London are the opposite of flexible. Take the Olympic Park – a very controlled site which had a rubric and an agenda laid down on it driven by the needs of Westfield before it was even built. With the best will in the world, the people behind the legacy, the Development Corporation, can't do that much, because cutting through the Olympic Park is a two-lane highway. I advocate a much more flexible approach which takes account of more than economic benefit and will look at other things, for example, affordable space on the high street. London's high streets are being killed off by high business rates. Flexible urbanism, of course, is easier in cities like Manchester and other European post-industrial cities where empty spaces have been taken over and colonised by unusual and exciting uses. But the context in London is different; London is so developed now, the land values are much higher, and therein the pressures on land. I have talked about unplanned urbanism, and what I was getting at was the importance of empty space, of wastelands, being allowed to have a purpose that is not always about profit. This is really hard in London where everywhere is a space for investment. Some spaces in London need to be free spaces, for unplanned urbanism rather than investment. We need to allow planners to be open-minded about alternative uses, alternative ways of doing things, to approach alternatives with a 'yes' rather than a 'no', but at the same time to protect spaces from the rampant loosening of planning regulations. The planning system has always been, in my mind, about striking that kind of balance.

EDITORS: The issue of course in London is that when a planning application comes in, development companies and builders dominate it.

ANNA MINTON: Yes, I think planners have limited authority and power. I think one of the problems about alternatives is that it's so hard for community groups who do come up with alternatives, who do work them through, who work incredibly hard on them, to get a proper hearing from local authorities. I mean, temporary uses have become quite trendy, but they have to be done by somebody with an institutional foothold.

EDITORS: But beyond pop-ups and temporary use, it's about developing alternatives that have longevity?

ANNA MINTON: Yes, all of the much needed public services, which are being savagely cut, libraries, youth services, old person services, they can come back into all the empty spaces on London's high streets. But it needs political will. Public libraries are so hugely important and I think there's going to be more around that. But public money basically goes into private pockets these days. Even if there was public money, if there's no political will to direct that public money into an alternative way of doing things, it will not happen. New York's High Line Park is a good example of an alternative that has been a hugely successful poster project for a different way of doing things, even if it has also had all sorts of downsides. You've got to work on two levels simultaneously: you've got to win the argument about alternatives and you've got to get working on alternative schemes.

EDITORS: It seems that local communities wherever you look in London appear not to be really working on alternatives?

ANNA MINTON: Part of the issue is that everybody who's involved in this stuff is involved in a huge personal battle, which is really tiring. And it's also very focused on local circumstances. We need to try and widen the debate and link a lot of these individual struggles together, to have a bigger discussion about the sort of city that we want to live in. There are organisations like the London Tenants Federation who have that linking capacity but it's got to go wider than just council tenants. We also need to change the terms of the debate on the national policy stage. There isn't a voice on the national policy stage or even on the London stage for the sorts of themes that we've been discussing. There are enough people who are interested, but it's about creating new structures, which is a very challenging and difficult thing to do. You look back at old struggles and see a group of people in the 1980s who were talking about not dissimilar themes, but in a different London context, academics like Doreen Massey and the like, and the groups they had around them. Now it is new folk like you guys, and new groups. And you want to be more successful than they were, because basically they lost badly.

In terms of looking at alternatives, the third piece of work I've just done is looking at the role of public interest and the public good in planning in particular. In my mind, the idea of public benefit has become interchangeable with economic benefit, just to go back to our discussion of sustainability. But can we reinvent the 19th and 20th-century idea of the public good and public interest given its assault by the Right for standing in the way of the market and on the Left for imposing universal mindsets on a diverse society? I think yes, it is worth reinventing around the common goods and services of the comprehensive city ideal, which is currently under threat and we stand to lose. I have gotten increasingly interested in the 1947 Planning Act and betterment. The fact that the planning system has never worked as it was intended because development charges which were at the heart of the planning system, basically, were never imposed. Development land tax just disappeared. The whole issue has never been properly addressed.

EDITORS: London's planning system is premised on an understanding that the private sector land market is not to be tarnished or to be touched, but at the same time planning in a way has to try and accrue public benefit. Maybe we have to go back to old models? Maybe there needs to be much more centralised government intervention and control, maybe even land nationalisation, collectivisation? Communities can't do much if they can't control the land that is being developed on.

ANNA MINTON: This is why I find this discussion so interesting. One of the key quotes was that development charges were not about nationalising land; they were about nationalising the development value of land. I think a discussion around that really does need to be had. But I think we do have to be really wary of going back to a sort of postwar-type model. I think that was irredeemably hard.

EDITORS: In terms of sustainable development and people being able to live in places and maintaining themselves, a big problem is the privatisation of utilities – water, electricity, gas, sewers, you name it.

ANNA MINTON: There is a cultural failure to launch a proper debate around these topics. Policy makers, developers and local authorities hide behind vague rhetoric like sustainable development. There's a lot of vested interest, so they do not want to encourage a proper debate on all of this.

EDITORS: The way in which the Mayor and the GLA [Greater London Authority] are approaching the sustainable environment is interesting. One of the things they have done is to appoint 'London Leaders', who are supposed to galvanise and demonstrate through example what is possible and permissible in relation to different types of sustainable development policies. They're a range of individuals, about 12 or so, and they come from different walks of life, but primarily businesspeople.

ANNA MINTON: It sounds like a business improvement district or sort of politburo for London really. It very much depends on who the London Leaders are and the role that they play. It sounds like a gimmick. You know, we need to do something here, let's get these people involved, they'll help us out in x and y way. It's not addressing the real manifold issues. There is a lack of democracy and a lack of empowerment to people on the ground, and this scheme appears to be a complete smokescreen and diversion from these important matters.

EDITORS: The final question we have is, what do you feel are the main sustainable development challenges for London? Do you think the whole sustainable development agenda should be pushed to one side?

ANNA MINTON: I think it's entirely discredited. It amazes me that we still talk about it. What do you mean – what is the main sustainable development challenge?

EDITORS: That's a very good question. What do we mean by sustainable development challenges? We like the way that the design theorist and philosopher Tony Fry writes about the relationship between design, unsustainability and politics. He argues that we need to eradicate the term 'sustainable development', and he uses a different language, like the word 'sustainment', that has overtones with a notion of necessity and need and not with want or aggrandisement. The term 'sustainable development' has been politically neutered and disassociated from politics, and Fry looks to re-associate it with politics and political discourse and debate. There's a politics to be played here in terms of challenging the particular definitions of it in London, normalising the definitions of it and saying, actually, we don't take that. What we want to do is to say this is how we understand it. Sustainable development for us is about providing individuals with possibilities and ensuring they have a baseline of material living and lifestyle. It is also about self-determination.

ANNA MINTON: So I would like you to reframe your question and then I'll happily answer it, without using the term 'sustainable development'!

EDITORS: The book itself, in a way, is trying to throw it away and to replace it with the notion of the 'good city', which in some ways is even more problematic a term. But it has an interesting lineage in (re)connecting the self to a basis of material living that is no more than consuming what one needs. Some of the thoughts about the good city, from people like Lewis Mumford, provide a sketch to flesh out what the possibilities for London might be.

ANNA MINTON: I think that says something. So again, social justice?

EDITORS: Yes, social justice issues. It's the whole raft and range of these. We would like to see a public transportation system that actually works as a public transportation system, that doesn't just go down one singular route, but is one that is actually connected up.

ANNA MINTON: Absolutely. Then you would have to have a model behind it which dealt with the fact that if you put this in the hands of private providers, they're going to cluster all the profitable routes and they're going to ignore the other ones. You say you like the good city. I was getting sort of hung up on public goods and common goods, but it's the same sort of territory. I came to the conclusion that maybe the public good is too much of a contested term anyway.

If we get back to your question, what are the main sustainable development challenges for London? If we bend sustainable development and say what the main social justice challenges are, I think it's quite clear that the main challenge is the accelerating trend towards the increasing polarisation of the capital in terms of housing, and that's without even discussing Housing Benefit cuts and changes in the definition of affordable housing. We are really accelerating a trend towards the creation of ghettos of poverty in peripheral parts of London, in boroughs like Barking and Dagenham. We're storing up huge, huge problems for the future. The vision of the London Plan a while back was to create a more mixed and balanced city. We're going rapidly in the opposite direction. That's the London crisis really.

Notes

[1] Section 106 agreements can be waived for sites where the Planning Inspectorate assesses that the affordable housing requirement has rendered the whole project unviable (www. gov.uk/government/publications/section-106-affordable-housing-requirements-review-and-appeal).

[2] The Conservative Party has published various documents defining open source planning as the decentralisation and streamlining of the planning system to 'allow it to focus on promoting sustainable development that local communities want' (Conservative Party, 2010).

[3] For further details about this comment, see the report in *The Guardian* newspaper at www.theguardian.com/politics/2010/oct/28/boris-johnson-kosovo-style-cleansing-housing-benefit

[4] For further details of this policy initiative, see www.securedbydesign.com

References

Conservative Party (2010) *Open source planning*, Policy Green Paper, No 14.
Minton, A. (2012) *Ground control: fear and happiness in the 21st century city* (2nd edn), Harmondsworth: Penguin.
Minton, A. and Aked, J. (2013) *Fortress Britain: high security, insecurity and the challenge of preventing harm*, London: New Economic Foundation.

THREE

Just Space:
towards a just, sustainable London

Robin Brown, Michael Edwards and Richard Lee

Just Space is a network of action groups influencing plan making in London, to ensure public debate on crucial issues of social justice and on social, economic and environmental sustainability. Operating mainly through mutual support among member groups, we are active across all spatial scales of London – at neighbourhood, borough and London-wide strategic levels. What brought us together was a need to challenge the domination of the planning process by developers and public bodies, the latter often heavily influenced by property development interests. We see little to indicate that the planning system's formal commitment to community participation is more than lip service: the gap between policy and practice is immense where democratic engagement is concerned. Just Space is doing a bit to close that gap.

The influence of academic work on Just Space has been limited and indirect – via cooperation with researchers who have shared their learning environment. We would mention Arnstein (1969), Castells (1983), Healey (1992) and Mayer (2011) as influential gateways to research on participation processes in city planning. On the specific issues of London – and especially the polarisation, displacement and gentrification processes – we have drawn on Porter and Shaw (2008), Edwards (2010), Imrie et al (2009) and Aldridge et al (2013).

Just Space works by:

- bringing together diverse participants representative of various interests and, through consensus forming, marrying expertise with direct experiences to formulate activities and collective views;
- providing co-learning and sharing information and knowledge by briefing papers, meetings, seminars/workshops and conferences;
- facilitating the voices of local communities/groups in public consultation, plan making and formal scrutiny opportunities provided by the statutory planning system;
- building links with researchers and students in universities aiming to harness their skills and capacities to meet community needs.

As an illustration, for the 2010 London Plan Examination in Public (EiP), Just Space coordinated or facilitated an unprecedented 60 community organisations that appeared and gave evidence.

The UK's statutory system of land use planning (now renamed 'spatial planning') is almost the only field where procedures for public participation are embedded by law as compulsory elements of public decision making, and this has been the case for some decades. In London it applies to the plans produced by the 33 boroughs and, since 2000, to the new Spatial Development Strategy (London Plan) produced by the Mayor of London. The Greater London Authority (GLA) created in that year has planning and various other strategic powers which are exercised by the directly elected Mayor and also comprises a small Assembly whose powers are limited: it can 'scrutinise' the Mayor, must approve the Mayor's budget and could – by a two-thirds majority – reject the London Plan (Rydin et al, 2004).

Just Space is a fluid coming-together of community groups and concerned independent organisations, several of who are pan-London bodies. It does not yet have legal status, and only recently adopted a constitution.[1] In the first few years it consciously strove to maintain its informal structure and operation, but the desire and need to survive and develop, in the face of changes in the operations of the planning system and institutions, meant that a few of the features of formalised organisations had to be adopted. This chapter presents a narrative of the formation and evolution of Just Space, highlights its main successes and failures, and reflects on some of the issues confronting Londoners as they seek to influence, or even take control of, their city. The word 'sustainability' is used with care and caution since we so often find it being emptied of meaning, used to whitewash or greenwash policies and actions whose true sustainability is questionable.

Origins of Just Space

Just Space came together in a project in 2007 by the London Civic Forum, a body founded in 2000 and charged with developing civic engagement among Londoners. With some grant aid, we facilitated networking, information and other support to voluntary and community groups so they had the opportunity to take part in the EiP of the Mayor's 2007 Alterations to the 2004 London Plan. The network was strengthened by the inclusion of the London Tenants Federation (LTF), which had been an active participant in the 2006 Alterations and in local campaigns, environmentalists and other activists who (as the London Social Forum) had mounted a public conference on 'Alternative futures for London' at City Hall in October 2005.

The groups that coalesced in that process had benefited from collaborative working and had secured a place and role in the statutory scrutiny of Alterations to the London Plan. They made significant interventions in the debate on the future of London on equalities, gender, disability, age, the needs of poor BME (black and minority ethnic) communities in regeneration and in relation to housing. They presented evidence of how London's dearth of affordable homes manifested in a much higher proportion of housing-related problems for those seeking advice in London than in other parts of England. Proposals on the spatial needs of older people, put forward by Age Concern London, were accepted by the Mayor's Planning Team for incorporation. The case for greater retention of industrial land – under pressure from an inflated housing market – was accepted. The groups argued for a social justice framework in relation to the 2012 Olympics decision making and legacy, and for more sustainable models for suburbs and town centres, trying to tie down the London Plan to precise statements that would enable London communities to sustain themselves in situ. They also reasoned that the Plan should have proposals that would actually achieve carbon reduction targets, reduce the need to travel and improve air quality, not just rely on aspirational statements.

It was collectively decided (26 July 2007) to build on this by establishing a network known as Just Space to strive for effective community involvement and effective delivery of spatial planning to communities, not only at the strategic level, but also locally throughout London. This was done in response to a commonly held view among these representative organisations that change brought about by the spatial planning and development process can and often does have an adverse impact on local communities. Planning practice, particularly in respect of marginalised communities and areas subject to development pressures, requires critical reassessment, and for community and voluntary groups to have a strong voice. Furthermore, this voice needs to be firmly grounded in the needs and issues facing Londoners, but that can also speak the language of planners and other decision makers.[2]

To tackle these issues, Just Space embarked on a diverse range of 'capability sessions', workshops, events and conferences, all intended to create capacity within communities and to support their networks to cascade, influence, challenge and sustain involvement in spatial planning, related strategies and development management. Potentially, they could have a significant impact on statutory and non-statutory plans emerging from the planning system.

Resources and organisation

This work was carried on with Just Space only minimally constituted, and under the wing of the London Civic Forum. However, it emerged that the Forum itself would close, and Just Space decided to do the minimum necessary to become formally constituted and open its own bank account. Nevertheless, efforts have been made to embed principles of diversity, mutual support and empowerment within a horizontal organisation in the Constitution (see Box 3.1). There are no elected chairs or other officers, save for a treasurer, decisions are based on seeking consensus, and tasks such as chairing meetings are rotated.

Meetings are open to everyone from the community sector with an interest in planning issues. As to decisions, we do not take a vote; we ask if everyone is in agreement. Our experience is that voting is not the best model for a community organisation seeking a participatory approach. Where there is disagreement, we aim to overcome this through discussion and compromise, rather than risk people feeling excluded and wanting to leave because they are out-voted. Of course,

Box 3.1: An extract from the Just Space Constitution

The Just Space ethos is one of grass-roots networking, informing and supporting local communities so that their contributions to planning policy are empowering and effective. It does this by:

- Maintaining an overview of strategic planning issues and their implementation
- Providing mutual support to community organisations engaging in the London Plan EiP process
- Raising awareness of London planning policies at local level
- Cascading learning to the local level in a way that informs involvement in Local Plans
- Working in partnership at the local level to develop new links between voluntary and community sector groups, groups concerned with equalities and active residents
- Developing plain language information that is accessible for all Londoners.
- Coordinating the skills and expertise of members where possible.

Source: http://justspace.org.uk

we disagree on some things and there are tensions to overcome. There is, for example, a potentially strong tension between the protection of green space and the need for more housing, so we have tended to avoid – so far – the issue of building on the Green Belt. However, by discussion, we increase understanding and sensitivity, and find that housing groups value green space and environmental groups recognise the social need for housing, so the conflict is not as intractable as many of us had imagined.

Just Space retains a self-employed community consultant who has operated effectively as Just Space's coordinator since its inception and, together with other participants, has been the focus for the organisation's essential organisational memory and core capacity. Just Space does not have an office, but draws on its members to contribute such resources. Within its membership, it is able to draw on a wide range and depth of knowledge and experience at applied, academic and professional levels in planning, community organising, the environment and housing. The strength of Just Space lies in the diversity and enthusiasm of its participating members.

Member organisations and groups vary from time to time. As a snapshot, the following were active participants in Just Space at the beginning of 2010: The London Forum of Amenity and Civic Societies, LTF, Hayes and Harlington Community Forum, King's Cross Railway Lands Group, London Gypsy and Traveller Unit, Race on the Agenda, London Voluntary Service Council, Women's Design Service, London Civic Forum, Friends of the Earth, Black Neighbourhood Renewal and Regeneration Network, Age Concern London, Third Sector Alliance and Spitalfields Community Association. Others were technical support organisations: Planning Aid for London and The Bartlett School of Planning at University College London (UCL). New organisations have joined at intervals and some members, hit by economic pressures and political cuts in funding, have ceased to exist or been unable to remain active in Just Space, in particular, groups advancing equality and social justice.

The London Plan

At the strategic level, Just Space aims to sustain the momentum of community involvement in spatial planning that has developed since 2007. The London Plan sets the strategic framework for development throughout Greater London, and in turn has an impact on the practices of the 33 London boroughs since their Local Plans have to be brought into general conformity with the London Plan. The London Plan is also supposed to guide the Mayor when he makes decisions on planning applications of 'strategic importance' where he has power to override borough decisions. The current Mayor, Boris Johnson, brought forward the Draft Replacement London Plan for EiP in 2010, and subsequent revisions in 2012; challenges were made both times by a wide range of groups, individuals and organisations.

During the three months of public consultation on the London Plan in 2010, the Mayor's office undertook limited engagement activity – presentations to local government and business interests, some display boards at transport interchanges and some information on the Mayor's website. For many people, therefore, it was only community activity that made them aware of the London Plan and prompted written comments. We organised two major conferences and a number of workshops enabling member organisations to develop and refine their own submissions. These workshops formed the basis for Just Space to formulate its own statements where there was widespread consensus, and especially where distinct issues needed to be linked.

What crystallises our participation is that the Mayor must, by law, organise an EiP of the proposed Plan (or Alterations) following procedures set out in national regulations. The purpose is to 'objectively test' the document, with a series of roundtable discussions led by one or more independent examiners appointed from the Planning Inspectorate. About 25 people take part in each day's debate, selected by the Inspector from among those who have submitted written statements during the consultation period. To be invited to speak they will have raised points of substance likely to add to an informed discussion around those matters and questions that the Inspector considers need exploring. Just Space does a lot of work encouraging and supporting community groups to make effective written statements which gives them the opportunity to take part in the debates, helping to maximise the range of groups that can present their evidence.

The last full EiP of the London Plan in 2010 had 35 days of roundtable discussions. Just Space supported 60 different community groups to take part. Many had their own seats at the table, but Just Space itself secured a 'hot seat' for most days of the EiP shared by a range of community groups that would not otherwise have been able to participate, an innovation that successfully brought an unprecedented diversity of voices to the table.

The planning process is complicated, with a great deal of jargon, formal documents and technical burdens, all of which make it difficult to assimilate information and to take part. Just Space stands for a democratic and deliberative process: we take care of the process side so that community groups can concentrate on the issues they want to raise. Before Just Space began this networking and organising, those taking part in the EiP had been mainly landowners, developers and public bodies, but we changed the balance and ensured that at the 2010 EiP one-third of the representation on any typical day was from the community. This was achieved without any financial support from the Mayor of London or other government bodies. It is a major achievement because the prevailing orthodoxy about London and its future is so powerfully embedded in the web of pressure groups (led by London First), professions and property interests whose influence on London Plans has for years been almost unchallenged (Edwards, 2001, 2010).

Issues raised by Just Space

Key elements giving a flavour of the Just Space representations can be seen in the opening statement on Day 1 (see Box 3.2).

Box 3.2: Just Space opening statement

...Our aim in this initial statement is to summarise why we consider that the draft plan is not—as it stands—fit for purpose.

What we have in common is a central concern with environmental and social sustainability and our focus in social terms is on those who are poor, exploited or in some ways excluded from the full enjoyment of what this wonderful city has to offer. We don't claim to be the only representatives of the London victims of globalisation but we are grateful to the panel for acknowledging that the Plan must serve everyone, acknowledging it by inviting us and many of our member organisations on their own account to appear at the EiP.

The main challenge faced by all global cities is how to limit the extremes of inequality which such cities generate and—where we can't limit them—how to mitigate the effects. Housing is an especially severe challenge because all of us live in the same or interconnected housing markets. And the challenge is especially severe in the UK because we have mostly become so passionate about protecting what we call the countryside and that makes space scarce – and thus attracts ever more speculative investment to inflate housing and land markets.

We consider that the Draft Plan before us today is unfit for purpose for reasons which we can group under 4 headings:

- Environmental sustainability;
- Its treatment of inequalities;
- Its inadequacy as a way through the economic crisis;
- The uneven playing field among stakeholders.

Source: http://justspace.org.uk

The fundamental issues raised were:

- major development and 'regeneration' does not benefit existing low-income communities, who are often exported out of the area to make way for the entry of the middle class;
- lack of supply of low-cost rented housing, with the result that people's housing needs are not met;
- questioning the economic model that has increased the gap between rich and poor. We argued for economic diversity and alternative economic strategies;
- inadequacy of policies to achieve targets of reduced carbon emissions, to improve air quality and to achieve environmental justice.

The evidence that Just Space and its member groups submitted was not primarily academic and it was not presented by speakers playing 'expert witness' roles. Most of the written submissions were a combination of critical evaluation of GLA and other available data and needs assessments, combined with narrative descriptions of the experiences of members as Londoners – with housing, accessing services, battling pollution and traffic, confronting and challenging inequalities, and so on.

The impact of these submissions was sometimes quite strong, and the Inspectors invited Just Space or other community groups to open the discussion of some topics, notably on urban regeneration. For example, the LTF was asked to draw on tenants' grass-roots evidence and case studies published in the *Briefing note on Inner London* (LTF, 2010b) and the *London Plan Examination in Public conference report 2010* (LTF, 2010c).[3]

Deficiencies in London Plan preparation, evidence and analysis had already prompted criticisms of its methodology – no alternative scenarios, no linked forecasts, no cross-border analysis, weak local and collaborative evidence collection – and around its likely achievement of a recovering economy that would be more diverse and low carbon, with greater equality and wellbeing as outcomes. Just Space recommended further research to the London Plan team (Just Space, 2010), but without any detectable results. In the actual EiP sessions, Just Space contributions gained their main impact from a combination of critical understanding of the issues and strong direct experience, simply delivered.

> "The session … relating to Areas for Regeneration … was nothing if not lively. Particularly devastating in their critique were the members of the Just Space network … banded together to offer a concerted assault on many of the key assumptions on which the plan is predicated. The group's presentation focused on the experiences of social housing tenants living in areas that have undergone extensive developer-led regeneration over the past decade. We heard about residents … tenants … friends and neighbours of a lifetime's standing who had simply been dispersed across London for good", wrote Building Design Magazine. (Woodman, 2010)

By holding the Mayor to account on these fundamental issues, and ensuring that a large number of community voices were heard over the six-month period of the EiP, some progress was made. We succeeded in persuading the Mayor to strengthen policy on protecting local shops, extending green infrastructure and promoting Community Land Trusts and Development Trusts. However, the listing of services and facilities that a local neighbourhood needs was not incorporated, but the concept that embodies this approach, 'Lifetime Neighbourhoods', was, albeit not at the level of specificity sought. On the major issues of affordable housing, road user charges, air quality and avoiding displacement of ordinary Londoners from 'regeneration' areas, they had convinced the Panel of their arguments, but the Mayor rejected the Inspectors' recommendations.[4]

Regeneration policy

In the 2010 EiP, Just Space and the LTF made a concerted effort to challenge the Mayor's policies on regeneration areas and the closely linked opportunity areas. Bringing together academic evidence (some of it gathered and digested by student volunteers) with LTF analysis and the direct experience of speakers from many parts of London that had been subject to 'regeneration', we argued that the main beneficiaries of the process tended to be property interests, while the deprived populations in whose name regeneration is always initiated usually lost heavily, their communities dispersed and their voices not carrying weight. The argument was made powerfully enough to convince the Panel of Inspectors (EiP Panel report, 2011), as outlined in Box 3.3.

Box 3.3: Extracts from the EiP Panel Report, 2011

§2.96 It was alleged that 'regeneration' of these areas followed a largely similar pattern involving the displacement of existing settled communities and their widespread dispersal mostly to unsuitable areas. Some of those affected (including elderly residents) had been impelled to make their own and often very unsatisfactory housing arrangements, or had effectively been forced to make themselves 'homeless', because dereliction of the estates during the decanting process had made their homes uninhabitable or the local environment unsafe. This was followed with redevelopment to provide mainly market housing with much smaller numbers of affordable units (and especially social rented housing) than the operation of London Plan 2008 affordable housing policies would require, and which were not available for the original community to return to. The affected communities consider that the only beneficiaries are developers and Borough finances. Moreover, it was put to us that the whole process is based on two false premises. Firstly, that the existing communities were 'deprived' (this being an almost unavoidable finding given that the existing tenants are mainly elderly, so by definition workless, or existing occupants of social housing, so inevitably on low incomes). Secondly, that the outcome was that deprivation had been cured (when in reality all that had happened was that a new wealthy community had supplanted the original one, which had been simply moved elsewhere to create new areas in need of 'regeneration').

§2.97 ... the community representatives, in response to the Panel's question, did not argue that the identification of Areas for Regeneration was inappropriate, or that some other spatial approach to the subject should be developed. Rather, within the areas identified, the principal points put to us by community representatives were that they:

· want involvement in the future plans for their areas;
· oppose wholesale and permanent displacement;
· want to contribute to, as well as derive benefit from, regeneration through new housing provision, local job opportunities and skills training, better environments and from improved community infrastructure of sufficient capacity and appropriate utility for all; and
· should be subjected to processes that are not unreasonably drawn out in implementation.

§2.98 We do not see those as unreasonable aspirations.

...

§2.101 If the risk of disadvantage being increased and intensified in other areas is to be avoided, however, the aim in regeneration should be to secure the same quantity of affordable housing within the areas concerned at the end of the process as there was at the beginning, even if the 'mix' (expressed as a percentage of affordable homes to market homes) changes. Although this affordable housing may not be wholly available to the original community (many of whom may by then have put roots down elsewhere and may be regarded, in a statutory sense, as suitably re-housed) it should at least be available for those displaced from regeneration projects nearby. The appropriate 'split' (expressed as the proportions of affordable housing that are to be social rented or intermediate) can then be tailored, by the housing providers in consultation with the Boroughs concerned, to meet the needs of the incoming community. We accordingly recommend that Policy 2.14 be modified by addition of a requirement that the aim should be no net loss of affordable housing within individual regeneration areas.

Source: EiP Panel Report (2011), GLA

On the other community group demands, the Panel either accepted the Mayor's existing policies or urged better borough-level consultation. However, this key recommendation for a strengthening of Policy 2.14 was a substantial victory, although the Mayor refused to accept it, and inserted a new wording which, while appearing to be a compromise, entirely circumvented the intentions of the community groups and the Panel: 'Policy 2.14.... These plans should resist loss of housing, including affordable housing, in individual regeneration areas unless it is replaced by better quality accommodation, providing at least an equivalent floor space' (Mayor of London, 2011, Policy 2.14). The 2011 Plan thus permits net losses of (units of) housing, and of affordable housing where the replacement is more luxurious and no smaller in total floor space: exactly what we were trying to prevent.

Rent levels in 'affordable' housing

The major focus of the next (2012) EiP was on Alterations proposed to the Plan to bring it into line with the Coalition government's National Planning Policy Framework (NPPF) (DCLG, 2012) for England and various other contextual changes. Our main target in this was to challenge the applicability in London of a new government definition of 'affordable' housing to be let at rents up to 80 per cent of local open market rents. This new definition would, of course, put such housing in London out of the reach of poor households and, in many boroughs, out of the reach of middle- and some quite high-earning households (see LTF, 2012). These new rents were to become the variable required by policy and would supersede prevailing social rents (also known as 'target rents') charged by councils and housing associations at (in London) much lower and fairly affordable levels. Many organisations thus came together to challenge the Mayor.

Just Space, the LTF and others argued strongly that the new, high 'affordable housing' rents would totally fail to meet the mounting needs of large proportions of Londoners without growing reliance on Housing Benefit – and that government restriction of these benefits, coupled with a cap on the total of all benefits, meant that this safety valve was not available. We therefore called for the retention of existing definitions of affordability as expressed in social rents, and that social rented housing should continue to have its own separate target setting (and monitoring of outputs).

The Inspector concluded that the Mayor's proposed Alteration was not based on evidence but 'is a pragmatic approach in the circumstances' (EiP, 2013, Section 13). On that rather frail – and highly arguable – ground, he decided not to recommend a change. The Inspector did, however, recommend a change to a related proposal by the Mayor, to prevent boroughs from capping rent levels of 'affordable housing' at levels lower than the London norm established by the London Plan – something that Islington and Tower Hamlets had already started to do. This proposed prohibition had attracted the ire of many boroughs, nine of which (a mixture of Conservative and Labour-controlled) formed a consortium to object. They argued that, where local evidence showed that the need was for social rents, or rents lower than 65–80 per cent of local market levels, they should be free to set these levels in borough plans. They demonstrated that they could secure development at these lower-rent levels through creative use of their own land and resources. The Inspector recommended that the prohibition of borough rent caps should be deleted from the proposed Alterations to the Plan.

The Inspector's report, promised for January 2013, is actually dated 19 June, and was finally published by the Mayor, along with his response, on 14 August 2013 in the middle of the summer holidays. The Mayor rejected the Inspector's recommendation, and insisted that what is effectively a ban on borough autonomy in setting rent caps within borough spatial plans should be implemented. At the London Assembly Extraordinary Meeting of 3 September 2013 a motion to reject the Mayor's Revised Early Minor Alterations (REMA) in light of the views expressed against the revised policies on affordable housing by, among others, 21 boroughs, and to ask for further revisions incorporating the recommendation of the independent Inspector, was put to the vote. While there was a 'simple' majority to reject at 13 to 9, this was not the required two-thirds majority, so the Assembly was deemed not to have rejected REMA. As evidence of the strength of feeling on this issue, eight boroughs have subsequently formally notified the Mayor that they will launch judicial review proceedings.

Somewhat overshadowed, another vote was won 13 to 9 calling on the Mayor to bring forward further Alterations to include a definition of sustainable development along the lines of the government's five guiding principles.[5] This definition had been proposed by the Mayor in Note ED16 to the EiP in response to representations by the Friends of the Earth, but on 11 October 2013, *REMA consistency with the National Planning Policy Framework* became operative as formal Alterations to the London Plan – without fulfilment of the Mayor's undertaking. More extensive Further Alterations were in the course of preparation, and these address the unprecedented rise in London's population and the development pressures that this brings with it. More than a million additional people are expected to live in the capital over the next decade, representing double the rate of growth previously predicted (Mayor of London, 2014).

These two summaries of the debates of 2010 and 2012 triggered by Just Space and its member groups give some flavour of what we do, although not the range of topics that we have addressed in the London Plan. Representations also covered air quality and global warming, green space, the defence of markets and local shopping, the needs of gypsies and travellers, use of waterways, space standards in housing and many aspects of transport.

Link with the local level

To be effective in influencing the London Plan, we need to be active at the borough and neighbourhood levels, raising awareness of London Plan policies and monitoring what is happening on the ground. Thus, Just Space's regional partnership has a local reach covering a diversity of issues and people. This link between geographic scales in community engagement has eluded cities around the world, and so London has an opportunity to break new ground.

At borough level for the last four years, Just Space has provided planning support to London's voluntary and community sector under London Civic Forum's 'Policy Voice' campaign (funded by London Councils). This support has been provided typically through borough-based workshops, empowering the local voluntary and community sector to respond to consultations on borough planning documents and to prepare for the EiPs of these policies, as in the cases of, for example, Hillingdon, Newham, Tower Hamlets and Lewisham.

In Hillingdon, community workshops were attended by some 150 people representing community groups, or as individuals, generating wider awareness and interest in the forthcoming Local Plan. As a consequence, issues articulated by the 56 written representations from the community were broadly based, soundly evidenced and reasoned. At the hearings the prior coordination meant a focused discussion and best use of the resources deployed by the Council and Planning Inspectorate. The community now has a better understanding of the opportunities and limits of planning, and is carrying this forward with a Community Planning Forum. The Council is committed to improving its consultation process to avoid a feeling of exclusion, embracing the Localism Act and giving more say to residents, including involvement in neighbourhood planning (Planning Inspector's report to Hillingdon Council, Section 14).

All borough-based workshops have raised awareness of the contribution of the Mayor's London Plan. This has empowered groups to raise regional policy at the local level and also to raise local policy concerns at the regional level through engagement with the London Plan EiPs. As well as supporting local groups to participate in EiPs, we try to build up planning expertise within communities. Some groups then gain interest in wider planning and become involved with Just Space in London-wide activity. Other local groups gain strength from contact with other localities fighting similar battles, and become involved in supporting each other across the city.

Substantial work at the local level on regeneration, neighbourhood plans, the formation of community planning networks and the local economy is illustrated through examples of recent projects.

Community and regeneration

In partnership with Professor Loretta Lees, then at King's College London, Just Space, the LTF and Southwark Notes Archive Group (SNAG) worked on a project to gather data on resident and business displacement in urban 'regeneration'. The project, funded through an Activist Scholar Award from *Antipode*, also considered the tools necessary to oppose demolitions and to develop community-led alternatives (see Lees et al, 2014).

On four council estates in London – the Heygate and Aylesbury Estates in Southwark, the Pepys Estate in Lewisham and the Carpenters Estate in Newham – former tenants were interviewed to find out why and how they were displaced, where they went and the experience of moving. Researching the displacement of local businesses was also important, given the rhetoric of new employment opportunities provided by regeneration.

The regeneration process tends to be top-down – controlling – imposing development on local communities rather than engaging them in meaningful decision making. This approach produces high-density, mainly market housing and employment that addresses only the highly skilled and fails to meet the needs of existing deprived communities. Just Space has proposed that social impact assessments be carried out and development proposals only approved when it is shown that established populations living in and around the area will benefit.

As part of this project, the 'Developing alternatives for communities facing gentrification and displacement' Conference took place in January 2013. Eighty representatives from tenants' and other community groups took part, many of whom had been involved in campaigning against top-down regeneration/gentrification/demolition and displacement.

The Conference considered approaches to preventing displacement and alternatives to the gentrification of these schemes. Demolition rather than refurbishment is promoted in 'regeneration' schemes without evidence that the existing housing is structurally unsound and without other costs being factored in. For example, these costs include embodied carbon costs and the social costs related to new build and displacement, such as disruption to children's education, and losing family and community networks. At a time when social rented homes are being replaced – at best – with homes rented at up to 80 per cent of open market level (as explained earlier), the need is greater than ever to protect existing stocks of social rented housing. Our next priority is developing a sound community-based model for analysing the price tag of demolition versus refurbishment that includes both long-term environmental and social costs.

The Conference also considered how new, genuinely affordable, house building could be organised through housing cooperatives, self-build and Community Land Trusts. Across Europe, housing cooperatives provide a significant proportion of accommodation for people from all walks of life – up to 20 per cent in some countries. In Britain the proportion is much lower, less than 1 per cent, and mostly aimed at social housing tenants. Housing cooperatives, other tenant-led and self-build housing are a means of providing affordable housing and community facilities, and give communities greater control of both homes and neighbourhoods. The vision for self-build projects goes well beyond housing and includes fair rents, mutual funds and credit unions, education, workspace, healthy eating cafes and land for food.

Through examination of Community Land Trust developments in the UK and the US and with contributors from new trusts in London, the Conference considered Community Land Trusts as a bottom-up community-based initiative, covering housing, enterprise and community facilities and amenities. The Conference explored its viability in London, and whether successful examples may support pressure being brought on the London Mayor and London Councils to release public land for further Community Land Trust schemes that would be genuinely and permanently affordable, enabling communities to sustain themselves in the long term.

The Conference also explored how local communities can use the concept of Lifetime Neighbourhoods as a positive tool to help define local development needs and ongoing long-term community stewardship of a neighbourhood. The concept, in a rather undeveloped form, is already present in the London Plan, but is in need of elaboration in relation to public and private services and for suburban as well as inner-city contexts. When tenants were asked, 'What is a community? What does it need?', they created a practical list of community needs, and emphasised the importance of people's involvement and ownership. The LTF definition of Lifetime Neighbourhood includes housing, community centres, amenities for young and old people, a range of social facilities, well-maintained public and green spaces, access to affordable public transport, allotments and a vibrant local community (LTF, 2010d).

Neighbourhood planning

Just Space, through its members and the events it organises, has contact with many community groups interested in developing Neighbourhood Plans, a kind of planning newly formalised by the Localism Act 2011. The support needs are immense and include the difficulty of producing an integrated plan and the need for community engagement skills, a community involvement strategy and a shared understanding of sustainability. To address some of these support needs, we have done substantial work with The Bartlett School of Planning at UCL, linking students with community groups. Whereas the early rounds of Neighbourhood Forum activity in London had been heavily concentrated in middle-class areas, these initiatives are well distributed between different types of areas and predominantly in less affluent districts.

An example where student support has been delivered is the Elephant & Castle. UCL students assisted with workshops at an event held by the Elephant Amenity Network in January 2012, and joined walkabouts with residents to explore sites of interest for the Neighbourhood Plan. The students provided mapping support and advice on design issues. There has been particular interest from students in a walkabout to map Latin American sites at the Elephant & Castle (retail, educational and other community facilities). Just Space has supported the formation of the Unity Neighbourhood Forum in Brent, including defining a clear geographical boundary for the Forum and for the Plan, organising walkabouts, mapping businesses and street design work. We are providing similar technical and community engagement support, with considerable input from LTF, UCL students and funds from the *Antipode* Activist Scholar Award mentioned earlier, for the production of a Community Plan for the Carpenters Estate in Stratford, interviewing residents and businesses, holding workshops and organising an exhibition of the draft Community Plan.

With London Civic Forum and Community Development Network London (CDNL), Just Space organised an all-day event, 'How Neighbourhood Plans work' (March 2012) to explore the potential of Neighbourhood Plans to enable community groups to have greater control over planning in their local areas. The event had 45 representatives from community organisations, housing associations and academics from across London, and considered:

- the legislative framework in the Localism Act;
- the importance of a community development approach to neighbourhood planning;

- how community groups can enter into mutually beneficial collaborations with professional organisations when developing Neighbourhood Plans.

Follow-up support was then provided through local workshops. In Kensington and Chelsea, two workshops were held, one with One Voice about how the Localism Act could be used to protect African Caribbean heritage in the borough using the 'right to bid' for assets of community value and a Neighbourhood Plan; the other with Action Disability Kensington and Chelsea about how to ensure neighbourhood planning in the borough was accessible and inclusive.

One outcome was that One Voice commented on the draft Planning Brief for some land under the Westway. In their response, they raised the fact that the Plan could emphasise the development of community assets, and they felt that the Planning Brief could offer the opportunity to develop social and community space that would specifically celebrate the history and culture of the African Caribbean community, which has been established in the area since the Windrush era.

Community planning networks

Just Space is committed to communities having an enduring involvement in the planning of their localities, boroughs and city. We recognise that the activities outlined above inevitably call for and are best responded to by the emergence of community planning networks. This is in order to reap the continuing benefits of mutual support and co-learning to sustain the necessary dialogue, as well as maintaining democratic representative legitimacy.

Currently, Just Space is supporting LTF in a Trust for London-funded project to set up community planning networks in three boroughs and in three London Plan opportunity areas where major developments are planned. All are relatively disadvantaged areas with many marginalised and excluded communities where the need to encourage tenant and other community groups to influence or challenge development plans is at its greatest. Just Space also provided support to Tower Hamlets Tenants Federation (THTF) to deliver a programme of events on community planning aimed at Tenants and Residents Associations (TRAs) in the borough. An event on neighbourhood planning was attended by representatives from 15 TRAs and from the Mayor of Tower Hamlets Office, Limehouse Community Forum, UCATT trade union, East London Community Land Trust, Quaker Social Action and Turk's Head (a local charity). THTF felt there was a huge information and consultation gap to overcome. They put together a plan for spreading the word about neighbourhood planning, through area forums, and by providing a space at THTF meetings for planning officers to collaborate with TRAs.

The session also identified three potential projects that THTF would like to deliver if the resources could be found:

- to assist one of its member associations to develop a pilot Neighbourhood Plan that would have lessons for all TRAs in the borough;
- to collaborate with the council in producing recognition criteria for a Neighbourhood Forum and guidance on the involvement and consultation that should be expected for a Neighbourhood Plan;
- to undertake an educational project on neighbourhood planning and the Localism Act with the large Bengali community in Tower Hamlets.

Economies of London

It became apparent through all these deliberations and activities that a deeper consideration of the economic life of London was needed. If economic development is to be sustainable, it needs to value the different ways of organising economic activity, and make connections between the economy and the rest of social life, for example, recognising the contribution of local shops and markets to the local economy and protecting industrial land against conversion to housing and the loss of local employment that goes with this.

In response, Just Space organised the event 'Alternative strategies for economic development in London' (March 2013) as a first step to creating a space to discuss economic planning at a metropolitan level, so as to influence the next set of Alterations to the London Plan and to support local groups in challenging the economic ideas behind major developments. Nineteen community and voluntary sector representatives and 10 university-based researchers attended, with discussions focused on alternative measures of economy, reindustrialisation and strategies for local economic development.

Patria Roman Velazquez (City University) set out her research with Latin American communities, in the Elephant & Castle and Seven Sisters. She explained the role of small retailing as a route to economic progression for Latin Americans in London. Many small retailers are women, and the work they do is important in enabling immigrants to integrate into London, contributing to a sense of belonging and identity, as well as generating economic assets for London. Pauline Rowe (Friends of Queen's Market in Newham) described a report on the economic value of the market from the New Economics Foundation. This had found, among other things, that the market delivered twice as many jobs per square metre as a food supermarket.

The Mayor of London's focus on growth of what economists measure as the market value of output (gross domestic product, GDP) and the amount of market value 'added' per worker (gross value added, GVA per capita) leads to an emphasis on particular parts of the economy – especially financial and business services – at the expense of all other economic activity which is portrayed as undynamic or unproductive. So, for example, people may be employed at Queen's Market, they may provide an important service for the local population, but somehow they do not have any visibility or priority in the GLA perspective. They are not seen; it is as if they do not exist or are waiting to be modernised out of existence.

To tackle this and other issues, Just Space is now hosting bi-monthly meetings on 'Economy and planning'. The intention is that the meetings develop a culture of collaboration between community groups and researchers on economic thinking that addresses social and environmental issues and what is actually happening at the grass-roots level.

Challenges and prospects for London

Just Space can provide, perhaps uniquely, an approach that harnesses our firm grounding in the requirements and issues of London's communities, coupled with academic and professional knowledge and experience. Specific strengths include:

- Integrated analysis and action on housing, planning and regeneration, taking forward a substantial body of work in London Plan Opportunity Areas (with a focus on affordable housing and Lifetime Neighbourhoods).
- Capacity building support for community groups on planning processes and policy, building on strong links from previous Just Space works in a number of boroughs (Hillingdon, Greenwich, Tower Hamlets, Newham, Brent, Haringey, Hackney, Barnet, Kensington and Chelsea, Southwark, Lewisham, Bexley).
- Existing links with groups in other boroughs through our members (particularly The London Forum of Amenity and Civic Societies and Friends of the Earth) and through our London-wide activities.
- Access to university planning expertise and skills (both academics and students, mainly planning and geography) that brings in more resources for community groups and opportunities for research funding bids.
- The production of briefing papers on planning policy issues, which, with funding, could be disseminated much more widely.

Just Space has studiously avoided aligning itself with any political party – or indeed becoming anything like a party, with manifestos, membership requirements and so on. It might perhaps be regarded as an 'urban social movement' (Mayer, 2011), but it is probably more accurate to describe it as a kind of organisational infrastructure for grass-roots urban activism and effective public participation. It is thus in a position to facilitate alliances and movements without becoming one.

Just Space is not an organisation given to theoretical discussion, and has not collectively considered whether its perspectives are 'post-political' (Swyngedouw, 2009), but we rarely find our positions aligned with any of the main political parties. We have, on occasions, invited individual politicians to speak at our meetings, and have made practical alliances sometimes with individual elected members of the London Assembly or borough councils. Many people assume that community groups of the kind we have as members will tend to support Labour Party politicians and councils, but the authors of this chapter take the view that, on key issues of urban policy, regeneration and environment, Labour boroughs can be as subordinated to property development interests as Conservative or Liberal ones, and just as reluctant to pay serious attention to community needs.

What we do could create significant capacity to support a very positive engagement with spatial planning that can begin to address the needs of diverse sections of the population and to ensure that policies are more sustainable, equitable and inclusive. Just Space partners are well placed to cascade learning and practices developed in such work into other areas of their own activity, and to encourage others to support it in other parts of London. They have a range of skills, have strong user involvement, are accessible and often represent those hardest to reach. Although the process of community involvement in strategic spatial planning is continuing, it is demanding and the need for support – especially for formal consultation events – is largely unmet.

A major challenge is resources to sustain ourselves and to provide free and open access to events and to consultation and research documents. We find fewer and fewer opportunities to access public money to support our work, but have been successful in securing grants from some of the charitable bodies active on London-wide or localised problems of poverty or deprivation. We are now also finding that some of our work supporting Neighbourhood Forums attracts payment on a small scale.

Universities have sometimes been helpful financially in recognition of their need to integrate community perspectives and associated skills in professional training and in the formulation of research that has an impact on real social needs. Despite the alarming trends for universities to become ever more business-oriented, many have allocated budgets for 'public engagement' from which we benefit through joint projects. We are proud of the *Research protocol on collaboration between community/activist groups and university staff and students on housing and planning issues*, a document that is being used elsewhere in Britain and abroad (Just Space website, 2010).

Our interactions with large non-governmental organisations (NGOs) have tended to be difficult: some have become bureaucratic and managerial, lacking the skills and habits of real grass-roots engagement. Many have become so dependent on government or similar grants that they are reluctant to support major challenges to the established orthodoxy that prevails in London policy communities.

In many ways our greatest challenge is the orthodoxy surrounding the triumphal view of London as a global city, 'inward investment' as an unquestioned goal of policy and market criteria as the test of 'viability' (for example, of social housing provision). Although we may not yet have secured major changes to the plans we engage with, we have at least ensured that displacement and other regressive policies do not go unchallenged.

There is perhaps some hope in that even very mainstream commentators (outside formal politics) are beginning to agree that Britain's headlong pursuit of debt-fuelled ('financialised') accumulation of land and property asset values is destructive, destabilising and a major driver of inequality. Since many of London's most acute housing, planning and environmental problems flow from that orthodox trajectory, some major realignment may be in prospect. We take some cheer from the tenacious citizens who know that the future of the city is what we, collectively, make it. There are alternatives, whatever we are told by our media and most politicians.

Notes

[1] See http://justspace.org.uk/about/constitution and Box 3.1 for an extract.

[2] '...the types of issues raised by London Civic Forum and London Tenants Federation are important and difficult to address', wrote Planning Inspectors to the Mayor of London (EiP, 2007, §5.137, Panel report, September).

[3] These papers were preceded by the *Response to consultation on the draft Replacement London Plan* in January 2010 which cited academic research and other reports on, inter alia, regeneration, housing provision, choice and affordability, health inequalities and mixed and balanced communities (LTF, 2010a).

[4] 'Just Space network made two simple, but I believe, vital requests ... that any regeneration project should incorporate a social impact assessment to establish the correlation between the transformation of buildings and the transformation of lives. The other ... a definition of regeneration that recognises that the ... concern is not merely with the renewal of its buildings but also with the social and economic renewal of its existing community' (Woodman, 2010). 'Social impact assessment' is nowhere to be found in the London Plan.

[5] Namely, living within the planet's environmental limits; ensuring a strong, healthy and just society; achieving a sustainable economy; promoting good governance; and using good science responsibly. These five principles are from the UK Sustainable Development Strategy *Securing the future* 2005 that was archived by the Coalition government but resuscitated in 2011. The principles are also found in NPPF 2012, after Section 5.

References

Aldridge, H., Bushe, S., Kenway, P., MacInnes, T. and Tinson, A. (2013) *London's poverty profile 2013*, London: New Policy Institute.

Arnstein, S. R. (1969) 'A ladder of citizen participation', *Journal of the American Institute of Planning*, vol 35, no 4, pp 216-24 (http://lithgow-schmidt.dk/sherry-arnstein/ladder-of-citizen-participation.html).

Castells, M. (1983) *The city and the grassroots: a cross-cultural theory of urban social movements*, Berkeley, CA: University of California Press.

DCLG (Department for Communities and Local Government) (2012) *National Planning Policy Framework*, London: DCLG.

Edwards, M. (2001) 'Planning and communication in London', *City*, vol 5, no 1, pp 91-100.

Edwards, M. (2010) 'Do Londoners make their own plan?', in K. Scanlon and B. Kochan (eds) *London: coping with austerity*, LSE London Series, London: London School of Economics and Political Science, pp 57-71.

EiP Examination in Public (2007) *Draft Further Alterations to the London Plan Panel Report*, 2007 (available from www.london.gov.uk/priorities/planning/london-plan/examination-in-public/previous-eips/london-plan-furtheralterations-eip-2007).

EiP Examination in Public (2010) *Draft Replacement London Plan Report of Panel*, 2010 (available from www.london.gov.uk/priorities/planning/london-plan/examination-in-public/previous-eips/replacement-london-plan-examinationin-public).

EiP Examination in Public (2012) *Report on the Examination into the Revised early Minor Alterations to the London Plan*, 2013 (available from www.london.gov.uk/priorities/planning/london-plan/examination-in-public/previous-eips/replacement-london-plan-examinationin-public).

Healey, P. (1992) 'Planning through debate: the communicative turn in planning theory and practice', *Town Planning Review*, vol 63 pp 143-62.

Imrie, R., Lees, L. and Raco, M. (eds) (2009) *Regenerating London: governance, sustainability and community in a global city*, London: Routledge.

Just Space (2010) 'London Plan commentary' (http://justspace2010.wordpress.com).

Just Space (2012) 'UCL working with Just Space' (http://ucljustspace.wordpress.com).

Just Space (2013) http://justspace.org.uk

Lees, L., Just Space, LTF (London Tenants Federation) and SNAG (Southwark Notes Archive Group) (2014) 'Challenging "the new urban renewal": the social cleansing of council estates in London', in B. Campkin and R. Ross (eds) *Urban Pamphleteer# 2 'London: Regeneration Realities'*, London: Urban Lab, University College London.

LTF (London Tenants Federation) (2010a) *Response to draft Replacement London Plan* (www.londontenants.org/publications/responses/LTF%20Response%20-%20Draft%20replacement%20London%20Plan.pdf).

LTF (2010b) *Briefing note on Inner London* (for 2010 EiP) (www.londontenants.org/publications/other/Matter%202D%20P2%209%20-%20LTF%20briefing%20note.pdf).

LTF (2010c) *London Plan Examination in Public June 2010 conference report* (www.londontenants.org/framesets/ftb&sinformation.htm).

LTF (2010d) *Lifetime Neighbourhoods, tenants' definition* (for 2010 EiP) (www.londontenants.org/publications/other/LTF%20Lifetime%20neighbourhoods.pdf).

LTF (2012) *The affordable housing con* (www.londontenants.org/publications/reports/LTF%20-%20afordable%20housing%20con%20final%20xxx.pdf).

Mayer, M. (2011) 'The "Right to the City" in the context of shifting mottos of urban social movements', in N. Brenner and M. Mayer (eds) *Cities for people not for profit*, London: Routledge, pp 63-85.

Mayor of London, GLA (Greater London Authority) (2004) *The London Plan*, London: GLA.

Mayor of London, GLA (2011) *The London Plan*, London: GLA.

Mayor of London, GLA (2014) 'Draft Further Alterations to The London Plan'. London: GLA.

Porter, L. and Shaw, K. (2008) *Whose urban renaissance? An international comparison of urban regeneration strategies*, London: Routledge.

Rydin, Y., Thornley, A., Scanlon, K. and West, K. (2004) 'The Greater London Authority – a case of conflict of cultures? Evidence from the planning and environmental policy domains', *Environment and Planning C Government and Policy,* vol 22, no 1, pp 55-76.

Swyngedouw, E. (2009) 'The antinomies of the postpolitical city: in search of a democratic politics of environmental production', *International Journal of Urban and Regional Research,* vol 33, no 3, pp 601-20.

Woodman, E. (2010) 'Fixing the regeneration game', *Building Design Magazine,* Leader article, 1 October.

Part 2

SUSTAINING LONDON IN AN ERA OF AUSTERITY

FOUR

Sustainable governance and planning in London

Emma Street

Introduction

The UK government's Sustainable Development Strategy calls for 'necessary decisions now to realise our vision of stimulating economic growth and tackling the deficit, maximising wellbeing and protecting our environment, without negatively impacting on the ability of future generations to do the same' (Defra, 2011a, p 2). This is the latest iteration of UK sustainable development (SD) policy in which SD is presented as a 'realizable condition gained through the convergence of environmental, social and economic action' (Fry, 2009, p 44). This chapter explores how this 'triple bottom line' definition of SD continues to shape the parameters for development and planning in London today.

The UK economy has been in a fragile state since the global credit crunch began in 2008. Yet national SD policy continues to be informed by what Fry (2009, p 41) terms a '"capital logic" proposition that the future can be secured via continual economic growth.' With that said, the current government's construction of SD does differ subtly from earlier strategies that focused on growth *management*. In light of the economic downturn, the recent White Paper, *The natural choice: securing the value of nature* (Defra, 2011b), frames SD not around economic growth per se, but rather the notion of economic *recovery*. In a context of deepening ecological and economic scarcity, the paper calls for the contribution the natural environment makes to quality of life and economic success to be quantified in economic terms: 'valuing nature properly holds the key to a green and growing economy' (Defra, 2011b, p 2).

In London, Mayor Boris Johnson's definition of SD rests upon creating a dynamic climate of economic growth. The assumption is that growth will deliver wider social and environmental benefits, not only for the city and its inhabitants, but for the whole of the UK. Greater London Authority (GLA) publications, including the (2009) *Climate Change Adaptation Strategy*, and the overall strategic plan for London (London Plan), 'welcome and support growth and development' (GLA, 2011, para 1.49). This growth and development is deemed *sustainable* in that it meets the 'immediate needs of the city and its people and providing foundations for lasting development and improvement for future generations of Londoners' (GLA, 2011, para 1.49).

This discourse has proven to be remarkably stable in recent years. It even appears to have withstood the fallout of the global financial crisis; an event which has called into question assumptions of economic growth that have informed policy making since the mid-1990s (see Raco and Street, 2012). While economic growth continues to be seen as the way to deliver social and environmental sustainability goals, Mayor Johnson's recent policies feature less of the aggressively pro-*global city* discourse deployed by his predecessor Ken Livingstone, who linked the future of London closely to the expansion of the financial services sector. In Johnson's London Plan (2011) the global city is invoked, but is tempered somewhat by the softer language of *quality of life*. This phrase features prominently, and a key goal is 'ensuring all Londoners enjoy a good, and improving quality of life sustainable over the life of this Plan and in the future' (GLA, 2011, para 1.1A; see also Holman, 2010).

However, Johnson and his colleagues at the GLA are under no illusion that *achieving* sustainable development objectives depends on securing (hard) investment in infrastructure to facilitate London's growth. The logic is unequivocal; financial investment here (as opposed to other cities and regions) offers the best way to secure the future (economic) sustainability of the UK. As Johnson argues, investing scarce resources in London 'pays for itself' (GLA, 2013a, p 59; see also GLA, 2011).

For some, this kind of 'low-level political pragmatic', in which the concept of sustainability remains anchored to the pursuit of economic growth, is problematic. Fry (2009, p 42) argues that so long as action to address climate change and chronic resource depletion remains orientated towards maintaining *business as usual*, efforts towards change will be 'weak' and 'fragmented'. Others have called for the concept of SD to be rejected altogether as a result of its failure to challenge the 'promethean economic growth paradigm' (Martínez-Alier et al, 2010, p 1741).

How to manage and direct (or even reverse[1]) growth, to minimise the negative impacts on the physical or natural environment and to maximise the wellbeing of urban populations is a perennial concern for planners. Today these tasks are often expressed in the language of SD, which, as authors such as Swyngedouw (2009) and Whitehead (2007) note, can obscure the contested nature of planning *for* sustainability. As the next section shows, the thinking that has informed SD planning has evolved over the years. For example, in contrast to current plans that seek to *stimulate* an economic recovery in order to deliver wider social and environmental goals, plans produced in the inter and postwar years were focused on *containing* growth that threatened Londoners' quality of life and the surrounding English countryside. The key task for planners at the time was clear: to establish 'how far and in what direction is it possible to direct … the enormous growth of London' (GLRPC, 1929, p 8).

The remainder of this chapter examines the dominant logics that have informed the concept of SD in London as it has evolved as a discrete policy goal towards the latter part of the 20th century. The focus is on how sustainability, as an emerging set of (sometimes disparate) ideas, has been framed in policy and plans dealing with London's future growth. Following a review of past and present approaches to SD planning, a case study of the ways in which SD has been framed and governed in London's South Bank area is presented. This localised example shows how multi-sector partnerships have worked to broker a coherent SD strategy to inform development in the neighbourhood. This process, which hinges on capturing the 'benefits' of economic growth accrued through intensified development for the local community, has been used to produce a consensual vision about what the area's future should consist of. The chapter concludes by speculating on how sustainable development policy in London may evolve in light of ongoing reforms to local governance and deepening economic, social and environmental uncertainties.

Framing the future growth of London

Planning for the SD of cities is an exercise in governing an *unknowable future* (Anderson and Adey, 2012, p 1530). Yet, despite an obvious orientation towards the future, planning is an activity that is informed by the modes of thinking and values that dominate at a given time. This section considers how the concept of urban sustainability has evolved since the interwar period, when a series of plans were produced that outlined a clear pathway for the city's future development. Plans and policies are based on, and mobilise (selective) *urban imaginations*, or conceptions about how urban spaces should function. As Raco (2007) notes, these are often based on diagnoses about 'problems' and the 'solutions' deemed necessary to address them. In this sense, plans and policies are not value-free and static objects, but rather are representative of particular ways of thinking about cities (and aspirations for their future development) that materially shape urban futures (see Healey, 2002; Dikeç, 2007).

While planning for London's future expansion in the inter- and post-world war years significantly pre-dated the emergence of the global *sustainability agenda*, there are parallels to be found with contemporary iterations of SD policy. For example, the importance postwar planners placed on strategic matters such as the protection of open space and quality of life remain central concerns for London's governing bodies (see GLA, 2011). Today, much is made of the need for community participation in the creation and governance of sustainable places, however, during the 1930s–1950s, this was a task that remained in the hands of professionals such as planners, architects and engineers. Their attempts to manage the long-term growth of the city are now perceived to represent a highly *interventionist* and *comprehensive* style of planning. As this approach has fallen from favour in recent years, more local-level and/or 'bottom-up' modes of engagement in planning and policy making have been promoted (see Healey, 1997).

The main goal of planning strategies for London produced during the interwar years was to *manage*, and in some instances curtail, growth, for the long-term benefit of the physical and social environment. More specifically, planners were tasked with preserving undeveloped or 'open land' in the face of population growth and increased personal mobility facilitated first, by the expansion of suburban railways, and latterly, by the widening availability of the automobile. As the Greater London Regional Planning Committee report (1929, p 9) states: 'Regional Planning consists primarily in the laying down of an appropriate design for urban growth.' The management of growth in central London, large swathes of which had been devastated by bombing during the Second World War, was to be facilitated by relocating Londoners to new towns or existing regional centres, outside of the urban core. According to the Greater London Plan, 'the natural evolution of orderly growth can be shaped into some semblance of ordered design, both for population grouping, land use, transport and public services.' (Abercrombie, 1944, p 7).

Planners' ambitions extended beyond the delivery of 'harmonised' urban and social forms. London's built environment was seen as nothing less than a physical expression of the power of the British Empire, with plans required to be 'worthy of the central idea, London, the capital of the Empire' (Abercrombie, 1944, p 17). While the 'gigantic' nature of this task was acknowledged, planners were nonetheless confident that London's role as the engine of national growth and political heart of the Commonwealth could be delivered, goals that were facilitated by new technologies and infrastructure investment (Abercrombie, 1944). The *problem* was merely how best to direct and order growth without threatening the surrounding English countryside, and improving the quality of life for Londoners.

While such challenges are rarely accompanied by straightforward or clear 'solutions', planning for London's future was nonetheless represented as a predominantly technical (and not political) exercise. Indeed, Swyngedouw (2009, p 611) observes that 'sustainability' continues to be treated as something outside of the political domain, and manageable 'by means of a series of technological, managerial and organizational fixes'. This *depoliticising* tendency is compounded by the contemporary language of consensus, good governance and inclusivity that emphasises the possibility of a harmonious future, while underplaying the inherently political nature of sustainability planning (Swyngedouw, 2009; see also Whitehead, 2007; Fry, 2009).

The postwar town planning movement, which culminated in the Town and Country Planning Act 1947, the basis for the modern planning system, emphasised the 'connectedness of the physical environment, the health of the populace and the smooth future development of society', in comprehensive masterplans that were designed to sweep away the vestiges of Britain's industrial past (Rees and Lambert, 1985, p 67). As Essex and Brayshay (2007, p 417) point out, the 'lofty, visionary ideals' that characterised these postwar plans often went unrealised. However, the impacts of what Baeten (2000, p 293) calls 'the hyperactive geography of postwar capitalism' on some areas of London's inner city were nonetheless significant.

In London's South Bank neighbourhood, postwar planners' ambitions were expressed in extensive, detailed and ambitious plans that aimed to dispense of the area's (pre-)Victorian industrial functions. Instead the South Bank was envisioned as a place that:

[M]ight well include a great cultural centre, embracing, amongst other features, a modern theatre, a large concert hall and the headquarters of various organisations. It might accommodate, too, a number of blocks of offices with, at the eastern extremity, tall blocks of flats and other buildings. (Abercrombie and Forshaw, 1943, p 128)

These plans, outlined in the 1943 County of London Plan, were never implemented. Yet Abercrombie and Forshaw's vision of the South Bank's future was, in some ways, prophetic; the area is now home to several of the features identified in the plan, including the South Bank (cultural) Centre, and a number of tall buildings that include commercial headquarters. Its past identity as a centre for riverside industry and workers' housing has been almost entirely lost (see Street, 2012).

In the postwar years, the population of inner London began to fall as commuter transport networks and satellite towns, including the New Towns, expanded. From a population of 4,010,000 in 1939, by 1951 the population of inner London stood at 3,346,000. By 1961 it had fallen further still to a total of 3,198,000 (ONS, 2012). Thinking about what London's future should consist of, and how transitions towards this should be governed, shifted accordingly. In 1969, the Greater London Development Plan (GLDP) was published by London's regional governing body, the Greater London Council (GLC). Established under the Government Act 1963, the GLC was created to reflect the needs of the diverse (and expanding) areas of Outer London, and to offer strategic governance alongside the 32 newly formed London boroughs.

The GLDP was intended to be a conceptual plan, addressing issues such as 'population, housing, employment, roads, transportation, areas for comprehensive development and other matters of strategic significance' (GLC, 1969, p 9). Unlike earlier London Plans that included detailed land use strategies, the GLDP's proposals were felt to be lacking in 'specific operational aims … and vision' (TCPA, 1970, p 13). This is likely to have been, at least in part, a response to critiques of the *rational-comprehensive* style of planning that characterised the postwar period.

Planning for London's future during the late 1960s and early 1970s began to embrace a more *collaborative* way of working that recommended the participation of a number of different actors, including local residents (see Healey, 1997). Key documents such as the Skeffington report (1969) were published, as part of a wider recognition that planning was a contested domain made up of multiple interests. Such thinking influenced legislation such as the Town and Country Planning Act 1971 that required local authorities to consult with local residents on planning matters.

Land use decisions made in London during the 1970s were increasingly acknowledged to involve 'questions of social advantage to particular groups which needed to be resolved as well as the achievement of "planning" goals' (Elkin, 1974, p 186). While planning had yet to adopt the language of *social sustainability*, a term that is frequently used when examining the (un)equal distribution of resources among populations (Littig and Griessler, 2005), the *politics* of planning for the city's future was recognised. A series of high-profile and controversial planning decisions in London, including the Coin Street campaigns where residents and developers battled for more than a decade for the development rights to a strategic South Bank site, illustrate how contested this arena had become (see Brindley et al, 1996; Street, 2012).

Margaret Thatcher's Conservative government, elected in 1979, ushered in a new era of planning and policy making, reflecting the belief that the role of the state should be to 'attract and to facilitate private development ... not to exercise undue control so as to delay or frustrate it' (Property Advisory Group, 1983, cited in Lloyd and Newlands, 1988, p 11). The Thatcher government's pro-market ideology was a significant departure from the thinking that informed the Town and Country Planning Act 1947, designed to contain the 'worst excesses of the private property development sector to the overall net benefit of society' (Lloyd and Newlands, 1988, p 11). The Thatcher government, guided by neoliberal thinking, made a series of dramatic changes to the way in which planning and development was governed, including the abolition of the GLC in 1986. Pro-development initiatives, such as the creation of the business-led urban development corporations (UDCs), were designed to unlock the growth potential of ex-industrial sites such as the London Docklands. The UDCs were granted semi-autonomous governance status, including some planning powers, in order to bypass obstructive local authorities and deliver economic growth (see Imrie and Thomas, 1995; Florio and Brownill, 2000).

While the predominant narrative in London plan making during the 1980s was pro-economic growth, at the global governance scale the *sustainable development agenda* was gaining momentum. Landmark publications from global institutions and think tanks such as the Club of Rome's *The limits to growth* (Meadows et al, 1972), and latterly, *Our common future* (or Brundtland report) (WCED, 1987), called for coordinated action across the international community to mitigate the negative impacts of development on the environment and communities. These reports were followed by a series of global summits with the aim of securing political commitment to SD. While the UK government did not publish its first SD strategy until 1999 (Defra, 1999), the concept began to inform planning practice and urban policy from the early 1990s. However, as the next section shows, the goals of SD frequently sat uneasily alongside other narratives, namely, the *global city* agenda that also began to gain traction around this time.

Imagining and governing a sustainable global city

Following the abolition of the GLC in 1986, governance arrangements in London became highly fragmented. Functions such as land use planning were carved up between central government, the London boroughs and a series of unelected quangos (quasi-autonomous non-governmental organisations), including the UDCs (Jones and Evans, 2008; see also Pimlott and Rao, 2002; Thornley et al,

2005). The incoming New Labour government, elected in a landslide victory in 1997, was acutely aware of the fragile status of London governance and made reform a priority (IPPR and KPMG, 1997). Under the Greater London Act 1999, a new regional governing body, the Greater London Authority (GLA), was established. Legislation set out the conditions for the election of a Mayor and a London Assembly of 25 members (Pimlott and Rao, 2002; see also IPPR and KPMG, 1997). The GLA was not meant to be a direct replacement for the GLC, however, reflecting the belief that London's increasingly diverse social, economic and environmental needs could no longer be met by a 'general city-wide service provider' (IPPR and KPMG, 1997, p 3).

London elected its first Mayor, Ken Livingstone, in 2000. Livingstone, who was Leader of the GLC at the time of its demise during the 1980s, established the London Sustainable Development Commission (LSDC) in 2002 to advise him on 'making London an exemplary sustainable world city' (LSDC, undated). While Livingstone's *formal* powers were relatively weak – the 32 London boroughs retained key decision-making powers in areas such as planning and education – his influence over what McNeill (2002) terms the 're-imagining' of London's future was significant (see also Sweeting, 2002).

Livingstone's vision, set out in the (2004) London Plan, featured SD as an 'overarching policy' within which 'all [London Plan] policies … are set' (GLA, 2004, p xxi). This vision was built upon the assumption that London's population, economy and its status as a leading *global city* (Sassen, 1992) would continue on an 'upward' trajectory. SD was to be achieved through the expansion of key sectors such as financial services, and strategic intensification in designated Opportunity Areas. This growth strategy would be complemented by 'iconic' *starchitect*-designed developments, such as Norman Foster's Swiss Re ('Gherkin') building, signalling London's intentions on the global stage (Charney, 2007).

Livingstone, no doubt influenced by supra-national bodies such as the European Union (EU) and United Nations (UN) who were pushing the global sustainable development agenda, set up a series of initiatives designed to tackle London's contribution to climate change. This included the launch of the Climate Change Agency (CCA) in 2005 (now subsumed into the GLA), the Congestion Charging Zone, designed to incentive the use of sustainable modes of transport, and the Cycle Hire scheme, later implemented under the mayoralty of Boris Johnson. The LSDC, a voluntary collection of 'experts' from a range of sectors, oversaw much of this activity, including the monitoring of annual Quality of Life indicators. These activities were actioned in line with the LSDC's Sustainable Development Framework for London which set out the following vision:

> We will achieve environmental, social and economic development simultaneously; the improvement of one will not be to the detriment of another. Where trade offs between competing objectives are unavoidable, these will be transparent and minimised. (LSDC, 2002, no page)

While the Framework acknowledges that 'trade-offs' will be necessary in working towards social, economic *and* environment goals, the implicit assumption is that they *can* be achieved simultaneously. However, as Whitehead (2003, p 1201) points out, the reality is that sustainable development strategies can be exploited as a 'basis for economic restructuring', particularly in a context of intensifying *inter-urban competition.*

In addition to being shaped by the emergent global climate change agenda, the LSDC Framework was also informed by national SD policy produced by the Labour government during the late 1990s-early 2000s. The Sustainable Communities Plan (SCs Plan) (ODPM, 2003) was the central document in a broad-based sustainable development agenda that set out a series of *soft* (lifestyle) goals, such as *good governance* and greater *community engagement*. These sat alongside a series of more quantifiable *hard* goals such as house-building targets and job creation measures. The *breadth* of the SCs Plan, which some argue acted primarily as a rhetorical device with little real substance (see Cochrane, 2006, 2007), also helped to ensure that environmental concerns did not unduly detract from the pursuit of a national growth strategy (Haughton and Counsell, 2004).

Governing sustainable development

In addition to instigating a range of policy measures, the Labour government created new governance frameworks designed to enhance local-level control over SD. Multi-sector partnerships, such as the Local Strategic Partnerships (LSPs), assumed responsibility for the preparation of local strategies in which long-term development visions, gathered through a collaborative process involving residents, councillors and local authority actors, and businesses representatives, were set out.[2]

The role of non-governmental actors, including businesses, in the creation of SCs was strengthened through initiatives such as the Business Improvement Districts (BIDs). Introduced under the Local Government Act 2003, BIDs aim to harness private sector resources at a local level and give businesses a greater say in the planning and governance of neighbourhoods (Ward 2007; Cook, 2009). While business and residential groups may have very different goals, particularly in relation to planning and development, the SCs Plan reflected the former government's belief that mutually beneficial visions of sustainable urban futures were achievable (Street, 2012).

For Swyngedouw (2009, p 611), the danger of such thinking is that, in the process of striving for a harmonious (but ultimately impossible) vision of sustainability, conflict becomes something that is only permitted at the 'margins of political debates'. Urban policy agendas, such the LSDC's Sustainable Development Framework, are, Swyngedouw (2009, p 613) argues, part of a process of closing down debate over urban futures in which 'vague concepts like the creative city, the sustainable city, the green city, the eco-city, the competitive city and the inclusive city replace the proper names of politics.'

As this chapter has argued, planning and development decisions are aligned to particular, time-specific, visions of the future. Yet they are often presented, in plans and in policies, as beneficial for, and representative of, wider (community) interests. The effect is to discursively cast futures planning as a neutral process, in which full consensus around a set of shared (but necessarily selective) priorities is possible (Southern, 2001). Whitehead (2007, p 5) argues that terms such as SD, which indicate that social, economic and environmental harmony is possible, are part of this depoliticising, and their use skims over the 'stories, struggles and values that cut across the history of sustainable development'. The remainder of the chapter explores some of these ideas in the context of SD planning in a central London neighbourhood.

Governing sustainable growth at the local level

This section examines the ways in which SD has been framed and governed in the South Bank area of London. It outlines some of the historic tensions that have existed between local residents and business leaders, whose understandings of what a sustainable future should consist of, and how it should be delivered, have diverged on some key issues. The case study shows how two development visions have been brought together by key actors as part of an attempt to broker a coherent local development strategy to inform future growth and deliver benefits 'for all'.

London's South Bank (see Figure 4.1) spans a 160-hectare area of inner London, bordering the River Thames. The area is characterised by a diverse set of land uses, including international business headquarters such as the riverside Shell Tower, cultural organisations such as the National Theatre, and smaller businesses, shops and offices located in and around the UK's busiest rail station, Waterloo (London Borough of Lambeth, 2011). It is home to a growing residential population of 9,194, which, following a period of decline, has increased by 35.3 per cent since 1991 (London Borough of Lambeth, 2011). Approximately 50,000 people work in the South Bank, and today it is one of London's most visited locations, attracting around 19 million tourists a year (SBP, 2006).

The South Bank has been identified as a frontrunner in neighbourhood working, and attempts to instigate a partnership-led approach to sustainable community building, mainly driven by local businesses, have been feted by consecutive governments (see DCMS and DCLG, 2009). In July 1997, the newly elected Prime Minister Tony Blair visited the area to open the newly regenerated Spine Route, a local arterial route-way. The project was one of the first public realm improvement projects to be delivered by a business-led partnership called South Bank Employers' Group (SBEG). Active in the area since 1991, SBEG is a not-for-profit company governed by a board of directors appointed by its members. These are representatives, generally at senior manager or director level, of the major businesses, cultural and public sector bodies situated in the South Bank area.[3]

Figure 4.1: The South Bank

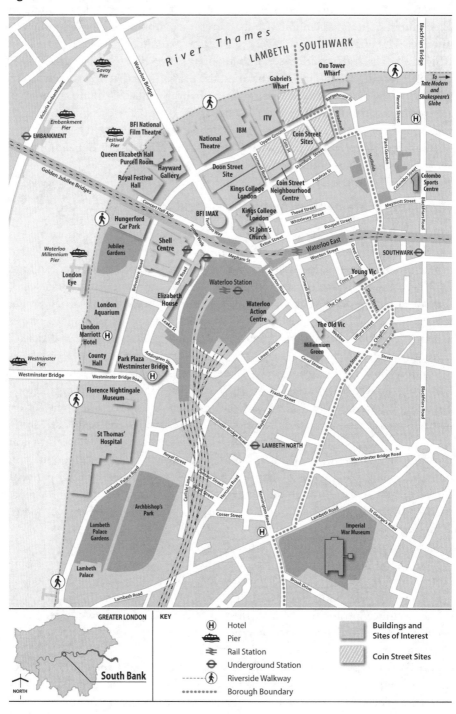

Source: SBEG (2009)

SBEG members pay an annual membership fee that is channelled into a range of activities, such as the operation of security patrols and street cleaning services, the delivery of public realm improvements and place-marketing initiatives. While it represents both public and private sector companies, SBEG self-identifies as a 'business-led' group with the remit of creating a 'better South Bank for all' (SBEG, undated). As Tony Blair commented on his visit to the South Bank in 1997, '[t]his is a model of how local people and private business can work in partnership. You can mix the two together and create a sustainable community' (SBEG, 1998, p 3).

The harmonious community that Blair refers to here is something that cross-sector partnerships such as SBEG have been trying to create since the early 1990s. As the South Bank's regeneration potential became clear, local business leaders began working together with the express aim of moving beyond past conflicts (such as the Coin Street campaigns) that were felt to be impeding the area's development (see Street, 2012). Although the South Bank is now widely recognised as a globally significant cultural, visitor and commercial centre, until relatively recently, many perceived it to be an 'under-developed' place with an 'image problem'. In an article published in 1994, *The Independent* newspaper's architecture critic, Jonathan Glancey, described the South Bank thus:

> This is the land of weather-stained concrete, of rain-swept walkways, urine-soaked stairs, ugly undercrofts and, most of all, of brutal Sixties architecture. (Glancey, 1994, no page)

The planner, Patrick Abercrombie, made similarly sweeping comments about the area's short-comings some 50 years earlier:

> It is one of the great anomalies of the capital that while the river, from Westminster eastwards, is lined on the north side with magnificent buildings and possesses a spacious and attractive embankment road, the corresponding south bank ... should present a depressing, semi-derelict appearance, lacking any sense of that dignity and order appropriate to its location at the centre of London and fronting on to the great waterway. (Abercrombie and Forshaw, 1943, p 129)

In interview,[4] local business and community representatives described the 'governance vacuum' that emerged following the abolition of the GLC, a body that had taken a special interest in the development of the South Bank. This situation was compounded by weak leadership from Lambeth and Southwark, the two London boroughs with shared responsibility for the area. As one interviewee put it, until relatively recently, local government was not "the hell interested in the area". For several local business representatives, this 'vacuum' was another factor in the South Bank's failure to 'capitalise' on the development opportunities associated with its prominent central London location.

SBEG has positioned itself as the frontrunner in securing a sustainable future for the South Bank area, and has sought to establish a system of local governance through which residents and businesses can broker a coherent set of SD priorities. Producing a vision to guide the area's future growth has entailed, as one SBEG member described:

> '[T]alking about what was wrong with the area, creating a positive vision and then, if you like, promoting that, signing people up to it, and then lobbying for public support of that.'

Delivering improvements to the public realm was seen, certainly by most members of the local business community, as the most effective way to create a more positive spatial identity for the South Bank. This reflected the belief that the South Bank's poor quality public realm was a 'problem' that acted as a disincentive to potential investors. The 'solution', public realm regeneration, would deliver a safer, cleaner and greener environment. Which, in turn, would stimulate further inward investment that could be captured through mechanisms such as Section 106,[5] to enhance the wellbeing of employees, visitors and local residents alike (see Box 4.1). Similar goals were enshrined in national SD and *place-shaping* strategies which called for local government, community and business actors to work together to 'promote the general wellbeing of a community and its citizens' (Lyons, 2007, p 3).

SBEG's well-connected membership helped the group to gather support for its development vision. However (and typically, given the contested terrain of urban sustainability), they are not the only local stakeholder group with views about what the South Bank's future development should consist of. Residents' organisations, notably the Waterloo Community Development Group (WCDG), a planning advisory group formed in 1972 that played a central role in the Coin Street campaigns, has a vision of the South Bank's future that, while similar to SBEG's in many respects, also departs from it in some notable ways.

Box 4.1: South Bank Employers Group's sustainable development vision

We will promote and improve the South Bank neighbourhood for the benefit of those who work, study or live in the area, as well as the millions who visit each year, with the aim of making South Bank:

- A desirable destination for cultural pursuits, business, education and leisure
- A place which supports and encourages investment and business growth
- A place with a flourishing and cohesive residential community
- A place which welcomes visitors
- A friendly, clean, colourful, safe, dynamic and diverse neighbourhood

Source: SBEG (2009, no page)

Articulated around New Labour's SCs agenda, WCDG's vision (see Box 4.2) calls for more affordable housing and improved residential facilities, rather than an improved public realm, per se. Unlike SBEG's vision, which is more *strategic* in focus, the WCDG's is more policy-specific, and targets what are typically seen as 'local' issues such as children's play facilities, parking arrangements and retail provision.

Box 4.2: Waterloo Community Development Group Sustainable Development Strategy

The policies of WCDG are for:

1. Retaining a viable and permanent residential community in Waterloo
2. Redressing the imbalance of land uses (too little useful open space and permanent
3. Increasing the amount of permanent housing, especially for young families
4. Increasing and improving the amount of useful, green open public space
5. Retaining and increasing useful retail shopping (that which supports family life)
6. The viability of Lower Marsh shopping centre and the market stalls
7. Retaining and improving the library service in Waterloo
8. A better environment; safer, greener, cleaner
9. Better indoor and outdoor facilities for local children and young people
10. Better facilities to support community activities (free meeting places etc.)
11. An increase in safety and reduction in crime
12. Controlling traffic pollution and reducing through traffic
13. Reducing non-resident parking
14. Relocating the bus garage
15. A ban on coaches waiting or parking
16. No land being used for off-street parking
17. Safe and convenient ground level crossings for pedestrians
18. Good planning policies to achieve the above
19. Consistent implementation of these policies
20. Effective and thorough consultation with the residential community

While much of this list is 'in tune' with the development agenda put forward by SBEG, WCDG has a complex attitude towards the matter of more intensified (high-density and volume) development in the South Bank, and has openly questioned the benefits that this type of development will deliver for local residents. The question of whether the South Bank is a 'suitable site' for tall buildings is something over which the group has been particularly conflicted. A WCDG representative offered this perspective in relation to a planning application:

> '[The proposed building] is tall ... and that is antithetical to everything
> we'd fought for, for 30 years ... tall buildings are, you know, they
> fail in so many different ways. They fail at ground level, they fail in

microclimate, they don't serve a local community well, that's our experience based on evidence.'

The WCDG's reluctance to fully embrace the goal of intensified (high-rise) development puts it in direct opposition to regional planning and economic development strategies that set a clear precedent for tall buildings (Charney, 2007). The South Bank and Waterloo area is identified in the (2004) London Plan as one of 28 Opportunity Areas suitable for more intensified development, including tall buildings. This vision was developed further in the *Waterloo Opportunity Area Planning Framework* (GLA, 2007) which also set quantifiable targets for local growth, including 15,000 new jobs and 500 homes in the area by 2016, with a particular focus on high-density development in and around Waterloo station.[6]

While the WCDG's reservations about tall buildings sets it apart from planning policy, the group has nonetheless embraced the consensual language of SD which it uses to communicate its views about the area's future development. As a member of WCDG commented, the arrival of the (2003) SCs Plan was something that the group welcomed:

'[T]his [was] fabulous to me ... because this is absolutely what we believe that ... buildings are for people and spaces are for people and they're only defined in terms of people, man is the measure.'

Despite claims from both the WCDG and SBEG to represent the interests of the whole South Bank community, their visions show signs of fracture on the strategic (and highly contested) matter of tall buildings and intensification. They also place different levels of importance on affordable housing provision and public realm regeneration. However, a more immediate challenge to SC building in the area was the deep mistrust that existed between some members of the community. Residents and businesses had often been on opposing sides in past disputes around local development, and improving relations was deemed critical if the South Bank was to capitalise on its Opportunity Area status and secure a 'sustainable future'.

SBEG's solution was to create a new partnership that incorporated elected representatives, in the form of local MPs and ward councillors, alongside personnel from SBEG, Lambeth and Southwark Councils, the (now defunct) London Development Agency and the Metropolitan Police. The South Bank Partnership (SBP) aims to promote 'effective neighbourhood working across borough boundaries and political alignments' (SBP, 2006, no page). Described by a SBEG representative as the group's 'political wing', bringing elected representatives onto the SBP board was important for three reasons. First, it provided a way for local businesses to ensure that their voice was heard by local authorities and elected representatives. Second, it provided a way to bypass those residents who refused to engage with business representatives and their vision of the South Bank's future. And third, it provided a way to generate buy-in for a growth-focused SD plan that would exploit the South Bank's status as a central London growth zone for the benefit of the 'wider South Bank community'.

For some residents, the SBP, which hosts quarterly public meetings on development matters in the area, was a welcome intervention. As an interviewee explained, the SBP provides a mechanism to feed local people's views through to the business-led SBEG, which he considered to be the most powerful force in local place-making: "we're isolated from SBEG, it's Kate [Hoey MP] that makes them listen to us. We're quite lucky, we have three good councillors and good MPs." However, others were less positive, describing the SBP as a: "Non-existent fantasy group. I have never seen a terms of reference or set of minutes of who the South Bank Partnership is." This interviewee's concern was that, despite the SBP's claim to represent the interests of the whole South Bank community, in reality, key decisions were made behind closed doors: "I don't even know what they do … I see the levers, which is SBEG."

These more critical comments echo those made by Baeten (2009, p 246), who argues that the use of 'institutionalised channels of partnerships' to create a singular discourse about development futures reduces alternative views to 'sheer background noise'. Despite the reservations of some community members about its format and function, the SBP has been officially recognised by both Lambeth and Southwark Councils, and praised as a model of good practice by the GLA and other regional and national governing bodies.

The SBP's most notable activity to date has been to publish *Under pressure and on the edge – London's South Bank: a manifesto for action* (SBP, 2006). The manifesto, which was updated in 2010, is an ambitious document that seeks to secure the sustainable future of the area by harnessing 'the pressures of change to the benefit of the people, businesses and activities of the South Bank and of the wider community of which we are on the edge' (SBP, 2006, p 3). In so doing, it invokes the idea of a cohesive community, emphasising the mutual gains that will flow from neighbourhood regeneration, and outlining the following priority areas:

- economic growth, new developments and new jobs;
- improved schools and training, especially to benefit local people without work;
- a safe, clean and accessible environment for all;
- an efficient transport interchange and improved gateway to London;
- increased opportunities for culture, sport, recreation and shopping.

The SBP's 'can-do' approach towards community development was recognised by the UK government's Department for Communities and Local Government (DCLG) who adopted the manifesto as a model for Local Charters,[7] while Jim Fitzpatrick, former Minister for London, commented:

> South Bank Partnership represents real neighbourhood leadership and delivery in action. I praise their proactive and comprehensive

partnership approach and believe that many areas in the capital could benefit from adopting their self-help attitude. (SBP, 2006, no page)

As Raco (2003, p 241) identifies, in recent years, the idea of the (pro-)active and responsible community has gained currency with governments who have rewarded bodies 'seen to be positive in their attitudes towards development projects', while less receptive groups have often seen their views side-lined. This was evident in South Bank, and several members of both the residential and business community reflected on the dwindling influence of the 'more combative' community members, who were the driving force of anti-development campaigns during the 1970s. Some saw this as symptomatic of how the parameters of planning debates have changed in recent years. Certainly in the South Bank context, the idea that incoming development can be resisted is seen as an increasingly 'out-dated' and 'unrealistic' perspective (see Dyrberg, 2009).

These anecdotes seem particularly apt in light of the current government's reorientation of the planning system towards a presumption in favour of *sustainable development*. These changes have involved major planning policy reforms that are aligned to a view of planning as a flexible force *for growth*:

> In order to fulfil its purpose of helping achieve sustainable development, planning must not simply be about scrutiny. Planning must be a creative exercise in finding ways to enhance and improve the places in which we live our lives. (DCLG, 2012, p i)

The revised South Bank manifesto (SBP, 2010, p 3) continues to be underpinned by the belief that the development opportunities offered by the area's growing reputation as a cultural and commercial hub will benefit 'the people, businesses and activities of the South Bank ... the wider communities of Lambeth and Southwark, and [contribute] to the success of London as a world city.' The SBP argues that development opportunities have been 'delayed by the planning process, especially [by] heritage issues, and stalled by the [economic] downturn.' This has 'denied us many of the economic and community benefits which we counted on to flow from development' (SBP, 2010, p 3). The straightened economic climate thus intensifies the need to reach consensus around development priorities. While the manifesto acknowledges the tensions that still exist particularly between business and residential communities, accepting higher-density development in strategic sites is presented as the only viable way to secure the South Bank's 'sustainable future'. This 'TINA' logic[8] may explain why recent planning applications for more intensified development in the form of tall buildings (namely, the Shell Centre redevelopment and the Elizabeth House scheme) have not been opposed by the residential community. Or, on the other hand, it may support the contention, expressed by members of the business community, that strong cross-community consensus on the best way to deliver sustainable growth (intensification) now exists. The next phase in the visioning of the South Bank's future, under the guise of *Neighbourhood Planning*,[9] (DCLG, 2012) is now under way, and may provide further clues as to the inclusivity of the South Bank's SD strategy.

A sustainable future for London

The South Bank, like many neighbourhoods across the UK, is facing an uncertain future. However, as a central *London* neighbourhood, the South Bank has several odds stacked in its favour. While in the immediate aftermath of the credit crunch there were fears that London might bear the brunt of the crisis, the city's economy has proven to be remarkably resilient (Raco and Street, 2012). Post-crash, London's economy has, to a large extent, returned to a state of 'business as usual'. This is despite calls – perhaps most visibly expressed by the Occupy movement – to challenge the role of global financial apparatus in the reproduction of social injustices (see Harvey, 2010).

Development-led models of regeneration, as endorsed in local-scale strategies such as the South Bank manifesto, have largely been upheld, particularly in the South East of England. In London, mega-events such as the London 2012 Olympic Games, and major infrastructure schemes such as Crossrail, have seen billions of pounds of investment channelled into the city's infrastructure. The investment, in London 2012, at least in Mayor Boris Johnson's eyes, represents 'value for money', not just for London, but for the whole of the UK:

> When you add up the benefits in jobs, growth, infrastructure, the boost to east London and the positive glow it has given to the brand of London and the UK – that £9.3bn looks like one of the most sensible and pragmatic investments in the history of British public spending. (GLA, 2013a, p 4)

This investment, along with the continuing presence of overseas investors, has meant the London economy, and its property market in particular, has remained buoyant. This has done little to destabilise growth-led models of SD, despite growing concerns about *unsustainable* levels of income inequality within the city (see *Financial Times*, 2013). The challenges of meeting the needs of a growing population, including housing an additional one million Londoners by 2021, as the gap between house prices and earnings ratios continues to widen, are acknowledged in the Mayor's *2020 Vision* (GLA, 2013a). Yet, as in earlier plans, the language is uncompromisingly ambitious, with Johnson arguing there is a need to 'lengthen London's lead as the greatest city on earth' (GLA, 2013a).

As this chapter has shown, urban sustainability, and how best to achieve it in the London context, has been influenced by wider narratives including growth management, neoliberalism, partnership working and community participation. Planners and policy makers' thinking has, certainly in recent decades, remained consistently supportive of the idea that economic growth should not be seen as a threat to social equality or the quality of the physical environment, but rather is the best or only way to deliver a range of social and environmental goals. Recent policy documents such as the UK government's White Paper *The natural choice* (Defra, 2011b), which seeks to quantify the economic 'value' of nature, only reinforce this tendency. This, for authors such as Martínez-Alier et al (2010), underlines the need for a wholesale re-evaluation of the notion of SD given the deepening climate crisis and rising levels of global inequality (see also, Fry, 2009).

While, as Healey (2002, p 1789) points out, the 'strategic capacity to debate the urban is not owned by any one agent', the South Bank case reflects a common scenario wherein some groups and/or coalitions of individuals take the lead in the process of 'imagining the city'. It is in the *soft spaces*, represented by structures such as the SBP, in which futures planning is increasingly enacted, yet these may lie outside of formalised democratic systems of governance (Allmendinger and Haughton, 2012). This is important given that unelected bodies, such as the recently formed Local Enterprise Partnerships (LEPs), are being invited to play a central role in local place shaping, economic strategy making and SD planning, under the banner of the *localism agenda* (see Heseltine, 2012).

The promotion of these modes of governance is framed in the language of decentralisation and local empowerment, but has the potential to serve to reinforce existing (and unequal) power dynamics in the negotiation of sustainable futures. For this reason, it is critical that we pay close attention to the struggles over the framing of urban futures at the local level as they are revealed in and through new governance arrangements, such as Neighbourhood Planning. As Massey (2007) points out, these localised instances highlight that, even in a *global city* like London, struggles over 'the local' remain important and can tell us much about the direction that sustainable urban futures may take.

Notes

[1] The notion of *de-growth* has been proposed by some as a way to foster 'the equitable and democratic transition to a smaller economy with less production and consumption' (Martínez-Alier et al, 2010, p 1741).

[2] Following the abolition of Local Area Agreements (LAAs) by the Coalition government in 2010, many LSPs were disbanded. LAAs set out a framework from which local government and partners (acting as LSPs) could select 35 priority targets to guide local strategy making. The abolition of the LAAs was accompanied by the dissolution of other policy measures including Comprehensive Area Agreements (CAAs), regional planning apparatus and a range of organisations often referred to as 'quangos'.

[3] SBEG currently has 18 members: Braeburn Estates, British Film Institute, British Rail Board (Residuary), Coin Street Community Builders, EDF Energy London Eye, Elizabeth House Partners, Ernst & Young, Guy's and St Thomas' NHS Foundation Trust, ITV, King's College London, London Duck Tours, London South Bank University, National Theatre, Network Rail, Park Plaza Hotels, Shell UK, South Bank Centre and Whitbread PLC.

[4] Fifty-two interviews were conducted with a range of local stakeholders, including SBEG staff, members, local community representatives, local councillors and local authority representatives between September 2008 and November 2009. An additional follow-up interview was conducted with SBEG in April 2013.

[5] Planning obligations (under Section 106 of the Town and Country Planning Act 1990) focus on mitigating the impact of development, and are commonly used to deliver community 'benefits' such as infrastructure or affordable housing.

[6] These targets were reviewed as part of the revisions to the London Plan overseen by current Mayor, Boris Johnson. The (2011) Replacement Plan identifies a minimum number of 1,900 new homes, and an indicative employment capacity of 15,000. It does not review progress towards these targets – this is part of an ongoing assessment of Opportunity Area Planning Frameworks (see GLA, 2013b).

[7] A voluntary partnership agreement on local development priorities between communities, local authorities and other service providers, Local Charters, were part of the Labour government's neighbourhood working agenda. Similar ideas are currently being developed in the form of Neighbourhood Planning (DCLG, 2012).

[8] 'There Is No Alternative' (TINA) is a phrase associated with Margaret Thatcher's Conservative government, and has been used to disregard alternatives to a free market ideology.

[9] Introduced under the Localism Act 2011, neighbourhood planning is designed to offer local communities (including businesses) the power to make local development plans.

References

Abercrombie, P. (1944) *The Greater London Plan*, London: HM Stationery Office.

Abercrombie, P. and Forshaw, J. (1943) *County of London Plan*, London: London County Council.

Allmendinger, P. and Haughton, G. (2012) 'Post-political spatial planning in England: a crisis of consensus?', *Transactions of the Institute of British Geographers*, vol 37, no 1, pp 89-103.

Anderson, B. and Adey, P. (2012) 'Guest editorial', *Environment and Planning A*, vol 44, pp 1529-35.

Baeten, G. (2000) 'From community planning to partnerships planning. Urban regeneration and shifting power geometries on the South Bank, London', *GeoJournal*, vol 51, pp 293-300.

Baeten, G. (2009) 'Regenerating the South Bank: reworking the community and the emergence of post political regeneration', in R. Imrie, L. Lees and M. Raco (eds) *Regenerating London*, London: Routledge, pp 237-53.

Brindley, T., Rydin, Y. and Stoker, G. (1996) *Remaking planning: the politics of urban change*, London: Routledge.

Charney, I. (2007) 'The politics of design: architecture, tall buildings and the skyline of central London', *Area*, vol 39, pp 195-205.

Cochrane, A. (2006) 'Devolving the heartland: making up a new social policy for the "South East"', *Critical Social Policy*, vol 26, pp 685-96.

Cochrane, A. (2007) *Understanding urban policy, a critical approach*, Oxford: Blackwell.

Cook, I.R. (2009) 'Private sector involvement in urban governance: the case of business improvement districts and town centre management partnerships in England', *Geoforum*, vol 40, pp 930-40.

DCLG (Department for Communities and Local Government) (2012) *National Planning Policy Framework*, London: DCLG.

DCMS (Department of Culture, Media and Sport) and DCLG (Department for Communities and Local Government) (2009) *World class places*, London: DCMS and DCLG.

Defra (Department for Environment, Food and Rural Affairs) (1999) *A better quality of life,* London: Defra.

Defra (2011a) *Mainstreaming sustainable development: the government's vision and what this means in practice*, London: Defra.

Defra (2011b) *The natural choice: securing the value of nature*, London: Defra.

Dikeç, M. (2007) *Badlands of the republic: space, politics and urban policy*, Oxford: Blackwell.

Dyrberg, T.B. (2009), 'What is beyond right/left? The case of New Labour', *Journal of Political Ideologies*, vol 14, pp 133-53.

Elkin, S.L. (1974) *Politics and land use planning: the London experience*, Cambridge: Cambridge University Press.

Essex, S. and Brayshay, M. (2007) 'Vision, vested interests and pragmatism: who remade Britain's blitzed cities?', *Planning Perspectives*, vol 22, pp 417-41.

Financial Times (2013) 'London and the world: Part 3: city under pressure', *Financial Times*, 10 September.

Florio, S. and Brownill, S. (2000) 'Whatever happened to criticism? Interpreting the London Docklands Development Corporation's obituary', *City*, vol 4, no 1, pp 53-64.

Fry, T. (2009) *Design futuring: sustainability, ethics and new practice*, Oxford and New York: Berg.

GLA (Greater London Authority) (2004) *The London Plan*, London: GLA.

GLA (2007) *Waterloo Opportunity Area Planning Framework*, London: GLA.

GLA (2009) *Leading to a greener London: an environment programme for London*, London: GLA.

GLA (2011) *The London Plan*, London: GLA.

GLA (2013a) *2020 vision: the greatest city on Earth*, London: GLA.

GLA (2013b) *London Plan Implementation Plan 1*, London: GLA.

GLC (Greater London Council) (1969) *Greater London Development Plan*, London: GLC.

Glancey, J. (1994) 'Architecture: action, it's the South Bank show', *The Independent*, 2 February (www.independent.co.uk/arts-entertainment/art/news/architecture-action-its-the-south-bank-show-masterplans-are-afoot-to-transform-the-capitals-unloved-arts-complex-in-a-design-competition-jonathan-glancey-gives-a-cautious-welcome-1391431.html).

GLRPC (Greater London Regional Planning Committee) (1929) *First report*, London: GLRPC.

Harvey, D. (2010) *The enigma of capital and the crises of capitalism*, London: Profile Books.

Haughton, G. and Counsell, D. (2004) 'Regions and sustainable development: regional planning matters', *The Geographical Journal*, vol 170, pp 135-45.

Healey, P. (1997) *Collaborative planning: shaping places in fragmented societies*, Basingstoke: Palgrave Macmillan.

Healey, P. (2002) 'On creating the "city" as a collective resource', *Urban Studies*, vol 39, pp 1777-92.

Heseltine, Lord (2012) *No stone unturned in pursuit of growth*, London: Department for Business, Innovation & Skills.

HM Government (1971) *Town and Country Planning Act 1971*, London: HM Stationery Office.

Holman, N. (2010) 'The changing nature of the London Plan', **in K.** Scanlon and B. Kochan (eds) *London: coping with austerity: a review of housing, planning and public policy issues*, London: London School of Economics and Political Science, pp 29-48.

Imrie, R. and Thomas, H. (1995) 'Urban policy process and the politics of urban regeneration', *International Journal of Urban and Regional Research*, vol 19, no 4, pp 479-92.

IPPR (Institute for Public Policy Research) and KPMG (1997) *The Greater London Authority: principles and organisational structure*, London: Corporation of London.

Jones, P. and Evans, J. (2008) *Urban regeneration in the UK*, London: Sage.

Littig, B. and Griessler, E. (2005) 'Social sustainability: a catchword between political pragmatism and social theory', *International Journal of Sustainable Development*, vol 8, no 1, pp 65-79.

London Borough of Lambeth (2011) www.lambeth.gov.uk/NR/exeres/241D9235-B094-416A-A141-5EA2709644EF.htm

Lloyd, G. and Newlands, D. (1988) 'Business and planning: a privatised planning initiative', *Planning Practice and Research*, vol 2, no 4, pp 11-14.

LSDC (London Sustainable Development Commission) (undated) www.londonsdc.org

LSDC (2002) *Sustainable Development Framework* for *London*, London: LSDC.

Lyons, M. (2007) *Lyons enquiry into local government. place-shaping: a shared ambition for the future of local government*, London: The Stationery Office.

Martínez-Alier J., Unai, P., Franck-Dominique, V. and Zaccai, E. (2010) 'Sustainable de-growth: mapping the context, criticisms and future prospects of an emergent paradigm', *Ecological Economics*, vol 69, pp 1741-7.

Massey, D. (2007) *World city*, Cambridge: Polity Press.

McNeill, D. (2002) 'Livingstone's London: Left politics and the world city', *Regional Studies*, vol 36, no 1, pp 75–91.

Meadows, D.H., Meadows, G., Randers, J. and Behrens III, W.W. (1972) *The limits to growth*, New York: Universe Books.

Ministry of Housing and Local Government (1947) *Town and Country Planning Act 1947*, London: HMSO.

ODPM (Office of the Deputy Prime Minister) (2003) *Sustainable communities: building for the future*, London: ODPM.

ONS (Office for National Statistics) (2012) *Estimated resident population mid-year*, Newport: ONS.

Pimlott, B. and Rao, N. (2002) *Governing London*, Oxford: Oxford University Press.

Property Advisory Group (1983) *The climate for public and private partnerships in property development*, London: HMSO.

Raco, M. (2003) 'New Labour, community and the future of Britain's urban renaissance', in R. Imrie and M. Raco (eds) *Urban renaissance? New Labour, community and urban policy*, Bristol: Policy Press, pp 235–50.

Raco, M. (2007) 'The planning, design, and governance of sustainable communities in the UK', in R. Atkinson and G. Helms (eds) *Securing an urban renaissance: crime, community and urban policy*, Bristol: Policy Press, pp 39–56.

Raco, M. and Street, E. (2012) 'Radical resilience? Sustainability planning, economic change, and the politics of post-recession development in London and Hong Kong', *Urban Studies*, vol 49, no 5, pp 1065–87.

Rees, G. and Lambert, J. (1985) *Cities in crisis: the political economy of urban development in post-war Britain*, London: Edward Arnold.

Sassen, S. (1992) *The global city: New York, London, Tokyo*, Princeton, NJ: Princeton University Press.

SBEG (South Bank Employers' Group) (1998) *South Bank at the crossroads*, London: SBEG.

SBEG (2009) *Business plans and accounts 2009-2012*, London: SBEG.

SBEG (undated) www.sbeg.co.uk

SBP (South Bank Partnership) (2006) *Under pressure and on the edge – London's South Bank: a manifesto for action*, London: SBP.

SBP (2010) *The South Bank manifesto 4 years on: a renewed call for action*, London: SBP.

Skeffington, A. (1969) *People and planning: report of the Committee on Public Participation in Planning*, London: HMSO.

Southern, A. (2001) 'What matters is what works? The management of regeneration', *Local Economy*, vol 16, pp 264–71.

Street, E. (2012) 'Reshaping the South Bank, the (post)politics of sustainable place-making in London', Unpublished PhD thesis, London: King's College London.

Sweeting, D. (2002) 'Leadership in urban governance: the Mayor of London', *Local Government Studies*, vol 28, no 1, pp 3-20.

Swyngedouw E. (2009) 'The antinomies of the postpolitical city: in search of a democratic politics of environmental production', *International Journal of Urban and Regional Research*, vol 33, pp 601-20.

TCPA (Town and Country Planning Association) (1970) *London under stress: a study of the planning policies proposed for London and its region*, London: TCPA.

Thornley, A., Rydin, Y., Scanlon, K. and West, K. (2005) 'Business privilege and the strategic planning agenda of the Greater London Authority', *Urban Studies*, vol 42, pp 1947-68.

Ward, K. (2007) 'Business improvement districts: policy origins, mobile policies and urban liveability', *Geography Compass*, vol 2, pp 657-72.

WCDG (Waterloo Community Development Group) (undated) *Our policies* (www.wcdg.net/content/about-us).

WCED (World Commission on Environment and Development) (1987) *Our common future* (Brundtland report), New York: United Nations.

Whitehead, M. (2003) '(Re)analysing the sustainable city: nature, urbanisation and the regulation of socio environmental relations in the UK', *Urban Studies*, vol 40, pp 1183-206.

Whitehead, M. (2007) *Spaces of sustainability: geographical perspectives on the sustainable society*, London: Routledge.

FIVE

Privatisation, managerialism and the changing politics of sustainability planning in London

Mike Raco

Introduction

The governance of London has long been an issue of contention and subject to upheavals, shifting logics and competing ideological projects. The city's overwhelming dominance of national economic, political and cultural life in the UK has been widely documented, as have its 'global city' credentials. Its unique circumstances reflect, and are in part reproduced by, a particular assemblage of local, metropolitan, national and global public and private sector organisations that sit in a sometimes uneasy co-existence. It is simultaneously lauded by some as one of the great democratic cities of the world at the same time as others characterise its politics as confusing and contradictory. Indeed, at its most extreme, writers such as Travers (2004) curiously describe London as an 'ungovernable' city, as if its governance is somehow dysfunctional in relation to a utopian view of governance efficiency and cohesiveness.

These contrasting views of London's politics are evident in current debates and strategies over sustainability planning. London has seen something of a renaissance in its government structures during the 2000s. It is the only city in England in which a relatively powerful Mayor has control over key policy fields. The 32 London boroughs[1] also play an important role in coordinating and shaping local welfare and sustainability strategies. In short, representative government in the city matters in a way that is perhaps not so true of other English cities where the powers and responsibilities of local government are less well developed. On the international stage London is often put forward as an exemplar or model for others to follow. It is perceived to be a city that promotes vigorous economic growth, a high quality of life and a political system based on democratic openness and accountability.

And yet, at the same time, as this chapter will show, a paradox is emerging. Despite the empowerment of government bodies, the city has undergone a quiet revolution in its governance arrangements. Surreptitiously, and in the name of wider visions of 'Good Governance' and sustainability, private companies and experts have taken ownership of a growing proportion of the city's key public infrastructure. Under private finance initiatives (PFIs), private companies now build, finance and operate much of what is commonly understood to be the 'public sector'. These PFIs are underpinned by inflexible contracts that can last for 30-40 years, with private contract holders effectively insulated from democratic demands and disruptions. Governance is, therefore, becoming more fragmented, with a growing assemblage of global private sector actors having a direct stake in local policy making and implementation. This, arguably, is helping to create a greater dissonance between citizens and state bodies. In some neighbourhoods even streetlights and waste management services are now financed and operated by private companies, all in the name of enhanced 'efficiency'. A new breed of private investor has emerged to take advantage of emerging opportunities with global hedge funds companies such as Innisfree and Semperian moving in to take control of ever greater portions of the city's 'public' assets.[2] It is a process that has remained stubbornly under-researched in academic work on urban governance, much of which is content to deconstruct official policy statements and discourses while underplaying the state structures and practices through which policies are constructed and implemented.

This chapter develops its arguments through three areas of discussion. First, it sets out some of the key relationships between conceptual understandings of governance reform and sustainability. It argues that the so-called Good Governance agendas that underpin contemporary, sustainability-based visions inexorably lead to output-focused forms of contract-based expert governance and privatisation. It highlights some of the connections between state reform and new progressive modes of governance. Second, it then uses the example of PFIs to explore some of the governance challenges created by recent shifts towards privatisation. It explains how private involvement in state practices and structures has evolved, and the implications for democratic governance. Privatisation is, in itself, a utopian construct that equates democracy with the delivery of tangible outputs and the mobilisation of new forms of expertise. For advocates of reform, any mode of governance that is seen to 'deliver' projects on the ground is, by default, more democratic, accountable and 'Good'. Third, it uses the example of sustainability planning in London to explore these dynamics. It quantifies some of the changes that have taken place in the city, and highlights their impacts on governance agendas and frameworks. It also looks at possible future trends and highlights some of the possibilities open to citizens to challenge and disrupt dominant models.

Governing sustainability, privatisation and the changing nature of the state

Governance reform has always been at the heart of global sustainability discourses since their emergence in the 1970s. A global utopian movement emerged that equated 'being modern with the acceptance of democracy and liberal values' (Gray, 2013, p 40). Sustainability rapidly became elided with liberal calls for the wholesale modernisation of Keynesian governance structures. Traditional forms of representative democracy and decision making were seen as outmoded and should be replaced by more participative processes in which citizens and communities would take on greater responsibility for policy making, implementation and (ideally) their own welfare. It is an agenda that has been pursued by global bodies, such as the United Nations (UN) and The World Bank, who now claim that the era of govern*ment* is over. The call, instead, is for the establishment of network-based Good Govern*ance* systems that operate efficiently if, according to the UN Economic and Social Commission for Asia and the Pacific (UNESCAP) (no date, p 1), they are:

- participatory
- consensus-oriented
- accountable
- transparent
- responsive
- effective and efficient
- equitable and inclusive
- and follow the rule of law.

The effects of this Good Governance agenda have been felt far and wide. Its core principles have underpinned the drawing up of sustainability and modernisation programmes in countries across the world. They appear to be non-political and consensual and if followed, it is argued, then 'corruption is minimized, the views of minorities are taken into account and the voices of the most vulnerable in society are heard in decision-making. It is also responsive to the present and future needs of society' (UNESCAP, no date, p 1). Control should rest with *local* communities and citizen groups, rather than governments and bureaucracies.

During the 1990s and 2000s, this modernising vision evolved into a direct concern with the delivery of public policy and the ways in which state actors could enlist private operators to take on more governmental responsibilities. Sustainability was equated not so much with citizen empowerment but with the efficient delivery of infrastructure and services. It became a managerial vision of governance and took on a central role in the modernising discourses of third way and self-proclaimed 'neo-progressive' thinkers (see, for example, Pearce and Margo, 2007). Government, it was claimed, could *only* be legitimate if it could provide clear, tangible *outputs*, such as new infrastructure and/or reformed services. In Scharpf's (1999) terms, the legitimacy of modern states depends on their ability to produce these visible outcomes. It does not reside, as imagined by many political theorists, with the quality and openness of democratic inputs into decision making. For modernising governments, it didn't matter *how* projects were delivered; all that mattered were the perceived results. As leading moderniser and Good Governance advocate Tony Blair (2010) recalls in his memoires,

> the problem for all progressive parties was that by the 1960s ... citizens on the ladder of opportunity didn't want more state help; they wanted choice, freedom to earn more money and spend it.... They wanted a different relationship with the state: as partners or citizens, not as beneficiaries or clients. (2010, p 90)

It was claimed that through privatisation and the delegation of responsibility to private sector experts, citizens would see the state 'working' around them and become supportive of governments and the political process.

This ability to demonstrate a tangible return from policy interventions has been particularly pertinent in relation to sustainability planning. There has been much scepticism over the value and utility of abstract imaginations concerning the needs of future generations when citizens have been facing pressing short-term needs of their own. It therefore became a priority for neo-progressive governments to demonstrate that their sustainability programmes were seen to be realistic and delivering results (see Giddens, 2009, for a full discussion). In Jacques Rancière's (2005, p 8) terms, policy makers therefore adopted a managerial *politics of the possible* characterised by a 'strange mixture of realism and utopia'. This sees sustainability as a policy outcome that can be implemented through the application of 'realistic' management principles. For Rancière (2005), this shift reflects a wider anti-utopianism in which political idealism has been equated with Keynesian governance failures and top-down control. The net result is that,

> ... we no longer believe in promises. We have become realists. Or, in any case, our governments and wise experts have become realists for us. They stick to the "possible", which precisely does not offer a great deal of possibilities. This "possible" is made of small things that progress slowly if they are handled with caution by those who know. (2005, p 9)

The outcome, as Rancière notes, is that as citizens we are implored to be realistic in our expectations and to allow things that were formally in the public sphere to be managed by private experts, because 'the realism which pretends to liberate us from utopia and its evil spells is itself still a utopia. It promises less, it's true, but it does not promise otherwise' (Rancière, 2005, p 11). The radical possibilities opened up by sustainability thinking become limited by a 'submission to the law of the present and the merely possible' (Rancière, 2005, p 10; see also Swyngedouw, 2009a, 2009b; Žižek, 2011, 2012).

A well-functioning state apparatus that promotes the principles of sustainability is increasingly presented as one that acts as an effective *manager* of projects and contracts. Its core function is to negotiate project outcomes and delivery mechanisms with private operators and experts. The public interest has been equated with good managerial skills and the implementation of processes that put democratic demands to one side and mobilise private sector experts as delivery actors. Surreptitiously, and through quiet accretion, state services and assets have subsequently been converted into investment spaces for private finance and corporations. These interests have, in turn, become adept at pushing their claims for more fundamental forms of privatisation in the name of modernisation, sustainability and Good Governance. Indeed, in many instances, global corporations now even write sustainability strategies for cities and are able to push their own visions for 'smart city' growth sustainability on to governments and populations (see, for example, PwC, 2012). It is in this wider context of governance reform that contemporary changes in sustainability planning and thinking in London have to be understood, and it to these that the chapter now turns.

Planning for sustainability and the emergence of a London model

As chapters in this book and elsewhere (see Imrie et al, 2009) have demonstrated, London's position as both a capital city and a global city means that planners and citizens face acute challenges. Policy is complicated by the fact that national government has a particularly strong presence in London and the city has been at the centre of accumulation strategies operating over multiple scales. Its economic primacy has generated real tensions over sustainability between the discourse of sustaining economic success versus the broader objective of protecting the environment and promoting equality and democratic transparency. Despite the rhetoric of some organisations and politicians (see London First, 2010), much of this primacy has been underpinned by public spending. Official data shows that in 2011/12 the UK state spent £9,613/capita in the city, a figure that is higher than in any other English region and well above the English average of £8,491 (see Bardens and Webb, 2012). And this, of course, excludes the billions of pounds used to support London's financial services through bank bailouts. It reflects the impact of state-funded projects in the city, such as the 2012 Olympics and investments in the London Underground. But it is also fuelled by the presence of government bodies and other state-funded agencies in the city with their own requirements in terms of infrastructure, skilled workers and urban development. This, provides direct economic benefits, but, as we will see in the discussion of privatisation below, it can also generate tensions and fuel inequalities.

In addition to public spending, London has also become a magnet for flagship investments by international investors. The *Financial Times* (2012) estimates that more than £22 billion of foreign investment was made in London's commercial property sector during 2011/12 – a figure that exceeds that invested in the property markets of any other European *country*. A similar story is true for residential property, with research by Knight Frank (2013) showing that prime central London property has increased by 53 per cent in value between March 2009 and January 2013, fuelled by overseas investments in luxury property. Average house prices by September 2012 had reached the staggering figure of £461,018[3] (see BBC Online, 2012). London is also one of the world's great commercial centres with some of the busiest international airports and economic sectors that are connected to global networks. It possesses business elites who are relatively disconnected from everyday life in the city. New forms of 'enclave urbanism' are emerging in which powerful global elites live in exclusive and increasingly gated and gentrified parts of the city (see Douglass, 2012, for a wider discussion). All of this makes planning for sustainability for the majority of citizens a particularly challenging task.

Given this context, it is perhaps surprising that London has become something of a role model for city authorities around the world. The city's congestion charge, for example, is seen as a leading example of car management control schemes, even though its sustainability credentials are highly questionable given that it legitimates the use of urban space for motor vehicles. Its politicians have played a leading role in the international C40 Group under the leadership of both Mayors Livingstone and Johnson. In cities such as Taipei and Hong Kong London's approach to sustainability planning has provided a template for local initiatives and strategies (see Raco and I-Lin, 2012). In more specific terms there are three identifiable elements to what might be termed a London model of sustainability planning emerging, all of which reproduce particular forms of managerial knowledge and practice.

First, there has been a long-running attempt to establish sustainability indicators that can be used to shape planning practices on the ground and core policy priorities. Box 5.1 lists the most recent version of these that relate to the London Plan 2011 (Mayor of London, 2011). As is common with sustainability indicators, the range of topics covered is enormous, drawing in targets for public health, pollution, energy use, the built environment, employment and transport. The tensions between these targets are underplayed, as is the wider politics of policy selectivity and prioritisation. The win–win–win discourses of sustainability overplay the very real costs and losses associated with any form of policy implementation (see Swyngedouw, 2009a). Nonetheless, targets and monitoring have become an integral part of sustainability thinking and practices in London, and have paved the way for some of the wider shifts towards privatisation and governance 'modernisation' discussed later in the chapter. In contrast to the rest of England, a metropolitan governance structure exists that has the capacity to produce plans and to monitor their impacts.

Second, sustainability discourses have been linked to urban development policy in the city, both in terms of strategic planning and project management/ delivery. Since the first London Plan of 2004, major urban projects have been concentrated in so-called Opportunity Areas and areas of intensification. There is a requirement that projects re-use brownfield land and are located in or around existing transport nodes or local centres. Planning controls are therefore being used to try and shape patterns of future spatial development across the city. The impacts of these projects on London's economy, labour force and environment have, of course, been far from sustainable, but there have been real efforts to try

Box 5.1: Indicators for monitoring the sustainability effects of the London Plan

1. Maximise the proportion of development taking place on previously developed land.
2. Optimise the density of residential development
3. Minimise the loss of open space
4. Increase the supply of new homes
5. An increased supply of affordable homes
6. Reducing Health Inequalities
7. Sustaining economic activity
8. Ensure that there is sufficient development capacity in the office market.
9. Ensure that there is sufficient employment land available
10. Employment in Outer London
11. Increased employment opportunities for those suffering from disadvantage in the employment market
12. Improving the provision of social infrastructure and related services.
13. Achieve a reduced reliance on the private car and a more sustainable modal split for journeys
14. Achieve a reduced reliance on the private car and a more sustainable modal split for journeys.
15. Achieve a reduced reliance on the private car and a more Replacement sustainable modal split for journeys
16. Achieve a reduced reliance on the private car and a more sustainable modal split for journeys
17. Increase in the number of jobs located in areas with high PTAL values
18. Protection of biodiversity habitat
19. Increase in municipal waste recycled or composted and elimination of waste to landfill by 2031
20. Reduce carbon dioxide emissions through new development
21. Increase in energy generated from renewable sources
22. Increase Urban Greening
23. Improve London's Blue Ribbon Network
24. Protecting and improving London's heritage and public realm

Source: Adapted from Mayor of London (2011, pp 13-16)

and ensure that development takes place in some of the most deprived and most contaminated post-industrial areas of the city.

Third, in more practical terms, major urban regeneration projects have also become subject to greater regulatory oversight in terms of their sustainability credentials. The London Olympics, for example, promoted itself as the most sustainable Olympic Games of all time. Contractors and sub-contractors had to demonstrate how their practices connected to wider sustainability plans and targets (see Raco, 2014, for a thorough discussion). Indeed, the legacy that is now being created around the Games is primarily one of efficient project management, with toolkits and best practice guidelines being produced for infrastructure managers in the city and elsewhere. The Olympic Delivery Authority has even launched a Learning Legacy Agenda that promotes the 'sustainable practices' of the Olympics, and the UK government uses these materials to demonstrate British 'expertise' to potential investors and governments in other parts of the world. In addition, an independent Commission for a Sustainable London was established by the Greater London Authority (GLA), the Mayor and others to provide further oversight on the sustainability features of the Olympic plans. It produced a series of critical reports throughout the Games, and policy makers frequently refer to its insights as a check and balance on their actions. Similar systems are now being rolled out in relation to other development projects such as Crossrail and King's Cross.

Such examples present London as a 'model' to follow, founded on the utopian belief that sustainability interventions can be identified, compartmentalised and implemented through the effective deployment of managerial techniques and practices. It promotes a vision in which sustainability obligations and objectives can be converted into effective contracts that shape behaviour and policy outcomes. It is an output-centred vision that has the potential to be transferable to other cities around the world. And yet, the paradox is that while a London model along these lines has emerged, the logical consequence of its implementation has been a push towards the privatisation of service delivery and asset ownership. This, as the next section demonstrates, precludes future possibilities for more integrated and accountable modes of sustainability planning at the same time as it appears to promise improved policy outcomes. Despite the relative strength of government bodies in London vis-à-vis other English cities and regions, the city is undergoing a systematic revolution in the ownership and control of large parts of its welfare infrastructure in the name of quality delivery and sustainability. The next section uses the rise of PFIs to analyse and illustrate some of these wider shifts. It begins by outlining the emergence of the PFI model. It then provides evidence of the scale and significance of PFI investments for the planning system and sustainability practices in London as a whole. A final section then looks at potential ways forward and the role that empowered government can play in fostering more effective and efficient forms of policy. This conclusion is clearly at odds with the Good Governance frameworks that underpin the politics of sustainability planning across much of the world, and their utopian calls for government hierarchies to be broken up and their powers and resources handed over to a range of alternative actors.

The coming of the Private Finance Initiative to London

The PFI was an invention of John Major's Conservative government of the early 1990s. The administration was trying to cope with the damaging effects of a recession on public finances, and access to private finance seemed to represent one possible solution to growing public debt. Under the PFI, private companies and investors would be allowed to finance, build, manage and operate state infrastructure, and then rent this back to state authorities under long-term contracts normally lasting for 25–30 years, and in some cases even longer (Smyth and Edkins, 2007). PFIs therefore include both the capital costs associated with financing and building infrastructure, and the service maintenance costs over the period of the long-term contracts. In the short term they are politically appealing as new investments are undertaken with little immediate cost to state budgets. Moreover, the financial liabilities of PFI do not count towards official government debt, thereby providing a further incentive for governments to leverage in short-term private finance, even if this means greater long-term costs.[4] This is, of course, in *direct opposition* to the core principles of sustainability planning discussed above that clearly and repeatedly state that policy interventions should *not* compromise the wellbeing of future generations. The argument was used that through private sector efficiencies PFIs would represent good value for money, both now and in the future, a claim that has been systematically undermined by researchers who highlight the inflated costs associated with private finance and the expanding costs of long-term liabilities (see Parker and Hartley, 2002; Spackman, 2002; Hellowell and Pollock, 2009; Public Accounts Committee, 2011).

Despite this, the PFI has relentlessly expanded since the early 1990s, along with its long-term burdens. PFI projects have been funded by government departments, state quangos (quasi-autonomous non-governmental organisations) and/or local authorities such as London boroughs. Treasury figures as of 2012 show that total UK PFI contractual liabilities and costs now exceed a remarkable £300 billion, an enormous burden given that the UK's total GDP in 2013 is measured at £363 billion (ONS, 2013). When the contracts expire, the infrastructure returns to the public sector, sometimes at 'market rates' that are yet to be negotiated, thus leading to further uncertainties and liabilities in the public sector. In the meantime, assets under PFI are not technically 'owned' by the state or by electorates. Any changes to the infrastructure *and/or* the services they provide require often complex and expensive contractual changes, costs, delays and the mobilisation of yet more costly private sector experts. PFI contracts typically possess clauses that make their early termination prohibitively expensive, with risks transferred from the private to the public sector. All risks, liabilities and uses of welfare infrastructure can be commodified, repackaged and sold on to investors such as hedge funds and investment banks under so-called 're-financing' deals, that further complicate structures of ownership, management and accountability (see NAO, 2006).

These changes have many implications. In order to make investments appealing to private investors, contracts are both long term and relatively insulated from changing democratic demands. Rather than simplifying governance arrangements within the welfare state, as envisaged in the facile language of Good Governance, the introduction of private actors has created new forms of complexity and rigidity. As we will see in specific project examples in London, a whole network of global actors have now become directly involved in decision making and, by default, future planning. They are coordinated not by government bodies or even welfare managers, but by elaborate expert-written contracts and global financial rules. The role of state actors becomes one of contract negotiation and management on a project-by-project basis. Democratic demands have to be converted into contractual demands. Politics becomes a process of contract writing and litigation, with wider policy ends, such as the creation of more 'sustainable cities', being put to one side or converted into the legalistic language of management obligations and risks.

This, in turn, is shaping how democratic processes work at the local and metropolitan scales and the boundaries of sustainability planning. Any form of democratic intervention requires coordinated action, implemented by accountable state bodies with the capacity to implement change in response to shifting democratic demands and needs. The existence of so many PFI projects effectively undermines these capacities. Thus, while sustainability discourses promise the wide-scale devolution of power and responsibilities to local communities and citizens, the reality is that privatisation, in the name of output-centred governance, corrodes local control and the ability to think and plan strategically. There is a clash of logics that cannot be overcome by simple post-political recourse to 'partnership' working. The longer-term and more inflexible the PFI contracts, the more appealing they are to private investors. This, however, runs against traditional notions of the public interest and longer-term sustainability planning that requires flexibility in asset management and leaves open clear avenues of accountability and change. Whereas private investors want more state and less government, citizens would be better served by more government and less state. The next section now turns to the situation in London in more detail, and explores and assesses the implications of PFIs for the city's longer-term planning.

PFI in London and the restructuring of the welfare state

During the 1990s and 2000s the ownership and management of large sections of London's welfare infrastructure have shifted from public control to private ownership. This has happened to such an extent that London is now seen by global accountancy firms and other PFI advocates as a trailblazer for others to follow. As of September 2012 there were 102 PFI projects in London covering a wide variety of infrastructure. The combined total value of the capital and the unitary payments is an extraordinary £53.4 billion, or approximately 18 per cent of the total costs of PFI for the UK as a whole. Figure 5.1 highlights the distribution of spending between different government departments. It shows that the key welfare sectors of health, transport and education have been recipients of the largest number of PFIs. Health has been a particularly lucrative sector for privatisation, with total PFI spending to date of £23.7 billion, or 44 per cent of the London total. This consists of capital costs of £2.8 billion and unitary payments of £20.9 billion.

Part of the reason for London's pre-eminence as a location for PFI spending is the presence of core government functions and state departments. Many of

Figure 5.1: Total PFI capital costs and unitary payments in London by policy sector as of September 2012 (£ billion)

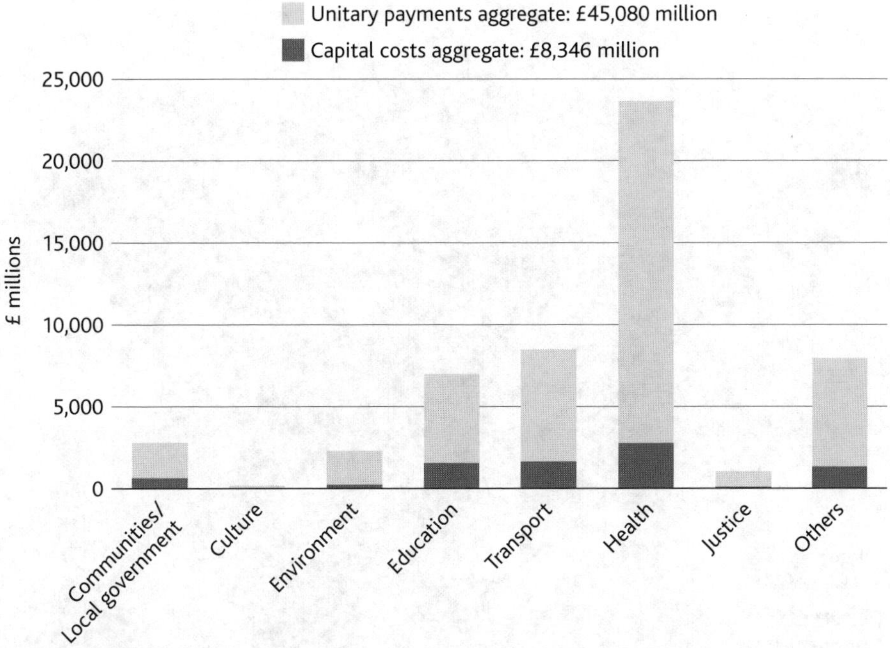

Unitary payments aggregate: £45,080 million
Capital costs aggregate: £8,346 million

Source: Data taken from HM Treasury (2012)

these were housed in offices constructed during the 1960s and 1970s that were in urgent need of re-location or major refurbishment. The PFI provided one obvious avenue through which such projects could be funded. A new building for the Home Office, for example, has been constructed at a capital value of £326 million, with repayments over 27 years of £1.14 billion. HM Revenue & Customs' office refurbishment, carried out by Bermuda-registered investment firm Mapeley, similarly involved capital outlay of £182 million, with repayments of an astonishing £4.2 billion over 20 years, a figure that is likely to dwarf the 'costs' of maintenance. Figure 5.2 shows the distribution of PFI projects across London, with a concentration in central London, and fewer in the suburbs largely because of such projects and the concentration of flagship welfare services such as leading hospitals and universities. Alongside these projects, recent capital spending on transport, including sections of the M25 Orbital Motorway and some parts of the Docklands Light Railway (DLR), have also been paid for through PFI contracts.

There are also more pragmatic reasons for this expansion. Much of the city's welfare infrastructure is antiquated and dates from the Victorian era when large-scale investments were undertaken by local government bodies. By the late 1990s there was clearly a policy problem to be tackled. After decades of neglect, many state buildings were dilapidated and in desperate need of refurbishment. New technologies also create demand for new buildings. The PFI seemed to

Figure 5.2: Number and geographical distribution of PFI projects in London, 2012

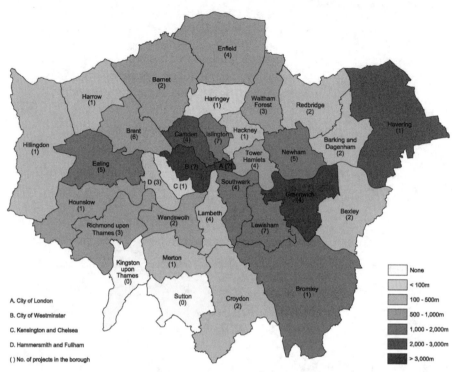

Source: Data taken from HM Treasury (2012); map produced by Sonia Freire Trigo, Bartlett School of Planning, UCL.

provide an ideal solution. It could be used to fund public sector projects with the pre–austerity expectation that welfare spending would continue to rise as it had during the 1990s and 2000s. This, it was hoped, would enable welfare managers to meet expensive long-term repayments while also guaranteeing quality service provision in new, upgraded infrastructure. Citizens, it was argued, would have no interest in who was providing and funding these services. All that would matter was that they would be seen to be working.

And yet, the impacts of these PFIs on the planning and management of the city are already being felt, and they are clearly not 'working' as planned. The example of the healthcare sector illustrates better than most the impacts of these changes on service provision, governance flexibility and the planning system as a whole. Changes are particularly significant given the drive to create healthier cities and the importance of healthcare to sustainable community planning and a wider sense of citizenship (see also Chapter Thirteen, this volume). London has long been a centre for world-leading and pioneering healthcare. Its teaching and research hospitals are among the best in the world, but have been subject to infrastructure problems given the costs of land and the physical difficulties of accommodating expansion. The PFI seemed a particularly appealing solution to these identified needs. Projects such as the refurbishment of St Bartholomew's

(St Barts) Hospital have become some of the biggest individual PFIs to be found anywhere in the world. Treasury figures show that in the St Barts case, capital spending of £1.15 billion was raised from relatively expensive private funds.[5] This figure, along with the tied maintenance and service costs on the site, will be paid back under a contracted repayment schedule lasting for 43 years (2006-49), and will total a remarkable £7.14 billion. The repayment schedules are outlined in Figure 5.3, and highlight the relentless increases that are required over the lifetime of the project. The hospital will not revert to full public ownership until 2049, meaning that until then, one of London's most significant hospitals is to be governed and managed under contracts signed in the early 2000s. All requirements for the hospital need to have been agreed at that time. The utopianism of PFI thinking and contractual governance is enshrined in such projects in which it is imagined that policy makers, technical experts, citizens and others can predict the needs and requirements of healthcare and health technologies for a period of decades.

Moreover, an examination of the ownership structures of these hospitals illustrates the sheer scale of the governmental problems that are being created for planners, communities and welfare managers. A special purpose vehicle, named Capital Hospitals Ltd, was established by private firms to obtain the PFI contract and to build and manage the hospital. It also received a loan of £250 million from the European Investment Bank (EIB), meaning that this 'private' development was effectively supported by money provided by EU nation states (see EIB, 2012).

Figure 5.3: Unitary costs repayments to be made on the St Bartholomew's Hospital Project, 2006-49 (£ million)

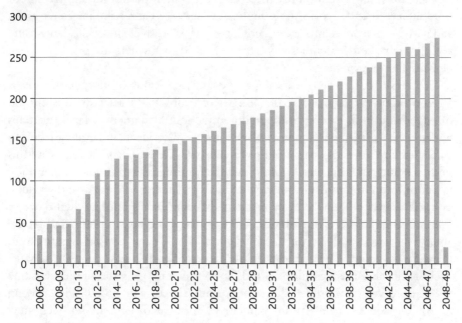

Source: Data taken from HM Treasury (2012)

Three global companies specialising in PFI projects make up the owners of Capital Hospitals. They are the American firm Innisfree (with a 35 per cent stake), the American–Scandinavian multinational Skanska (35 per cent) and Equion, part of the John Laing and Henderson Investment Group (30 per cent). In the company's annual accounts (Capital Hospitals, 2010) credit risks are downplayed. The Directors' Statement notes that the hospital trust will be able to pay its obligations to the private firms, and that even in the event of bankruptcy, various guarantees are underwritten by the Secretary of State for Health and central government budgets. The hospital has become a state-backed commodity, with almost zero risk for global private investors, who have no incentive or requirement to adapt the conditions of the original contract, whatever the wider economic, social and political changes taking place within London between now and 2049.

What is also revealing is the way in which privatisation draws together a wide-ranging network of beneficiary companies who organise and facilitate the process. Multinational companies have been directly involved in organising the St Barts project at every stage. A Partnership UK (2011) database search revealed that PricewaterhouseCoopers (PwC), Davis Langdon consultants, the legal firm Allen & Overy, Jardine Lloyd Thompson Risk Solutions, and the insurer, Integrated Building Services, all acted as public sector advisers in the early stages of the contract-writing process at undisclosed cost. Another seven firms received contracts to design and build the infrastructure: namely, the multinational firms Carillion, Skanska, Rashleigh, Weatherfoil Facilities Services, Siemens, Synergy and the architects Hellmuth, Obata & Kassabaum. These actors have a significant impact on shaping policy, but despite the wider rhetoric of citizen empowerment and sustainability that justifies their involvement, little is ever known about how such influence works, how much it costs or what advice has been given and acted on. Commercial confidentiality acts as a direct break on democratic accountability and precludes any pretence of local 'ownership' on the part of citizens and electorates.

The result of this privatisation process and the input of so many actors is an enormous escalation of costs and an inflexibility in asset ownership and management, both for expansion and contraction. St Barts now faces shortfalls in expenditure and is the subject of major cuts in services, in large part due to escalating and non-negotiable PFI payments (see *The Guardian*, 2013a). And this story is being repeated across London where in some cases hospitals have already gone bankrupt in paying off PFI liabilities and are facing cuts to staff and services. Sustainable healthcare policies are increasingly being dictated not by clinical needs, policy changes or the demands of different citizens and communities, but by the ability of services to cope (or to fail to cope) with the costs of privatisation and the inflexible contracts used to facilitate change. Services have emphatically *not* become 'localised' as a result of Good Governance reforms and modernisation.

The same is true for the wide variety of other sectors in which PFI is playing a growing role. Current projects include: waste management services, new streetlights, fire engines, social housing renewal projects, new police stations and prisons. Policy is now discussed and thought about in relation to what is contractually possible, rather than what should be done in terms of planning priorities and citizen demands. The 2011 Census indicates that London's population increased by an unprecedented 14 per cent between 2001 and 2011, and that demand for services and infrastructure can change rapidly and are impossible to predict, even over the short term. A truly sustainable planning system needs to be adaptable and flexible in order to manage change. What privatisation has meant is that it is increasingly difficult to act in this way. These pressures will only become more acute in the wake of austerity cuts and shrinking budgets.

The future of sustainability governance in London and the disruptions of democracy

The growth of PFI projects in London, and the wider privatisation agendas of which they are a part, raises some fundamental questions about the nature of democracy and the ways in which state practices are being transformed. It would be wrong to claim that some of the changes outlined above are beyond reform and set in stone. The corrosive effects of change are beginning to mobilise citizen protest, while simultaneously exposing the scale of the accountability gaps that have been created. London is home to a vociferous formal and informal politics with state actors and third sector social movements and communities seeking to assert core democratic demands. These demands may create *moments of disruption* in which utopian, managerial reforms are rejected and disrupted. In places such as Lewisham in south east London, the financial ruin brought to local hospital services through PFI repayments and the loss of local ownership and control of assets has stirred up popular protests which have had some impact (see *The Guardian*, 2013b). The utopian vision of an output-centred politics is fragmenting as its output failures become apparent. Attempts to insulate private investors and contractual decisions from democratic scrutiny and change cannot be accepted as given. State policies change, as do structures of accountability and decision making. It may be that future governments decide, for example, to guillotine contracts or even default given the scale of the debts that need to be paid off and the long-term economic prospects for countries such as the UK. In a context of austerity, even state-backed contracts may not be risk-free.

There is already some evidence of this happening, and in many ways London provides a test-bed for the emergence of a different type of politics and perhaps one that is closer to some of the more utopian understandings of sustainability that were fostered in the 1970s and 1980s. Much of this has been led by government institutions. The Mayor's executive body, Transport for London (TfL), for instance, has either bought itself out of some PFI contracts and/or changed contractual relationships so that companies take on 'concession contracts' that can be terminated at any time. The delivery of the electronic Oyster card scheme in London represents a good example of such changes. The system was originally set up in 2003 under a 17-year PFI handed to a private consortium named TranSys.

This included global firms such as Fujitsu and WS Atkins. The scheme worked well initially, but the consortium had no need to be flexible or entrepreneurial, and were unwilling to expand the scheme beyond their contractual requirements. After a period of growing frustration, in 2010 TfL decided to buy out the contract at a cost of £101 million. This, it was argued, would actually save money in the longer term as the PFI debt repayments were so significant. By taking control of the Oyster card system TfL now has plans to expand it and to make it more of a smartcard. It is hoped that by making the scheme more user-friendly, more people may make use of public transport, thereby contributing to wider sustainability objectives. As an accountable and strategic government body it is able to be flexible, adaptable, dynamic and innovative. It can respond to new demands to reorganise public transport systems to meet wider objectives. These characteristics are the opposite of those enshrined in inflexible, contract-based PFI privatisation schemes.

Further privatisations of the public transport network, such as those relating to the DLR, now involve different types of contract as investments are not privately financed and are much easier for government actors to change or break. In the case of a contract signed to manage the DLR services, between TfL and Serco, the former have maintained control of the concession agreements, and there are a number of ways in which they are able to terminate the contract in the event of 'a change of law which renders illegal or impossible ... the Franchisee's obligations' (TfL, 2006, p 109), or if national government decides that the contract should be terminated, then it can be. Serco is paid a set fee for performance, and failure to adhere to this means fines and possible termination of contract. Moreover, the state still maintains control over the assets, a fundamental prerequisite for any meaningful form of sustainability planning (TFL, 2010).

Such interventions may represent one way in which governments and citizens can re-establish control over key assets and services. But many local authorities in London are now facing significant austerity cuts. They are under growing pressure to embark on local PFIs in order to maintain state services in the short term. In addition, new regulatory demands for sustainability initiatives, such as improved recycling or waste management schemes, may only be met with further rounds of privatisation. The rewards for private companies are potentially enormous. On current trends, and with the managerial/privatisation models of sustainability governance in the ascendancy, it seems unlikely that there will be any major reversal in recent trends in the near future. Local welfare budgets will have to renegotiated with a shift away from service provision to the repayment of private finance to global investors.

Conclusion

This chapter has argued that the rolling out of sustainability planning in London is fundamentally conditioned by the structures of governance and accountability that exist within the city. It has documented recent changes that have seen contradictory trends. On the one hand, the London case is represented as a 'success story' in which new models of effective sustainability management and governance have been rolled out by relatively powerful elected government bodies. The city has played a leading role in international debates over the meaning of urban sustainability, and has used its urban development projects to pioneer contract-based forms of sustainable management. Sustainability planning is presented as a governance problem that can be 'fixed' through effective modes of expert-driven intervention. London is championed as a leading exponent of these governance solutions, and widely praised as an example of where democracy 'works'. On the other hand, London's model of sustainability management has ushered in a series of changes that preclude integrated, long-term planning. Privatisation in the pursuit of short-term policy delivery targets has fragmented governance relationships in the city and transformed the role of the state into that of a contract manager, whose principal concern is with the drawing up of managerial frameworks and the establishment of public–private partnerships. Decisions have increasingly been taken in behind-the-scenes technical negotiations free from the 'interference' of democratic scrutiny. The result has been that large parts of the city's infrastructure have undergone a change of ownership and control during the 1990s and 2000s, with private operators, many of which are global corporations, playing an expanded role. Modernising reforms that promise realistic outcomes have generated new degrees of separation between citizens and decision-making structures.

Moreover, the chapter has also demonstrated that privatisation and managerialism have undermined some of the core precepts of sustainability thinking. The repayment costs of privately financed investments *will be met by future generations*, even though the benefits, in terms of new infrastructure, are being made available to existing governments and citizens. State spending is, in effect, being mortgaged out to private investors. As with all long-term loans the repayments will be much greater than if projects had been funded through short-term, current account payments (see Murphy, 2011). Any pretence that governance arrangements in cities such as London have become more focused on sustainability is undermined by these structural transformations in financing, governance and welfare management.

One further lesson from the London case is, therefore, that the rolling out of a sustainability-driven, Good Governance agenda can *increase* the distance between citizen demands and policy-making processes. Paradoxically, it is where stronger government bodies in London have acted to protect the public interest that the demands of citizens have been best protected. Where government control has been weakened, it is private companies that have moved in to fill the governance gap, rather than active and empowered citizens. In this respect the London experience has far wider implications. The managerial utopias of delivery thinking that have driven reform may reflect Žižek's (2011) wider concern that a new authoritarianism is driving contemporary governance reforms across the EU and the Global North. Disruptive democratic demands are seen as a 'problem', to be managed and controlled through the process of output-driven contractualisation. Official public policy discourses and formal strategies are becoming less significant. Power increasingly lies in the ability to shape contracts in terms of their formulation, content and legal framings. Any disruptions to this governance model require an understanding of often complex judicial and regulatory processes, and require a new type of engagement that is very different from the utopian dreams of sustainability thinkers of the late 20th century.

Notes

[1] In addition, there is also the Corporation of London that governs the City of London.

[2] By 2012, Semperian alone had 106 projects in the UK and oversaw contracts for 282 separate public assets, with a combined value of £106 billion.

[3] Or approximately US$600,000 or €510,000.

[4] The Major government quietly re-wrote civil service and financing rules, then known as the Ryrie Rules, that had previously ensured that all private debt used for government projects would appear in official accounts as public sector debt.

[5] One consistent criticism of PFIs is that private firms have to borrow funds from private markets at relatively high interest rates, whereas state bodies can borrow money at much lower rates of government debt.

Acknowledgements

Many thanks to Sonia Freire Trigo for compiling and analysing the PFI data for this chapter, and for reading and commenting on a draft of the original text. Thanks also to Emma Street, Rob Imrie and Loretta Lees for their thoughtful and valuable comments on an earlier version. Final responsibility for the chapter is, of course, the author's alone.

References

Bardens, J. and Webb, D. (2012) *Public expenditure by country and region*, Note: SN/EP/4033, 28 November, London: House of Commons Library.

BBC Online (2012) 'UK house prices: July–September 2012' (http://news.bbc.co.uk/1/shared/spl/hi/in_depth/uk_house_prices/regions/html/region10.stm).

Blair, T. (2010) *A journey*, London: Hutchinson.

Capital Hospitals Ltd (2010) *Directors' report and financial statements*, London: Companies House.

Douglass, M. (2012) 'Local city, capital city or world city? Civil society, the (post-) developmental state and the globalization of urban space in Pacific Asia', in M. Steger (ed) *Globalization and culture*, Cheltenham: Edward Elgar Publishing, p 109.

EIB (European Investment Bank) (2012) *EIB loan for the Royal London and Barts Hospitals* (www.eib.org/projects/press/2006/2006-041-eib-loan-for-the-royal-london-and-barts-hospitals.htm).

Financial Times (2012) 'Foreign money seeks London property' (www.ft.com/cms/s/0/6e206aa0-185b-11e2-80af-00144feabdc0.html#axzz2KljjUWal).

Giddens, A. (2009) *The politics of climate change*, Cambridge: Polity Press.

Gray, J. (2013) 'Respect your elders – civilisation's gains and losses', *The New Statesman*, 25-31 January, pp 40-1.

Guardian, The (2013a) 'London HNS hospital trust Barts Health losing £2million a week' (www.theguardian.com/society/2013/jul/17/barts-health-trust-losing-2m-week).

Guardian, The (2013b) 'Lewisham hospital illegal cuts plan thrown out by judge' (www.theguardian.com/society/2013/jul/31/lewisham-hospital-services-decision-reversed-judge).

Hellowell, M. and Pollock, A. (2009) 'The private financing of NHS hospitals: politics, policy, practice', *Institute of Economic Affairs Publication*, March, pp 13-19.

Imrie, R., Lees, L. and Raco, M. (2009) 'London's regeneration', in R. Imrie, L. Lees and M. Raco (eds) *Regenerating London: governance, sustainability and community in a global city*, London: Routledge, pp 3-23.

Knight Frank (2013) *Spring 2013 – London residential review*, London: Knight Frank.

London First (2010) *Tax policy – supporting UK growth*, London: London First.

Mayor of London (2011) *Replacement London Plan – sustainability statement*, London: Greater London Authority.

Murphy, R. (2011) *The courageous state – rethinking economics, society, and the role of government*, London: Searching Finance Ltd.

NAO (National Audit Office) (2006) *Update on PFI debt refinancing and the PFI equity market*, London: HMSO.

ONS (Office for National Statistics) (2013) *Gross domestic product, quarterly estimate Q2 2013* (www.ons.gov.uk/ons/rel/gva/gross-domestic-product--preliminary-estimate/q2-2013/stb-gdp-preliminary-estimate--q2-2013.html#tab-Key-points).

Partnership UK (2011) www.pppdatabase.co.uk/ accessed 8 March 2011, webpage now defunct.

Parker, D. and Hartley, K. (2002) 'Transaction costs, relational contracting and public private partnerships: a case study of UK defence', *Journal of Purchasing and Supply Management*, vol 9, pp 97-108.

Pearce, N. and Margo, J. (eds) (2007) *Politics for a new generation – the Progressive Movement*, London: Palgrave.

Public Accounts Committee (2011) *12th report – government's use of consultants and interims*, Hansard, London: House of Commons.

PwC (PricewaterhouseCoopers) (2012) *Smart cities – from earthen walls to smart grids*, London: PwC.

Raco, M. (2014) 'Delivering flagship projects in an era of regulatory capitalism: project management, contractualism, and the London Olympics 2012', *International Journal of Urban and Regional Research*, vol 38, pp 176–97.

Raco, M. and I-Lin, W. (2012) 'Urban sustainability, conflict management, and the geographies of postpoliticism: a case study of Taipei', *Environment and Planning C: Government and Policy*, vol 30, pp 191-208.

Rancière, J. (2005) *Chronicles of consensual times*, London: Continuum International Publishing Group.

Scharpf, F. (1999) *Governing Europe: effective and democratic?*, Oxford: Oxford University Press.

Smyth, H. and Edkins, A. (2007) 'Relationship management in the management of PFI/PPP projects in the UK', *International Journal of Project Management*, vol 25, pp 232-40.

Spackman, M. (2002) 'Public–private partnerships: Lessons from the British approach', *Economic Systems*, vol 26, pp 283-301.

Swyngedouw, E. (2009a) 'The zero-ground of politics: musings on the post-political city', *New Geographies*, vol 1, pp 52-61.

Swyngedouw, E. (2009b) 'The antinomies of the postpolitical city: In search of a democratic politics of environmental production', *International Journal of Urban and Regional Research*, vol 33, pp 601-20.

TfL (Transport for London) (2006) *Franchise agreement – Docklands Light Railway and Serco Ltd* (www.tfl.gov.uk/assets/downloads/franchise_agreement.pdf).

TfL (2010) 'TfL secures ownership and control of Oyster brand and ticketing system' (www.tfl.gov.uk/info-for/media/press-releases/2010/april/tfl-secures-ownership-and-control-of-oyster-brand-and-ticketing-system).

Travers, T. (2004) *The politics of London – governing an ungovernable city*, London: Palgrave.

Treasury, HM (2012) 'PFI database 2012' (http://data.gov.uk/dataset/private-finance-initiative-pfi-data).

UNESCAP (United Nations Economic and Social Commission for Asia and the Pacific) (no date) *What is good governance?* (www.unescap.org/pdd/prs/ProjectActivities/Ongoing/gg/governance.pdf).

Žižek, S. (2011) *Living in the end times*, London: Verso.

Žižek, S. (2012) *The year of dreaming dangerously*, London: Verso.

SIX

Sustaining a global city at work: resilient geographies of a migrant division of labour

Cathy McIlwaine and Kavita Datta

Introduction

Researchers have long documented the increased reliance of global cities on – and indeed some would argue *addiction* to – migrant labour (Sassen, 1991; Wills et al, 2010; Spencer, 2011). This is clearly evidenced in the global city of London where, over the past two decades, economic restructuring involving deregulation and sub-contraction, political reform associated with declining access to welfare and the imposition of an increasingly restrictive immigration regime have combined to produce a distinct 'migrant division of labour' at the bottom end of the city's economy. While scholars have documented the multiple vulnerabilities that low-paid migrant workers endure in global cities like London, emerging research suggests that these workers have been further marginalised since the on-set of a protracted recession from 2008 onwards which has been associated with growing labour market insecurity as well as anti-migrant sentiments (Wills et al, 2010; Datta, 2011). This said, it is also clear that migrant workers' experiences of the recession vary significantly. In the UK, this is partly attributable to British immigration policies that have progressively entrenched differences *between* migrant communities, creating distinct hierarchies of labour market and residency rights that particularly distinguish between migrants originating from an expanded European Union (EU) and those coming from poorer parts of the world in the Global South.

Based on extensive research with migrant men and women from EU and non-EU origins employed in London's low-wage economy,[1] this chapter begins by documenting the emergence of a migrant division of labour in London during a period of economic prosperity before considering the implications of the subsequent economic downturn on migrant workers and on the migrant division of labour itself. Drawing on empirical research conducted with Bulgarian and Latin American migrants from a range of countries, it highlights the material spatialities that underpin migration flows to the city as well as the experiences of recession among migrants and how they cope once settled. We argue that while the migrant division of labour remains firmly intact in London during economic downturn, migrants are experiencing even more vulnerability than during the boom years. As a global city going through an economic downturn, London continues to need low-paid, flexible labour to sustain it, with migrants providing this in ever more deleterious circumstances. It becomes clear that a consideration of the role of migrant labour is central to conceptualising sustainable development in relation to a city such as London. Indeed, both highly skilled and low-paid migrant labour is essential to the sustainable functioning of London's labour market, although the arguably active exploitation of the latter resonates most strongly in terms of the need to ensure social justice that underpins a truly sustainable city. Another conceptual dimension of the chapter is the need to take into account much more explicitly the inherent geographies of how economic recession plays out transnationally and locally for low-paid migrant workers in cities. In turn, these geographies further undergird the sustainability of the city, again, often at the expense of low-paid migrants' wellbeing. Therefore, the idea of 'sustaining a global city at work' rests squarely on the shoulders of low-paid migrant labour and the migrant division of labour of which they are a core element.

'The migrant division of labour': from boom to bust

Immigration was at historically high levels on the eve of the recession in the UK, with much of what is referred to as 'new migration' occurring under the New Labour government, and a longer-term increase in net immigration dating back to the early 1990s (Datta, 2012). Recent analysis shows a doubling of the UK's foreign-born population between 1993 and 2011, from 3.8 million to 7 million. Correspondingly, the foreign-born citizen population increased from 2 to 4.5 million in the same period (Rienzo and Vargas-Silva, 2012). In turn, London as a global city has historically served as a significant destination for migrants such that by 2001, 42 per cent of those who had arrived in the UK had settled in the city. By 2006, just under a third (31 per cent) of the city's population and just over a third (35 per cent) of its working-age population had been born overseas (Spence, 2006; Fix et al, 2009). By 2011, there were 2.6 million foreign-born people in London, comprising 42 per cent of the population (Rienzo and Vargas-Silva, 2012). Migrants have therefore been critical in shaping London's national and ethnic 'super-diversity', with important differences between migrant groups in relation to labour market integration, immigration status and gender, ethnic, religious and class composition (Baker and Mohieldeen, 2000; Vertovec, 2007). Furthermore, while 30 per cent of London's migrants originate from high-income countries, 70 per cent are from developing countries (Spence, 2005).

This increase in net immigration was shaped by economic and political priorities from the 1990s onwards. Wills et al (2010) document how London's pre-recession labour market was characterised by simultaneous professionalisation, economic inactivity as well as the growth of the 'working poor' (see also May et al, 2010). These changes were themselves the product of over three decades of neoliberal reform and associated deregulation and sub-contracting which led to the transformation of the British economy, from one dominated by heavy industry to one based predominantly on services. In turn, this transformation was evident at both ends of London's labour market, with a concomitant growth in highly skilled jobs at the apex – particularly evidenced in the growth of financial services located in the City of London and Canary Wharf – as well as a smaller but still significant rise in the proportion of workers labouring at the very bottom end in sectors such as hospitality and care (May et al, 2007; Wills et al, 2010). In turn, jobs at the bottom end of the city's economy were associated with part-time 'flexible' working, low and stagnating wages, deteriorating conditions of work as well as an erosion of the bargaining power of workers (Somerville and Sumption, 2009; Wills et al, 2010). Perhaps unsurprisingly, then, this segment of the labour market was also characterised by a rising number of vacancies as attempts to marshal the long-term native unemployed into these jobs through New Labour's twin agenda of a 'work ethic' mantra and reform of the benefit system proved to be remarkably ineffective (Rogers et al, 2009).

Within this context, a growing reliance on migrant workers or a 'migrant division of labour' was identified in London (May et al, 2007; Wills et al, 2010). This refers to the reliance of the economy and employers on migrant labour because of its flexibility and acceptance of working conditions that 'native' workers would not necessarily accept (Wills et al, 2009). As an illustration, in 2001, it was estimated that 46 per cent of London's low-wage jobs were occupied by foreign-born workers (Spence, 2005). Indeed, this dependence on migrant workers was even more significant in certain sectors of the city's economy such that it was clear that some parts of London's low-wage economy could no longer function without the labour of migrants (Wills et al, 2010). Exploring this specifically within migrant-dependent sectors of the economy, the percentage of cleaners born abroad rose from 40 per cent in 1993/94 to almost 70 per cent in 2004/05. Similar trends were evident in the hospitality industry, with 29 per cent of chefs and cooks born abroad in 1993/94 increasing to 76 per cent in 2004/05 (Wills et al, 2010).

This concentration of migrant workers in low-end low-skilled jobs was also shaped by a radical overhaul of the British immigration system. Efforts to control immigration into the UK began in earnest almost as soon as migration to the country increased, and crystallised in the 1990s around a set of 'managed migration' policies. These reflected three key immigration priorities: first, recruitment of the 'right' kinds of migrants from a global pool that the British economy needed to maintain its competitive edge; second, a clamping down on so-called 'bogus' asylum seekers, refugees and irregular migrants; and third, an encouragement of EU migration over migration from the Global South (Anderson et al, 2006; Markova and Black, 2007; Datta, 2009; Wills et al, 2010). As such, the guiding principles of immigration reform were that certain types of migration were beneficial for the British economy, and while this was originally conceived in terms of highly skilled workers, there was an appreciation that workers were also needed for low-skilled jobs. Furthermore, the demand for migrant labour had to be 'sold' to the British public through harsh restrictions on the migration of those who were considered burdensome, while facilitating the migration of those who would contribute to economic growth in the country (Flynn, 2003).

To a large extent, these immigration priorities were facilitated by the expansion of the EU, first in 2004 to incorporate the Accession 8 (A8) countries[2] and then again, in 2007, to include Romania and Bulgaria (the A2 countries). Despite concerns among older members of the Union that A8 enlargement would lead to uncontrolled East to West emigration, the UK was one of only three European countries to grant A8 nationals immediate access to its labour market, a decision that was largely guided by the Treasury's view that this migration would be beneficial to the UK economy and would fill significant labour shortages identified in low-skilled jobs such as construction, hospitality, transport and public services, as well as care work including nursing (Anderson et al, 2006; McDowell, 2009; Finch and Goodhart, 2010; Wills et al, 2010).[3] As Spencer (2010) argues, subsequent high employment rates among A8 migrants (81 per cent versus 74 per cent for UK-born workers) support the argument that there were plentiful jobs to be had.

This said, the scale of A8, and in particular Polish migration to the UK, was largely unanticipated, with 345,000 workers registering for employment in the space of just over a year between May 2004 and December 2005 (Anderson et al, 2006).[4] It is estimated that by 2009, nearly 1.5 million A8 workers had migrated to the UK where they comprised half of the labour immigration flow, with the Polish emerging as the largest migrant community (having been 13th in 2003) (Fix et al, 2009; Somerville and Sumption, 2009). This 'invasion from the East', as it came to be depicted in certain segments of the media, had a strong bearing on the UK's position on the subsequent enlargement of the EU in 2007 to admit Romania and Bulgaria, whose nationals received a much more guarded and cautious welcome (MAC, 2008). In particular, the government chose to restrict A2 nationals' access to the British labour market along the lines set prior to their accession to the EU via temporary worker schemes (Simeonova, 2004; MAC, 2008; Markova, 2009). Initially imposed for two years, these restrictions were reviewed and extended at the end of 2008 and then again to 2014, on the advice of the Migration Advisory Committee (MAC), a decision that was shaped by the looming economic downturn, the unknown implications of lifting restrictions as well as the fragile state of these two economies. Importantly, while European migration has been facilitated and tolerated to varying extents, flows from the Global South have been progressively restricted and even criminalised (see below).

Once in the UK, and in cities such as London, research has highlighted the poor working conditions endured by many low-paid migrant workers. Focusing on sectors such as construction, care, cleaning and food processing, Wills et al (2010) illustrated low levels of pay, long working hours, significant incidences of working in two or more jobs and limited entitlements in relation to sick pay, holidays and maternity leave. This said, migrants' economic and social precarity has arguably intensified during the recession, when pre-existing labour market inequalities have been amplified (Rogers et al, 2009). Within advanced economies, the UK was identified as being particularly at risk of a severe and protracted downturn (Wearden, 2009; IMF, 2010). While the recession occurred after an unusually long period of growth, its onset was very rapid (Sumption, 2010). Experiencing a significant contraction of its GDP (gross domestic product), the first headline casualty was the financial sector, as evidenced by high-profile redundancies, with employment in finance in London shrinking by a third, from a peak of 360,000 jobs in 2008, and a corresponding decline in the sector's contribution to national wealth (Allen, 2010; French et al, 2010). Furthermore, the concentration of migrant workers in sectors that were particularly exposed to the recession – including construction, manufacturing and retail – has meant that workers located in lower-end jobs have also been affected (Rogers et al, 2009). Migrant workers have faced considerable economic insecurity (shaped by labour market, job and income insecurity), erosion of wages and working conditions and unemployment (Anderson and Pontusson, 2007; Campbell et al, 2007; Jayaweera and Anderson, 2008). Broader research suggests that migrant workers who are the 'last hired' are also the 'first fired', and face higher than average unemployment as employers seek to distinguish between core workers and more disposable temporary/agency/sub-contracted workers (Rogers et al, 2009; Castles, 2009; Dobson et al, 2009; Cavanaugh, 2010). Taken as a whole, while unemployment in the third quarter of 2008 was 6 per cent, it was 20 per cent higher among migrant workers (at 7.2 per cent) and 40 per cent higher for non-OECD (Organisation for Economic Co-operation and Development) migrants (Somerville and Sumption, 2009). Thus, migrants – and particularly those coming from poorer parts of the world – are likely to fare the worst, with recent arrivals potentially becoming detached from the labour market for a long period of time, which has significant repercussions on their subsequent integration into the labour market (Martin, 2009; Somerville and Sumption, 2009).

Given that migrants' access to welfare and benefits is restricted, periods of unemployment not only exacerbate their financial and economic vulnerability, but also push them into taking on *any* job, rendering them further vulnerable to an erosion of working standards during economic downturns (Fix et al, 2009; Somerville and Sumption, 2009). Rogers et al (2009) identify workers employed in food processing, hospitality and low-wage manufacturing as being particularly at risk of worsening conditions due to the high levels of sub-contracting, small workplaces, basic contracts and high turnover endemic in these sectors. Workers may be pressurised to work longer hours within the context of a broader intensification of work, accept wage freezes or cuts and experience a further erosion of their bargaining power vis-à-vis their employers. Competition between migrant and British-born workers may also intensify, leading to greater hostility. It is also posited that the economic downturn may have changed native workers' lack of interest in low-paid low-skilled jobs. Glossop and Shaheen's (2009) study of the impact of A8 migration to the British cities of Bristol and Hull illustrates the shifting dynamics of local labour markets as a result of the recession, as evidenced by fewer job vacancies as well as an increase in the number of people on Jobseeker's Allowance.[5] Documenting the experience of Polish migrants in Ireland, Krings et al (2013) highlight an overall decline in 'new' migrations, from 215,000 at the beginning of 2008 to 177,000 in 2012, which they partly attribute to deteriorating economic conditions, particularly in the construction sector. Furthermore, they document that those migrants who remained in Ireland endured intensification of work in terms of longer hours of work and extension of working duties as well as reduced opportunities for promotion.

However, there is also evidence that different migrant communities have fared differently during the recession. Sumption (2010) argues that if migrants are taken as a whole, then the crisis does not appear to have affected them disproportionately in relation to UK-born workers, because the former have historically experienced higher unemployment and lower employment rates. However, some migrant communities have coped with the recession better than others, which Sumption attributes to education levels, English language ability, ethnicity, age, gender and level of economic development in the home countries (Sumption, 2010). Moreover, McCollum et al (2013) illustrate that while the economic downturn has increased the availability of native workers, both quantitatively and qualitatively, the demand for migrant labour has remained resilient in certain sectors of the British economy, such as agribusiness. They attribute this to the fact that in certain cases, migrant labour is complementary rather than substitutive of native workers (see also Findlay, Geddes and McCollum, 2010; McCollum, 2012; Findlay and McCollum, 2013). Given the 'global' nature of the recession, and deteriorating economic circumstances in their own countries, certain types of migration flows (from East and Central Europe, for example) have continued while migrants have delayed the decision to return back home.

We explore these varied experiences of the recession in London in greater detail below, first, in relation to the complex geographies of how transnational migrants arriving and settling in London deal with economic crises; and second, looking at the local experiences of and mechanisms by which migrants deal with the economic crisis in London. We argue that the transnational and local practices developed by migrants serve to bolster London's migrant division of labour in remarkably resilient and sustainable ways, albeit with personal costs to migrants themselves.

Transnational geographies of the migrant division of labour during recession in London

Despite the growing body of work outlined above on the ways in which international migrants respond to economic crisis, the focus has primarily been on conditions in destination contexts alone. As such, there has been little consideration of the spatialities of these responses in a more holistic manner, or recognition of the relational processes that underpin international labour migration to global cities such as London.

One important and somewhat obvious, yet overlooked, issue in relation to migrant labour during times of recession is that migration is invariably prompted by the search for economic opportunities abroad in light of crisis in home countries. Among Latin American migrants in London, although the reasons for migration were a complex combination of material, social and political factors, 40 per cent stated that they moved primarily in search of economic improvement that was impossible back home. Delmar, 32 years old and from Ecuador, noted: "I came here because of the economic crisis in my country … it's still better here now although this country takes away with one hand and gives with another, but here I can make plans." Thus, as indicated above, migration from poorer economies to advanced industrialised nations such as the UK continues despite economic recession in the latter. For example, our research with Bulgarians showed that 50 per cent had arrived in London since 2007, one year before the onset of the economic crisis, while 25 per cent of Latin Americans had migrated since 2008. The fact that 96 per cent of the Bulgarians and 85 per cent of the Latin Americans interviewed were working further corroborates the notion that the migrant division of labour remains intact during recession, albeit with modifications and at considerable costs to the migrants themselves (see below). Indeed, these particular migrant groups that tend to be concentrated in the lower echelons of London's labour market have substantially higher employment rates than other foreign-born residents in the city (55 per cent), and compared with the London population as a whole (61 per cent) (McIlwaine et al, 2011). However, the sustainability of London's migrant division of labour that we argue rests on the exploitability of low-paid migrant labour appears to be largely unique in the European context, as our discussion of the Spanish situation below illustrates.

Another related yet still neglected spatial dimension of the effects of recession on migration is the intensification of transnational flows of people, goods and services within what can be termed 'transnational social spaces' (Faist, 2000) or 'transnational social fields' (Levitt, 2001; Levitt and Glick-Schiller, 2004). On the one hand, the secondary movement of people tends to increase during times of crisis, and on the other, the tangible and intangible ties among migrants in different countries (not necessarily home countries) also multiply (McIlwaine, 2012). In the context of migration to London, research among Latin Americans has clearly shown increased intra-European migration prompted by the economic crisis. Again, the issue here is the recognition that the economic downturn has been largely global and has certainly affected other countries in ways even more marked than the UK. Among Latin Americans, the severe economic collapse in Spain has been a primary force behind their movement to London. With initial movement from Latin America to Spain (in particular from Ecuador) growing in the early 2000s due to the booming economy and labour demand in domestic care work, construction and agriculture, together with an immigration regime that facilitated the entry of migrant labour (Fix et al, 2009), this changed after 2008 as the Spanish economy collapsed, resulting in the loss of one million jobs in 2008, and in the highest unemployment rate in the EU of 17 per cent (and over 20 per cent among non-EU migrants) (Rogers et al, 2009). This was integral to the exodus of 120,000 migrants in 2006, rising to 232,000 in 2008 (Fix et al, 2009).

The migratory effects of this were felt in London. Among Latin Americans, our research shows that 36.5 per cent had migrated from an intermediate country before arriving in the UK, and that 38 per cent of these people had come from Spain. The intensification of movement via Spain after the crisis is exemplified in the words of 44-year-old Francisco from Ecuador: "The main reason that I migrated from Spain to London was because of the global economic crisis.... I'm going to stay in London until the crisis passes but for two years maximum." Not surprisingly, the majority moved to London in search of work. Liliana, 45 and from Colombia, had lived in Gran Canaria for 11 years before moving to London in 2009. She decided to move to London when her hours of work in her job as a security guard in a shopping mall were reduced by half due to the recession, and she found it difficult to provide for her three daughters. Because she had previously regularised her immigration situation and obtained a Spanish passport (which was relatively easy in Spain), she was able to enter the UK as an EU citizen and find work (as a cleaner) quite quickly and easily.

However, many were not as fortunate as Liliana in terms of being able to enter the UK legally. Indeed, our research shows that not only was there a shift towards entering with an EU passport, but irregular entry increased after the recession. Indeed, 24 per cent of all irregular Latin Americans had entered between 2008 and 2009. However, most of these entered the UK legally in the first place, primarily on student or tourist visas, and over-stayed. Although the majority of these irregular migrants were able to secure work, as has been widely documented elsewhere (Engbersen, 2001; Vasta, 2008), they are invariably the most exploited in the labour force. This was especially in relation to not being paid for work undertaken, as Melia, a 28-year-old from Bolivia, recounted, in relation to her recent job as a chambermaid in a hotel:

> 'I worked in a hotel but after a month they didn't pay me. When I asked for my wages, they said no and I was illegal so I could do nothing. They treated me horribly; I think that they would treat a dog better.'

This abuse also included sexual harassment, as Mercedes, 27 years old from Bolivia, discussed, in terms of her cleaning job. Her supervisor regularly 'took liberties' with her in a sexual manner, and when she threatened to report him, he stated that he would denounce her to the authorities. Because she needed her job, she put up with it. Therefore, irregular migrants face particular challenges in terms of hardship in a more restricted labour market during times of downturn (see also below). This also has very severe negative ramifications for migrants' wellbeing psychologically, as explained by 52-year-old Emilio from Ecuador, who arrived in London in 2009 with a false Spanish passport that he has subsequently returned to the 'broker': "It's an oppression, you don't feel secure in anything, you can't be relaxed even at home, you can't do anything, you are like a type of ghost, you are not secure. Psychologically it affects you, you get depressed" (see also Wright and Black, 2011; Wright, 2012).

One final ramification of the spatialities of recession among migrants is the creation of ever more complex transnational household structures. While the creation of transnational households is well documented (Parrenas, 2005; Hondagneu-Sotelo, 2007), this research focuses on the relationships between home and destination countries. In contrast, our research shows how multiple transnational household arrangements have emerged, often underpinned by economic recession. This has especially been the case in light of the Spanish mortgage crisis whereby migrants had been able to access cheap mortgages during the boom years, only to find themselves with mortgages they were unable to pay back after the crash in the housing market (Moser, 2009). This situation has led to the creation of transnational fathers and mothers, as one parent migrates in search of work to attempt not only to get by but also to pay back debts. Daniel, 44 and from Ecuador, lost his construction job in Spain and moved to London in 2009. However, he had to leave his wife and children behind, creating a transnational household as well as undermining his wellbeing: "Economics, that was the reason I moved to London – for work and I have to pay off my housing debts there. But my emotional life has changed because I had to leave my wife and children in Spain."

These processes highlight how we need to adopt a much more nuanced perspective on the multiple effects of recession that play out in spatial ways across borders. Not only does economic crisis prompt migration from home countries, but it also fuels secondary and irregular migration, with all their associated vulnerabilities. Furthermore, London as a destination for migrants, especially from the Global South, continues to provide employment opportunities as the migrant division of labour is maintained, albeit in modified form and to the further detriment of the migrant workers themselves in terms of their wellbeing. While it is beyond the remit of this chapter, it is also worth noting that the movement of highly qualified people to London also has detrimental effects on the labour markets in the home countries (Datta et al, 2007). Again, this highlights the importance of how understanding the sustainability of cities such as London entails consideration of the material spatialities of the migrant division of labour far beyond the confines of the city itself, with international and transnational ramifications. The chapter now turns to address migrants' everyday experiences of recession in London itself, both locally and transnationally.

Surviving the migrant division of labour during recession in London

With London continuing to provide economic opportunities for low-paid migrants in the lower reaches of the labour market, especially from the A2 countries and those from the Global South, this section examines migrants' experiences in the labour market during recession as well as the ways in which they have coped with the greater entrenchment of precarity that recession has brought about.

Although London's migrant division of labour has remained intact during recession, and migrants are still attracted to the city because of labour opportunities as employment rates among migrants remain high, economic uncertainty still looms large for many. Many migrants feared not only their own unemployment but also that of their clients, especially among those working in domestic cleaning and other personal services. For example, Ivana, from Bulgaria, who worked as a cleaner and as a personal assistant in the financial sector, pointed out: "I am afraid the financial sector could collapse. That is my only concern. But I know that this cannot happen. I also loose clients because not all people can afford cleaning services anymore." Feelings of economic insecurity were especially marked among Bulgarian men in particular who, unlike many Latin American men or indeed, other male migrants, were reluctant to move into what they viewed as 'feminised work' such as cleaning and caring, preferring instead to work in construction and related building occupations (McIlwaine, 2010; Datta, 2011; see also Datta et al, 2009). The recession also resulted in professional migrants having to take on menial jobs, as was the case with Danilo from Colombia, who initially worked as an architect on arrival in the UK before the recession, but who ended up working as a waiter: "Because of the crisis ... construction was affected and so were architecture companies ... the large projects stopped and so they began to let staff go." Yet, reflecting the discussion above, he still felt it was better to stay in London rather than return home: "to have a salary as an architect there [in Colombia] that is really low or to have a salary the same or better as a waiter here, I prefer to be here."

A very marked effect of the recession for migrants was the erosion of wages and changes in the expectations of work. The experiences of Ivan from Bulgaria, who worked in the construction sector, echoed those of many others migrants:

> 'I am paid less for the same work I did before and the cut is both as payment per hour and as cut of number of hours I am paid for. It is hard to manage financially, especially lately in the time of the crisis. I started feeling it six months ago. I work as a sub-contractor, they [the agency he works for] call me when there is work for me, they cut the hours and the money per hour lately. The payment was £11 per hour, now it is £9 per hour. I am paid for 8 hours per day, and we work 10 hours, they do not pay the time envisaged for rest now, and they used to pay it before.'

The downturn has also affected small business owners, as 57-year-old Agustin from Ecuador, who owned a small shop selling Latin American food products, noted: "To be honest, the crisis has affected me badly and my sales have gone right down. It's not what I had hoped for." These processes were also accompanied by a wider deterioration in working conditions, such as failure to pay various types of leave and abolishing any benefits, as Dario, a 26-year-old chef from Bolivia, pointed out: "Not only have my hours been reduced, we no longer get food in the cafe; they are trying to serve less food to save money."

Another key aspect of the effects of recession was deteriorating relations among workers. Several people noted increasing competition among the workforce, especially between regular and irregular migrants. For example, José, 45 and from Colombia, working as a cleaner, noted: "There are more people coming to London now and the legals are taking the jobs. If someone is working without papers they have to leave to let the legal ones work. The recession is making it really hard for illegals at work and the legals look down on those with no papers." There also appeared to be more tension between migrants and British-born people as the latter behaved more like migrants. In particular migrants commented that British-born people were also cutting back on consumption and leisure activities in a bid to save money. In the opinion of Diddi from Bulgaria: "I see it, the recession – the bars are empty, people do not spend as much, as they did, they are nervous, they become more like us Bulgarians, there are more people in Primark – it is not accidental." In addition, in a focus group discussion, several male participants from Bulgaria who worked in the construction sector commented that despite no overt open hostility between migrant and native workers, migrant workers were more likely to be made redundant.

Such economic insecurity also served to further undermine the wellbeing of migrants in relation to physical and mental health. This also had ramifications for people's relationships. A Bulgarian man who participated in a focus group told us how:

> 'Insecurity with work and finance leads to stress which affects personal life, people tend to be more impatient with their partners and the availability of extra time gives more opportunities for arguments. In many cases one of the parties has to carry most of [the] financial burden and if the union is not strong enough, it causes problems.'

Yet migrants were certainly not completely passive in the face of these challenges (see also Datta et al, 2007; Datta, 2011; McIlwaine, 2013). Although most had little option but to accept their changing working conditions, migrants invariably addressed any shortfalls in incomes by securing additional jobs or working longer hours, as shown in the case of Danilo, above. Angelina, a 49-year-old Bulgarian who was working as a waitress, reported that: "there is less work lately which is less money so I have to find more sources to get money. It is psychologically difficult. I am considering going for cleaning." Similarly, Alberto, 58 and from Ecuador, who worked in office cleaning, stated that: "You have to tighten your belt, to eat less, that's the strategy and to work more."

Returning to the notion of the inherent geographies of the ramifications of economic downturn, an option open to migrants is to return back home. Some respondents reported the desire to return themselves, or noted that other compatriots were going home. However, there was also a widespread opinion among many regardless of their country of origin that the situation was generally worse back home. One Bulgarian focus group participant discussed this: "People are returning back to Bulgaria but [they] can't find work for low-qualified [skilled] labour as the crisis has hit Bulgaria much later then the UK. [However] at least the cost of living there is lower and most of the people have their own accommodation, which is the biggest expense in London." Furthermore, several also said that they planned to stay longer in London because they now needed more time to save up money before they could return. This was the case for 40-year-old Cesar from Ecuador, who was a dentist: "It [the recession] has affected me yes, I wanted to return home much faster, but now I need to wait longer until my new project comes through and I make more money."

Another dimension of the spatialities of recession for migrant workers in London is the effects of recession on remittances. Although it is now widely acknowledged that after an initial decline in remittance sending around the world, the effects of the global downturn were not as severe as was first assumed (Sirkeci et al, 2012), our research certainly highlighted a marked decline in the amounts remitted. Dario, the Bolivian chef (above), pointed out: "Now it isn't like before. Before I sent a lot of money, but in the last three months, I have reduced it and I've sent less. Before I sent 60 per cent of my salary, now I send 40 per cent." Furthermore, there was also evidence of reverse remittance sending, as in the case of Cesario from Colombia, who had lived in London since 2008 after living in Spain for 10 years. After losing his cleaning job, his wife in Colombia sent him a monthly allowance from their savings to tide him over until he secured another job (whereas previously he had sent £3,000 back to Colombia per year). In turn, the global nature of the crisis also meant that migrants felt even greater pressure to send money home in order to allow their families to survive, as reported by Alfonso from Bolivia: "What I sent before used to cover the needs of my family, but now no. For example, if I sent 500 dollars three years ago, now I have to send 1,000 to buy the same things."

Conclusion: sustainable London, sustainable migration?

This chapter has explored how a migrant division of labour sustains London's economy. Although a marked migrant division of labour emerged during the boom years of London's growth, we have argued that this has proved to be remarkably resilient during times of austerity and economic downturn. This is partly because of the particular nature of the evolution of the UK's welfare and migration regime over the past decade, as well as the continued demand for labour in the lower echelons of the economy. With many native-born British people still unable or unwilling to work in the jobs defined as 'dirty, dangerous and degrading', it is left to migrants to continue to fill these positions. However, this is not to say that the recession has not had deleterious effects for migrants concentrated in the low-paid sectors of London's economy. As we have shown, working conditions have worsened, and jobs have become even more exploitative, with negative ramifications for the wider wellbeing of migrants and their families, both locally and transnationally. This leads us to the other core argument of the chapter, which is the importance of taking the spatialities of recession into account when assessing the effects on migrants. As illustrated, the UK recession has not occurred in a vacuum from the rest of the world, and the reasons why migrants continue to migrate to London in the first place is because of economic hardships in their own countries in Europe and beyond. Indeed, the uneven geographies of development that underpinned the functioning of the economies of advanced industrial nations and global cities such as London during times of growth have been sustained during crisis. In turn, not only has the migrant division of labour been resilient to the economic crisis in a negatively modified form, but the consequences have also been felt, both locally and transnationally, beyond London. As such, we suggest that the very sustainability of London's economy is predicated on the continued and sustained migrant divisions of labour, underpinned by people who are willing to work for low wages and in poor conditions for as long as there is demand for work and as long as the global economy continues to function in geographically uneven and unjust ways. Therefore, conceptualising urban sustainability of cities such as London needs to recognise the spatialities and resilience of such a migrant division of labour.

Notes

[1] This chapter draws on two research projects undertaken between 2009 and 2011: *Migrants and their money* (Datta, 2012) and *No longer invisible* (McIlwaine et al, 2011). Both projects included a number of migrant communities drawn from East and Central Europe, Africa and Latin America. The projects deployed mixed methods frameworks ranging from questionnaire surveys, in-depth interviews and focus groups. In this chapter, we particularly draw on our work with Bulgarian migrants (54 questionnaires, 24 in-depth interviews and one focus group; 9 participants: 6 men and 3 women) and with Latin Americans from a range of different countries (1,041 questionnaires and 50 in-depth interviews).

[2] This included the Czech Republic, Estonia, Hungary, Latvia, Lithuania, Poland, Slovakia and Slovenia.

[3] In an effort to allay public misgivings, encourage formal labour market participation as well as restrict access to welfare, a Worker Registration Scheme (WRS) was established in the UK which A8 migrants were required to sign up to within a month of starting to work. A8 migrants were then eligible for certain benefits after a year of being registered on the WRS (Anderson et al, 2006).

[4] Up to 30 per cent of those who registered on the WRS may already have been in the UK prior to May 2004 as undocumented or irregular workers (Anderson et al, 2006; Garapich, 2008).

[5] The Jobseeker's Allowance is designed for people of working age who are either out of work or working less than 16 hours per week, and who are available and actively looking for work (www.jobseekers-allowance.com/what-is-JSA.html).

Acknowledgements

We would like to thank the Trust for London, the Latin American Women's Rights Service and Friends Provident Foundation for funding the projects included here. We are also deeply grateful to all the researchers who conducted the interviews as well as the people who agreed to participate in the surveys, interviews and focus groups.

References

Allen, J. (2010) 'The City and finance: changing landscapes of power', in N. Coe and A. Jones (eds) *The economic geography of the UK*, London: Sage Publishing.

Anderson, B., Ruhs, R., Rogaly, B. and Spencer, S. (2006) *Fair enough? Central and East European migrants in low wage employment in the UK*, Report written for the Joseph Rowntree Foundation, published as a COMPAS Report, COMPAS, University of Oxford.

Anderson, C. and Pontusson, J. (2007) 'Workers, worries and welfare states: social protection and job insecurity in 15 OECD countries', *European Journal of Political Research*, vol 46, pp 211-35.

Baker, P. and Mohieldeen, Y. (2000) 'The language of London's school children', in P. Baker and J. Eversley (eds) *Multilingual capital*, London: Battlebridge.

Campbell, D., Carruth, A., Dickenson, A. and Green, F. (2007) 'Job insecurity and wages', *The Economic Journal*, vol 117, pp 544-66.

Castles, S. (2009) *Migration and the global financial crisis: a virtual symposium. Update 1.A: an overview* (www.age-of-migration.com/uk/financialcrisis/updates/1a.pdf).

Cavanaugh, M. (2010) 'Numbers matter', in T. Finch and D. Goodhart (eds) *Immigration under Labour*, London: Institute for Public Policy Research, pp 30-3.

Datta, K. (2009) 'Risky migrants? Low paid migrants coping with financial exclusion in London', *European Urban and Regional Studies*, vol 16, no 4, pp 331-44.

Datta, K. (2011) 'Last hired and first fired? The impact of the economic downturn on low-paid Bulgarian migrant workers in London,' *Journal of International Development*, vol 23, pp 565-82.

Datta, K. (2012) *Migrants and their money: surviving financial exclusion in London*, Bristol: Policy Press.

Datta, K., McIlwaine, C., Evans, Y., Herbert, J., May, J. and Wills, J. (2009) 'Men on the move: narratives of migration and work among low paid migrant men in London', *Social and Cultural Geography*, vol 10, no 8, pp 853-73.

Datta, K., McIlwaine, C., Wills, J., Evans, Y., Herbert, J. and May, J. (2007) 'The new development finance or exploiting migrant labour? Remittance sending among low-paid migrant workers in London', *International Development Planning Review*, vol 29, no 1, pp 43-67.

Dobson, J., Latham, A. and Salt, J.C. (2009) *On the move? Labour migration in times of recession: what can we learn from the past?*, Policy Network Paper, Barrow Cadbury Trust (www.policy-network.net/publications_detail.aspx?ID=3194).

Engbersen, G. (2001) 'The unanticipated consequences of panopticon Europe: residence strategies of illegal immigrants', in V. Guiraudon and C. Joppke (eds) *Controlling a new migration world*, London: Routledge, pp 222-46.

Faist, T. (2000) 'Transnationalization in international migration: implications for the study of citizenship and culture', *Ethnic and Racial Studies*, vol 23, no 2, pp 189-222.

Finch, T. and Goodhart, D. (2010) *Immigration under Labour*, London: Institute for Public Policy Research.

Findlay, A. and McCollum, D. (2013) 'Recruitment and employment regimes: migrant labour channels in the UK's rural agribusiness sector, from accession to recession', *Journal of Rural Studies*, vol 30, pp 10-19.

Findlay, A., Geddes, A. and McCollum, D. (2010) 'International migration and recession', *Scottish Geographical Journal*, vol 126, no 4, pp 299-320.

Fix, M., Papademetriou, D., Batalova, J., Terrazas, A., Yi-Ying Lin, S. and Mittelstadt, M. (2009) *Migration and the global recession*, Washington, DC: Migration Policy Institute.

Flynn, D. (2003) *Tough as old boots? Asylum, immigration and the paradox of New Labour policy*, JCWI Immigration Rights Discussion Series, London: Joint Council for the Welfare of Immigrants.

French, S., Lai, K. and Leyshon, A. (2010) 'Banking on financial services', in N. Coe and A. Jones (eds) *The economic geography of the UK*, London: Sage, pp 61-78.

Garapich, M. (2008) 'The migration industry and civil society: Polish immigrants in the United Kingdom before and after EU enlargement', *Journal of Ethnic and Migration Studies*, vol 34, no 5, pp 735-52.

Glossop, C. and Shaheen, F. (2009) *Accession to recession: A8 migration in Bristol and Hull*, London: Centre for Cities.

Hondagneu-Sotelo, P. (2007) *Doméstica: immigrant workers cleaning and caring in the shadows of affluence*, Stanford, CA: Stanford University Press.

IMF (International Monetary Fund) (2010) *World economic update: restoring confidence without harming recovery*, 7 July (www.imf.org/external/pubs/ft/weo/2010/update/02/index.htm).

Jayaweera, H. and Anderson, B. (2008) *Migrant workers and vulnerable employment: a review of existing data*, COMPAS report for TUC Commission on Vulnerable Employment, Oxford: COMPAS, University of Oxford.

Krings, T., Bobek, A., Moriarty, E., Salamońska, J. and Wickham, J. (2013) 'Polish migration to Ireland: "free movers: in the new European mobility space', *Journal of Ethnic and Migration Studies*, vol 39, no 1, pp 87-103.

Levitt, P. (2001) 'Transnational migration: taking stock and future directions', *Global Networks*, vol 1, no 3, pp 195-216.

Levitt, P. and Glick-Schiller, N. (2004) 'Conceptualizing simultaneity: a transnational social field perspective on society, *International Migration Review*, vol 38, no 3, pp 1002-39.

MAC (Migration Advisory Committee) (2008) *The labour market impact of relaxing restrictions on employment in the UK of nationals of Bulgarian and Romanian EU member states*, London: MAC.

Markova, P. (2010) 'Impact of the Global Economic Crisis on Social Exclusion in Bulgaria', *European Social Watch Report* (www.socialwatch.eu/wcm/Bulgaria.html).

Markova, E. and Black, R. (2007) *East European immigration and community cohesion*, York: Joseph Rowntree Foundation.

Martin, P. (2009) 'Recession and migration: a new era for labour migration?', *International Migration Review*, vol 43, no 3, pp 671-91.

May, J., Wills, J., Datta, K., Evans, Y., Herbert, J. and McIlwaine, C.J. (2007) 'Keeping London working: global cities, the British state and London's migrant division of labour', *Transactions of the Institute of British Geographers*, vol 32, pp 151-67.

May, J., Wills, J., Datta, K., Evans, Y., Herbert, J. and McIlwaine, C. (2010) 'Global Cities at Work: Migrant labour in low paid employment in London', *The London Journal*, vol 35, pp 85-99.

McCollum, D. (2012) 'Investigating A8 migration using data from the Worker Registration Scheme: temporal, spatial and sectoral trends', *Local Economy*, vol 28, no 1, pp 35-50.

McCollum, D., Shubin, S., Apsite, E. and Krisjane, Z. (2013) 'Rethinking labour migration channels: the experience of Latvia from EU accession to economic recession', *Population, Space and Place*, vol 19, no 6, pp 688-702.

McDowell, L. (2009) 'Old and new European economic migrants: whiteness and managed migration policies', *Journal of Ethnic and Migration Studies*, vol 35, no 1, pp 19-36.

McIlwaine, C. (2010) 'Migrant machismos: exploring gender ideologies and practices among Latin American migrants in London from a multi-scalar perspective', *Gender, Place and Culture*, vol 17, no 3, pp 281-300.

McIlwaine, C. (2012) 'Constructing transnational social spaces among Latin American migrants in Europe: perspectives from the UK', *Cambridge Journal of Regions, Economy and Society, vol 5, no 2, pp 271-88.*

McIlwaine, C. (2013) 'Prácticas de subsistencia desplazadas entre los colombianos en Londres', in F.O. Esteban (ed) *Espacios transnacionales de la migración latinoamericana en Europa*, Buenos Aires: Editorial Antropofagia, pp 101-24.

McIlwaine, C., Cock, J.C. and Linneker, B. (2011) *No longer invisible: the Latin American community in London*, London: Trust for London.

Moser, C.O.N. (2009) *Ordinary families, extraordinary lives*, Washington, DC: Brookings Institution.

Parrenas, R.S. (2005) *Children of global migration: transnational families and gendered woes,* Stanford, CA: Stanford University Press.

Rienzo, C. and Vargas-Silva, C. (2012) *Migrants in the UK: an overview,* Oxford: Migration Observatory, University of Oxford (www.migrationobservatory. ox.ac.uk/sites/files/migobs/Migrants%20in%20the%20UK-Overview_0.pdf).

Rogers, A., Anderson, B. and Clark, N. (2009) *Recession, vulnerable workers and immigration: background report,* Oxford: COMPAS, University of Oxford.

Sassen, S. (1991) *The global city: New York, London, Tokyo,* Princeton, NJ: Princeton University Press.

Simeonova, D. (2004) *The negative effects of securitizing immigration: the case of Bulgarian migrants to the EU* (www.migrationonline.cz).

Sirkeci, I., Cohen, J.H. and Ratha, D. (eds) (2012) *Migration and remittances during the global financial crisis and beyond,* Washington, DC: The World Bank.

Somerville, W. and Sumption, M. (2009) *Immigration in the United Kingdom: recession and beyond,* London: Equality and Human Rights Commission, Migration Policy Institute.

Spence, L. (2005) *Country of birth and labour market outcomes in London: an analysis of Labour Force Survey and Census Data,* London: Greater London Authority.

Spence, L. (2006) *A profile of Londoners by language: an analysis of the Labour Force Survey data by language,* London: Greater London Authority.

Spencer, S. (2010) 'Economic gain, political cost', in T. Finch and D. Goodhart (eds) *Immigration under Labour,* London: Institute for Public Policy Research, pp 19-20.

Spencer, S. (2011) *The migration debate,* Bristol: Policy Press.

Sumption, M. (2010) 'Foreign workers and immigrant integration: emerging from the recession in the UK', in D.G. Papademetriou, M. Sumption and A. Terrazas, with C. Burket, S. Loyal and R. Ferrero-Turrion (eds) *Migration and immigrants two years after the financial collapse: where do we stand?,* Washington, DC: Migration Policy Institute, pp 47-62.

Vasta, E. (2008) *The paper market: 'borrowing' and 'renting' of identity documents,* WP-08-03, Oxford: COMPAS, University of Oxford.

Vertovec, S. (2007) 'Super-diversity and its implications', *Ethnic and Racial Studies,* vol 30, no 6, pp 1024-54.

Wearden, G. (2009) 'UK faces worse recession than US and Europe IMF warns', *The Guardian,* 18 March.

Wills, J., Datta, K., Evans, Y., Herbert, J., May, J. and McIlwaine, C. (2010) *Global cities at work: new migrant divisions of labour,* London: Pluto Press.

Wills, J., May, J., Datta, K., Evans, Y., Herbert, J. and McIlwaine, C. (2009) 'London's migrant division of labour', *European Urban and Regional Studies,* vol 16, no 3, pp 257-71.

Wright, K. (2012) 'Constructing human wellbeing across spatial boundaries: negotiating meanings in transnational migration', *Global Networks,* vol 12, no 4, pp 467-84.

Wright, K. and Black, R. (2011) 'Poverty, migration and human well-being: towards a post-crisis research and policy agenda', *Journal of International Development*, vol 23, no 4, pp 548-54.

SEVEN

Sustaining London's welfare in an age of austerity

Chris Hamnett

Introduction

Like other major developed world cities, London presents a paradox of inequality in that it contains a disproportionate share of the most affluent and wealthy, as well as a large number of people who are unemployed, poor or on a low income. The existence of poverty in London is well known (Hamnett, 2003; MacInnes et al, 2011). What is less well known in mainstream academia is how the poor survive day to day. In the 19th century many of those who were unemployed, sick or poor would have struggled to get enough to eat, to rent basic accommodation or even just to survive. The alternative was the workhouse. But after the Beveridge report and the development of the modern British welfare state since 1947, unemployment, disability and poverty have not condemned these groups to near starvation levels. Instead, they are now supported by a large number of different welfare benefits, ranging from pensions and child benefits to Jobseeker's Allowance, housing and incapacity benefits, which collectively added up to £200 billion in 2012. In 2010, however, the Coalition government announced its intention to radically cut welfare benefits. This chapter specifically focuses on the impact of some of these cuts, particularly the impact of both the Housing Benefit cap and the general benefits cap, both of which are discussed in more detail below. It is argued by critics of the cuts that they are likely to displace significant numbers of low-income households, potentially running into some tens of thousands, from the private rented sector in central and inner London. In this respect we look in particular at government welfare cut-generated residential displacement.

The significance of these cuts highlights the fact that no discussion of world or global cities can be complete without analysis of the role of government and state spending and taxation. Contrary to some claims made by global city theorists, the state and national politics, as well as global capital, has a big impact on living conditions and living standards in global cities. While it could be argued that welfare spending cuts are an inevitable response to the global financial crisis and a climate of austerity, this is questionable, and it can be strongly argued that they are, in fact, a result of local political choices and decisions that we should not see as inevitable (Peck, 2012; Hamnett, 2014).

While there has been extensive research on the deprived and low-income groups in London both currently and historically (Steadman-Jones, 1974; Green, 1986, 1995; Hamnett, 2003; MacInnes et al, 2011), there has been relatively little urban research on the role, scale and importance of welfare benefits, but beyond the world of the healthy, the employed, the (relatively) well-paid, there is another world, that of those who are economically inactive, unemployed, sick, disabled, poor or living on a low income. And these groups are in receipt of a variety of benefits (Beatty and Fothergill, 2011a, 2011b, 2013), which are extremely important and contribute a significant proportion to household income in some areas. Welfare benefits play a crucial role for low-income groups in helping to maintain a basic standard of living and enabling the recipients to get by economically and to keep their heads above water. To this extent, they play a key role in social reproduction and social sustainability. Without benefits, or with much lower benefits, it is very likely that many households would struggle to maintain a basic standard of living, to pay their housing costs and to feed themselves. As some authors have pointed out (Walker and Huby, 1989; Mohan, 2003; Hamnett, 2009a), it is possible to conceive of 'spatial divisions of welfare' in terms of spending and incidence of benefit. Some regions or areas have much higher percentages of beneficiaries and levels of support than others. The Data Management Analysis Group (DMAG) of the Greater London Authority (GLA) (2007) noted in its report *Who benefits?* that:

> While London has the highest levels of average income of any region, this embraces the highest proportion of individuals in both the highest and lowest income quintiles after housing costs. Social security benefits make up around 60 per cent of gross income for the poorest fifth of households nationally, compared to only two per cent in the top fifth. London has local authority areas with both the highest and the lowest rates of means-tested benefit receipt in the country. And while the rate of receipt of means tested benefits has decreased over the last few years across the country as a whole, this decrease has been less marked in London. (GLA, 2007, p 6)

Scale and distribution of benefits

The Institute for Fiscal Studies (2012) estimated that total government spending on welfare benefits in Britain totalled £200 billion in 2011-12. This comprised £37 billion in benefits for families with children, £42 billion for people on a low income, £85 billion for older people (of which state pensions made up £74 billion), £32 billion for those who were sick or disabled, and £5 billion for those who were unemployed. The benefits for people on low income included Income Support (£6.9 billion), Working Tax Credit (£6.9 billion), Housing Benefit (£22 billion) and Council Tax Benefit (£4.9 billion). Taken collectively, such benefits accounted for 25 per cent of total British government spending in

2012. The level of government spending on social security has risen from about 4 per cent of GDP in 1957 to 14 per cent in 2012. The proportion of households including one or more members in receipt of a social security benefit, including State Pension and Child Benefit, averages a remarkable 65 per cent in Britain (ONS, 2007).

While child benefits and pensions are distributed fairly evenly across Britain as a whole, reflecting the distribution of both children and retired people, benefits targeted at unemployment, incapacity and low incomes tend to be focused on what can be termed the economically depressed, ex-industrial areas of Britain, such as Scotland, South Wales, the North East and North West, along with the inner areas of some of Britain's major cities. An analysis of benefit distribution

Table 7.1: Government benefit expenditure, 2011-12

Major DWP benefit expenditure heads	London
Attendance Allowance	467
Bereavement Benefit/Widow's Benefit	58
Carer's Allowance	211
Council Tax Benefit	789
Disability Living Allowance	1,272
of which children	151
of which working age	783
of which pensioners	337
Employment and Support Allowance	453
Housing Benefit	5,884
Incapacity Benefit	404
Income Support	1,225
of which on incapacity benefits	677
of which lone parents	445
of which carers	44
of which others	58
Industrial Injuries Benefits	34
Jobseeker's Allowance	761
Maternity Allowance	68
Over 75 TV Licences	50
Pension Credit	1,208
Severe Disablement Allowance	75
of which working age	60
of which pensioners	15
State Pension	5,982
Statutory Maternity Pay	367
Winter Fuel Payments	203
Total	19,510

Source: DWP Benefit Expenditure Tables

by household and region shows that the incidence of some benefits, particularly Incapacity Benefit, is much higher in the ex-industrial and coal-mining areas where employment has collapsed, and many workers are affected with health problems, making work difficult. This can be shown in terms of both incidence of specific benefits and the relative financial importance of different benefits in different regions (see Figure 7.1). It is also possible to see the relative importance of welfare benefits in household income. Family Resources Survey (FRS) data for 2009 shows that, excluding pensions and pension credits, social security benefits as a percentage of household income ranged from 4-5 per cent in the South East and East of England to 10-11 per cent in Wales, the North East and North West. Add in pensions and Pension Credit, Income Support and other sources, the percentage of household income from the state varied, from a low of 15 per cent in inner London, to a high of 30 per cent in Wales, and 25 per cent in some other ex-industrial regions. At a local authority level the percentages are even greater. This highlights the dependence of some regions and areas on various forms of government social security spending. The Centre for Social Justice (2013) calculated that the total amount of government welfare spending

Figure 7.1: The percentage spent on different benefits, by region, 2009-10

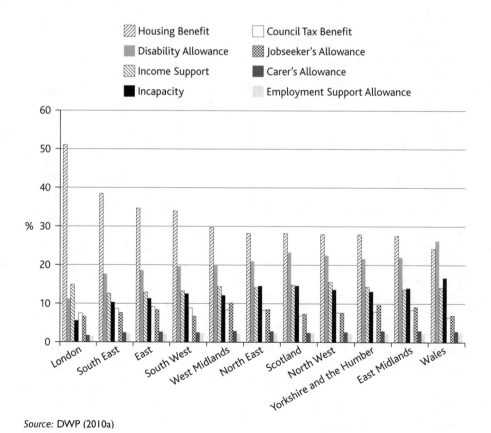

Source: DWP (2010a)

totalled over £5,000 per capita in some local authorities including Barking and Dagenham, Newham, Enfield and Waltham Forest in London.

Although London has a relatively low incidence of incapacity and disability benefits, it scores highly in terms of some other benefits, notably Housing Benefit, as a result of the extremely high cost of housing in London which has an impact on rents. It also has substantial numbers of poor people. Taken collectively as a result of its large population, London accounts for almost 14 per cent of total benefit spend in Britain, and it has a much higher percentage of its population claiming Housing Benefit than most other areas of Britain (Hamnett, 2009a, 2010). The overall structure of welfare spending in London has been analysed in detail by DMAG (GLA, 2007) and so will not be reiterated here. The focus here instead is on the impact of government welfare benefit cuts. It is noteworthy, however, that DMAG (GLA, 2007) found that almost twice as many households (29.4 per cent) in inner London were in receipt of Housing Benefit compared to outer London (16.9 per cent) and Britain (16.2 per cent) as a whole. Similarly, 28 per cent of households in inner London were in receipt of Council Tax Benefit compared to around 20 per cent in outer London and Britain as a whole. Twenty-eight per cent of children in London, and 36 per cent in inner London, live in households dependent on key welfare benefits compared to just under a fifth nationally (see Table 7.2). While the figures are slightly dated, it is unlikely that they are indicative of significant differences between parts of London and Britain as a whole.

Table 7.2: Claimant rates by benefit type, 2005

Benefit type	Great Britain	London	Inner London	Outer London	Population base
Income Support	6.1	7.7	9.3	6.5	Age 16-59
Jobseeker's Allowance	2.4	3.2	3.9	2.7	Working age
Incapacity Benefit	6.5	5.6	6.5	5	Age 16-64
Housing Benefit	16.2	21.3	29.4	16.9	All households
Council Tax Benefit	20.3	22.2	27.8	19.6	All households
Pension Credit	21.8	24.8	33.4	20.8	Age 60+
State Pension	96.5	91.9	86.5	94.5	Pensionable age
Children dependent on benefit	19.5	28.1	36.2	23.4	Age 0-18

Source: GLA (2007)

Nature and impact of government welfare cuts

While the previous Labour government had struggled to reduce some aspects of welfare spending, notably the rapid growth of Incapacity Benefits that were paid to three million claimants nationally, the importance of welfare spending and its social and geographical impact was given fresh impetus by the decision of the newly elected Coalition government in Britain in May 2010 to embark on major cuts to a range of welfare benefits, including the introduction of household caps on some benefit payments, notably Housing Benefit and overall benefit payments, as well as the introduction of tighter medical criteria for disability and incapacity benefits. Taken collectively, these changes have led to major debates and considerable opposition (Collins, 2012, 2013; Goodhart, 2012; Ganesh, 2012, 2013; Cavendish, 2013; Byrne, 2013). They can be seen as part of a wider process of tightening up, or rolling back, welfare policies and costs in a number of western countries since the mid-1990s, and have been linked to a policy shift that has been termed 'welfare to work'. The attempt to cut welfare spending began under New Labour in 1997, in order to reduce the number of people claiming Incapacity Benefit, and the background to the cuts, and the rationale, has been discussed in detail elsewhere (see, for example, Beatty and Fothergill, 2013; Hamnett, 2014). What is unclear is what the precise impacts of the new cuts will be, although there is widespread agreement that one of the impacts will be to squeeze the low-income welfare benefit-dependent groups out of expensive housing areas such as central and inner London, where previous levels of Housing Benefit payments have been relatively high (Hamnett, 2009a; Hamnett, 2010). This could lead to a change in the pattern of residential segregation in London, with the central and inner areas becoming increasingly the preserve of high-income groups. In this respect we are looking at state-led residential displacement as a result of welfare cuts. This chapter examines some of these issues. First, however, it is important to examine the scale and incidence of some key benefit spending in London.

Current structure of welfare expenditure and the incidence of benefits by region

Department for Work and Pensions (DWP) figures for benefit expenditure in Britain show that out of a total of £158 billion of expenditure by the DWP in 2011-12 (excluding Child Benefit and tax credits, which account for a further £42 billion), London accounted for £19.5 billion or 12 per cent of national benefit spending. This is slightly below London's 14 per cent share of the British population, and reflects the fact that benefit spend per capita in London is below the national average. This broadly reflects the relative health of the London economy and below average levels of unemployment. Consequently, London has a level of workless families well below the national average, and below average levels of population on incapacity benefits. Both of these measures are much higher in the old, ex-industrial regions of Scotland, Wales, the North East and North West (see Figures 7.2 and 7.3).

Where London stands out as well above average is in terms of the level of spending and the incidence of Housing Benefit. This is a benefit designed to offset the cost of housing for low-income households. The reasons for this are relatively simple and reflect the very high cost of housing in the capital and the shortage of affordable social housing. Of a total national bill for Housing Benefit of £22.8 billion in 2011-12, London accounted for £5.88 billion

Figure 7.2: Value of benefit expenditure (£ million), by region and benefit type, 2010

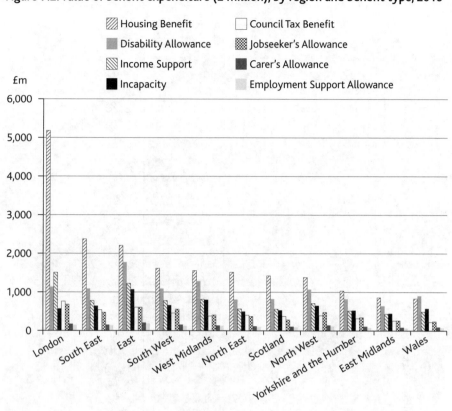

(25.8 per cent), about twice its share of national population. In January 2013 London had 853,000 Housing Benefit recipients, just under 17 per cent of the national total. Of these, almost 570,000, or 67 per cent, were in social housing, and the other 33 per cent in private rented housing. The average weekly cost of Housing Benefit per recipient in Britain in March 2011 was £87 compared to £127 in Greater London. But for unregulated private tenants it was £108 in Britain against £187 in London. The explanation is that rents in London are much higher than elsewhere. The very uneven distribution of Housing Benefit in 2011–12 shows that London local authorities dominate the national ranking in terms of the absolute amount of Housing Benefit expenditure (see Figure 7.3). At the top, not surprisingly, is Birmingham, Britain's second largest city, at £500 million, but the next four local authorities in terms of total spending are all London boroughs. They are followed by Liverpool, Manchester and Leeds, but of the top 30 local authorities, no fewer than 24 are London boroughs. This is an indication of the remarkable concentration of Housing Benefit in London (DWP, 2013). Housing Benefit spending is disproportionately high in London because of its very high rents.

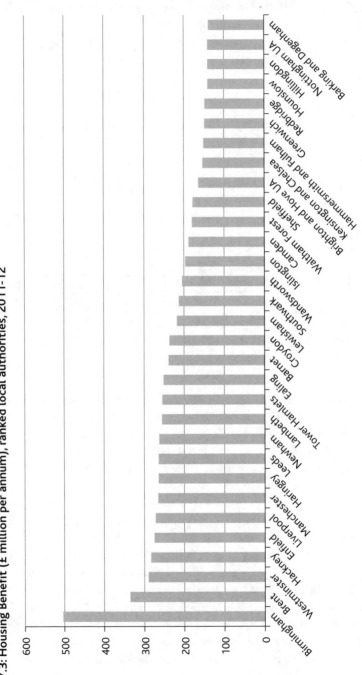

Figure 7.3: Housing Benefit (£ million per annum), ranked local authorities, 2011-12

Source: DWP (2013)

More generally, the DMAG (GLA, 2007) report *Who benefits?* provides a useful, if rather dated, baseline survey. It noted, regarding the percentage of children who are dependent on benefits, that:

> Twenty eight per cent of children in the capital are dependent on key social security benefits, compared to less than a fifth nationally. And the distribution between the types of benefits is markedly different compared to other regions, with 88 per cent of receipt in the capital being solely income-based. In no other region do means–tested benefits alone contribute to more than 77 per cent of the total. Part of the explanation lies in the difference in rates of receipt among different types of households with dependent children. For example, around 57 per cent of lone parent households in London are reliant on Income Support, the highest rate for any region. Overall, nearly a quarter of London's children (23 per cent) are living in families dependent on Income Support. This compares with 15 per cent in Great Britain and is by far the highest rate for any region. In addition, the proportion of children in households reliant on income-based Jobseeker's Allowance is the highest of all regions. (GLA, 2007, p 6)

Another measure of the importance of Housing Benefit in London is DWP statistics on Housing Benefit caseload (or beneficiaries) as a percentage of households. The data (see Figure 7.4) indicate that once again London boroughs dominate the league table. At the top no fewer than 42 per cent of all households in the London Borough of Hackney claim Housing Benefit, followed by Haringey, Tower Hamlets and Newham (37 per cent), and then a string of other boroughs at over 31 per cent. This compares to a British average of 19 per cent and lows in some prosperous rural areas in the South East of under 10 per cent. It is clear that most London boroughs have a significant proportion of households dependent on Housing Benefit. This has made London particularly vulnerable to restrictions on housing benefits.

Housing Benefit, along with Incapacity Benefit, has become a key political issue in the debate over welfare spending because, until April 2012, there was no effective limit on Housing Benefit claims, and a small number of claimants were claiming extremely large sums. The distribution of claims by amount is shown in Table 7.3. What it indicates is that a small number of claimants, about 5,300 nationally (<0.1 per cent) were claiming more than £25,000 per annum (about £500 per week) in Housing Benefit, a very small number, about 2,000, were claiming more than £30,000 pa, and a tiny number (380) were claiming more than £40,000 pa, with 10 claimants (all in London) claiming more than £100,000 pa. Claims of this size are astonishing on any basis and difficult to justify. Consequently, in 2010, before the General Election, Yvette Cooper, then Labour Minister for Housing, announced the Labour government's intention to cap Housing Benefit at £50,000 pa. This policy, and associated Labour attempts

Figure 7.4: Housing Benefit caseload as a percentage of households, March 2012, top 27 local authorities

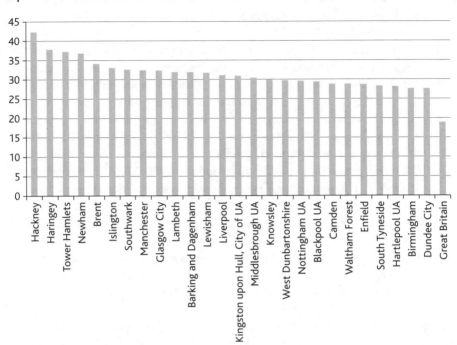

to reduce numbers of Incapacity Benefit claimants, were overtaken by the election of the new Coalition government in May 2010, which made cuts to welfare spending a priority to help reduce the level of the budget deficit post-financial crisis. This highlights the issue of social and housing sustainability in London given the massive inflation in London house prices in recent decades (Hamnett, 2009b), which has intensified of late as a result of the large number of wealthy overseas buyers and investors, and has pushed up rents. This means that renting in London for many low-income families is now only financially possible with the aid of Housing Benefit. This is not sustainable for the future, and government benefit cuts pose major problems in this area.

The Coalition government's welfare cuts

One of the first measures announced by the Coalition government elected in May 2010 was sharp cuts to welfare spending. The Chancellor of the Exchequer, George Osborne, stated that 'Britain was going to cut welfare benefits which the country could no longer afford' (Osborne, 2010). It can be argued, however, that the government saw the financial crisis as an opportunity to make some long desired cutbacks to welfare spending, and particularly what the government saw as a high level of welfare dependency (Hamnett, 2010, 2014). In some respects, the government can be seen to have taken forward the welfare changes that the previous Labour government had begun to make, in particular, a shift from welfare to work. The Coalition, however, has taken them much further and faster, generating strong debate. Some commentators (Cavendish, 2013; Collins, 2013; Ganesh, 2013) argue that the government should seriously restructure the welfare state and reduce the levels of benefit or eligibility or both.

The broader case for reform was outlined by Iain Duncan Smith, Secretary of State for Social Security, in the Foreword to the government White Paper, *Universal Credit: welfare that works* (DWP, 2010b). In it he claimed that:

> Successive governments have ignored the need for fundamental welfare reform, not because they didn't think that reform was needed but because they thought it too difficult to achieve. Instead of grasping the nettle, they watched as economic growth bypassed the worst off and welfare dependency took root in communities up and down the country, breeding hopelessness and intergenerational poverty.

He went on to assert that:

> The welfare bill has become unsustainably expensive, but the real price of this failure has been paid by the poorest and the most vulnerable themselves. Today, five million people are on out-of-work benefits in the UK, and 1.4 million of them have been receiving out-of-work benefits for nine out of the last ten years. Not only that, but we now have one of the highest rates of workless households in Europe, with 1.9 million children living in homes where no one has a job.... [T]oo much of our current system is geared toward maintaining people on benefits rather than helping them to flourish in work; we need reform that tackles the underlying problem of welfare dependency. That is why we are embarking on the most far-reaching programme of change that the welfare system has witnessed in generation. (DWP, 2010b)

It is not necessary to agree with this analysis, but it is necessary to understand its importance. The Conservatives have long desired to cut welfare spending, and welfare dependency is a recurrent element in right-wing thinking, but the political and economic circumstances have never been right. In this respect, the financial crisis provided a perfect justification for the government to cut welfare. The ideological rationale for the cuts has been analysed elsewhere (Hamnett, 2014), and so will not be reiterated here. What is important here is to identify the cuts that will have a major effect on London, although the list of welfare cuts is long and includes many policies that will have an impact across the country as a whole. These include the restriction on Child Benefit to households where no one earns more than £60,000 pa and the freezing of annual inflation-linked benefit uprating to 1 per cent for three years. (For a useful summary list of cuts, see Beatty and Fothergill, 2013, and Centre for Social Justice, 2013.) It is difficult to analyse the impact of all individual cuts on London, but three cuts in particular can be identified that will have an effect. The first is the cap on Housing Benefit and the reduction in Local Housing Allowance levels that the government introduced in April 2012. The second is the overall weekly benefit cap that was introduced in April 2013 in four local authorities and was rolled out nationally in 2013. The third is the change to Council Tax Benefit. I now deal with each in turn.

Cuts to Housing Benefit

The rationale for the cuts to Housing Benefit is that it had risen to £22 billion pa in 2011–12 (just over 10 per cent of total benefit expenditure), and that previously there was no limit to the amount that a household could claim. This was particularly marked in London, where rents are very high. Analysis of the distribution of Housing Benefit claims in late 2010 shows that while the majority (75 per cent) were under £5,000 pa, 96 per cent were under £10,000 pa, and 99.4 per cent were under £20,000 pa (about £400 pw); there was a very small tail of very high claims (0.25 per cent) of over £25,000, with 160 claims of over £50,000 pa and just 10 of over £100,000 pa (see Table 7.3). These are remarkable figures, and they almost all relate to families with large numbers of children living in large properties in central or inner London. Such claims are hard to justify on any basis, and some Conservative-controlled London councils objected to the large sums being claimed. The first announcement of the new Coalition government in May 2010 was the imposition of a graduated Housing Benefit cap, ranging from £150 pw for a single room to £400 pw (£20,800 pa) for a four-bedroom property. The previous five-bed allowance was abolished.

Table 7.3: Housing Benefit caseload by average yearly award, November 2010

Average yearly amount of Housing Benefit	Number	% of total
£0-5,000	3,602,090	75.1
£5-10,000	1,001,800	20.9
£10-15,000	128,960	2.7
£15-20,000	34,610	0.7
£20-25,000	6,460	0.1
£25-30,000	3,250	0.1
£30-35,000	820	0.0
£35-40,000	920	0.0
£40-45,000	150	0.0
£45-50,000	70	0.0
£50,000+	160	0.0
Missing Housing Benefit values	19,050	0.4
Total caseload	4,798,340	100

Source: DWP (2011)

The caps were estimated to hit about 18,000 households in total, some 14,000 of which were in London (DWP, 2010c). In addition, the government introduced other measures, one of the toughest being that in the private rented sector, Local Housing Allowance would only be paid up to a maximum of the 30th percentile of local rents compared to the previous median. This was expected to hit far more households, effectively restricting most households to the bottom 30 per cent of the private rented sector in terms of rent levels.

Taken collectively, these changes led to fierce opposition by London local authorities and housing charities, arguing that they would squeeze large sections of the poor in private rented housing out of central and inner London into the cheaper outer London boroughs and beyond (Hamnett, 2010; London Councils, 2011a; London Councils, 2011b; London Councils, 2011c; Fenton, 2012). There was a fierce debate between those who argued that the government cuts amounted to a form of welfare-based 'social cleansing' and those, generally on the Right, who argued that the poor had no right to expect to be housed in the most expensive housing areas of the capital. This debate is extremely important. On the right, Marin (2010) argued that while the state has a responsibility to support people on low incomes and to help them pay for housing, there is no obligation to house them in the most expensive areas of cities. The implication of this is that in the most expensive areas of London, many low-income, benefit-dependent households will not be able to meet their rents and may have to move out of the city altogether. On the left it is argued that social mix is important, and that it is unjustifiable to displace low-income households from areas they may have lived in for a long time and where they have social networks and their children may be at school. But it can be argued that households that are not benefit-dependent necessarily adjust their housing and residential options to their budgets, and the great majority cannot live in expensive residential areas even if they wanted to, so why should this option be available to those on benefits? But the inevitable consequence of this shift is that living in central and inner London will increasingly become the preserve of high-income groups, which raises issues of social sustainability. Some of the debate is summarised in an earlier analysis of the impact of Housing Benefit cuts (Hamnett, 2010). The full effects will only become clear in a year or more, but it raises important issues related to the 'right to the city' debate. Increasingly it would seem that the 'right to reside' is reverting to being income-related. A major fear is that many low-income households will be forced out of London entirely, to live in lower housing cost areas of the outer South East or other parts of the country.

Welfare benefit cap

Following the introduction of Housing Benefit caps, in 2011 the government announced its intention to introduce an overall household welfare benefit cap. The rationale for this proposal was based on the notion of 'fairness', specifically, that the overall level of benefit support should not be excessive in relation to those in employment on low incomes. Consequently the benefit cap was implemented specifying a maximum level of benefits equivalent to median household post-tax earned income. In 2012 this was £26,000 pa, or £500 pw for married couples and single parents and £350 pw for single people. While certain benefits will be excluded from this, notably, pensions and certain disability benefits, most are included, and the cap essentially means that most households will not be able to claim more than £26,000 pa in total. This is a substantial sum, but it will hit many households. The government's own preliminary impact assessment (DWP, 2012) estimated that 56,000 households would be affected, 49 per cent of which were located in London. For the most part these households are those with three or more children and 50 per cent are single-parent households. Subsequent analysis (DWP, 2013) suggested a total of 88,600 households affected, of whom some 42,000 or 47 per cent are in London. The boroughs with the largest number of households were Westminster, Brent, Ealing, Enfield, Newham and Tower Hamlets, all with more than 2,000 households potentially affected. Given that the benefit cap system will be operated via housing benefits, it is likely that most of those affected will suffer a reduction in the level of Housing Benefit payable. In extreme cases, where households were receiving over £500 pw in Housing Benefit alone, they will experience major benefit cuts. Figure 7.4 shows the likely number of households affected, by local authority. What is remarkable about the list is that while some of Britain's major cities, such as Birmingham, Manchester and Liverpool, feature at the top, the list is overwhelmingly dominated by London boroughs, accounting for some 20 out of the top 27 local authorities in terms of absolute numbers. Given that most of these boroughs have populations of <300,000, much smaller than provincial cities, this indicates housing costs in London.

The welfare cap took effect in April 2013 in four local authorities and it was introduced nationally in July 2013. There are currently competing claims about its impact. Charities and local authorities claim that they have seen significant upheaval and displacement. The government claim, by contrast, that they are seeing significant attempts by households to look for work. It has subsequently been suggested that the government are considering further reductions in the maximum level of benefits (down to £400 pw) in order to further cut the size of the welfare bill, but as the financial savings are unlikely to be significant, the principal purpose is perhaps disciplinary and punitive (Elliott and Savage, 2013). At the time of writing it is impossible to determine with accuracy the impact of the Housing Benefit and overall welfare caps on households, but some London local authorities report they are seeing a significant increase in rent arrears, with the consequent risk of loss of housing.

Council Tax Benefit

Finally, it is important to note that under the guise of the localism agenda, from 2013 the government passed responsibility for the management of Council Tax

Benefit to local authorities. Council Tax Benefit is paid to low-income households to enable them to pay Council Tax, the British tax levied by all local authorities to help pay for local services such as waste collection, education, social services and so on. It is levied on all households in Britain and is based on the valuation band of property. Council Tax Benefit has 5.9 million recipients in Britain, at an average of about £16 pw. The sting in the tail is that the government has told local authorities that it will cut the total amount paid (£4.9 billion) by 10 per cent, and give total discretion to local authorities over how they allocate the money, as long as pensioners and people with disabilities are protected. These proposals have been strongly criticised on the grounds that the localisation policy is simply a smokescreen to cut costs and to pass the burden onto local authorities. The government's plans for Council Tax Benefit effectively take it out of Annually Managed Expenditure (AME), which allows for budget flexibility to account for variable demand, and moves it as fixed grant (with a 10 per cent reduction) to the Department for Communities and Local Government's Local Government Departmental Expenditure Limit (LG DEL), which is a fixed funding pot. Analysis by London Councils of the impact over the five-year period 2005/06 to 2009/10 shows that the cost to London councils was £400 million, an effective 17 per cent cut in budgets given the requirement to protect pensioners and those who are unemployed. The impact on top of the Housing Benefit and benefit cap will be to increase housing costs for low-income families, and to further squeeze housing affordability in London for these groups.

Summary and conclusion

Government social security benefit expenditure accounts for 25 per cent of total government spending and is now around £200 billion per year. It comprises a big part in household income for many low-income households, and some households are totally dependent on welfare benefit income to pay for rents and living costs. This is particularly marked in areas of high unemployment where those who are economically inactive and unemployed are concentrated. In such areas, a very high proportion of households are in receipt of benefits. In this context, the government welfare cuts put in place from 2010 onwards to help reduce the government budget deficit and to cut welfare dependency are likely to have a very major impact. This is particularly so in high rent areas, notably in London, where households are in receipt of high levels of Housing Benefit. The introduction in 2012 of the Housing Benefit cap and then in 2013, the overall benefit cap, means that households in receipt of over £20,000 pa in Housing Benefit or over £26,000 in total welfare benefits, will experience a cut in the level of benefits they receive. In some cases these will be very considerable. This has major implications for the ability of low-income households to afford housing in central and inner London. There has been considerable debate about the potential numbers of households likely to be affected, but in terms of Housing Benefit caps, it could be around 14,000 in London and around 40,000 in terms of the overall benefit cap. These groups will see cuts in the level of benefits that may be very significant and could lead to them being forced out of their accommodation and out of London entirely. This raises important issues about long-term social sustainability and about the 'right to the city' debate. While it can be argued that no one has a right to be subsidised to live in expensive housing in expensive areas of the city, the implications of a shift towards a more market-driven form of housing allocation will be that over time, central and inner London will increasingly become the preserve of the more affluent and higher income groups. This has been happening for some decades as gentrification has increased, but the impact of welfare cuts will be to intensify this process of social segregation.

References

Beatty, C. and Fothergill, S. (2011a) *Benefit reform: the local, regional and national impact*, Sheffield: Centre for Regional Economic and Social Research, Sheffield Hallam University.

Beatty, C. and Fothergill, S. (2011b) *Tackling worklessness in Wales*, Sheffield: Centre for Regional Economic and Social Research, Sheffield Hallam University.

Beatty, C. and Fothergill, S. (2013) *Hitting the poorest places hardest: the local and regional impact of welfare reform*, Sheffield: CRESR, Sheffield Hallam University.

Byrne, L. (2013) 'Not only heartless, but hopeless: why Tory benefit cuts won't work', *The Observer*, 7 April.

Cavendish, C. (2013) 'Our welfare bill has run wildly out of control', *The Times*, 17 January.

Centre for Social Justice (2013) *Signed on, written off: an inquiry into welfare dependency in Britain* (www.centreforsocialjustice.org.uk/UserStorage/pdf/Pdf%20reports/CSJ_Signed_On_Written_Off_full_report-WEB-2-(2).pdf).

Collins, P. (2012) 'Labour must cut its dependency on welfare', *The Times*, 7 December.

Collins, P. (2013) 'Who benefits from welfare?', *Prospect Magazine*, 22 May.

DWP (2010a) *Family Resources Survey 2009-10*, London: DWP.

DWP (2010b) *Universal Credit: welfare that works*, Cm 7957 (www.dwp.gov.uk/docs/universal-credit-full-document.pdf).

DWP (2010c) *Impacts of Housing Benefit proposals: changes to the Local Housing Allowance to be introduced in 2011-12*, London: DWP.

DWP (2011) *Housing Benefit by level of awards*, London: DWP.

DWP (2012) *Benefit cap (HB) regulations 2012, impact assessment of the benefit cap*, London: DWP.

DWP (2013) *Housing Benefit expenditure tables* (www.gov.uk/government/collections/benefit-expenditure-tables).

Elliott, F. and Savage, M. (2013) 'Miliband links benefits to behaviour', *The Times*, 22 August.

Fenton, A. (2012) *Housing benefit reform and the spatial segregation of low-income households in London*, Cambridge: Centre for Housing and Planning Research, University of Cambridge.

Ganesh, J. (2012) 'Britain needs a grand vision tailored to what it can afford', *Financial Times*, 8 December.

Ganesh, J. (2013) 'Britain's two gambles in welfare reform', *Financial Times*, 7 January.

GLA (Greater London Authority) (2007) *Who benefits? An analysis of benefit receipt in London: summary of findings*, London: Data Management and Analysis Group, GLA.

Goodhart, D. (2012) 'Goodbye Beveridge – the end of British welfare approaches', *Financial Times*, 29 September.

Green, D. (1986) 'A map for Mayhew's London: the geography of poverty in the nineteenth century', *The London Journal*, vol 11, no 2, pp 115-26.

Green, D. (1995) *From artisans to paupers: economic change and poverty in London, 1790-1870*, Aldershot: Scholar Press.

Hamnett, C. (2003) *Unequal city: London in the global arena*, London: Routledge.

Hamnett, C. (2009a) 'Spatial divisions of welfare: the geography of welfare benefit expenditures and of housing benefit in Britain', *Regional Studies*, vol 43, no 8, pp 1015-33.

Hamnett, C. (2009b) 'Spatially displaced demand the changing geography of house prices in London, 1995-2006', *Housing Studies*, vol 24, no 3, pp 301-20.

Hamnett, C. (2010) 'Moving the poor out of central London? The implications of the government cuts to housing benefits', *Environment and Planning A*, vol 42, no 12, pp 2809-19.

Hamnett, C. (2014) 'Shrinking the welfare state: the structure and geography of British government welfare cuts', *Transactions IBG* (forthcoming).

IFS (Institute for Fiscal Studies) (2012) 'Reforming council tax benefit', *IFS Commentary 123* (www.ifs.org.uk/comms/comm123.pdf).

London Councils (2011a) *Council tax changes won't benefit Londoners* (www.londoncouncils.gov.uk/news/current/pressdetail.htm?pk=1420).

London Councils (2011b) *Does the cap fit? An analysis of the impact of welfare reform in London* (www.londoncouncils.gov.uk/policylobbying/welfarereforms/benefitcap/welfarereformresearch.htm).

London Councils (2011c) *The impact of housing benefit changes in London*, London: London Councils.

MacInnes, T., Parekh, A. and Kenway, P. (2011) *London's poverty profile 2011*, London: Trust for London and New Policy Institute.

Marin, M. (2010) 'The palatial injustice that shelters in housing benefit', *Sunday Times*, 31 October.

Mohan, J. (2003) 'Geography and social policy: spatial divisions of welfare', *Progress in Human Geography*, vol 27, no 3, pp 363-74.

ONS (Office for National Statistics) (2007) *Regional trends*, ONS: Southampton.

Osborne, G., (2010) 'Chancellors statement to the House of Commons', 20 October, www.hm-treasury.gov.uk/spend sr2010 speech.htm

Peck, J. (2012) 'Austerity urbanism: American cities under extreme economy', *City*, vol 16, no 6, pp 626-55.

Steadman-Jones, G. (1974) *Outcast London*, Harmondsworth: Penguin.

Walker, R. and Huby, M. (1989) 'Social security spending in the United Kingdom: bridging the north–south economic divide', *Environment and Planning C*, vol 7, no 3, pp 321-40.

Part 3

THE CHALLENGES FOR A SOCIALLY SUSTAINABLE LONDON

EIGHT

The death of sustainable communities in London?

Loretta Lees

Social sustainability and social mixing

Sustainability is based on the idea that 'marginal and poor groups should not disproportionately bear the costs of public or private activities or policies' (Manzi et al, 2010, p 9). Yet planners are now concerned primarily with creating 'sustainable cities that balance environmental concerns, the needs of future populations and economic growth (Beauregard, 2005, p 204). Planners seem less concerned with the traditional ideals of social justice and of balancing the market and social interests in the public good. Social sustainability is usually defined in relation to environmental and economic sustainability, but Kearns and Turok (2004) argue that it has a more anthropogenic quality that considers human needs and quality of life issues. Polese and Stren (2000, pp 16-17) define it as: 'development (and/or growth) that is compatible with the harmonious evolution of civil society, fostering an environment conducive to the compatible cohabitation of culturally and socially diverse groups while at the same time encouraging social integration, with improvements in the quality of life for all segments of the population.' But a 'clear theoretical concept of social sustainability is still missing' (Littig and Griessler, 2005, p 68), and in sustainability policy issues of social equity are often addressed by vague, qualitative platitudes such as sense of place, community, diversity and vibrancy (see Raco, 2005, pp 333-4).

Social sustainability has been very influential in British housing policy; it is perhaps most evident in the policy of creating mixed-income communities, mixing tenures and social classes in 'affordable' and market rate housing. Indeed, throughout the 1990s and into the 2000s neighbourhood regeneration was bound tightly to the rhetoric of social sustainability that was encapsulated in mixed communities policy. The concept of 'mixed communities' or 'social mix' re-emerged in the 1990s in reaction to the large concentrations of socially homogeneous populations of poor people residing in the inner cities of Western Europe and North America. Social mix policies have had one dominant objective, to de-concentrate or dilute large concentrations of low-income/poor households. The welfare programmes that built large council estates in the 1950s and 1960s have been blamed for creating monolithic, socially segregated areas of poverty and social deprivation in the inner city. In the British context, mixed communities policy sought to both de-concentrate poverty *and* tackle social exclusion on these estates.

Drawing heavily on the US Federal Department of Housing and Urban Development's (HUD) HOPE VI (Home Ownership and Opportunities for People Everywhere) program (see Cisneros and Engdahl, 2009), the British Social Exclusion Unit, under the then New Labour government, and the Urban Task Force promoted mixed communities as the solution to large concentrations of poor people on British council estates (see Lees, 2008; Bridge et al, 2011). The promotion of social mix informed urban regeneration policy and early programmes, such as the late 1990s New Deal for Communities, which were launched to tackle social exclusion in deprived areas. The goal of New Labour's social engineering was to create a new moral order of respectable and well-behaved (middle-class) residents.

Mixed communities policy came to the forefront of spatial planning under New Labour's Sustainable Communities agenda (ODPM, 2003a), and the Mixed Community Initiative of 2005 went a step further in promoting a more privatising, entrepreneurial and instrumental approach to social mixing in a new wave of roll-back neoliberalism (see Watt, 2009; Raco, 2012). The Local Government White Paper (DCLG, 2006a) recommended that local authorities act as strategic enablers, using land use planning mechanisms to achieve socially, economically and culturally mixed communities. Likewise, the 2006 Planning Policy Statement 3 (PPS3) (DCLG, 2006b) advocated mixed-income sustainable communities. Mixed communities policy has been especially revanchist on those large council estates in London being completely demolished and rebuilt as mixed communities (on 'revanchism', see Smith, 1996). In London, the contrast between disinvested local authority stock and the highly valuable land it sits on has created a 'state-induced rent gap', with massive capital accumulation potential (Watt, 2009, p 235). The reality is that 'social sustainability' in London is merely rhetoric used by local authorities to sell the wholesale demolition of council estates and their 'regeneration' as mixed communities. The end result is the displacement of low-income populations from inner London, state-led gentrification and social polarisation/segregation (see Bridge et al, 2011). In this chapter I discuss how state-led gentrification is not creating but rather is destroying sustainable communities in London. I look at how misguided policy at the national and local level has damaged local community life in London (for the US context, see Williamson et al, 2003). To exemplify this I highlight the case of the Heygate Estate in Elephant & Castle. I also look at attempts to fight this gentrification in what has amounted to a bottom-up fight for social sustainability.

Top-down social sustainability: mixed communities policy in London

Most of inner London is now gentrified, and council estates and their tenants have become the final gentrification frontier. There is a continuing but pepper-potted geography of social class division in London between the professional middle classes and low-income groups in low-paid jobs or on benefits. Processes of industrial and occupational restructuring have not yet erased this social division. Buck et al (2002) have identified widening social inequalities in London. Commenting on the British government's Index of Multiple Deprivation in 2000, they argued that: 'deprived people are far more likely to be found in Inner London than in Outer London' (Buck et al, 2002, p 47). It is this population of deprived people in inner London that the state has set out to gentrify, using mixed communities policy.

Social sustainability is a dominant element in discourses on urban regeneration in London (Imrie et al, 2009), and regeneration programmes across London have sought funding on the basis of creating mixed and sustainable communities. The first London Plan (GLA, 2004) developed by Ken Livingstone wanted to underline the city's economic growth and global city prosperity along with reinvesting in the city's infrastructure, increasing social inclusion and improving London's environmental sustainability. Social sustainability was encapsulated in Livingstone's vision: 'social inclusivity to give all Londoners the opportunity to share in London's future success' (p xii). The London Plan ambitiously set out to do what few cities have done, to balance economic growth with sustainability and social equity. Ken Livingstone's most powerful redistributive tool at the time was his ability to negotiate planning gains beyond those recommended by central government (McNeill, 2002), and he set a goal of 50 per cent affordable housing for all new developments in London, exceeding the commonly used national benchmark of 25 per cent. The Department for Environment, Transport and the Regions (DETR, 1998) defined affordable housing as: '… both low cost market housing, and subsidised housing (irrespective of tenure, ownership or financial arrangements) that will be available to people who cannot afford to occupy houses generally available on the local market.' This definition has allowed a significant amount of flexibility over what comprises affordable housing (indeed, Livingstone's 50 per cent affordable housing was only 35 per cent social rent; the other 15 per cent was intermediate), and who is eligible for it, something that was highlighted as a problem in the Office of the Deputy Prime Minister's (2003b) review of affordable housing provision in South East England because it allows local governments to excessively manipulate an urban renaissance.

Similarly, Boris Johnson's 'new' London Plan (GLA, 2011) has continued with mixed communities policy (as we will see later in this chapter); he has kept the policy that council estates should be mixed, but stopped supporting social housing in areas of owner-occupation, and designated a number of 'regeneration areas' – channelling funding and initiatives to the 20 per cent most deprived wards in London, according to the 2007 Index of Multiple Deprivation, where it assumes that deprivation is at its most severe because it is concentrated (GLA, Mayor of London, 2009). London's 33 'Opportunity Areas', identified in the previous London Plan, are on brownfield land with significant capacity for new housing, commercial and other development.

It is both interesting but also worrying that mixed communities policy has been enacted in London (and indeed elsewhere) in the face of growing evidence (especially from the numerous evaluations of HUD's HOPE VI program in the US) about its poor performance with respect to its claims about aiding the social and economic mobility of the poor. Cheshire (2009) undertook a thorough evaluation of mixed communities policy in the US and called it 'a faith-based *displacement* activity'. He is clear that the evidence to date indicates that mixed communities policy does not improve the life circumstances of poorer residents, either those few who get to remain or those who are moved out. He goes on to state that there seems to be quite persuasive evidence that specialised neighbourhoods have labour market advantages, even for the poor – indeed, particularly for the less skilled who rely on personal contacts to a greater extent to find jobs.

In addition, a recent London-based study by Arbaci and Rae (2013), that explored the extent to which social tenants in 10 mixed-tenure neighbourhoods across London had greater life chances in terms of opportunities and access to resources than those in 10 concentrations of social housing, echoed both Cheshire's (2009) conclusion and those of other evaluations from around the world (see Bridge et al, 2011). They conclude that mixed communities policy in London has exacerbated social inequality and masked deprivation. Using the Indices of Multiple Deprivation indicators utilised by the government as evidence for area-based funding initiatives in deprived areas, they found, perhaps not surprisingly, that social tenants did experience some socio-economic opportunities and access to resources, but that these were not dependent on, or improved by, the level of tenure mix within the neighbourhood. Rather, it was decommodified access to neighbourhood and welfare services, such as education, training and employment opportunities, that was crucial – services that can be better targeted and more cost-effectively provided in areas of concentrated need. In one of their study areas in Islington they found that affluent professionals were replacing low-income Greek and Somalian populations, and that social tenants were being pushed further out of London to places such as Enfield and Cheshunt in Hertfordshire. The social tenants who remained were trapped and restricted in a new community, and they could not afford or gain access to any other accommodation within Islington – creating, not solving, a lack of housing choice and undermining any social sustainability. Moreover, the much touted shared ownership schemes in the Islington 'mixed community' were taken up almost exclusively by young professionals from outside of the neighbourhood, thus limiting the progression of housing careers, which was/is one of the selling points of the mixed communities initiative:

> Islington is a representative case of a mixed neighbourhood that does not provide greater opportunities and resources for social tenants but instead increases inequality, enhances school segregation and constrains housing careers within the neighbourhood, resulting in entrapment or outflow to peripheral outer-London neighbourhoods. Mixing between private and social housing residents appears to be one of

distant observation rather than shared investment of social capital. (Arbaci and Rae, 2013, p 474)

Here Arbaci and Rae's (2013) research echoes the findings of the research undertaken on new build gentrification along the River Thames (see Davidson, 2008, 2010), where many of the new developments were built as mixed communities:

> The biggest thing I've seen in terms of benefit is the young girls getting jobs working at the hotel [incorporated within a 'mixed-use' new development]. You know, as maids. So it has given work.... But saying that, they will never be able to live here. When they get a bit older, get married and that, unless the council starts putting up new houses, they will have to leave. I think that is a pattern.... It is nice for the girls to have work, but you could ask if it fulfil promises. You certainly don't have the vibrant working community where we all knew each other now. (interview, cited in Davidson and Lees, 2010, pp 405-6)

Davidson and Lees (2005, p 1170) discuss the different types of displacement – both direct and indirect – associated with the new build developments being constructed along the Thames. They argue that the displacements being triggered by the new build developments, which have been built on brownfield sites and as such do not displace a pre-existing population, are indirect, a form of 'exclusionary displacement', where lower-income groups are unable to access property because of the gentrification of the neighbourhood, and that this goes in tandem with 'sociocultural displacement' as gentrifiers take control of community apparatus. But there are other, even more disturbing, displacements afoot in central London, akin to the more simple 'eviction and rent hike' displacement common to the gentrification literature. Significant numbers of low-income tenants have been, and are in the process of being, displaced from their homes and communities in inner London through the guise of mixed communities policy (see Figure 8.1)

For example, the Heygate Estate in Southwark had 1,212 council properties, including those that were leasehold (through the Right to Buy). Tenants have been moved out (198 of whom moved out under the shadow of a possession order; see the maps of this displacement in Lees et al, 2013), but a very small number of the 179 leaseholders refused to move (I turn to closer analysis of the Heygate Estate later in this section). The estate, which is now being demolished, is to be replaced with 2,535 new homes, of which none will be council rented and only 79 will be social rented! The adjacent Aylesbury Estate to be 'regenerated' by Notting Hill Housing Trust had 2,700 council homes; the new plan will build 4,200 new homes of which 50% will be 'affordable', three quarters of these will be social rent not council rent and the rest shared ownership or equity. The physical regeneration of the estate as suggested in current plans will displace

Figure 8.1: The socially cleansed London council estates

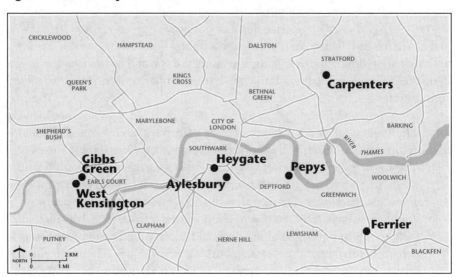

© Loretta Lees

approximately 20 per cent of the existing households, the people whom, ironically, the regeneration process is being targeted at. In addition the 600[1] leaseholders who bought under the Right to Buy will also be priced out (see Lees, 2013). And there are currently plans to include the new 'affordable' rent product in the category 'social rented', so the vast majority of the new social rented homes on the Aylesbury Estate could end up being up to 80 per cent of market rent! The Pepys Estate in Deptford saw the displacement of 600 or so residents from the 158 flats in the infamous Aragon Tower (see the BBC documentary, *The Tower: A Tale of Two Cities*, 2007, at www.bbc.co.uk/programmes/b007rq1p). They were evicted by Lewisham Council as vacant possession was one of the requirements of the developers, Berkeley Homes, buying the building for £11.5 million, which they then subsequently gentrified into the Z apartments that are now acting as a beachhead for gentrification around the Pepys Estate (see Davidson and Lees, 2010). Adjacent council tenants on the Pepys Estate were also either 'kicked out' or rehoused by the Hyde Housing Association that took over from the council. The Ferrier Estate in Greenwich, where demolition is now complete, consisted of approximately 1,732 council homes and 174 privately owned (through the Right to Buy) residences. The new £1 billion 'Kidbrooke Village' to replace it includes the construction of 4,398 new homes, approximately 610 properties for social housing, 750 for shared ownership and 2,500 for private ownership. On the West Kensington and Gibbs Green Estates, the much touted mixed communities regeneration programme will create up to 7,583 new homes, of which 760 will be replacement council homes and 740 will be additional intermediate affordable homes; 800 council tenancies will be lost. The residents lodged legal proceedings against the council. And finally, the Carpenters Estate, adjacent to the 2012

Olympic site – in 2012 Newham Council accepted University College London's (UCL) £1 billion proposal to build a new campus in Stratford,[2] which would have meant the demolition of the Carpenters Estate, displacing hundreds of people and radically changing the area and forcing out those who live in the area through rent hikes. In May 2013 UCL pulled out, and tenants on the Carpenters Estate have been working hard to design their own neighbourhood plan.

Echoing Hamnett's (1994, 2003) professionalisation thesis, Butler, Hamnett and Ramsden (2008) have argued that since 1981 London has become increasingly middle class, and that, as a consequence, 'old' class relations are in decline, if not entirely absent (see Watt, 2008). Reasserting Hamnett's (1994) thesis about *replacement* rather than *displacement*, they argued: '[W]hilst the old manual working class groups may have declined, they have not left a vacuum but have been *replaced* by these new groups of middle- and lower-middle class non-manual working households' (p 84; emphasis added). This characterisation of a significant decline in the working-class/lower-income population of London was underlined by Butler's (2007, p 162) call for gentrification 'to decouple itself from its original association with the deindustrialisation of metropolitan centres such as London and from its associations with working-class displacement.' Paul Watt (2008) has argued that both Butler and Hamnett's 'thesis' of socioeconomic change in London associates the decline of traditional working-class occupations with the decline of the working-class population, demonstrating what Loic Wacquant (2008) calls the 'literal and figurative effacing of the proletariat in the city...' (p 199). This chapter lends weight to this debate, for the direct displacements occurring on these estates *are* large-scale, they *are* significant and deserve our attention. The numbers of working-class displacees from these estates, and here I've only mentioned those I have been working on,[3] are in their thousands! I discuss this in detail in the next section.

Displacement from the Heygate Estate in Southwark

The Heygate Estate is located in Elephant & Castle in Southwark, which, in 2011 (when demolition of the Heygate Estate began), was ranked 3rd out of all 32 London boroughs for income inequality – the average household income was £29,800 and the median £16,800 (London's Poverty Profile, 2011). Elephant & Castle itself suffers from very high levels of poverty and is a dense area for social housing. The demolition of the Heygate Estate is part of a wider plan to regenerate the area around the Elephant & Castle road junction and shopping centre (see Campkin, 2013, Chapter 2, for a discussion of the wider regeneration in Elephant & Castle). Efforts to regenerate the Heygate Estate began in the 1990s with New Labour's Single Regeneration Budget; the masterplan for the demolition of the estate was adopted by Southwark Council in 2004, and in 2007 Lend Lease (an Australian property development company with a global portfolio and a controversial track record; see www.newstatesman.com/2013/02/southwark-accidentally-leaks-confidential-information) was chosen as the developer.[4]

Figure 8.2: Graffiti representing the demolition and rebuilding of the Heygate Estate

© Loretta Lees

Demolition began in 2011, but the estate is still undergoing demolition, before being completely rebuilt as a new 'mixed community' (see Figure 8.2). Southwark Council sold Heygate for £50 million (they had not yet even finished paying off the building of the original estate), and then spent a further £44 million moving 1,000 residents out. Southwark Council's expected capital receipts from Heygate land are almost equal to the costs incurred in emptying and demolishing the buildings! Three-quarters of the homes in these new developments will not be for Heygate tenants, despite this being an explicit rationale for their inclusion in the Southwark Plan (see www.southwark.gov.uk/info/856/planning_policy/1241/the_southwark_plan/1); they will be for private sale, prompting MP Simon Hughes to call for the planning application to be withdrawn.

As part of the decantment of the Heygate Estate, the council set out to 'persuade' the tenants into accepting new housing association properties in the Heygate area (with no security of tenure, more expensive rents and less controls over housing associations) or council properties outside their local district of Walworth. Council tenants were asked to find homes themselves through the council's Homesearch waiting list and bidding scheme (no mean feat!), and were given only six months to do so:

> '… it took six times because you know, if you don't accept any of the bidding you go back, you know, you go to the bottom again. But you know, I think I got mine after the third bidding.' (ex-Heygate council tenant who was displaced, interview, 2013)

Then the council began to issue eviction notices over the heads of those who failed to find their own council place or who had refused the council's offer of alternative housing.

Some tenants and leaseholders were offered flats in the nearby 'socially mixed' Strata Tower (newly constructed in 2010 at 147 metres tall, it is currently the tallest residential building in London; see Figure 8.3). Floors 2-10 and the adjacent three-floor pavilion of this new 'mixed', 'sustainable' high-rise (praised by Bill Clinton for its sustainable credentials as part of the Climate Positive Development Program of the Clinton Climate Initiative) is 'intermediate affordable housing' run by the Family Mosaic Housing Association. They offered part-rent, part-buy flats, and applicants needed to purchase at least 25 per cent of the flat, and also had to earn between £18,000-£60,000. The Strata Tower was the only retained-equity scheme offered, but the service charges alone were unaffordable to most former Heygate residents. The new housing association occupiers in the Strata include young professionals such

Figure 8.3: The Strata Tower, SE1

© SNAG

as teachers, a website manager, software development engineer and partner relationship manager and large numbers of Asian students (the Strata was advertised in Hong Kong) (McSweeney, 2013). All of the floors above floor 10 are for private owner-occupiers/tenants. Despite Southwark's Affordable Housing Supplementary Planning Document (SBC, 2008),[5] stating that 'housing should not reinforce social distinctions' (p 2) and that 'there should be no difference in the appearance and quality of affordable units and market units' (p 27), social distinctions are reinforced because the housing association and private residents have separate lifts! Moreover, how can separate lifts promote 'community cohesion and good relations between different groups', as Southwark's 2008 Planning Document specifies. A private resident from floor 14 interviewed by McSweeney (2013) said that they knew no one by name on the housing association floors, and were 'unlikely to talk to anyone' (p 31). Residents on the higher floors often used their flats as a base during the week when working in London, and had houses in places like Brighton that they returned to at the weekend, echoing the findings in Davidson and Lees (2005) about the lack of investment and interest these new residents have in their new, local community. Ironically, McSweeney (2013, p 33) found more social mixing among the housing association tenants because those flats were 'effectively owner-occupied' in contrast to the private flats where 'at least half' were rented out. In fact, when the Strata flats were being sold off plan, 75 per cent of the sales were to private investors as opposed to people buying who actually wanted to live in them. The Strata Tower is a symbolic indicator of the mixed community outcome. One leaseholder from the Heygate Estate who was offered a flat in the Strata Tower was given £150,000 for her three-bed flat on the Heygate Estate, but flats in the Strata Tower ranged from a studio flat at £240,000 to three-bed flats at £775,000. The two-bed penthouse is currently on the market for £1.6 million. Moreover, she had worked three jobs, seven days a week to pay off her mortgage, and saw her Right to Buy flat as an investment for her children. To buy in the Strata (or indeed elsewhere in London) she would need to get another mortgage – not easy on her low income and with insecure jobs and new mortgage restrictions – her life security and investment was consequently destroyed.

Only a small percentage of Heygate council tenants signed up for the 'right to return' (which means moving twice), some because they wanted to remain council tenants (even if it meant living elsewhere) – but the fact is the number will be smaller, as evidence from New Orleans shows[6] – once people have moved once and got their children into school and so on, they are loath to move again. In addition, a number of studies have underlined the difficulties that relocated public housing residents have in rebuilding social networks (see, for example, Clampet-Lunquist, 2004; Gibson, 2007), and this should come as no surprise given the many studies of displaced communities and social networks as a result of postwar slum clearance and urban renewal programmes (see Figure 8.4). A film was made about two tenants who were forced to move from the Heygate Estate (see southwarknotes.wordpress.com/heygate-estate – 'Janet and Larry Move Out' by King Chain Productions). It shows well the stress and upset that displacement causes. In 2009 the BBC's 'Inside Out' programme also featured displacement from the Heygate Estate (www.bbc.co.uk/insideout/content/articles/2009/03/05/london_heygate_s15_w8_video_feature.shtml). When the tenant mentioned earlier searching the Homesearch waiting list, who signed the

Figure 8.4: Social cleansing: the Heygate Estate

© Loretta Lees

'right to return', was asked: "And would you like to go back once it's finished, once it's completed?", she answered: "That one I'm not sure. Because I moved away from London and I'm in Kent … I had … friends when I was there but I lost contact … I still have their numbers but it's the distance and everything" (interview, 2013).

As mentioned earlier, leaseholders on the Heygate Estate were offered council buy-outs for their properties; these were below market value, but many caved in and left as the council tenants on the estate were quickly moved out. Adrian Glasspool was one of two leaseholders who held out on the mostly vacant and derelict Heygate Estate. He was offered £160,000 for his three-bed maisonette (an independent assessor valued it at £240,000). He said: "The council's surveyors disagreed with this … claiming that this is what similar properties on the Heygate and the soon to be demolished Aylesbury Estate had been selling for. Clearly, it is ridiculous to compare values with other properties that were earmarked for demolition." He refused to move. In what amounts to state Rachmanism[7] (see Figure 8.5) Southwark turned off the gas, electric and other utilities; he had no heat and ran a generator. While he is to be commended for asserting his right to stay put, unfortunately, he was forcibly evicted from his home of 16 years in November 2013.

The story is further complicated by so-called 'affordable housing'. Last year the London Tenants Federation (LTF) produced a document, *The affordable housing con* (LTF, 2012), showing that the government term 'affordable housing' used to refer to social rented, intermediate and affordable rent homes is deeply problematic. Indeed, the term is often used in mixed communities regeneration schemes to argue that councils/developers are building 'replacement' low-income housing, but as the LTF reveals, much of the housing coined as 'affordable' is out of reach of households earning even the median level of income in London – which stands

Figure 8.5: '21st century state Rachmanism' enacted by Southwark Council on the Heygate Estate

© Loretta Lees

at around £30,000 pa. The affordability issue that the LTF pointed to is in the process of being escalated by the rolling out of the Coalition government's benefit caps, Universal Credit and a 'Bedroom Tax' – it is likely that many households that had qualified for social rented housing in central and inner London will be unable to meet the cost of affordable market rents, even with access to benefits. State-led gentrification in London is in the process of being further escalated by these policies. Ironically, even Hamnett (2011) recognises this as the final block in the wall of gentrification for inner London. London Councils (2010) calculated that 15,000 people in London as a whole might lose their homes, and 67,000 might be at risk of eviction (9,900 alone could be forced from central London). Boris Johnson has called this 'Kosovo-style social cleansing' – not perhaps the best descriptor, but it does elicit the visceral and revanchist nature of the predicted population displacements. Johnson said that the 'great genius' of London is that it is a place 'where people of many different economic groups live together. The last thing we want to have in our city is a situation like Paris where the less well-off are pushed out to the suburbs' (see www.theguardian.com/housing-network/2011/aug/31/boris-johnson-london-plan-housing). But as the next section shows, this is a Mayor who continues to spout the mixed communities myth/rhetoric but who in reality has set about dismantling it.

The turn away from mixed communities policy in London

The turn away from mixed communities policy has not been a result of the critical evidence bases collected by academics such as those mentioned earlier; rather, it has been due to a change of government, a new London Mayor and the economic downturn triggered by the 2008 financial crisis. The major spending initiatives of the previous governments, including New Deal for Communities, have disappeared, and direct state intervention in the wellbeing of cities is no longer a government priority. The winning policy agenda of economic growth along with social justice (a mix of economic, social and environmental sustainability) has not, however, disappeared overnight, as Flint and Raco (2012) suggest; rather, it is fraying, gradually collapsing. The growth assumptions that underpinned urban planning and urban policies in the 1990s and 2000s have been undermined, but the moral rhetoric of mixed communities, diversity, social mixing and so on (see Lees, 2003) has not, as we see previously reflected in Boris Johnson's words. Mixed communities policy remains, for now, part of the 'new' London Plan and part of local authority policies and plans; the neoliberal policy orthodoxy (mindset) on mixed communities continues, but the mechanics of it are in a significantly (and increasingly) diluted form. This cynical, 'ideological mask' (see Žižek, 1989) is less interested in social justice and more interested in not losing this morally persuasive rhetoric to sell urban regeneration schemes to Londoners. The gradual withdrawal from mixed communities policy can already be seen in the new plans for the Heygate Estate, where the percentage of 'affordable' social housing to be built in the redevelopment has fallen from 35 to 25 per cent, and may yet drop further. There has also been withdrawal from building social housing in situ in new developments:

> Developers are now being allowed to buy their way out of having poorer people living in their new developments, for example, Southwark Council has recently taken £9 million from the builders of 197 flats behind the Tate Modern (the NEO Bankside development) rather than force them to sell 34 of the units to social housing providers, enabling the developer to build private homes for the rich alone. It seems then that the social experiment of using planning laws to mix communities across London is being abandoned by stealth. (Lees, 2013)

In 2013 the Coalition government removed the 'planning gain' requirement, forcing builders to include low-cost housing to get planning permission for their developments, and as outlined previously, developers can renegotiate their Section 106 requirements if they were signed before April 2010.[8] Local authorities and developers can now decide how many affordable homes they provide, and how many (or few) of them should be for social rent. In a nutshell, the scrapping of the London-wide target removes the only mechanism compelling developers to deliver affordable housing on individual sites across London. The changes are there for the next three years. The impact these changes will likely have on social inequality, social segregation and social mixing in the capital is profound.

Flint and Raco (2012, p 4) are right in arguing that as governments roll out austerity agendas, 'the principles and programmes that formed the heart of the postwar Keynesian welfare settlement have come under renewed attack, with significant implications for social justice and urban change.' One of these postwar Keynesian settlements – council housing and the benefits its tenants receive – has come under particular attack. The social housing budget was cut by 50 per cent, from £8.4 billion in 2007-10 to £4.4 billion 2011-14; in London the Mayor's initial proposal for a revised housing strategy (GLA, 2011) was to cut London's affordable housing budget by two-thirds (see www.london.gov.uk/sites/default/files/Revised%20Housing%20Strategy%20proposals.pdf). With housing policy now the responsibility of the Mayor, there was/is great pressure for Boris Johnson to bend regional and national policies. And interestingly, the Mayor's affordable housing policy does not sit well, and even conflicts with the new London Plan's overall strategy to create mixed communities. In the 'new' London Plan there has been a reduction in the overall proportion of affordable housing relative to market homes (a target of 39 per cent affordable homes, compared with the earlier 50 per cent target), and a shift between social and intermediate housing. On coming into office Boris Johnson made a point of attacking Ken Livingstone's 2004 policy that 50 per cent of all new residential developments across London should be affordable, and that 70 per cent of those should be for social rent. Indeed, the Mayor's 'new' London Plan (GLA, 2011) has not changed since Johnson first published his consultation draft in October 2009. Along with the government's housing and welfare policies, the new London Plan amounts to a wholesale attack on social housing and social segregation in London on an unprecedented scale. It is not socially sustainable.

We are clearly in a transitional, unstable phase where the core assumptions of the 1990s and 2000s are breaking down, where new forms of neo-Keynesianism are emerging and where there may, as I discuss below, be new opportunities for alternative, less growth-oriented agendas (see Raco, 2012). We have here both a complex dystopian and a utopian dialectic and future to get to grips with in urban studies.

Bottom-up fight for social sustainability: the case of the Southwark Notes Archive Group[9]

There are now hopes that the current crisis will open up new opportunities and possibilities for more socially just forms of urban sustainability (see, for example, Flint and Raco, 2012; Lees, 2013). But the social sustainability of communities appears to be increasingly dependent on private or individual resources in a context of major cutbacks in urban policy and other spending programmes. Sustainable development is entwined with the changing political and policy context of redistributing power, in which provision of goods, services and other material underpinnings for sustaining *people* is dependent, so government suggests, on the activities of individuals and local communities. Cameron (2009) describes this as 'galvanising, catalysing, prompting, encouraging and agitating for community engagement and social renewal.'

One community group that has galvanised, catalysed and agitated for social renewal is Southwark Notes Archive Group (SNAG), and their work makes for interesting 'reading' with respect to both the Coalition government's Localism Agenda and the recent proclamations in urban studies about 'the post-political city' (see, for example, Swyngedouw, 2007).

So what are the possibilities, as framed by the Coalition government and the 2011 London Plan, for the future sustainability of urban communities in London? The Coalition's Localism Act (DCLG, 2011) and the 'new' London Plan (GLA, 2011) came out in the same year, and on paper at least offer some possibilities for local communities, such as those in Southwark, faced with demolition and renewal. The Localism Act (2011)[10] sets out 'a series of measures with the potential to achieve a substantial and lasting shift in power away from central government and towards local people. They include: new freedoms and flexibilities for local government; new rights and powers for communities and individuals; reform to make the planning system more democratic and more effective, and reform to ensure that decisions about housing are taken locally' (DCLG, 2011). Significantly it introduced the possibility of 'Neighbourhood Plans' that allows local communities to shape new development by coming together to prepare their own plans. The 2011 London Plan is a mixed bag – there are possibilities: in particular, Opportunity Area Planning Frameworks (OAPFs), which are a joint production between the Mayor and the boroughs – these could be developed with a neighbourhood planning process at their heart. But there are problems, such as the weak provision for social rented housing in the plan, and the fact that it does not take account of the revised upwards London population forecasts, the economic crisis or changes in the benefits system.

SNAG are a group of local people in Southwark, totally independent of any political party or group, who are actively fighting what is going on in Southwark in the name of '*regeneration*'. They do not see regeneration as always a bad thing, but they do see it as a bad thing when local people's needs are 'only superficially understood and cared about' (see http://southwarknotes.wordpress.com). They are fighting for the retention of decent council housing (and in that, the 'right to stay put'), open spaces and local shops:

> Regeneration is always sold to us with the myth of the trickle-down theory of wealth creation. It's supposed to be in our interest as something might come our way. But what might come is always only mere crumbs from the table of those with the power and the money. Regeneration is often a forced and false consensus rather than a genuine public debate. Gentrification is never in our interest as it's the displacement of the original poorer inhabitants by wealthier ones. The result of this switch is always evictions for us, closure of local shops and amenities and deterioration of the communal life that is the lifeblood of us all. Where regeneration crosses over with gentrification is where the replacement of council estates with new mixed residential buildings results in a decrease in local social housing as land is sold off to private developers for profit. (http://southwarknotes.wordpress.com/where-we-are-coming-from)

SNAG's activities have been substantial. In addition to their anti-gentrification blog (see http://southwarknotes.wordpress.com), they have collated an archive that includes histories and notes on regeneration and gentrification in Southwark from 1900 to the present day – these are both online and hard copy material, and can be viewed in 56a InfoShop, a social centre (self-managed community space) in Walworth (see www.56a.org.uk). They have also organised a series of anti-gentrification walks (see Figure 8.6) over the last couple of years, walking around the sites of old and new gentrification in Southwark. In late 2012 they ran a full day workshop, 'The siege of the Elephant: convergence against the gentrification of the Elephant & Castle', bringing together locals, activists, academics and other researchers to share evidence and discuss alternatives to gentrification in Southwark. The morning was spent discussing displacement, the role of consultation and the spin of regeneration, and the afternoon focused on resistance – countering displacement, politicising consultation and proposing alternatives. 'The siege' was built on in a public engagement workshop at King's College London in early 2013, which considered the gentrification of council

Figure 8.6: SNAG's 2012 anti-gentrification walk

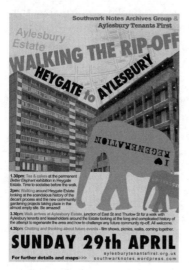

© SNAG

housing across London through the guise of mixed communities policy, and prioritised the full discussion of alternatives from community land trusts to cooperatives and Lifetime Neighbourhoods.[11]

In February 2013 members of SNAG were involved in the official representations made by Better Elephant and the Elephant Amenity Network to the Public Inquiry into the Compulsory Purchase Orders Southwark Council had issued to remaining Heygate leaseholders. The Planning Inspector, Wendy Fabian, looked through the evidence presented by Southwark Council, Lend Lease and local objectors – including Adrian Glasspool and the two other remaining tenants holding out on the Heygate Estate. The objectors argued that the Heygate scheme was not financially and socially viable, and that structurally sound social housing units were being replaced with very few social units in the new development. They argued that the redevelopment plans were not economically, socially or environmentally sustainable, and that 70 per cent of residents had been in favour of refurbishment rather than demolition (see http://betterelephant. org/images/HeygateCPOStatementOfCaseFinal.pdf). On the first day of the Public Inquiry, recognising the strength of feeling about the Heygate scandal, the council, fearful of trouble, provided elaborate crowd control measures that turned out not to be necessary. On the second morning of this lengthy Public Inquiry the Planning Inspector chose to visit the estate for herself with the objectors and council officers; she walked around the estate surrounded by private security and followed by a car!

The work of SNAG, and indeed other groups such as Better Elephant[12] and the Elephant Amenity Network, demonstrates the problematical nature of the 'post-political city' thesis (on post-political correctness, see Lees, 2013). Advocates of the post-political city and the post-democratic city argue that the city has become moribund as a site of public political encounter, democratic debate and radical dissent. The political has disappeared in the face of a city colonised by policy and the police (polic(y)ing) (see Rancière, 1998; Žižek, 2006). Proper urban politics, according to post-political commentators such as Swyngedouw (2008), fosters dissent, creates disagreement and triggers the debating of, and experimentation with, more egalitarian and inclusive urban futures. The activities of SNAG are, I would argue, proper urban politics. Their blog, anti-gentrification walks and their involvement in the Public Inquiry are all a form of urban intervention, radical resistance and proper urban politics. The political is not dead! In fact, in London it seems that anti-gentrification activity is not only alive and well (contra post-political commentators and gentrification authors such as Hackworth and Smith, 2001) – it is growing, gathering more support and getting more vocal. As we speak there are anti-gentrification activities across the organising spectrum – from Just Space (http://londonjustspace.wikispaces.com), LTF (www.londontenants.org), Defend Council Housing (www.defendcouncilhousing.org.uk), to squatting to fight gentrification and reclaim regeneration (see Self Organised London Social Space – www.facebook.com/selforganiselondon) to a 'right to the city' campaign being set up in London but with UK coverage (see www.righttothecity.org.uk).

Inner London is damned if they do mixed communities policy and damned if they don't…

The state-led gentrification and social cleansing of the final gentrification frontiers in inner London – both council estates and low-income tenants – has been ongoing since the late 1990s and continues today (see Lees, 2013). In London, poor and increasingly marginalised council tenants have borne, and are still bearing, the brunt of mixed communities policy. This is not sustainability – as outlined in the introduction to this chapter, sustainability is based on the idea that 'marginal and poor groups should not disproportionately bear the costs of public or private activities or policies' (Manzi et al, 2010, p 9). But since 2008, mixed communities policy has come up against both a severe economic downturn and a change of government. In addition, land and property values in London have continued to grow, unlike in the rest of the UK, driven directly and through ripple effects by demand coming from abroad. The result is that social sustainability is all but dead in London. There is no longer the money or national political interest in mixed communities (although there is residual local authority interest because they know that they have to *sell* urban redevelopment to their local communities). At play is both the *dilution* of low-income groups through neighbourhood densification and the building of housing for owner-occupiers in place of council housing, and also *displacement* – either through displacement into other social housing in the same borough or within other London boroughs (usually meaning they lose their secure tenancy status), or, as is increasingly the case, displacement to outside of London – often to other low-income areas in the South East, to places in Kent or even to small towns in the North of England. Add the new government benefit caps into this mix, and my prediction is that inner London will end up being an 'embarras de richesses', as Ruth Glass predicted in 1964. The fact is that London's final gentrification frontiers continue to face large-scale gentrification and displacement with or without mixed communities policy – they seem damned either way.

As such, contra Butler (2007) this chapter shows that any study of gentrification in London cannot divorce itself from the study of working-class/low-income population displacement, or class conflict. As Paul Watt (2008, p 209) has argued: 'The contemporary multi-ethnic London working class does not have as pronounced a class identity as its post-war Fordist equivalent[...]. However, it is present, not just as the demonic, phantasmic "other" in urban middle-class imaginations, but also in reality in the workplaces, schools and housing estates of the metropolis.' As Fuller (2012, p 914) argues, there needs to be a 'far greater engagement with the governance and politics of state-led gentrification, since this is the terrain in which decision-making ultimately produces gentrification, displacement and injustices.'

The sustainability agenda in London (as elsewhere) is the epitome of the post-political (Swyngedouw, 2007), and it simply sustains the status quo – uneven development and social inequality (Harvey, 2005), but like Davidson (2009, p 609), I would argue that if we ask the question 'what society do we want to sustain?', then a reconsideration of the 'social' offers a potential site for a progressive metropolitan politics. There needs to be much better debate around social sustainability and what it might offer London. McKenzie (2004, p 12) defines social sustainability as 'a life-enhancing condition *within* communities, and a process *within* communities that can achieve that condition' (emphasis added) In this guise social sustainability must be bottom-up and not top-down; it must be generated by communities, not government, local authorities or developers. It must restore politics over market forces, but it must also know what kind of society it wants to create and sustain. We need alternatives, because sustainability and social justice do not go hand in hand (Marcuse, 1998).

One (quite radical in the face of this 'new' urban renewal) alternative would be to refurbish these estates, most of which are structurally sound. At the Public Inquiry on the Heygate Estate, its original architect Tim Tinker and Twentieth-Century Society director (see www.c20society.org.uk/author/catherinecroft) Catherine Croft, both expert witnesses, both told the Planning Inspector that the Heygate Estate could easily be refurbished and brought up to 21st-century standards of insulation. In 2012 the global architectural consulting firm Gensler produced an entry for the Building Trust International HOME competition (focused on providing residents most at risk in developed cities with a safe place to live), showing that it would be possible to refurbish the Heygate Estate for just £14,000 per unit – costing in total less than half of what it has already cost Southwark Council just to empty the estate. Given that this is just marginally above the £13,000 grant available under the HCA (Homes and Community Agency) Empty Homes Grant Programme, this would be very appropriate for a community-led regeneration scheme on the Heygate Estate (and indeed elsewhere). The Gensler Heygate entry won an honourable mention in the competition; SNAG advertised this fact on their blog, but were asked by Gensler to remove the competition slides. Gensler are now working with Lend Lease (the new Heygate developers) on its new £1.3 billion commercial district on the edge of the Olympic Park in Stratford City.

Anne Power (2008) has considered the main social, economic and environmental benefits of refurbishment as compared to demolition in relation to the social issues of housing need and fuel poverty. Her conclusion was that refurbishment and infill building is more socially acceptable, cheaper and creates far lower environmental impact; it also reduces fuel poverty. Power is clear that the overall balance of evidence suggests that refurbishment makes more sense on the basis of time, cost, community impact, prevention of sprawl, reuse of existing infrastructure and the protection of existing communities. In conclusion, I want to argue very strongly that the refurbishment of council estates in London (many of which are structurally sound) could both upgrade council housing and keep low-income communities in place. Jane Jacobs (1961) stood up to the bulldozer and postwar urban renewal in New York City; it is time now for critical urbanists to stand up to the bulldozer and the 'new' urban renewal/state-led gentrification in London too.

Notes

[1] This was the 2009 figure; it is no doubt larger now.

[2] Rather than 'studentification' we have 'universification'!

[3] Some of the research presented in this chapter was funded by the 2012 Antipode Activist Scholar Award for a project titled 'Challenging "the new urban renewal": gathering the tools necessary to halt the social cleansing of council estates and developing community-led alternatives for sustaining existing communities'; the co-investigators were the London Tenants Federation (LTF), SNAG and Just Space. This project is collating data on gentrification induced displacement from four council estates in inner London being 'regenerated' as mixed communities (Heygate, Aylesbury, Pepys and Carpenters), and helping tenants on some of the estates to fight the process of gentrification (see Lees et al, 2013).

[4] See www.corporatewatch.org/?lid=4635 on the corrupt processes issued by Lend Lease.

[5] See www.southwark.gov.uk/downloads/download/2245/affordable_housing_spd

[6] Government reports confirm that half of the working poor, older people and people with disabilities who lived in New Orleans before Katrina have not returned. Read Arena (2012) on the transformation of New Orleans public housing from public to private.

[7] See Lees et al (2008, p 14) on Rachmanism in London in the 1960s.

[8] Section 106 agreements can be waived for sites where the Planning Inspectorate assesses that the affordable housing requirement has rendered the whole project unviable (www.gov.uk/government/publications/section-106-affordable-housing-requirements-review-and-appeal).

[9] There are other important groups too, such as Better Elephant and the Elephant Amenity Network. I focus here on SNAG because I got to know them better during the research project.

[10] See www.local.gov.uk/localism-act

[11] These events were both linked to the Antipode project.

[12] Better Elephant set up a form of guerrilla gardening called the 'Heygate Regeneration Scheme' (see http://now-here-this.timeout.com/2011/11/07/guerilla-gardening-elephant-and-castle%E2%80%99s-heygate-estate).

References

Arbaci, S. and Rae, I. (2013) 'Mixed-tenure neighbourhoods in London: policy myth or effective device to alleviate deprivation?', *International Journal of Urban and Regional Research*, vol 37, no 2, pp 451-79.

Arena, J. (2012) *Driven from New Orleans: how non-profits betray public housing and promote privatization*, Minneapolis, MN: University of Minnesota Press.

Beauregard, R. (2005) 'Introduction: institutional reforms', *Planning Theory*, vol 4, no 3, pp 203-7.

Bridge, G., Butler, T. and Lees, L. (eds) (2011) *Mixed communities: gentrification by stealth?*, Bristol: Policy Press.

Buck, N., Gordon, I., Hall, P., Harloe, M. and Kleinman, M. (2002) *Working capital: life and labour in contemporary London*, London: Routledge.

Butler, T. (2007) 'For gentrification?', *Environment and Planning A*, vol 39, pp 162-81.

Butler, T., Hamnett, C. and Ramsden, M. (2008) 'Inward and upward? Marking out social class change in London 1981-2001', *Urban Studies*, vol 45, no 2, pp 67-88.

Cameron, D. (2009) 'The Big Society', Hugo Young Memorial Lecture, 10 November [transcript: www.respublica.org.uk/item/ResPublica-mentioned-in-Camerons-speech-ggtc].

Campkin,B. (2013) *Remaking London: decline and regeneration in urban culture*, London: I.B. Tauris.

Cheshire, P. (2009) 'Policies for mixed communities: faith-based displacement activity?', *International Regional Science Review*, vol 32, no 3, pp 343-75.

Cisneros, H. and Engdahl, L. (eds) (2009) *From despair to hope: HOPE VI and the new promise of public housing in America's cities*, Washington, DC: Brookings Institution Press.

Clampet-Lunquist, S. (2004) 'HOPE VI relocation: moving to new neighborhoods and building new ties', *Housing Policy Debate*, vol 15, pp 415-48.

Davidson, M. (2008) 'Spoiled mixture – where does state-led "positive" gentrification end?', *Urban Studies*, vol 45, pp 2385-405.

Davidson, M. (2009) 'Social sustainability: a potential for politics?', *Local Environment*, vol 14, no 7 pp 607-19.

Davidson, M. (2010) 'Love thy neighbour? Interpreting social mixing in London's gentrification frontiers', *Environment and Planning A*, vol 42, no 3, pp 524-44.

Davidson, M. and Lees, L. (2005) 'New build "gentrification" and London's riverside renaissance', *Environment and Planning A*, vol 37, no 7, pp 1165-90.

Davidson, M. and Lees, L. (2010) 'New build gentrification: its histories, trajectories, and critical geographies', *Population, Space and Place*, vol 16, pp 395-411.

DCLG (Department for Communities and Local Government) (2006a) *Strong and prosperous communities, the Local Government White Paper*, Cm 6939-I, London: DCLG.

DCLG (2006b) *Planning policy statement 3: housing*, London: DCLG.

DCLG (2011) *A plain English guide to the Localism Act* (www.gov.uk/government/uploads/system/uploads/attachment_data/file/5959/1896534.pdf).

DETR (Department for Environment, Transport and the Regions) (1998) *Circular 6/98: Planning and affordable housing*, London: DETR.

Flint, J. and Raco, M. (2012) (eds) *The future of sustainable cities: critical reflections*, Bristol: Policy Press.

Fuller, C. (2012) '"Worlds of justification" in the politics and practices of urban regeneration', *Environment and Planning D: Society and Space*, vol 30, pp 913-29.

Gibson, K. (2007) 'The relocation of the Columbia Villa community: views from residents', *Journal of Planning Education and Research*, vol 27, no 1, pp 5-19.

GLA (Greater London Authority) (2004) *The London Plan: Spatial Development Strategy for Greater London*, London: Mayor of London, GLA.

GLA (2011) *The London Plan*, London: Mayor of London, GLA.

GLA, Mayor of London, (2008) *The London Plan: Spatial Development Strategy for Greater London* (consolidated with Alterations since 2004), London: GLA.

GLA, Mayor of London, (2009) *The London Plan: Spatial Development Strategy for Greater London (draft replacement)*, London: GLA.

Glass, R. (1964) 'Introduction: aspects of change', in Centre for Urban Studies (ed) *London: aspects of change*, London: MacKibbon & Kee, pp xiii-xxiii.

Hackworth, J. and Smith, N. (2001) 'The changing state of gentrification', *Tijdschrift voor Economische en Sociale Geografie*, vol 22, pp 464-77.

Hamnett, C. (1994) 'Socio-economic change in London: professionalisation not polarization', *Built Environment,* vol 20, no 3, pp 192-203.

Hamnett, C. (2003) 'Gentrification and the middle-class remaking of Inner London, 1961-2001', *Urban Studies*, vol 40, no 12, pp 2401-26.

Hamnett, C. (2011) 'The reshaping of the British welfare system and its implications for geography and geographers', *Progress in Human Geography*, vol 35, no 2, pp 147-52.

Harvey, D. (2005) *A brief history of neoliberalism*, Oxford: Oxford University Press.

Imrie, R., Lees, L. and Raco, M. (eds) (2009) *Regenerating London: governance, sustainability and community in a global city*, London: Routledge.

Jacobs, J. (1961) *The death and life of Great American cities*, New York: Vintage.

Kearns, A. and Turok, I. (2004) *Sustainable communities: dimensions and challenges*, ESRC/ODPM Postgraduate Research Programme, Working Paper 1, London: Office of the Deputy Prime Minister.

Lees, L. (2003) 'Visions of "urban renaissance": the Urban Task Force Report and the Urban White Paper', in R. Imrie and M. Raco (eds) *Urban renaissance? New Labour, community and urban policy*, Bristol: Policy Press, pp 61-82.

Lees, L. (2008) 'Gentrification and social mixing: towards an inclusive urban renaissance?', *Urban Studies*, vol 45, no 12, pp 2449-70.

Lees, L. (2013) 'The urban injustices of New Labour's "new urban renewal": the case of the Aylesbury Estate in London', *Antipode*.

Lees, L., Slater, T. and Wyly, E. (2008) *Gentrification*, New York: Routledge.

Lees, L., Just Space, LTF (London Tenants Federation) and SNAG (Southwark Notes Archive Group) (2013) 'Challenging "the new urban renewal": the social cleansing of council estates in London', in B. Campkin, D. Roberts and R. Ross (eds) *Urban Pamphleteer #2 'London: regeneration realities'*, London: Urban Lab, University College London, pp 6-10.

Littig, B. and Griessler, E. (2005) 'Social sustainability: a catchword between political pragmatism and social theory', *International Journal for Sustainable Development*, vol 8, no 1/2, pp 65-79.

London Councils (2010) *The impact of Housing Benefit changes in London – analysis of findings from a survey of Landlords in London*, London: London Councils.

London's Poverty Profile (2011) 'Income inequalities by wards within London boroughs', *London's Poverty Profile 2011* (www.londonspovertyprofile.org.uk/indicators/topics/inequality/income-inequalities-within-london-boroughs).

LTF (London Tenants Federation) (2012) *The affordable housing con* (www.londontenants.org/publications/reports/LTF%20-%20afordable%20housing%20con%20final%20xxx.pdf).

Manzi, T., Lucas, K., Lloyd-Jones, T. and Allen, J. (eds) (2010) *Social sustainability in urban areas: communities, connectivity and the urban fabric*, London: Routledge.

Marcuse, P. (1998) 'Sustainability is not enough', *Environment and Urbanization*, vol 10, no 2, pp 103-11.

McKenzie, S. (2004) *Social sustainability: towards some definitions*, Hawke Research Institute Working Paper Series, No 27, Magill, South Australia: University of Southern Australia.

McNeill, D. (2002) 'Livingstone's London: left politics and the world city', *Regional Studies*, vol 36, pp 75-80.

McSweeney, A. (2013) 'Social mixing? The Strata Tower, Elephant & Castle', Unpublished undergraduate dissertation, Department of Geography, King's College London.

ODPM (Office of the Deputy Prime Minister) (2003a) *Sustainable communities: building for the future*, London: ODPM.

ODPM (2003b) *Improving the delivery of affordable housing in London and the South East*, London: ODPM.

Polese, M. and Stren, R. (eds) (2000) *The social sustainability of cities: diversity and the management of change*, Toronto: University of Toronto Press.

Power, A. (2008) 'Does demolition or refurbishment of old and inefficient homes help to increase our environmental, social and economic viability?', *Energy Policy,* vol 36, pp 4487-501.

Raco, M. (2005) 'Sustainable development, rolled-out neoliberalism and sustainable communities', *Antipode,* vol 37, no 2, pp 324-47.

Raco, M. (2012) 'A growth agenda without growth: English spatial policy, sustainable communities, and the death of the neo-liberal project?', *Geojournal,* vol 77, no 2, pp 153-65.

Rancière, J. (1998) *Disagreement,* Minneapolis, MN: University of Minnesota Press.

SBC (Southwark Borough Council) (2008) *Affordable housing supplementary planning document,* London: SBC.

SBC (2011a) *London Borough of Southwark, Elephant & Castle supplementary planning document baseline information* (www.southwark.gov.uk/download/downloads/id/7058/baseline_information_background_paper).

SBC (2011b) *LDF core strategy,* adopted April 2011 (www.southwark.gov.uk/news/article/304/core_strategy_adopted).

Smith, N. (1996) *The new urban frontier: gentrification and the revanchist city,* London and New York: Routledge.

Swyngedouw, E. (2007) 'Impossible "sustainability" and the postpolitical condition', in R. Krueger and D. Gibbs (eds) *The sustainable development paradox: urban political economics in the United States and Europe,* London: Guilford Press, pp 13-40.

Swyngedouw, E. (2008) *Where is the political?* (www.socialsciences.manchester.ac.uk/disciplines/politics/research/hmrg/activities/documents/Swyngedouw.pdf).

Wacquant, L. (2008) *Urban outcasts: a comparative sociology of advanced marginality,* Cambridge: Polity Press.

Watt, P. (2008) 'The only class in town? Gentrification and the middle-class colonization of the city and the urban imagination', *International Journal of Urban and Regional Research,* vol 32, no 1, pp 206-11.

Watt, P. (2009) 'Housing stock transfers, regeneration and state-led gentrification in London', *Urban Policy and Research,* vol 27, no 3, pp 229-42.

Williamson, T., Imbroscio, D. and Gar, A. (2003) *Making a place for community: local democracy in a global era,* New York: Routledge.

Žižek, S. (1989) *The sublime object of ideology,* London: Verso.

Žižek, S. (2006) *The parallax view,* Cambridge, MA: The MIT Press.

NINE

From supermarkets to community building: Tesco PLC, sustainable place-making and urban regeneration

Rob Imrie and Mike Dolton

Introduction

The development and delivery of urban regeneration occurs through a panoply of organisations and governance arrangements, and has never been confined to any particular organisational type or context. While state-led, and publically funded, initiatives have been in the vanguard of regeneration, a whole mix of public and private institutions are key to facilitating outcomes, including major corporate organisations. This is particularly so in relation to retail-led regeneration, in which companies, such as Asda, Ikea and Tesco, are diversifying the portfolio of their activities by becoming increasingly active in commercial property development. For instance, in May 2012, Tesco completed the first phase of 94 affordable homes on behalf of Islington and Shoreditch Housing Association in London. The development is part of an 11-acre regeneration scheme that is expected to deliver 253 owner-occupied homes, 10 industrial units and 10 retail units anchored by a 38,000ft^2 Tesco store.

This development is not an isolated example, but is part of a broader phenomenon of retail organisations' involvement in urban regeneration, in ways that go beyond expanding existing store capacity or creating a new facility. One development, Strand East in Stratford, London, is occurring on land owned by Ikea. A recent planning application submitted by their development company, LandProps Holdings, is for 1,200 homes, a 350-bed hotel, office space, bars and restaurants. It has been described as a 'proto-type' town that is replicating 'historic, chic downtown neighborhoods' (Garun, 2012, p 1). Likewise, in the City of Bath, Sainsbury's has outlined plans to expand its existing 40,000ft^2 flagship store to 60,000ft^2, construct 300 new homes, with a mix of affordable and family housing, and provide offices, while rejuvenating underused land around a waterfront area. For Tim Watkins (2011), Sainsbury's development manager, 'this is not just Sainsbury's we are talking about, this is a whole regeneration project.'

The propensity for corporate retail companies to engage in urban regeneration, beyond the provision of store capacity, is significant in an economic context characterised by public expenditure cuts, and the dismantling by the Coalition government of urban policy programmes put in place by previous, New Labour, administrations. For some commentators, retail organisations can provide the resources and skills to uplift declining areas, redolent of philanthropic behaviour or self-help that may reduce the pressure on government to commit scarce public resources (see Lowe, 2005; Guy, 2008). For others, corporate retailers are motivated by, primarily, self-interest, and their involvement in urban regeneration is no more than a quid pro quo, or a means to lever store expansion (Friends of the Earth, 2006). The consensus view is, however, that retail organisations are significant in increasingly shaping the social and economic fortunes of places, and an important player in the politics of urban change (Lowe, 2005; Guy, 2008).

This view draws attention to Scherer and Palazzo's (2011) comments about the paucity of research about corporate activity in complex networks of governance. As they suggest, there is a need for better understanding of the public role of private organisations, including the political nature of business and its impacts on people and places. In seeking to build on their observation, we refer to a case study of a Tesco-led regeneration in Bromley-by-Bow (BB) in East London. We assess the company's involvement in influencing the politics and governance of urban policy programmes relating to regeneration in the locale. The case illustrates the blurring of boundaries between the economic and political activities of Tesco, and the significance of an enlarged role for private organisations in the provision of public infrastructure and related goods and services. This enlargement, at face value, is redolent of Deetz's (1992) thesis about the corporate colonisation of public life propagating regeneration dominated by particularist interests.

Such interests are not solely of Tesco's making but part of a broader political environment, characterised by a multiplicity of public and private actors involved in the propagation of post-democratic formations. We explore the co-construction of a political consensus relating to the regeneration of BB, and the attempt, by development partners, to neuter opposition to what were, in effect, partisan, property-led, proposals by Tesco. While Tesco and partners sought to propagate a post-political reading of the plans for BB, as part of a stakeholder politics allegedly inclusive of, and responsive to, the broadcloth of interests, the subsequent failure of the scheme to materialise highlights the potency of politics and the indeterminate nature of urban regeneration. While not underestimating the significance of corporate organisation to shape places, Tesco's involvement in BB's regeneration draws attention to the power of contingent socio-institutional relations in the (re)production of places.

Corporate governance and the politics of urban regeneration

A significant element of successful urban regeneration is seen as the involvement of the private sector in bringing their skills and resources to bear on the reconstruction of cities. Since the early 1980s, a political rhetoric about privatism has emerged in policy statements about regeneration, with successive government ministers extolling the virtues of private sector-led interventions. In a context of austerity, and declining public resources, private investment is often the only solution, or so it seems, in bringing land and buildings back into use, and opportunities have opened up for organisations not commonly thought of as serving a regeneration function. Wrigley et al (2002), for example, note how the resources of major retail companies may be made available by local authorities to redevelop declining district centres that many other types of investors might be unwilling to invest in. They identify Tesco as the most active supermarket chain in targeting the potential of the 'regeneration agenda' to expand its market share.

There are benefits in encouraging such activity, and Neate (2011) describes a Tesco-led regeneration in Toxteth, Liverpool, an area of high unemployment, high crime rates, and, historically, unattractive to inward investors. Tesco's investment was one of the largest ever in the area by a private company, creating 300 jobs and providing a third of these for people out of work for more than six months. Such investments, by Tesco and others, are increasingly part of mixed-use developments. Some see this as indicative of a corporate takeover of regeneration, involving diminution of public control and the propagation of property-led development promoting, first and foremost, the commercialisation of space. For others, private corporate involvement in regeneration is a welcome, and inevitable, part of post-austerity, by permitting organisations with key skills and resources to contribute to city building, while simultaneously enabling public authorities to reduce spending as part of debt management.

The involvement of Tesco, and other corporate organisations, in urban regeneration may be understood as part as part of broader shifts in governance, in which the state continues to withdraw from the provision of physical infrastructure, goods and services. A significant literature documents the reduced role of public authorities in shaping urban regeneration, and the rise of private involvement in, and control over, place-making (Boyle, 1999; Jessop, 2002; MacLeod, 2011; MacLeod and Jones, 2011). This, for Swyngedouw (2010, p 3), is 'governance beyond the state', characterised by the broadening of actors involved in urban governance, but also a narrowing of regeneration agendas, or what is deemed a permissible part of city building. This is the pursuit of economic growth by putting into place strategies to (re)commodify land and property markets, a policy orientation that Swyngedouw (2010, p 3) describes as enabling 'the imperatives of a globally connected neo-liberalised market economy' to emerge.

Such imperatives include the redirection of regeneration policy from redistributive objectives to investment in land and property, and encouragement of private sector entrepreneurship to facilitate job and wealth creation. Part of the process appears to be generating a political consensus about the efficacy of economic growth, in which the management of dissent, or counterviews to the propagation of a 'growth first' agenda, appears to be paramount. Observers suggest that contemporary urban politics is notable for the side-lining of political engagement, in which stakeholder engagement seeks to stifle views that run counter to the hegemony of privatism and land and property commodification (Rancière, 2001; Crouch, 2004; Butler and Ntseng, 2008). The outcome, so it is alleged, is a post-politics or the absence of overt political dissent in which, for

Swyngedouw (2010, p 4), urban governance is akin to oligarchic rule 'in which political power seamlessly fuses with economic might.'

While this is an insightful reading into the politics of urban regeneration, it does not capture, entirely, the specific, and situated, relations of corporate involvement in city building. As the case of BB will show, there is no necessary relationship between 'political power' and 'economic might'; the one does not necessarily entail the other. Nor is it clear, in the BB case and in other examples of regeneration, that an instrumental, managerial politics has superseded political, and politicised, engagement. Here, we concur with Gill et al (2012, p 509) that it is never possible to foreclose political contestation, and that, at best, post-politics, as a way of conceptualising contemporary urban politics, may fail to capture, and explain, the many local disputes and political subventions that are a recurrent feature of social struggles relating to people's rights to the city (see also Lees, 2013). Thus, from civil strife in Middle Eastern cities, to anti-gentrification movements in places such as Berlin and New York, urban political protests are a manifold, and manifest, part of cities.

This understanding disrupts notions that urban development is unilinear or is part of an undisputed neoliberalising project. However, much of the urban political literature, from the seminal work of Peterson (1981) onwards, seems to (re)produce an understanding of city politics as at the behest of corporate organisations and, in Swyngedouw's (2010, p 3) terms, is shaping 'consensually … the city according to the dreams, tastes and needs of the transnational economic, political, and cultural elites' (see also Mayer, 2006). Others interpret regeneration, including corporate capture of state instruments, as part of a market logic process. This is one whereby space shaping is a reflection of corporate power that, in Brenner and Theodore's (2002) terms, is the restructuring of urban space or the (re)production of a global competitive order (see also Swyngedouw, 2010). The outcome, so some suggest, is urban ubiquity characterised by the diminution of the public realm and the rise of privatised place-making.

The case of BB illustrates regeneration processes that do not necessarily accord with some of the totalising accounts of urban political analyses, outlined above. The complexity of socio-institutional relations in the BB area does not permit one to read, or understand, regeneration as derivative of, necessarily, neoliberalism's hegemony, or seeking to shape spaces for a corporate class. Rather, following McGuirk and Dowling (2009), and recent interventions by authors such as Peck et al (2013), we concur that pre-constituted theoretical frameworks, seeking to explain regeneration, need to be avoided or, otherwise, sensitised to the contingent pathways that shape development processes. Tesco's involvement in BB is not part of a master stratagem to 'neoliberalise' the locale; nor is it nurturing a post-politics where *all* dissent to its plans is absent or suppressed. Rather, Tesco's uneven insertion into the development politics of BB is illustrative of a highly charged, political process of urban transformation.

Regeneration and the (post-)politics of shaping places: the case of Bromley-by-Bow

The rest of this chapter is based on a discussion and analysis of the development proposals for a 4.6-hectare site located in BB in the London Borough of Tower Hamlets (LBTH). We document the intricate, micro, socio–institutional relations involved in the development of a spatial, place-making strategy for the site, and the role, and significance, of the major corporate organisation, Tesco, in seeking to shape both the process and outcomes. The data highlight how private sector, corporate, organisation and public sector state formations are conjoined in regeneration, in ways whereby the latter is often invoked in the service of the former. Tesco's involvement in BB is illustrative of how, privatised neoliberal values, or those propagating the commodification of land and buildings, may be deployed as part of a process to (re)define what the public interest is or ought to be, albeit a process that is highly uneven and contradictory.

The focus of our discussion is depicted in Figures 9.1 and 9.2 that outline the broader development locale and the BB site. On the eastern part of the BB site is the River Lea, and the southern part is occupied by two companies, TRAD Scaffolding (TS) and Crowley Ltd, overlooking a major arterial route, the A12. The north portion of the site is occupied by a Tesco store that opened in 1983, and a Tesco-owned petrol station and service yard. The store is 6,360m^2 in size, and in July 2011, it had a net sales area of 3,300m^2 for convenience shopping. The locale has, historically, been defined by its manufacturing and working-class roots, in which rapid deindustrialisation has led to high unemployment of more than twice the national average. This is part of a legacy described by the Greater London Authority (GLA) (2007, p 1) as 'derelict industrial land and poor housing ... land is fragmented and divided by waterways, overhead pylons, roads, and railways.'

Up until the late 1990s the site had been protected as an industrial employment area (see Figure 9.1). In the 1998 Tower Hamlets Unitary Development Plan (LBTH, 1998, para 4.3), it was stated that 'development will not normally be permitted in the vicinity of an existing industrial use where it is felt to be incompatible with that use and may give rise to pressure to curtail the industrial use.' However, by the early 2000s, rumours about the development of an Olympic Park in the vicinity, as part of London's bid for the 2012 Olympic Games, were part of a context whereby interest in the commercial redevelopment of the site intensified. In 2004 and 2006, TS submitted planning applications that were subsequently unsuccessful, including the 2004 version for a mixed-use scheme, including 478 dwellings, offices and retail.[1] This was followed by the production of a masterplan by LBTH, supportive of non-industrial development, and later, in January 2010, a planning application by Tesco was submitted for a scheme comprising a hotel, 454 residential units and a doubling in size of their existing store.

Figure 9.1: The development site

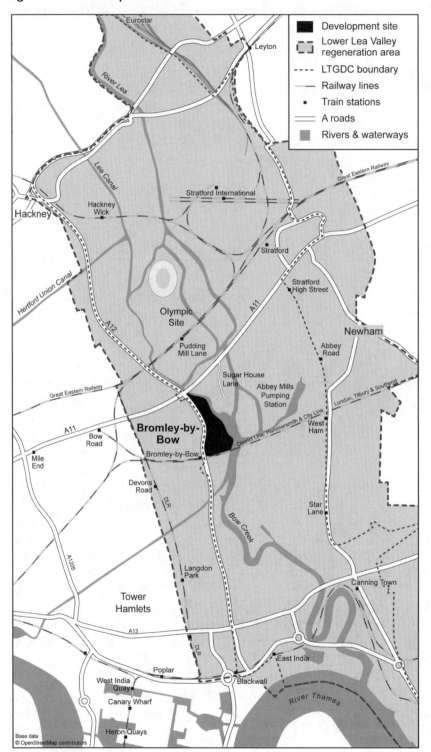

Source: Jenny Kynaston, Royal Holloway University of London using Open Street Map

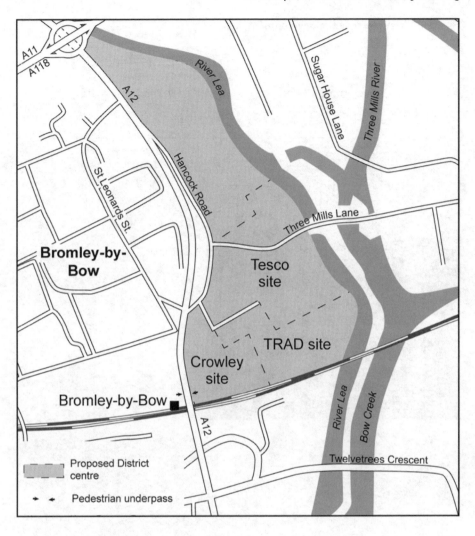

In seeking to understand Tesco's involvement in shaping the discourse of urban regeneration in BB, and, by implication, the interrelationships between corporate organisation and place-making, we conducted a 12-month study between February 2011 and January 2012, and it comprised two stages. The first was the collection of documents relating to the site's development history, including planning applications, the LBTH masterplan, planning inquiry reports, Tesco's statement of community engagement and numerous planning committee reports. The second stage was interviews with 14 key actors, including planners from LBTH, local councillors, the architects of Tesco's scheme, Collado Collins, Tesco's planning consultants, GL Hearn, and other development organisations, such as London Thames Gateway Development Corporation (LTGDC) and Leaside Regeneration Company (LRC). We also spoke with members from the local community, including residents and local activists.

Figure 9.2: Views across the development site

Figure (a) shows the existing Tesco store; (b) the Trad Scaffolding site; (c) depicts some of the industrial dereliction that typify lands and buildings adjacent to the site
© Rob Imrie

Figure (a)

Figure (b)

Figure (c)

The rest of the discussion is divided into three parts. First, we explore the significance of the (re)production of a spatial discourse of/about BB that, over a short time period, became part of the re-imagining of the locale's regeneration potential. This was the supplanting of its industrial heritage and commitment to enhancement of its manufacturing base and, instead, the propagation of a property-led vision entailing the commercialisation of local land and property markets. The scenario is a familiar one in regeneration, premised on what Harvey (2001, p 208) describes as the deployment of 'certain kinds of geographical knowledge' that renders what was previously impermissible as permissible. In the instance of BB, we highlight the role of state agents in the (re)production of discourse amenable to a neoliberalising logic of regeneration, and the subsequent changes in the socio-legal basis of planning and policy frameworks that altered, fundamentally, the understanding of what sustainable place-making is or ought to be.

Second, we outline the manufacturing of consent for Tesco's proposals, based on a process that, while appearing to broaden the sphere of governing, was, in the BB context, seeking to foreclose the possibilities for openly democratic decision making and outcome. Here, we refer to consultative practices, by Tesco and partners, as part of an endeavour to create a context for its development proposals to be conceived as rational and opportune, and commensurate with the interests of both local and London-wide constituents. Core to the process was the deployment of a stakeholder politics, or the formation of 'public opinion' by a collectivity of consensual partners, organised around Tesco's use of consultative techniques that did not encourage divergent viewpoints. While the process appears to be redolent of a post-politics, the data indicate that Tesco's management of dissent was never complete or wholly successful, as evidenced by the conflicts that broke out between the retailer and other local landowners.

Third, we consider the role of public instruments, including judicial process, in underpinning privatised property development, and in this instance, the sponsorship by a public authority of a Compulsory Purchase Order (CPO) to enable Tesco to be handed ownership of the BB site. While the CPO was sponsored by an unelected, ostensibly state or public organisation, that, theoretically, had the powers to side-step democratic scrutiny or controls, the subsequent failure for the CPO to be granted draws attention to the political, contested nature of the site's development. The CPO process was messy and indeterminate, hardly post-political, and the outcome, Tesco's failure to secure ownership of the site, highlights the potency of state, juridical interventions in shaping urban political relations. The failure of the process draws attention not only to the judicialisation of urban politics, but also to McGuirk and Dowling's (2009, p 176) observation, that neoliberal development 'has no unitary logic nor realizable state of completion.'

(Re)representing regeneration in Bromley-by-Bow

A focus of critical attention in urban studies is the politics of regeneration and the discourses of space and sustainable place-making. Integral to regeneration is the propagation of partial, or particular, geographical knowledges that, in and through their representations of place, may serve to naturalise urban development trajectories. These knowledges of place are shaped by professionals, such as architects and planners, laying claim to possessing legitimate knowledge of/about urbanism. In Lefebvre's (1991) terms, they are agents of the representations of space, influencing popular understandings of what places are or ought to be. By producing graphical and technical representations about urban futures, such as drawings and plans, these experts are purveyors of 'an organizing schema or a frame of reference for communication' (Schmid, 2008, p 37). In the BB case, Tesco's regeneration proposals only became permissible because of the deployment of expert techniques of plan making that re-represented what was possible for the area.

Here, the actions of LBTH and the GLA, alongside affiliate organisations such as the LTGDC, were part of a process to change the planning and policy contexts, or to re-represent the locale in ways whereby its future could be (re)imagined in ways previously not countenanced. What transpired were political leaders in the GLA and LBTH not only responding to pressures by global property investors to create conducive investment opportunities in BB, but also being pro-active in the production of a planning framework that made such a scenario realisable. This scenario, of a property-based, commercial redevelopment of BB, seemed unlikely in the early 2000s, with one of the major planning statements noting that plans for the Lower Lea Valley (LLV), including the BB site, were 'seeking a retention of employment/industrial uses' (Urban Practitioners, 2004, p 3). In an interview, an officer from LRC noted that these plans were not realistic and that the "industrial designation on this land meant that nothing was going anywhere fast."

The mayoral ambitions of Ken Livingstone, in the early 2000s, were part of a process that began to change the perception of BB as a declining, industrial place, to a focal point for regeneration. For Livingstone, London's future was identified as enhancing its world city, global status, and spreading the benefits of growth to places often bypassed by investors. As Livingstone said (2004, p xi), 'development has to be directed towards areas of social and economic deprivation … of historic neglect and future opportunity.' By mid-2004, such sentiments were enshrined in the first London Plan (GLA, 2004). It set out the Opportunity Area Planning Framework (OAPF) that identified 28 'Opportunity Areas' (OAs) in London, one of which was the LLV, including BB. The plan for the LLV OA was identified as creating a 'vibrant, high quality and sustainable mixed use city district' (GLA, 2007, p iii), and in interview, Tesco's planning consultant said that this "was the first document of any weight attaching redevelopment or regeneration proposals to BB."

In response to the OA designation, local politicians and planners in LBTH prepared a draft masterplan in 2006 to take advantage of the new regeneration possibilities, particularly those relating to the 'considerable development pressure … due to [BB's] prime location between Canary Wharf and the 2012 Olympic and Paralympic Games site' (Urban Initiatives, 2006, p 7). A regeneration officer we spoke to said that the "plan was driven by the fact that there were a lot of developers suddenly interested in the area", and "to get something meaningful" out of the situation required a clear direction or steer from the council. The subsequent steer was a break with the previous commitment, embedded into the council's Unitary Development Plan (LBTH, 1998), to protect and enhance the industrial nature of BB, and instead, it was noted in the masterplan the council's intent 'to ensure that new development delivers a step change within Bromley-by-Bow' (Urban Initiatives, 2006, p 2).

This step-change was defined by proposals for a mixed-use neighbourhood centre with an expanded Tesco store at its fulcrum.[2] The rationale was embedded into a series of strategic policy documents published between 2005 and 2010, including a re-draft of the London Plan (GLA, 2008), the BB draft masterplan (Urban Initiatives, 2006), the Leaside Area Action Plan (LAAP) (LBTH, 2007) and a Land Use Development Brief (LUDB), drawn up by LBTH and LTGDC in 2009. The LAAP (LBTH, 2007, para 4.32) characterised the area as comprising 'under-utilised industrial sites' and suggested that '[a] relocated Tesco's … at the gateway to an attractive, new neighbourhood centre would contribute to encouraging residents, shoppers and leisure visitors to the area.' The outcome, so the document claimed, would be the transformation of the Tesco site from an 'isolated – inward looking development' in an area lacking a 'strong identity', to a place of 'vitality that will ensure a mix of uses and activities during the day and evening' (LBTH, 2007, para 4.34).

The discursive (re-)representations of BB, from an industrial use to new commercial investments in retail, leisure and private residential development, were part of a broader corporatisation process that rejected piecemeal development for the site in favour of comprehensive renewal. The LUDB (LTGDC and LBTH, 2009, p 5) clarified intent by noting that a piecemeal approach would 'undermine efforts to deliver the mix of land uses ... required to create an integrated and sustainable community.' This directive was never likely to appeal to, or be resourced by, local businesses, or community and voluntary organisations. Instead, it is a (re)scaling of regeneration, requiring the deployment of resources by powerful global investors that have, in Harvey's (2001, p 115) terms, 'the money power'. This discursive construction of BB reflects uneven socio-political and economic relations in which particular, partial representations of space began to predominate, while others were marginalised and rendered invisible and impermissible.

The neutered language of the planning documentation conveys the reasonableness of Tesco's property-led approach, and the LTGDC's (2010, para 10.3) claim, that 'the proposed development is based on a coherent master plan that responds appropriately to the constraints and opportunities of the site', is illustrative of the use of language that is part of a smokescreening of its development intent. Meanwhile, the socio-material relations of poverty and inequality in BB remain a side-show, even an irrelevance, and barely part of the discourse of sustainable place-making. No matter that the average salary in Tower Hamlets has been calculated at £11,800 compared to the average of £95,000 in Canary Wharf (Tower Hamlets Food Bank – see www.towerhamletsfoodbank.org.uk), while the East Thames Group (Gaus, no date) estimate that '63 percent of Tower Hamlets households' are 'unable to reasonably afford a 2 bed property [at] Affordable Rent Model levels'.

Negotiating regeneration and post-welfare urban development?

The content of urban regeneration programmes can be understood, in part, by how they are deliberated and defined or subject to consultative and participative techniques and processes. A broad range of writings suggest that regeneration has rarely been subject to democratic process and is, increasingly, characterised by a post-politics that obfuscates issues of social equity and the distributive impacts of urban development (see Haughton and Allmendinger, 2011; Swyngedouw, 2011). Tesco's approach to the BB development provides insight into their political role in seeking to manage public feeling in ways whereby the company's agents sought to manage political dissent while simultaneously negotiating with local authority officers to assure the project's broader social relevance. The latter highlights the potency of post-welfare formations or, in the BB instance, the not uncommon acquiescence of local state agents to property-led development in seeking to lever private resources for public projects.

For LBTH, a corporate-led development was attractive because of the potential scale of resources it entails, permitting community benefits to be negotiated as part of the formal approval of a planning application. Such agreements, negotiated under Section 106 of the Town and Country Planning Act (1990), were complex in form and detail, and revolved around, primarily, securing from Tesco affordable housing, public space and a building for a local library. In a context of austerity, and public spending cuts, LBTH, with LTGDC, were as incentivised as Tesco to maximise development values as the basis for levering private funds for transfer to social or community projects. The rationale, at face value, appears to reflect Harvey's (2008, p 38) observations about neoliberal form of governance, that 'integrate state and corporate interests' where 'the disbursement of the surplus through the state apparatus favours corporate capital ... in shaping the urban process.'

The negotiations around Section 106 and, in particular, affordable housing, seem to support some, if not all, of Harvey's (2001, p 2008) understanding.[3] While Tesco was acting as a 'distributive agent', and providing some social resources, beyond a purely commercial venture, what was apparent was not an integration of state and corporate interests per se, but political dissension, or key points of difference, between Tesco and LBTH, and between different state actors, namely, LBTH and LTGDC (Néron, 2010). While Tesco's original plans promised to provide up to 50 per cent affordable housing, this was subsequently reduced to 24 per cent on the grounds that any higher a proportion would render the development of the site unprofitable. A LBTH politician expressed his exasperation at Tesco, noting the lack of power of the council: "what else can [LB] Tower Hamlets do?" This comment was also directed, in part, at LTGDC that, according to this respondent, had pushed through the Tesco proposal for affordable housing despite objections from LBTH.

Tesco's ability to shape broader community feeling towards the BB proposals was no less potent. Tesco set up a programme of community engagement in 2009, and deployed a series of instruments, or techniques, to garner support for the regeneration (see Green Issues, 2009). A community consultant, Green Issues (GI), was appointed to carry out the process, and they constructed a lay public around a select group of key stakeholders. These were primarily registered community groups identified by GI as representative of BB population. The stakeholders included members of local social enterprises, an arts trust, local ward councillors, community police, LRC, BB Community Forum and local Catholic and Church of England Church representatives. The BB Bangladeshi Forum and Muslim Cultural Centre is not cited as being invited (Green Issues, 2009).

Tesco's construction of a lay public, by recourse to stakeholder engagement, may be understood as a post-democratic manoeuvre, to neuter dissent and to manufacture consensus about the efficacy of BB's regeneration. The act of seeking to neutralise politics is, however, no less than a political action by the company, in which the public, and their values, are constructed as co-terminus with those of Tesco, or at least, that they have a stake in the successful regeneration of BB. Mackey (2006, p 2) understands the use of the stakeholder analogy by corporations as part of a 'life world colonisation', a term coined by Habermas (1976) to describe ideological interventions in local communities by 'powerful, self interested cliques'. In the BB context, the socio-cultural construction of the public, or at least some members of it, as 'stakeholders', serves to reduce the public to pre-set, definable groups, creating what Giddens (2000, p 152) describes as 'closed and clientelist' relations and decisions made by 'interlocking elites'.

The foreclosure of consultation was constructed around Tesco's understanding that their proposal was non-negotiable, and the focus was the provision of information and seeking to allay public concern and diffuse potential dissent. The process included a public exhibition in which leaflets were sent to 5,000 households inviting them to attend, and meetings with key stakeholders. A councillor felt the process was inadequate and reflected lack of effort by Tesco to get access to people: "I was not convinced that the tools were used to get local people's views…. We're not sure how local people's views are heard and how effective the process is." There was no feedback or follow-up by Tesco; no information was provided to the public about how far the consultative process had changed the plans for BB. A councillor felt that the process was not set up for this and that it was a public relations exercise: "Tesco gave us what all developers do, a presentation by consultants. We do not know if the community viewpoint is being reflected in what is happening."

The use of what Paddison (2009) refers to as techniques of consensual persuasion were evident including, at a public exhibition, the issuing of 'support cards' permitting consultees to fill in their name and address under the strap line 'I support Tesco's proposals for a new District Centre in Bromley-by-Bow, which will bring shops and community facilities, homes, jobs and training opportunities for local people' (Green Issues, 2009, p 26). This performative part of the process resonates with the managerialist, depoliticising, or post-political, use of consultation pioneered during the New Labour years in which lay publics were constructed to take part in deliberative democratic processes designed, at face value, to empower local communities and address the democratic deficit perceived to characterise local state/citizen relations (see Clarke and Newman, 1997; Paddison, 2009). A local councillor expressed distaste with the approach, by noting that "the community isn't that involved with the Tesco site development … they're not in a position to influence it."

This observation appears to signify the impotence of the local political system, and an acceptance, by this respondent, that the process was a fait accompli. A local activist concurred by noting the inability of LBTH to influence what was perceived as a LTGDC-led agenda: "I spoke to someone at Tower Hamlets about it … she agreed … that there was just nothing that they could do." Despite this, the process was not without dissent towards Tesco's proposals, and various local groups, including private landowners such as TS, were, and remain, a challenge to the prevailing order. For TS, the issue remains the potential threat to local landowners, particularly their removal or relocation from the site and associated job losses. However, their observations, like others, are part of a weak form of political activism demanding inclusion in the regeneration, and they do not challenge what Žižek (1999) refers to as the 'symbolic order', or the ideological (re-)representation of property-led renewal as 'a good thing', in and of itself.

Securing regeneration and the relevance of the state judicial process

While Tesco secured consent for the development through the formal planning system, and sought to legitimise its activities through a consultation that bore little resemblance to a transparent, democratic process, there was still the outstanding problem of the land ownership of the site. The implementation of Tesco's plans required it to acquire ownership of the BB site by negotiating with, and buying out, the two other landowners, TS and Crowley. TS did not want to sell to Tesco, partly because they were interested in developing the site themselves, but also because a costly relocation would be involved. Their reluctance to sell to Tesco, and Tesco's unwillingness to negotiate a joint project with TS, created an impasse. The solution, from Tesco's perspective, was the deployment of state judicial powers, or, in this instance, the use of compulsory purchase powers vested in the LTGDC. An officer from LTGDC said in interview, "we [wanted] a comprehensive approach ... particularly the Tesco scheme and these two sites brought into a single scheme."

Subsequently, in early 2011, an application for a CPO was submitted by LTGDC to the Secretary of State for Communities and Local Government in order to acquire the site for disposal to Tesco. In interview, Tesco's planning consultant, GL Hearn, outlined the rationale, that "the role of retail provision to kick starting the redevelopment of the area should not be underestimated." This view was echoed by the chief executive of the LTGDC (2006, p 9) in noting that the site was "a once in a lifetime opportunity" to transform the area. In both instances, Tesco was being positioned as best placed to secure the regeneration objectives for BB. This was recognition, by local state agents, that Tesco was *the* key political player in the locale, and more or less an immovable, irresistible, force. As an officer from LTGDC explained to us, "there were actually very few options given that you have to move Tesco in order to liberate the land that they occupy ... Tesco weren't going to move unless they were allowed to expand."

The realisation of Tesco's ability to resist relocation underpinned the understanding, by officers in LBTH and LTGDC, that the best, perhaps only, way to achieve their objective, 'to deliver exemplary sustainable development on a dramatic scale' (LTGDC, 2006, p 1), was to harness the company's economic power. The regeneration process was complicated by the conflict between TS and Tesco over rights to the BB site, and their intent not to work with one another, or negotiate a legal settlement to bring the land under sole ownership or otherwise parcel it together as a workable development. A senior planner at LTGDC noted that there was animosity between TS and Tesco, and rivalry between them about securing the rights to develop the BB site. In interview he said, "there was no prospect of any deal being done between the landowners, there was no prospect of us being able to acquire the land by private treaty, and so as a last resort, compulsory purchase was identified as the way forward."

The reputation of LTGDC, as a major land agent and instrument to deliver East London's regeneration, was also at stake in relation to the BB site, and this was part of their motivation to ensure nothing stood in the way of a comprehensive renewal. In a meeting with an officer from LTGDC, he outlined the issues to us: "we had CPO powers that we weren't afraid to use if the various land owners didn't negotiate and agree a land strategy themselves." LTGDC wanted to avoid delay to get development up and running prior to the Olympic Games, and as the officer said, "the prospects of being able to work with the other landowners, and Tesco, just seemed like an extremely expensive and difficult thing to embark on … working [just] with Tesco using a CPO was much easier." Tesco understood this, and the officer suggested that the company played an astute, political hand in manoeuvring the process so that LTGDC's application for a CPO became inevitable.

Here, Tesco were seeking to gain access to, and use, regulatory mechanisms to enable them to strengthen their negotiating position with other landowners. An officer from LTGDC felt that Tesco were exploiting their knowledge of the likely use of CPO in their favour, by more or less offering terms to other landowners that they knew were unacceptable. As he said: "the knowledge of having the Development Corporation potentially using their powers to help them realise their scheme … enabled Tesco to be very bullish in terms of what kind of offers they were making to those landowners which undoubtedly would have been well below the kind of sums of money they were expecting to receive." This purposive action by Tesco, in making a private land settlement more or less an impossibility on the BB site, draws attention to what Néron (2010, p 335) describes as 'the ways firms interfere in the political process, and therefore, in the shaping and reshaping of their regulatory environment.'

For Tesco, access to state, legal powers was their paramount objective, and the company was strongly lobbying at all stages for the deployment of a CPO. As the LTGDC officer said in interview: "Tesco kind of took the initiative to want to explore with us how they might be able to promote a comprehensive scheme and use our powers to help realise land assembly." The officer felt this was appropriate and part of the remit of the public sector or, as he observed, "it's what you can do to help the private sector respond in circumstances where they won't lay out [finance]." Others noted the significance of a state, legal instrument in shaping the regeneration or, as an officer from LTGDC outlined, we are "basically lending the private sector public powers." This is reflective, in part, of a decentred, dispersed form of governance, and the devolvement of state powers to facilitate a process of disbursement, and, in this respect, is no less than a subsidisation of private costs.

While Tesco's subsequent failure to secure the CPO seems to reflect a technical, judicial process, seemingly objective and neutral, it is more productive to view the outcome as constitutive of a politics of contestation in which people's livelihoods, and the rights to access and occupy space, were paramount in the inspector's deliberations. Tesco's ambitions, supported by LTGDC, were undermined by an over-zealous approach that appeared to be insensitive to existing users/occupiers of BB. This led to the CPO application being rejected on the grounds that the LTGDC had been slow to address issues of relocation, in particular the likely costs to relocatees, and had failed to provide a satisfactory relocation site for TS. LTGDC were therefore deemed to have failed to have 'reflected the guidance of Circular 06/2004' (Prentis, 2011, para 10.67), which notes that a CPO should only be the last resort and used only after a sponsoring authority has sought to acquire land through negotiation wherever this is practicable (see ODPM, 2004, para 24).

The episode highlights the non-linear, contradictory nature of urban regeneration, and how neoliberalising logics do not necessarily come to fruition. The failure, of LTGDC and Tesco, to secure the CPO, illustrates the power of the state to shape regeneration and, in particular, highlights the potency of its internal heterogeneity as a source of tension, even contradiction. In the BB case, the objectives of one state agency, the LTGDC, were challenged, and overturned, by another, the Planning Inspectorate and the Secretary of State for Communities and Local Government, and highlights how the state may operate in and against itself. While the immediate outcome is a foreclosure of redevelopment in BB, the issue is not that the principles of property-led regeneration have disappeared, but that they have been blunted until alternative means to assemble the site are constructed. In this instance, the failure of Tesco to secure the site reflects state power but it does not herald a radical politics or provide a basis for the production of egalitarian spaces.

Conclusion

The development and delivery of socially sustainable places in London, including the supply of low-cost, affordable housing, appears to be part of the portfolio of major corporate organisations, such as Tesco, who traditionally have not be in the vanguard of delivering urban regeneration. In the case of BB, the local authority was dependent on a private sector organisation to bring forward an ambitious regeneration, including the provision of social housing and other community facilities. This appears to be part of an ongoing trend. While the proposed scheme has stalled, temporarily, the process highlights significant difficulties for local authorities in dealing with social need in a context of public debt, and this makes a Tesco-style approach to regeneration attractive to local politicians. While many councillors in LBTH were cynical of Tesco's motives, they broadly supported their role in regeneration, as they did not see any alternative ways to providing much needed public benefit.

The process was lacking one of the cornerstones that some claim is important in sustainable place-making, that is, community involvement and a participative politics. Proclamations from The World Bank (2006) and United Nations (UN) (2002) have, over the years, argued the case for good governance, including citizens' participation, in sustainable development. In BB, however, the dominant role of Tesco, in seeking to cherry-pick the site while driving down their social contributions, weakens the already tenuous claims to democratic legitimacy of contemporary regeneration practices, if this legitimacy is premised on active shaping of regeneration by local citizens, including local businesses. For Tesco, the active management of potential dissent to the plans for BB was facilitated by stakeholder, consultative techniques that reflected less a post-political process and more a political manoeuvring to maintain a status quo, or a 'common interest' between powerful state and corporate agents.

This observation draws attention to the role of major corporations as *political actors* in shaping places, and, in the BB case, Tesco, in conjunction with LTGDC, was propagating a politics that, while not named as such, had the capacity to engender a redistributive process in relation to social goods and services (such as housing). Thus, from Tesco's reluctance to broker a deal with other local landowners over site assembly, to LTGDC's referral of the process to a judicial hearing, the political nature of corporate activity in urban policy processes is highlighted. Far from a post-politics in play, characterised by depoliticised forms of decision making, Tesco's filtration of key state organisations, coupled with its conflicts with TS, shows the significance of what Néron (2010, p 335) describes as 'the politicisation of the corporation'. Here, Néron (2010) is referring to the limits of analysis that conceive of organisations such as Tesco as depoliticised, as though there can be a clear separation between the economic and political activities of corporate behaviour.

The study also shows the significance of 'judicialisation' in shaping sustainable place-making (see Imrie and Thomas, 1997). The fact that Tesco failed to secure the regeneration was related to disputes between them and other landowners that led to a judicial review and, subsequently, the application for a CPO being turned down by a planning inspector. The fact that a judicial process stymied Tesco's proposals reflects Hirschl's (2006, p 721) observation that there is, globally, a 'profound transfer of power from representative institutions to juridical' or the 'judicialisation of politics'. This points towards new areas of research because if policy is becoming more judicialised, then it (a) creates new challenges for under-resourced communities to challenge policy decisions, particularly in the light of cuts to legal aid; (b) possibly creates new inequalities between groups with uneven capabilities at mobilising the law; and (c) may in the longer run benefit powerful interests that can meet the requirements of judicial review better than others and may push for new regulations/laws that only they can fulfil.[4]

Notes

[1] On 15 July 2004, TS submitted a planning application to LBTH to redevelop their site with a 5- to 18-storey mixed-use development comprising 549 residential units, office use and car parking and landscaping. This application was never determined by LBTH. On 29 January 2006 (ref: PA/06/00678) TS submitted another planning application to LTGDC for demolition of existing buildings and redevelopment to provide a mixed-use development of 544 residential units, commercial space and car parking. On 25 January 2007 the application was appealed on non-determination. On 22 November 2007, following a Public Inquiry, the Secretary of State dismissed the appeal on the grounds that it would prejudice the comprehensive redevelopment of the area.

[2] The notion of a neighbourhood centre is not clearly defined in planning documents issued by either LBTH or LTGDC. In the masterplan, the idea of a neighbourhood centre is defined as giving 'a focus to the area through the provision of local shops and community facilities' (Urban Initiatives, 2006, p 3).

[3] The Planning Advisory Service define Section 106 agreements as 'planning obligations ... a mechanism which make a development proposal acceptable in planning terms, that would not otherwise be acceptable. They are focused on site-specific mitigation of the impact of development' (see www.pas.gov.uk). The planning application by Tesco was underpinned by a major Section 106 agreement to provide social housing, transport infrastructure, a new school and a library.

[4] Our thanks to Mike Raco for these excellent observations.

Acknowledgements

Our thanks to Loretta Lees and Mike Raco who gave invaluable feedback that has been incorporated into a revision of the chapter. We would also like to thanks Jenny Kynaston who drew the maps for Figure 9.1.

References

Boyle, M. (1999) 'Growth machines and propaganda projects: a review of readings of the role of civic boosterism in the politics of local economic development', in A. Jonas *and* D. Wilson *(eds) The urban growth machine: critical perspectives two decades late,* Albany, NY: State University of New York Press, pp 55-70.

Brenner, N. and Theodore, N. (eds) (2002) *Spaces of neoliberalism: urban restructuring in Western Europe and North America,* Oxford: Blackwell.

Butler, M. and Ntseng, D. (2008) 'Politics at stake: as note on stakeholder analysis', *Pambazuka News,* 31 July, issue 392 (www.pambazuka.org/en/category/comment/49799 [Accessed 22 October 2013).

Clarke, J. and Newman, J. (1997) *The managerial state,* London: Sage.

Crouch, C. (2004) *Post democracy,* Cambridge: Polity Press.

Deetz, S. (1992) *Democracy in an age of corporate colonization: developments in communication and the politics of everyday life*, Albany, NY: State University of New York.

Friends of the Earth (2006) *Calling the shots: how supermarkets get their way in planning decisions*, London: Friends of the Earth.

Garun, N. (2012) 'Meet Strand East, an Ikea-designed town', *Digital Trends* (www.digitaltrends.com/international/meet-strand-east-an-ikea-designed-town).

Gaus, T. (no date) *Impact of the affordable rent model: Tower Hamlets*, East Thames Group (www.eastthames.co.uk/assets_cm/files/pdf/impact_of_the_affordable_rent_model_tower_hamlets.pdf).

Giddens, A. (2000) *The third way and its critics*, Malden, MA: Polity Press.

Gill, G., Johnstone, P. and Williams, A. (2012) 'Towards a geography of tolerance: post-politics and political forms of toleration', *Political Geography*, vol 31, pp 509-18.

GLA (Greater London Authority) (2004) *The London Plan: Spatial Development Strategy for Greater London*, London: GLA.

GLA (2007) *Lower Lea Valley Opportunity Area Planning Framework Summary*, London: GLA.

GLA (2008) *The London Plan: Spatial Development Strategy for Greater London: consolidated with alterations since 2004*, London: GLA.

Green Issues (2009) *Statement of community engagement: Tesco, Bromley by Bow* (http://planreg.towerhamlets.gov.uk/WAM/doc/Other-553902.pdf?extension=.pdf&id=553902&appid=&location=VOLUME4&contentType=application/pdf&pageCount=1).

Guy, C. (2008) 'Retail-led regeneration: assessing the property outcomes', *Journal of Urban Regeneration and Renewal*, vol 1, no 4, pp 378-88.

Habermas, J. (1976) *Legitimation crisis*, London: Heinemann Educational Books.

Harvey, D. (2001) *Spaces of capital: towards a critical geography*, London: Routledge.

Harvey, D. (2008) 'The Right to the City', *New Left Review*, vol 53, pp 23-40.

Haughton, G. and Allmendinger, P. (2011) 'Moving on: from spatial planning to localism and beyond', *Town and Country Planning*, vol 80, pp 184-7.

Hirschl, R. (2006) 'The new constitutionalism and the judicialization of pure politics worldwide', *Fordham Law Review*, vol 75, pp 721-54.

Imrie, R. and Thomas, H. (1997) 'Law, legal struggles and urban regeneration: rethinking the relationships', *Urban Studies*, vol 34, no 9, pp 1401-18.

Jessop, B. (2002) *The future of the capitalist state*, Cambridge: Polity Press.

LBTH (London Borough of Tower Hamlets (1998) *Unitary Development Plan*, London: LBTH.

LBTH (2007) *Leaside Area Action Plan: interim planning guidance*, London: LBTH.

Lees, L. (2013) 'The urban injustices of New Labour's "new urban renewal": the case of the Aylesbury Estate in London', *Antipode*, Early View, 3 May (http://onlinelibrary.wiley.com/doi/10.1111/anti.12020/pdf).

Lefebvre, H. (1991) *The production of space*, Chichester: Wiley.

Livingstone, K. (2004) 'Foreword', in GLA, *The London Plan: Spatial Development Strategy for Greater London*, London, GLA.

LTGDC (London Thames Gateway Development Corporation) (2006) *Corporate Plan 2006-2008*, London: LTGDC.

LTGDC and LBTH (London Borough of Tower Hamlets) (2009) *Bromley-by-Bow land use design brief*, London: LTGDC.

LTGDC (London Thames Gateway Development Corporation) (2010) *Planning Application For Determination by LTGWDC: Report of the Director of Planning*, 28 May, London, LTGDC.

Lowe, M. (2005) 'The regional shopping centre in the inner-city: a study of retail-led urban regeneration', *Urban Studies*, vol 42, pp 449-70.

Mackey, S. (2006) 'Misuse of the term "stakeholder" in public relations', *Prism*, vol 4, no 1 (www.prismjournal.org/fileadmin/Praxis/Files/Journal_Files/2006_general/Mackey.pdf).

MacLeod, G. (2011) 'Urban politics reconsidered: growth machine to post-democratic city?', *Urban Studies*, vol 48, no 12, pp 2629-60.

MacLeod, G. and Jones, M. (2011) 'Renewing urban politics', *Urban Studies*, vol 48, no 12, pp 2443-72.

McGuirk, P.M. and Dowling, R. (2009) 'Neoliberal privatisation? Remapping the public and the private in Sydney's masterplanned residential estates', *Political Geography*, vol 28, no 3, pp 174-85.

Mayer, M. (2006) 'Urban social movements in an era of globalization', in N. Brenner and R. Keil (eds) *The global cities reader*, London: Routledge, pp 296-304.

Neate, R. (2011) 'Tesco breathes new life into Toxteth', *The Guardian*, Tuesday 12 July (www.theguardian.com/business/2011/jul/12/tesco-brings-hope-to-toxteth).

Néron, P.-Y. (2010) 'Business and the *polis*: what does it mean to see corporations as political actors?', *Journal of Business Ethics*, vol 94, no 3, pp 333-52.

ODPM (Office of the Deputy Prime Minister) (2004) *Compulsory purchase and the Crichel Down rules*, ODPM Circular 06/2004, London: ODPM.

Paddison, R. (2009) 'Some reflections on the limitations to public participation in the post-political city', *L'espace politique*, vol 8 (http://espacepolitique.revues.org/1393).

Peck, J., Theodore, N. and Brenner, N. (2013) 'Neoliberal urbanism redux?', *International Journal of Urban and Regional Research*, vol 37, no 3, pp 1091-9.

Peterson, P.E. (1981) *City limits*, Chicago, IL: University of Chicago Press.

Prentis, D. (2011) 'Application by the London Thames Gateway Development Corporation for confirmation of the London Thames Gateway Development Corporation (Bromley by Bow) (South) Compulsory Purchase Order 2010', *CPO report to the Secretary of State for Communities and Local Government*, Bristol: The Planning Inspectorate.

Rancière, J. (2001) 'Ten theses on politics', *Theory and Event*, vol 5, no 3, pp 1-16.

Scherer, G. And Palazzo, G. (2011) 'The new political role of business in a globalized world: a review of a new perspective on CSR and its implications for the firm, governance, and democracy', *Journal of Management Studies*, vol 48, no 4, pp 899-931.

Schmid, C. (2008) 'Henri Lefebvre's theory of the production of space: towards a three-dimensional dialectic', in K. Goonewardena, S. Kipfer, R. Milgrom and C. Scmid (eds) *Space, difference, everyday life: reading Henri Lefebvre*, Abingdon: Routledge, pp 27-45.

Swyngedouw, E. (2010) 'Post-democratic cities: for whom and for what?', Paper Presented in Concluding Regional Studies Association Annual Conference, Pecs, Budapest, 26 May.

Swyngedouw E. (2011) 'Interrogating post-democratization: reclaiming egalitarian political spaces', *Political Geography,* vol 30, no 7, pp 370-80.

UN (United Nations) (2002) *Report of the World Summit on Sustainable Development*, A/CONF.199/20 and A/CONF.199/20/corr.1, New York: UN.

Urban Initiatives (2006) *Bromley by Bow masterplan*, London: Urban Initiatives.

Urban Practitioners (2004*) Lower Lea Valley Joint Area Action Plan and Opportunity Area Planning Framework interim draft (incorporating comments from London Borough of Hackney*, London: Urban Practitioners.

Watkins, T. (2011) 'Sainsbury's reveals £160m plan for Bath', *Bath Chronicle*, 24 November (www.thisisdevon.co.uk/Sainsbury-s-reveals-pound-160m-plan-Bath/story-13942912-detail/story.html#axzz2iI7HvA7e).

World Bank, The (2006) *Equity and development: world development report 2006*, Washington, DC: The World Bank.

Wrigley, N., Guy, C. and Lowe, M. (2002) 'Urban regeneration, social inclusion and large store development: the Seacroft development in context', *Urban Studies*, vol 39, pp 2101-14.

Žižek, S. (1999) *The ticklish subject: the absent centre of political ontology*, London: Verso.

TEN

Educating London: sustainable social reproduction versus symbolic violence?

Tim Butler

Introduction

Education has joined housing and transport as one of the 'crunch issues' if London is to sustain itself as a world-leading city. 'London world city' has inherited an education system from a past era when its largely working-class population left school to labour in its semi-skilled industries. Whereas 30 years back, a form of class sorting and sifting took place in which the relatively small middle class was apparently able to mould the education system to its needs, this is no longer the case. With de-industrialisation and widespread gentrification, London's greatly expanded middle classes and those aspiring to join them now form the largest population group in the city and, as a consequence, are having to compete ferociously for places in London's comparatively scarce high-performing schools. Gentlemanly systems of matching social classes to school places no longer apply such is the mismatch between supply and demand and the requirement that the ways in which pupils are allocated be transparent. In this emergent market in education, increasing numbers of parents feel it is their responsibility to garner the best educational assets on offer for their children.

In this situation, the ability to live near a high-performing school ranks as the single most important determinant of a child's success, at least for those who are being educated in the state, as opposed to the private, sector. This means, of course, that London's education system increasingly reflects existing privilege. While many parents would join with policy makers in promoting the ideal of education as the agent for equality of opportunity, in practice, this is regarded as largely utopian, particularly the nearer children come to the age of secondary school selection. Indeed, any such threat to the chances of 'my child' winning one of the coveted places at almost every stage of an educational career is regarded with deep suspicion as evidence of the evils of 'social engineering'.

This chapter engages some key themes being raised by the book about what is meant by sustainability through an examination of parental aspirations and the policy context of education in London. As the editors point out in their Introduction (Chapter One), 'sustainability' is one of those infuriating terms which cross the borders between academic, policy and everyday discourse with a warm, well-meaning aura, but which, when interrogated for even a moment, turns out to be largely meaningless. It is, in many respects, similar to the term 'community' whose misuses have been charted for decades by sociologists and others with no perceptible affect on its continued deployment. In this chapter, I argue that sustainability and education make an interesting pairing because in both cases they raise the question of 'for whom?'. Education is a socially useful good, but also the primary means by which all, except perhaps the very wealthiest and very poorest, hope to advantage their children in the next generation and/or to pass on and augment their relative advantage.

For both education and sustainability, there is a policy discourse about social justice and – in the case of sustainability – environmental justice, and an aspiration for a better life that comes up against the realities of 'possessive individualism' by which individual aspiration is articulated. In both cases, what is essentially a positional good, whose value lies in its scarcity, is jealously fought over and usually defended by those already in possession of advantage. NIMBYism ('not in my backyard') or the right to live in a school catchment area both pose serious challenges to a city's ability to guarantee itself a future. In terms of education and schooling, it is argued that a society is only sustainable if it finds ways to reproduce itself so that all the talents are mobilised for the benefit of all and not the few. In a class society, it is unsurprising that those owning desired assets try to garner them for their children which, at the same time, serves systematically to deny them to others, with the result that society (in this case, the city) becomes less able to sustain itself and often has to import from outside those skills it is unable or unwilling to nurture. By so doing, it creates cultures of privilege and deprivation.

As Pierre Bourdieu (Bourdieu and Passeron, 1990) has noted, those with such assets (cultural, economic or social capital) tend to disparage others not in possession of them in ways that render them largely invisible and ignorant. He terms this 'symbolic violence'. In this chapter, I argue that the battle over educational equality in London over the last 50 years is now showing clear signs of coming down on the side of an increasingly unequal system in which parents fight for a right to an ever decreasing allocation of educational resources. This is expressed in terms of there being 'good' and 'bad' schools in which, increasingly, 'good schools' are associated with 'good areas' – not just because (however tricky to define) they offer a 'good education', but because they attract the right kind of 'people like us'. Any school not regarded as good is therefore at risk of being demonised as 'bad', if not 'failing'.

While it might be argued "twas ever thus', the growing inequality in access to London's educational resources is doing nothing to meet the very real challenges London faces in meeting the twin – and often contradictory – goals of sustaining social cohesiveness while enhancing its economic competitiveness. London's schooling system is not only becoming more socially regressive but, in so doing, is also contributing to, rather than mitigating, London's failure to build itself a sustainable future by almost any definition of this very slippery term.

In this chapter, I outline how this situation has changed within two short generations of the city's gentrification and urban regeneration, which has helped to generate a schooling system increasingly geared to reproducing rather than reducing pre-existing social advantage. Increasingly education has become a primary field by which those who are already advantaged are able to manoeuvre to maintain that advantage inter-generationally through privileged access to high-quality and high-achieving schools. Such is the shortage of perceived high-quality schools in London, particularly in those areas that have undergone gentrification over the last 40 years, that it is not just the working classes and economically inactive, but also large swathes of the expanded middle classes who perceive themselves as being excluded from where they would like to be in this emerging market in education. The symbolic violence of exclusion is, however, increasingly mirrored by the interaction of London's housing and education markets, whereby scarce places in 'good schools' are rationed by the device of 'distance from school'. This, in effect, ensures that only those with access to advantaged housing markets are eligible for the best non-selective state schools. This coming together of social and economic advantage in the context of London's education markets is relatively new; whereas previously the middle classes were able to trade their cultural capital to nullify the disadvantage of distance, this is increasingly less the case – as I will show. This, I suggest, has direct implications for London's sustainability as a city of socially mixed communities.

In the next section, I present an account of how London's education system is structured into overlapping but distinct 'circuits of schooling', which I then contextualise in the changing class structure of London to present an argument that the increased competition for 'good' school places is resulting in greater social segregation in schooling based around housing market status. In the third section, I illustrate this process by drawing on research conducted in East London.[1] Finally, I draw some conclusions, and suggest that this process of 'symbolic violence' towards the already disadvantaged is likely to lead to London becoming a yet more unsustainable city.

Circuits of schooling and London's education market

In an influential paper, Ball et al (1995) argued that there were separate 'circuits of education' in which the working and middle classes pursued different strategies towards secondary school choice at age 11 (following six years of compulsory primary schooling). They argued that the middle classes were, for the most part, 'user choosers' who crafted individual strategies for their children in terms of selecting secondary schools that were deemed appropriate to the particular child's skills and interests. Having identified a number of appropriate schools – often, but not exclusively, ones that demand a degree of selection – these were presented to the child as 'options', and the child was then incorporated into building a narrative about why that particular school suited her/him and vice versa.

This then formed the basis of a well-rehearsed and individualised programme of preparation that would be undertaken over the year (or more) before the selection processes took place. Selection might include the taking of competitive examinations, the demonstration of particular aptitudes (in, for example, music) or more generally being a suitable middle-class child whose attributes mapped closely on to those that were projected by the school. In many cases, these strategies would involve a variety of target schools and a potentially lengthy journey to school. In many instances, this would involve the child in a separation from the friendship/year group that had been built up at primary school. For most such children, their primary school was local to where they lived because for most parents, including middle-class ones, that seemed the right thing to do with young children.

Ball et al argued that working-class parents, by contrast, adopted broadly an adaptive approach that was accommodative to their children's wish to go to a local school with their peer group. Thus, the authors identified two largely separate 'circuits of secondary schooling' operating in London, with middle-class parents strategising pro-actively to identify a set of secondary schooling options that would enable their child to be in an envisaged but yet-to-be-realised situation in several years time that might be very different from their present one, whereas the working-class parents were considerably more accommodative to their children's wish to proceed through a local schooling system alongside their peers. For this latter group, not only were expectations of how the child might emerge different, but they also placed more value on the convenience of a local school that seemed 'right' to them in terms of their own role and their child's happiness and desire to remain part of a local cohort. The middle classes, for their part, were not just prepared to travel large distances (or to enable their child to), but often implicitly put a lot of value on separating them from what might turn out to be an unsuitable peer group in favour of a different one in a 'yet-to-be-realised' situation that would equip them with what they identified as a suitable constellation of educational, social and cultural capital that would be well-matched to their particular set of attributes and interests.

Thus Ball et al described a London that was divided into circuits of (secondary) schooling that were not only 'classed' but had very different geographies. The working-class circuit was essentially local and respected the boundaries of the local education authority (LEA) of the London borough (LB) in which they lived. Almost universally the schools in this circuit would be non-selective 'comprehensive' ones drawing from their local area and the primary schools within it. The middle-class circuits were more complex and ranged across a number of different school types and were largely sub-regional (and in some cases regional and indeed, city-wide) crossing local authority boundaries. While the Education Act 1988 had enshrined the principle of parental choice in legislation, in practice it simply legitimated what the middle classes had been doing for many years, which was deploying their stocks of cultural, economic and social capital to their advantage in seeking out places in what they identified as the best schools that were most well-matched to their children's particular talents. While these schools might include non-selective comprehensives, for the most part they were schools that selected on the basis of ability to pay or the child's aptitude in meeting the individual school's stated (and/or unstated) entrance requirements.

Therefore, in addition to London's fee-paying schools, and the selective grammar schools in those (outer) London boroughs that had retained schools that selected at age 11 by academic testing, they also included faith schools, specialist schools (such as city technology colleges) and other grant-aided schools with formal (or informal) power to recruit the kind of children they wanted. These circuits of education spread across the city in complex ways with myriad ways of selecting pupils – ranging from the ability to pay to informal interviews where the child (and parent) were able to demonstrate that they were the 'right sort' and would match the school's 'ethos'. Even in the case of private education, it was often not simply a matter of getting out the cheque book – given the competition for places, there were examinations and interviews to be gone through. This not infrequently forced parents contemplating private secondary schooling to transfer their children at the age of seven from the local (state) primary school to a (private) preparatory school with close links to the target private secondary school (Butler and Robson, 2003).

It is important to contextualise the identification of these class-specific circuits of schooling into the larger picture of the structure of London's educational provision. There is a material basis for the middle-class strategising and the apparent working-class acquiescence in terms of secondary school choice that has its origins in the postwar social settlement. The sociologist John Rex noted that the postwar welfare state represented what he termed a 'truce situation' (1961, p 127) between labour and capital in which the state, in effect, sponsored separate spheres of provision – specifically in housing, as Rex and Moore (1967) noted in their study of 'race relations' in Sparkbrook in Birmingham. A similar truce situation was in operation with respect to education.

The Education Act 1944 sat alongside the 1942 Beveridge report, and was the vehicle for mitigating one of Beveridge's five 'Giant Evils' of 'Want, Disease, Ignorance, Squalor and Idleness'. For the first time, this offered a secondary education free to all and raised the school leaving age to 15. This was to be achieved through a tri-partite secondary schooling system consisting of grammar, technical and secondary modern schools designed to reflect the assumed talents of the population – academic, technical and a general education for manual labour. This was conceived as a system that operated on 'parity of esteem' in which these various talents were regarded as being different but of equal value in building a socially just society. Unsurprisingly, it turned out somewhat differently, with the grammar schools rapidly becoming colonised by the middle classes in which a grammar school education quickly became equated with *being* or *becoming* middle class (Jackson and Marsden, 1962). The nascent discipline of the sociology of education soon demonstrated that the chances of a working-class child getting into grammar school were considerably and systematically less than that for the middle-class child, and that Intelligence Quotient (IQ) test-based 11+ entrance examinations tested nurture rather more than nature (Banks, 1968; Halsey and Karabel, 1977).

Patterns of social mobility remained stubbornly static, reflecting existing privilege; Goldthorpe's calculation of the odds ratios for working-class and middle-class entry into the vastly expanded middle class of the 1960s showed a rate of 13:1 in favour of the middle-class boy – girls being a different story, with similar odds ratios but lower absolute rates (Goldthorpe, 1987). Goldthorpe demonstrated that absolute mobility of the working class into the middle class had more to do with the massive overall expansion of the occupational structure than with any change in the rates of mobility. Willis' (1977) study of working-class boys – undertaken in the early 1970s in the still-industrialised West Midlands – showed that the system was failing the working class rather than the other way around. The secondary modern, stereotyped in the comics of the time, such as the 'Bash Street Kids' in *The Beano*, emerged as providing a training for generalised manual labour in Willis' account in which resistance to authority rather than transferrable skills was the order of the day.

The emerging evidence that the selective system was failing working-class children and reinforcing the existing inequalities led to proposed changes in the structure of education in England and Wales in favour of non-selective secondary schools (so-called 'comprehensive' schools). Ironically, it fell to the incoming Conservative government and its Education Secretary, Margaret Thatcher, to implement it; individual LEAs were, however, permitted to retain a measure of selection if they so wished. A minority retained an element of selection, but by the 1980s, the overwhelming proportion of secondary schools had become non-selective.

London reflected these national patterns with some interesting variations. London carried through into the postwar period a class structure of a working-class city which also had a disproportionate number of upper and upper-middle-class inhabitants – mainly concentrated in the 'West End' central area, who traditionally sent their children to fee-paying private schools. Central London was well provided with such elite schools, although many upper-class children were also sent as boarders to the so-called public schools elsewhere in the country. There were also a small number of grammar schools – usually one to each of the relatively small London County Council (LCC) boroughs that catered for the middle classes unable or unwilling to send their children to fee-paying schools and that also attracted bright working-class boys on scholarships; for example the historian, the late Eric Hobsbawm, refers to the education he received at Marylebone Grammar School during the 1930s.

For the most part, however, London's schools were for its working-class population who, it was generally assumed, would leave school at the first opportunity to seek work. There was a broad distinction between inner London that was generally the poor and working-class part of London, and the outer London boroughs that were suburban, leafy and aspirational. Politically,

London traditionally divided Left–Right between inner and outer. With the re-organisation of London's boroughs in 1965 following the report by Herbert Morrison which set up the Greater London Council (GLC), education in inner London was provided by the Inner London Education Authority (ILEA) (see the area marked in Figure 10.1).

Figure 10.1: The Greater London Area showing the Inner London Education Authority

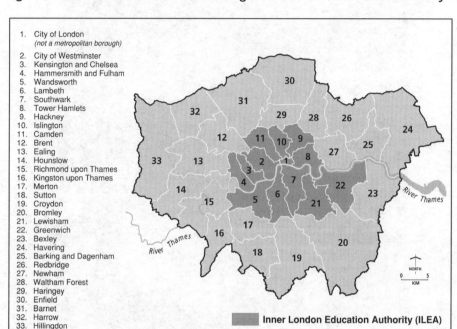

1. City of London
   (not a metropolitan borough)
2. City of Westminster
3. Kensington and Chelsea
4. Hammersmith and Fulham
5. Wandsworth
6. Lambeth
7. Southwark
8. Tower Hamlets
9. Hackney
10. Islington
11. Camden
12. Brent
13. Ealing
14. Hounslow
15. Richmond upon Thames
16. Kingston upon Thames
17. Merton
18. Sutton
19. Croydon
20. Bromley
21. Lewisham
22. Greenwich
23. Bexley
24. Havering
25. Barking and Dagenham
26. Redbridge
27. Newham
28. Waltham Forest
29. Haringey
30. Enfield
31. Barnet
32. Harrow
33. Hillingdon

Inner London Education Authority (ILEA)

Technically a sub-committee of the GLC, ILEA was in practice run by an elected group of councillors who were mainly Labour and responded enthusiastically to the call for comprehensive schooling by turning the whole of the ILEA area comprehensive. In the process, they built some iconic new schools that architecturally and educationally were intended to symbolise their commitment to equality of opportunity – Holland Park (Figure 10.2), Islington Green and Rising Hill were all examples of this brave new world, with high-profile headteachers, progressive educational policies and an alumni that included the children of the famous who have often gone on to become famous themselves (the Benns and the Milibands being obvious examples).

This was the highpoint of the victory of the liberal middle-class conscience that set out to prove that building such schools in the centre of the city could transform the educational experience and outcome of and for local working-class children, partly, at least, by not segregating out the middle class. By being inclusive and attracting such children, it was argued that the meritocratic ideal might truly be promoted. For a short period of time, it appeared that this was the case; the

Figure 10.2: Holland Park Comprehensive School

Source: City of London, London Metropolitan Archives

apparently altruistic middle classes who were the pioneer gentrifiers of the city sent their children to such schools with enthusiasm. These pioneers and their immediate successors did not consider schooling and the poor reputation of inner London's schools as a barrier to their settling there (Butler and Hamnett, 2011b). In so far as they considered schooling an issue – many were either single, in childless households or with pre-school-age children – they expressed a confidence that they could transform the local schools to meet their needs. The early gentrifiers in Islington included many teachers who taught in progressive local schools (examples might include William Tyndale, Islington Green and Highbury Grove [Figure 10.3]). Today, such a situation would be largely unimaginable – few young teachers could possibly consider living in any inner London borough given local house prices. For many of this early generation of gentrifiers (Butler, 1997; Butler

Figure 10.3: Highbury Grove Comprehensive School

Source: City of London, London Metropolitan Archives

and Robson, 2003; Lees et al, 2008), altruism and conscience were markers of the 'pioneer' spirit that set them apart from their suburban counterparts. The belief that if they set about improving a school to meet their needs it would improve the learning situation for local working-class and minority ethnic groups was also a matter of faith. This may not have been transformative of the schooling system, but in so far as it accommodated the incoming middle class, it also demonstrated the possibilities for a comprehensive system in which the different class and ethnic groups at least tolerated and worked beside each other at school. What is striking – and depressing – is how far that situation has changed in the intervening period.

Buck et al (2002) note that post-Second World War London would have seemed very white and working class to a contemporary observer. Gentrification, immigration and de-industrialisation had begun to change all that by the 1980s, and the process of change has been even more rapid over the last 30 years. In 1981, professionals accounted for only 4.1 per cent of the socio-economic group (SEG) total in inner London (and 4.7 per cent in outer London); by 2001 inner London's proportion had more than doubled to 10.2 per cent of the SEG total, while in outer London it grew by only 2 percentage points, to 6.7 per cent.[2] This is indicative of the continuing 'social upgrading' of inner London and a shifting social balance between inner and outer London. However, much of the highest rate of growth was in the intermediate group (SEG 5.1), which is not only the largest single group, but whose growth, in inner London, was nearly twice the rate for that of England and Wales. London's 'social upgrading' has therefore been happening at the top and at the lower end of the middle of its social structure (Butler et al, 2008).

Davidson and Wyly (2012; but see also Hamnett and Butler, 2013, for a detailed response) have disputed this analysis of London's changing class structure, although not the fundamental claim about the city's changing occupational structure As Davidson and Wyly's (2012) critique makes clear, these claims have considerable theoretical importance for understanding the processes of class change at work in London that are considerably wider than can be encompassed by the concept of gentrification. The rapid growth of the old SEG 5 is sociologically very important, and suggests that the changes in the structure of jobs has created an expanded new group of lower-level middle-class workers. It represents a new 'middle mass' of white-collar and routine non-manual workers, lending support to Pahl's (1988) thesis regarding the emergence of an 'onion'-shaped occupational structure in Britain. It is this group that is at the heart of the pressure on London's school system, competing for places in 'good' state schools with more affluent members of the middle classes, and trying to distance itself from those below them in the social structure. These divisions are both classed and ethnicised, and work through in complex ways in relation to education, as I show in the next section, in the context of recent research undertaken in East London.

East London and the competition for school places

East London has long been London's poorest quarter and, until comparatively recently, was the area of the capital most resistant to the gentrification that has affected the rest of London so dramatically over the last 30 or so years. One of the reasons that the UK won the right to stage the 2012 Olympic Games in East London was because of the claimed regeneration benefits from its legacy in what remains one of the poorest areas in the UK in one of the European Union's (EU) wealthiest regions. De-industrialisation (initially with the closure of the docks) and its subsequent re-industrialisation as a post-industrial economic space has transformed the economic base of the area. For many of its previous residents, the consequences have been devastating. Their redundant skills and lack of capital have placed them at a huge disadvantage in the changed labour and housing markets of East London – while some have moved out, others have simply failed to compete in the new economic, social and cultural environment.

In recent years, the area has undergone a dramatic ethnic transformation and witnessed the growth of a minority ethnic middle class. As such, it provides a fascinating lens through which to study the interaction of class, ethnicity and aspiration in an increasingly prescient preview of the kind of multi-ethnic city that London is now becoming; according to the 2011 Census, only 45 per cent of its population are white British-born. The story also raises some challenging issues about sustainability for existing groups – notably the white working class

– being unable to sustain and reproduce themselves in an area that has seen its economy undergo major restructuring. Only by moving have both these groups been able to address issues of their social reproduction in ways other than social deprivation. This group has been displaced from schooling, housing and employment as others with greater stocks of cultural, economic and social assets dominate these changed institutional sectors of social life.

This has been an apparently victimless transition, without huge protest; in precisely the same way that those who are 'gentrified out' melt away from social and social scientific view, so, too, in education do we see the practice of what Bourdieu termed 'symbolic violence'. Those who fail are simply those who don't 'make the cut', and the poor and powerless get blamed for their own failure in an exercise of 'soft power'. In what follows, we see this operate in two areas of East London in albeit different circumstances. An insidious part of this is how the process rolls out – for example, those displaced from the schooling and housing of Victoria Park in inner East London become the displacers and new gentry of Ilford in outer East London. There may be disputes about the nature and causation of gentrification – between, for example, those who emphasise *re*placement rather than *dis*placement – but what seems unambiguously clear is that when you have this degree of change, there is little sustainability.

Whereas the West End has long been the locus of wealth and power in London, the East End is equally that of poverty and deprivation. With the development of the docks, the working-class culture of East London became firmly established by the end of the 19th century and a bastion of London's working classes. With the exception of a few relatively upmarket areas, such as Barkingside, Wanstead and Woodford, East London retained its reputation through most of the 20th century as the poorest part of London, with an over-representation of the lower social classes and an under-representation of managerial and professional social classes (Willmott and Young, 1973). This was reinforced by the large-scale council redevelopment of much of Tower Hamlets and Newham after the Second World War in which streets of bomb-damaged terraced houses were replaced with high-rise or medium-rise 'deck access' council estates. By 1981, before the redevelopment of the Thames riverside for private housing, 85 per cent of households in Tower Hamlets lived in council housing – one of the highest proportions in Britain.

In 1957, when Young and Willmott (1962) published the first edition of their classic study of Bethnal Green, *Family and kinship in East London*, the East End of London was still a largely white, working-class residential area, with tight social links based around kinship and class. Although the more affluent were beginning to suburbanise out to Woodford and elsewhere (Willmott and Young, 1961), East London retained many of its traditional characteristics. In the last 30 years, however, East London has witnessed many dramatic economic, social and physical changes associated with de-industrialisation, starting with the closure of the docks from the late 1960s onwards, the redevelopment of Canary Wharf and associated riverside housing from the late 1980s onwards, and more recently the Olympics-related developments around Stratford. This development has transformed the area, bringing large numbers of white-collar jobs in financial and business services and new groups of residents who have bought or rented luxury apartments along the river (Butler, 2007).

While many of the traditional working-class manual occupations have disappeared and been replaced by employment in the rapidly expanding non-manual service sector, a parallel change has occurred in the ethnic structure of area. A predominantly white working-class population has, in large measure, been replaced by a new multi-ethnic one: many are still poor, but they are no longer largely white. Instead, large parts of East London, initially the inner boroughs, but more recently spreading to the outer ones, have witnessed one of the most dramatic ethnic transformations of any part of Britain in the last 30 years. Although the East End was subject to large-scale immigration in the 19th century, mostly by Eastern European Jews escaping persecution, the area retained its overwhelmingly white character. In the last half century, however, this has changed dramatically, with the immigration of large numbers from Asia, the Caribbean and Africa. Since 2004, and the accession of the Eastern European countries to the EU (the 'A8'), the area has also seen a major influx of East European workers.

The M25 orbital motorway now provides the *de facto* outer marker for London and its hinterland. Nowhere is this more apparent than in East London between the outer London boroughs and shire county of Essex. The marker between the outer London boroughs in which our research areas 4 and 5 are located and Essex used to be one of social class; it has increasingly now become one of ethnicity. The non-white (specifically Asian) populations of inner East London (particularly Newham) have been moving steadily outwards, replacing lower middle-class and working-class white populations who have moved further out across the white borderlands of the M25 (Butler and Hamnett, 2011a). Watt's (2009) ethnography of two estates on these white borderlands both sides of the M25 focused on the interweaving of aspiration, class and ethnicity, in which he demonstrates that many of these moves have been driven by the desire to maintain a sense of whiteness in what he terms, in a well-turned pun on Savage et al's (2005) eponymous concept, a sense of '[s]elective belonging'.

The place of those whites who have moved on has increasingly been taken by an aspiring black and minority ethnic (BME) middle class, many of whose members are themselves in flight from what they see as the long-term decline of the inner London boroughs in which they were – for the most part – born and raised.[3] The 'push' may be scenarios of decline, underachieving schools, new migrant groups and the spread of 'buy to let' housing; the 'pull' is one of high-achieving and, for the most part non–selective, schools and single-family semi-detached housing. Compared to its 'suburban whitelands' composition of just 30 years ago, Redbridge is now a very multi-ethnic place, yet, even in the remaining, predominantly white, boroughs of Havering and Barking & Dagenham, the proportion of *middle class* BME (particularly among Black Africans) is rising faster than that for the middle class as a whole (Butler et al, 2013). The proportion of non-white secondary school children is currently approximately three times the figure for the 2001 Census count of the population as a whole. This is indicative of the rapid rise in the BME population, which the 2011 Census showed as exceeding the predictions of most experts.

Education and schooling are, as I have suggested, central to this social and ethnic re-shaping of East London as inward-bound gentrifiers replace and displace outward-bound aspirationally driven suburbanisers (Butler and Hamnett, 2011a) and those stuck in a vicious cycle of deprivation and displacement, first, from housing (directly and indirectly) and now, from schooling (Butler et al, 2013). I examine how this has happened in two parts of East London. These two areas are formed by three of the five research areas (see Figure 10.4) that formed the basis for an Economic and Social Research Council (ESRC)-funded study on education, ethnicity and aspiration in East London (Butler and Hamnett, 2011a). Victoria Park (area 1) in inner East London and Redbridge (areas 4 and 5) in outer East London made up the ends of a transect across the north east of London; the dominant narratives were about social and spatial mobility, and how this varied by class and ethnicity and was articulated through the notion of aspiration. These are stories of class and ethnic change in which schooling informs the narratives of domination and exclusion – it is, I would suggest, a story of symbolic violence at work. The study involved a multi-methods approach and, in addition to intensive work on official and commercial data sources, we undertook a face-to-face survey of 300 respondents across our five areas and followed this up with 100 in-depth semi-structured interviews.[4]

Figure 10.4: The East London study area showing the five research locations

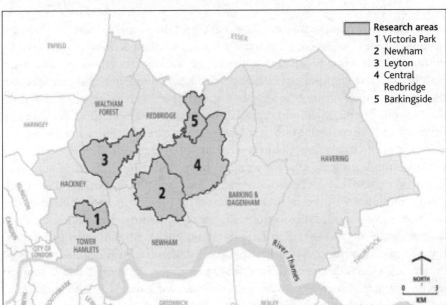

Victoria Park

Victoria Park in inner East London lies on the borders of Hackney and Tower Hamlets, and is a classic exemplar of London's gentrification, although it came to the scene 15 years later than the gentrification that occurred in Islington and Camden in the 1970s and early 1980s.[5] Direct displacement (Marcuse, 1985) was in evidence in the early stages – as landlords (including the Crown Estate) 'cashed out' and sold tenanted properties. In the early stage of its gentrification, the incomers tended to ignore the local schools and sent their children to the private schools in the City and elsewhere; more recently, however, they have tended to look to state schooling in the local area, particularly at primary school level. This has – at least symbolically – focused around Lauriston School that is regarded as the 'best school' in Hackney and has become the middle-class school of choice, with a catchment area of less than 200 metres.

> 'I think the biggest change since we've been here in this house – since '95 – is that people with children of school age are more prepared to stay here and educate them in Tower Hamlets than they used to be. Before we'd see people with young children coming up to secondary school and moving out when schooling became an issue, and so it was very difficult to keep families in the immediate area. But now virtually every single house in this street has a young family … it's lovely having all these young families and knowing that they are going to stay because, you know, as the children come up to secondary school age they are not moving away any more. So it has changed a lot.' (interview)

What happens when the middle classes fail to get their children into their school of choice? Our evidence suggests that there is a cascading process of displacement of those with less power by those with greater power; this includes people (both middle class and working class) feeling forced out of the area as they fail to get their children into a school which they would traditionally have regarded as their local school of choice. In addition, parents whose children fail to get into the favoured school experience feelings of disempowerment as 'their' school is labelled as 'unacceptable'. This denigration of what are sometimes well-performing schools comes through the power of the middle class to attach such labels (this is what Bourdieu means when he refers to 'symbolic violence'; see Bourdieu and Passeron, 1990). This ability of the relatively powerful to displace the less powerful from the 'better schools' occurs as a result of those with the necessary economic assets buying or renting property near to their target school. Perhaps more insidiously, if this is not possible, they work to get their children into faith schools despite their often-weak faith affiliations. At the same time, they simply 'blank out' (or render invisible) other schools because they do not have the 'right' social mix. All three behaviours were observed in Victoria Park (see Butler et al, 2013).

'A neighbour two doors down in the terrace – they're not short of money at all, extremely well-paid job, but he's got an ideological issue with private education so their children went to Lauriston, because that's the best primary school in the area. He's actually out of the catchment area but bought an investment apartment within the catchment area and registered that as his address just to get his kids in. And now the children have got to an age where they've left there they've gone to the new Mossbourne Academy which is the new school that was built from the ashes of the Hackney Downs former Grammar School because that was Hackney's new flagship school to register that they were going to turn around the education provision in the borough. It's got a new absolute top-class headmaster, there's no money being wasted or kept back in terms of provision of amenities or what have you. If that avenue hadn't been opened to them there's no way that they would have sent their children to, you know, Cardinal Pole or one of the other, you know, established Hackney secondary schools.' (interview)

This person, by getting his child into Lauriston, displaced a child who would otherwise have gone there; if they had genuinely lived in its catchment area, the child would not have subsequently got into Mossbourne, so there is a double advantaging happening. The victims of this process are not always the poor and disadvantaged, as the next respondent illustrates. She is middle class, but did not live sufficiently near to Lauriston to get her child in there. She was unwilling (and financially unable) to play the games practised by the parent quoted above. She takes up the story of what happened when she was turned down for a place. This account is a good illustration of the ability to render an alternative school unacceptable, albeit in an often self-reflexive manner:

'The only other one would have been Orchard.[...] I did know the school, and I think Orchard is actually really trying, and it has really improved an awful lot. But I honestly felt – and I read an Ofsted report that pulled this out – it wasn't very good at helping and supporting kids who didn't have any special needs. I think they just sort of say, thank god for them they're all right, and spend a lot of time nurturing a lot of kids that need a lot of help and there really are a lot of children there who need lots of support. But I thought I'm not sure that's going to serve my child. Because Orchard is the flip-side of Lauriston – it's a mirror image, it's you know, all the middle-class people get sucked into Lauriston and that leaves Orchard similarly skewed. And also it does look towards Hampton Park Estate, it's very ethnically mixed with lots of children on free school meals. I think once you get a proportion of middle-class kids that go there – a critical mass – then this area has to support more than one decent school, and at the moment Saint Elizabeth has become the kind of alternative school of choice that people are now [...] about, but a lot of people are locked out of it because they are not Catholic or church-going in some way. And whether Orchard will become the target for those people as it should … it's mad.' (interview)

Her analysis of Orchard is revealing:

'… Orchard is a three-storey Victorian building; it's very much a traditional Victorian school and it's a nightmare really as a school building now, it's full of stone staircases and big high classrooms that are badly designed for modern use. But anyway, so a friend tried to go and look round and the school were just really unhelpful, not consciously I don't think, but it didn't … Lauriston sells itself, it is the most cunning school for making sure its profile is really high.... They don't even have a website … they were really unhelpful. They said to people, you can't take a buggy around … you know a lot of people who are looking for a school for their older kid will have a younger one probably in a push chair....' (interview)

Orchard, in fact, has good results (in fact, one year it got better SAT scores than Lauriston), but it is felt to take the 'wrong kind of kids', from the 'wrong kinds of areas' with the 'wrong kinds of parents'. This respondent felt excluded from the community because she didn't get into Lauriston but she was not, however, going to Orchard because it was a working-class school, so she dusts off her religious credentials and gets her child into a faith school that wants to increase its middle-class intake. Others tell a similar story of not wanting their children to go to schools that are either too mixed (high Bangladeshi numbers) or insufficiently mixed (too white and working class), so they go for what might be termed the 'Goldilocks' solution which, in practice in this area, means 'going the faith route', as many of the respondents put it. The consequence of this is that these schools then become unavailable to the local working class who find themselves – whether they like it or not – at schools like Orchard that become schools for the poor and working class unable to get into schools elsewhere in the area. A similar story can be told at secondary level as the middle classes 'zero in' on a number of 'improved' schools. We have seen reference to the Mossbourne Academy in Hackney; a similar transformation can be seen in relation to Morpeth School in Tower Hamlets that has increasingly become a middle-class school of choice for Victoria Park parents wishing to remain in the state sector. The consequence has been that it has become increasingly inaccessible to those who might normally have expected to go there and now find that they live outside its *de facto* catchment area (see Butler et al, 2013).

What we have witnessed in Victoria Park is a process in which the middle classes (or at least those with sufficient assets) use their economic and cultural power to create some middle-class schools but equally to demonise others. The bigger picture argument is that displacement is not something that is narrowly confined to tenurial and class displacement, but has been transferred to schooling and social reproduction, and the players and victims are not simply the working class and the poor, but also members of the less-advantaged middle classes. The displacement cascades down from a relatively small upper-middle-class professional group to less-advantaged members of the middle class to the considerably disadvantaged. These groups (if they can) either displace those with less power than themselves or move out of the area or to schools that they would not previously have considered as being their local school. In our next case, we look at how this works out in an area that is considered to have good secondary schooling into which people have moved for precisely these reasons. The detail differs, but what we see is a similar 'sifting and sorting' of children which is ultimately determined according to the ability of their parents to buy access in the local housing markets surrounding the favoured schools. Many of those who moved to Redbridge have left areas like Victoria Park and Newham (albeit often for different reasons) because they are unable to participate at the level they would wish in their education markets. Having been displaced from one housing/education market in which they have insufficient power, they proceed to exercise their power in a less expensive market, but carrying with them the equity from a more expensive housing market. This allows them to buy into some of the most desirable school catchment areas in the whole of London, and their ability to do so prevents others from gaining access to these schools, thus starting a further chain of displacement.

Redbridge

The other side, therefore, of this manoeuvring for advantage is apparent among parents in Redbridge, many of whom moved to the area precisely because of its high-performing state schools – including two selective grammar schools.[6] For the most part, our interviewees were attracted by its non-selective comprehensive schools and, in particular, Seven Kings School. Many respondents were second and third generation British Asians who had themselves been upwardly socially mobile but felt frustrated by the poor educational provision in Newham (one of London's poorer performing boroughs) from where many came. Redbridge's attraction was that it had one of the best performances of any London LEA (see Figures 10.5 and 10.6).

Redbridge has a 'full suite' of selective and non-selective schools. *Prima inter pares* is Seven Kings High School, a non-selective comprehensive school with good, but not exceptional, results that stands at the top of the popularity stakes, with 10 applications for every place. This is followed by Valentines and the two selective grammar schools, Ilford County and Woodford County, each with around 6.5 applicants per place. Beal is the next most popular school, with a ratio of 5 applicants per place. There is then a slow fall off in popularity down to Hainault Forest High School, that has only 1.3 applicants per place and to which many

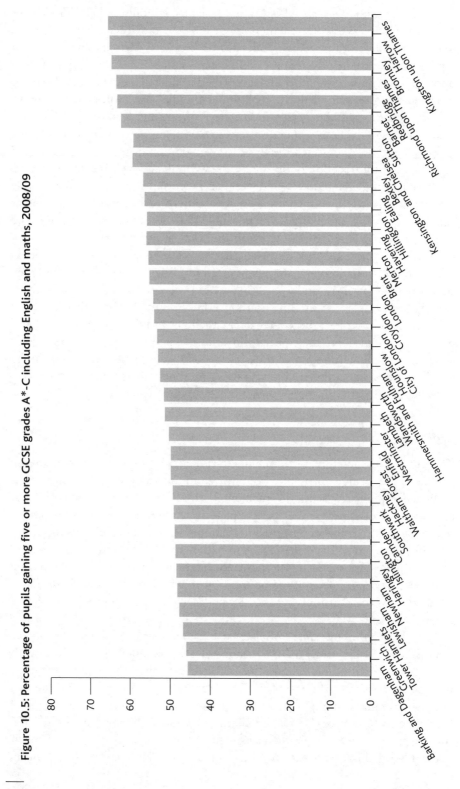

Figure 10.5: Percentage of pupils gaining five or more GCSE grades A*-C including English and maths, 2008/09

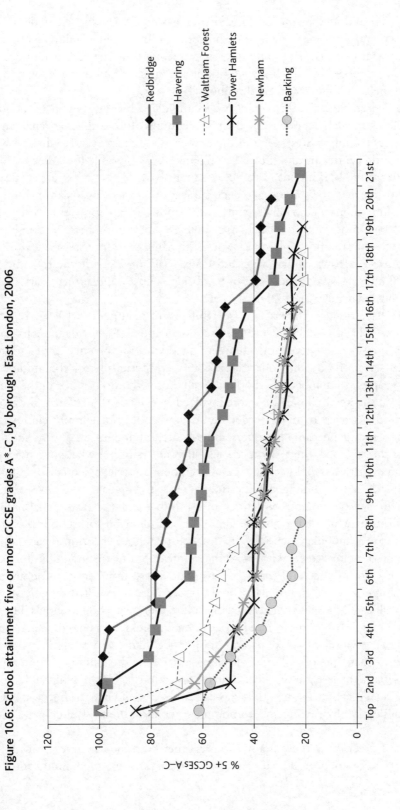

Figure 10.6: School attainment five or more GCSE grades A*–C, by borough, East London, 2006

pupils are allocated by the local authority as a way of balancing excess demand for more popular schools elsewhere in the borough. In fact, Hainault is an improving school with results that would impress in many of the neighbouring boroughs, but it is a school to which several of our respondents said that they would only send their children "over my dead body".

In the remainder of this section we examine how parents negotiate the supply of places in such schools, and their perceptions of how this particular market operates (and frustrates). One of the chosen research areas in Redbridge was in the south/centre, around Ilford/Seven Kings (area 4), while the other was in the north around Barkingside (area 5) (see Figure 10.4). These two areas are distinct; the former has, for some years, been subject to a process of Asian in-migration from inner London, notably Newham. In Barkingside this process has only begun to change more recently, partly as a spillover effect from a rise in house prices elsewhere in the borough, and partly as its white working class have continued to move east towards Havering and Essex. Barkingside is home to some large social housing estates and some of Redbridge's least popular secondary schools, notably, Hainault Forest High School.

We have discussed elsewhere (see Butler and Hamnett, 2010; Hamnett and Butler, 2011) parental perceptions of school quality in Redbridge; the focus here is on how the geography of catchment areas works in practice as the arbiter of social selection and thus of social mobility and, crucially for the argument in this chapter, to deny good schooling to all those who do not live in the school's 'golden shadow'. Choice therefore involved risk; it was this risk that most of the respondents tried to mitigate but found they could not entirely eliminate. As some respondents came to understand too late, catchment areas were not always what they seemed: there was a crucial difference between what you could apply for and what you might actually get. Catchment areas act as a qualifying, but not necessarily a determining, qualification for entry to popular schools in Redbridge; it is the *de facto* 'distance to school' measure that is the critical spatial rationing mechanism which balances the supply of, and demand for, school places. For 'good' (read 'popular') schools, the distance-to-school criterion meant living in the surrounding streets with the distance measured by geographic information systems from the school main gate to your house front door, using approved crossing places. For unpopular schools, places were often filled up only after the LEA allocated those who had failed to get into their first-choice schools (Hamnett and Butler, 2011). The ambiguity of catchment areas does not come across in all of the interviews, as not all parents grasped that living in a catchment area is, in fact, no guarantee of a place. In Barkingside, where the schools are not popular, the catchment area is ironically a kind of 'allocation cage' from which it is difficult to escape, precisely because the schools that they would like to choose are denied them despite their being able to nominate them on their list of choices:

> 'I don't think there is any choice, if they're in the catchment for the
> school, then for 90 per cent of parents that's where their child's gotta

go. I know parents try, occasionally they do, they plump for a school that's not, that they really don't stand a chance of getting into, but it's either one or the other'. (interview)

However, the actual home-to-school distance required to guarantee a place can (and does) change year by year, indicating that, in practice, a catchment area is not only dynamic but simply an 'enabling device' rather than a right. In the case of the ever-popular Seven Kings High School, to have any chance of getting in you need to live within a few hundred metres of the school:

> 'Seven Kings is quite a big school but it has a very small catchment so you have to be in specific roadsets, it's not like borough-wide or anything, it's tight, and you do find there are loads of people who are moving in, buying flats, etc, specifically to get their kids into the school. Obviously the prices of the houses rise and it has a knock-on effect.' (interview)

The rules of the game are clear: not opting for a first choice for which you have a realistic chance of success (by living well within its catchment area) is potentially very risky. If a parent fails to get her/his first choice, there is a danger that he or she may not get any of the schools on their list of preferences or, at best, one of the ones towards the bottom for which demand is not so high, and places are filled by the LEA. An understanding of this situation leads to a calculated assessment of risk in which an overambitious choice can result in an allocation to a lower ranked school.

As in Victoria Park, those with assets can 'play the system' quite shamelessly in order to maximise their chances and minimise the risk of not getting into a particular non-selective school:

> 'We did actually [laughing] have to rent a flat out for a whole year, but it was cheaper in the long run than actually sending him to a private school for the long term. It's making a sacrifice, a whole year of rent is like paying a second mortgage, but we thought that was better than sending him private which was 14,000 pounds a year, so in the long term it suited us, he is in the school where I wanted him to be. Unfortunately it is a little bit underhand but we had to do it.' (interview)

What we see in both Victoria Park and Redbridge is the working out of the struggles and strategic manoeuvring that parents feel obliged to undertake in London today. As the quotation above acknowledges, this involves all sorts of 'shady' and semi-legal activities necessary to play the game. This, however, is not a game in which those with insufficient assets can play; those with some assets can shift geographically – often trading distance from the centre (for example, from Victoria Park to Seven Kings) to gain power and traction in a less expensive housing/education market. This is simply a trading situation in which those with no power lose out and into only those with power can enter. The overall notion of sustainability for a city in which these class manoeuvres can occur is in itself unsustainable because the overall message is that the mechanism (equality of opportunity through equal access to education) has itself become the means for sifting and sorting its population. This, in subtly different ways, is what has been happening, both in Victoria Park and Redbridge, and is occurring across the city.

Conclusion

The conclusion to be drawn from this is simple and clear. Schooling and education should be the means by which people can realise their aspirations for their children and so achieve intergenerational social mobility. What we have shown is that, despite an often quite dramatic increase in overall rates of attainment by London's schools, there is evidence of a worrying trend towards clustering around the best schools by the culturally, economically and socially advantaged, which has the effect of excluding and displacing others. Given the well-known association between school performance and the social composition of its intake, this suggests that London is failing to provide the educational resources to enable its population to fulfil its potential. This is a denial of the equality of opportunity agenda that underlay the move to a comprehensive system 40 years ago, and arguably represents a *de facto* return to the days of selection where privilege shuts out all but the brightest minority from access to higher education. More generally, if we argue that sustainability − if it is to be anything other than a meaningless rhetoric − requires that a city (or nation state) is able to offer people the means to achieve social reproduction in line with their aspirations as well as their capabilities, then the trends identified here would suggest that London is rapidly becoming a less, not more, sustainable as a city.

It is nearly 50 years since maintenance grants and paid tuition fees enabled all to go to university, irrespective of their material circumstances. This is now a gone world in which higher education is structured by ability to pay, and the same is now happening with primary and secondary schooling. The sociology of this inequality is well known; what is now becoming apparent is its geography. London will probably cope economically, as it always has done, by attracting the 'brightest and the best' from elsewhere − at a cost to those places − but what is not clear is how it will cope with the frustrated ambitions of a population denied the right to participate in the wealth of the city. It is hard to see how, by any definition, this behaviour is sustainable. In the summer of 2011 we saw in the London riots that engulfed much of the inner city the consequences of frustrated aspiration through the withdrawal of the Education Maintenance Allowance that enabled many poor young people to stay on at school. If riots are the indicator of an unsustainable urban system, then attention needs to be focused on the methods of secondary school allocation which are imposing social segregation on the city; the advantaged middle classes are not only garnering the best of the educational assets, but are also actively avoiding having their children mix with the less advantaged. For their part, the latter will no doubt learn the lesson which was preached for much of the 19th and 20th centuries which is, that 'school is not for them'. This was the message encapsulated by Paul Willis (1977) in his ethnography of a working-class school in the distinction between 'the lads' and 'the earholes'. The tragedy was that both groups lost out. What we are doing in London is recreating that system, in which aspiration and resistance are both bound for failure.

Notes

[1] It should be noted that much of this research has been widely published elsewhere in a series of articles by myself and my colleague Chris Hamnett; in this chapter, I reflect on this research in light of the theme about sustainability. Readers interested in the detail should consult the individual papers (cited in the References at the end of this chapter) or, for a comprehensive overview, our 2011 book, *Ethnicity, class and aspiration: the making of the new East End* (Bristol, Policy Press).

[2] SEG 5, or intermediate social groups, consists of ancillary workers (SEG 5.1) and non-manual foremen and supervisors (SEG 5.2). This group forms a significant proportion of the national workforce and has become increasingly important over the two decades under examination. Between 1981 and 2001 the share of SEG 5 of the SEG (1-15) total in England and Wales more than doubled, from 10 to 22 per cent. SEG 5.1 covers a wide range of occupations in the health, teaching, scientific, engineering and financial occupations (Butler et al, 2008). These occupations include nurses, health technicians such as radiographers and opticians, social workers, health inspectors, quantity surveyors, accountants, artists, writers and graphic designers. All belong to the social class group 2 in the new social classification (NS-SEC) that allocates occupations according to whether they are responsible for managing others, the number of employees in the company and if they are self-employed. Under the new classification SEG 5.1 members are distributed among the 'Higher managerial and professional' (10 per cent) (NS-SEC 1), 'Lower managerial and professional' (75 per cent) (NS-SEC 2), the 'Intermediate' (9 per cent) (NS-SEC 3) and 'Small employers and own account workers' (5 per cent). The residual 1 per cent is allocated to lower social classes. SEG 5.2 covers occupations such as the police, fire and prison service officers, security guards, traffic wardens, sales assistants, telephone operators and a range of routine clerical workers and assistants. In the new classification they are allocated to the classes of 'Lower managerial and professional' (68 per cent) (NS-SEC 2) and 'Lower supervisors' (32 per cent) (NS-SEC 5) (Rose and O'Reilly, 1997, p 2). Thus a considerable proportion, roughly one-third, of SEG 5.2 is not typically middle class. However, SEG 5.2 only represents approximately 16 per cent of SEG 5 (Rose and Pevalin, 2005). Thus, 82 per cent of SEG 5 has been reclassified as higher and lower managerial and professional classes under the new system (NS-SEC 1 and 2), and only about 18 per cent of the old SEG 5 are not classified as middle class, with most being classified into NS-SEC 3.1 (Intermediate) (Butler et al, 2008).

[3] BME stands for black and minority ethnic; sometimes it is referred to as BAME, black, Asian and minority ethnic. How to refer to non-white groups is a political minefield, and many such terms rapidly become politically unacceptable. In Europe, such longstanding minorities are often referred to as 'immigrants', which would be unacceptable in the UK.

[4] The data was gathered in the context of an ESRC-funded research project that utilised a multi-method approach and involved analysis of several official data sources such as the census and Pupil Level Annual School Census (PLASC), and the linked National Pupil Database (NPD) to which we linked MOSAIC, a commercially available geo-demographic database that we used as a substitute for an indicator of social class which is missing from PLASC/NPD. In addition, we undertook 300 face-to-face interviews and a follow-up sample of approximately 100 semi-structured interviews (most of the quotations in what follows were taken from these).

[5] The content of this section is discussed in more detail in Butler et al (2013)

[6] See Butler and Hamnett (2010) and Hamnett and Butler (2011).

References

Ball, S., Bowe, R. and Gewirtz, S. (1995) 'Circuits of schooling: a sociological exploration of parental choice of school in social class contexts', *Sociological Review*, vol 43, no 1, pp 52-78.

Banks, O. (1968) *The sociology of education*, London: Batsford.

Bourdieu, P. and Passeron, J.C. (1990) *Reproduction in education, society and culture*, London: Sage.

Buck, N., Gordon, I., Hall, P., Harloe, M. and Kleinman, M. (2002) *Working capital: life and labour in contemporary London*, London: Routledge.

Butler, T. (1997) *Gentrification and the middle classes*, Aldershot: Ashgate.

Butler, T. (2007) 'For gentrification?', *Environment and Planning A*, vol 39, no 1, pp 162-81.

Butler, T. and Hamnett, C. (2010) 'You take what you are given: the limits to parental choice in education in East London', *Environment and Planning A*, vol 42, no 10, pp 2431-50.

Butler, T. and Hamnett, C. (2011a) *Ethnicity, class and aspiration: understanding London's new East End*, Bristol: Policy Press.

Butler, T. and Hamnett, C. (2011b) 'Location, education: place, choice and constraint', *Children's Geographies*, vol 9, no 1, pp 35-48.

Butler, T. and Robson, G. (2003) *London calling: the middle classes and the remaking of inner London*, Oxford: Berg.

Butler, T., Hamnett, C. and Ramsden, M. (2008) 'Inward and upward? Marking out social class change in London 1981-2001', *Urban Studies*, vol 45, no 1, pp 67-88.

Butler, T., Hamnett, C. and Ramsden, M. (2013) 'Gentrification, education and exclusionary displacement in East London', *International Journal of Urban and Regional Research*, vol 37, no 2, pp 556-75.

Davidson, M. and Wyly, E. (2012) 'Class-ifying London: questioning social division and space claims in the post-industrial metropolis', *City*, vol 16, no 4, pp 395-421.

Goldthorpe, J.H. (1987) *Social mobility and class structure in modern Britain*, Oxford: Clarendon Press.

Halsey, A.H. and Karabel, J. (eds) (1977) *Power and ideology in education*, Oxford: Oxford University Press.

Hamnett, C. and Butler, T. (2011) 'Geography matters: the role of catchment area and distance as key determinants of school allocation and educational access in East London', *Transactions of the Institute of British Geographers*, vol 36, no 4, pp 479-500.

Hamnett, C. and Butler, T. (2013) 'Re-classifying London: a growing middle class and increasing inequality', *City*, vol 17, no 2, pp 197-208.

Jackson, B. and Marsden, D. (1962) *Education and the working class; some general themes raised by a study of 88 working-class children in a northern industrial city*, London: Routledge & Kegan Paul.

Lees, L., Slater, T. and Wyly, E. (2008) *Gentrification*, New York: Routledge.

Marcuse, P. (1985) 'Gentrification, abandonment, and displacement: connections, causes, and policy responses in New York City', *Journal of Urban and Contemporary Law*, vol 28, pp 195-240.

Pahl, R.E. (1988) '"Is the emperor naked?" some questions on the adequacy of sociological theory in urban and regional research', *International Journal of Urban and Regional Research*, vol 13, pp 709-20.

Rex, J. (1961) *Key problems of sociological theory*, London: Routledge & Kegan Paul.

Rex, J. and Moore, R. (1967) *Race, community and conflict: a study of Sparkbrook*, Oxford: Oxford University Press.

Rose, D. and O'Reilly, K. (eds) (1997) *Constructing classes: towards a new social classification for the UK,* Swindon: Economic and Social Research Council and Office for National Statistics.

Rose D., Pevalin, D. and O'Reilly, K. (2005) *The NS-SEC: Origins, Development and Use*, Basingstoke: Palgrave.

Savage, M., Bagnall, G. and Longhurst, B. (2005) *Globalisation and belonging*, London: Sage.

Watt, P. (2009) 'Living in an oasis: middle-class disaffiliation and selective belonging in an English suburb', *Environment and Planning A*, vol 41, pp 2874-92.

Willis, P. (1977) *Learning to labour: how working class kids get working class jobs*, Aldershot: Gower.

Willmott, P. and Young, M. (1961) *Family and class in a London suburb*, London: Routledge & Kegan Paul.

Willmott, P. and Young, M. (1973) 'Social class and geography', in D. Donnison and D. Eversley (eds) *London: urban patterns, problems and policies*, London: Heinemann, pp 190-214.

Young, M. and Willmott, P. (1962) *Family and kinship in East London*, Harmondsworth: Penguin.

ELEVEN

Sustaining the public: the future of public space in London?

James Fournière

Introduction

Sustainability is somewhat of a nebulous concept (Evans and Jones, 2008; Davidson, 2010) which can be applied across a range of social, economic and environmental phenomena. However, its specific application to urban public space remains scarce. For example, Carmona and Wunderlich's (2012) comprehensive review of different types of contemporary urban public spaces within London makes no explicit reference to sustainability, be that environmental, economic or social. Allusions to sustainability arguably come through notions of diversity and the assumption that diverse public spaces are in some way socially sustainable, but again, this is implied and connected to larger and equally problematic concepts such as 'community' (see, for example, Project for Public Spaces, 2012).

Chiesura (2004) links the social sustainability of public spaces through their ability to improve the quality of life of users of the spaces. However, 'quality of life' has often been applied to selective groups of people at the expense of other users (for more on the use of 'quality of life' initiatives, see Mitchell, 2003; Vitale, 2008). A potentially more productive way of examining sustainability in relation to urban public spaces comes through the introduction of cultural sustainability and cultural reproduction. Low et al (2005), in their examination of urban parks, adopt Throsby's (1995) framework in which 'sustainability refers to the evolutionary or lasting qualities of phenomena, avoidance of short-term or temporary solutions, and a concern with the self-generating or self-perpetuating characteristics of a system' (Low et al, 2005, p 5). Within a social context, sustainability is thus viewed as 'maintaining and enhancing the diverse histories, values, and relationships of contemporary populations' (Low et al, 2005, p 5). This analytical framework is developed through three dimensions: place preservation, cultural ecology theories and cultural diversity (Low et al, 2005, p 5).

Diverse public spaces should thus allow and sustain diverse encounters, bringing different sections of society into contact and potential conflict with each other. This was formally recognised by the first Mayor of London, Ken Livingstone, in his '100 Public Spaces Programme', stating:

> Cities have always been places where people gather – to talk, to argue, to rest, to trade. Squares and streets, parks and other green spaces, foyers and public buildings form a city's public realm, the place where encounters – chance and planned – can occur. (Mayor of London, 2002, p 3)

The '100 Public Spaces Programme' was primarily concerned with upgrading the quality of existing public spaces in the lead-up to the London 2012 Olympic Games, projects specifically orientated for 'promoting urban renaissance' (Mayor of London, 2002, p 2; for a more critical assessment of the inclusiveness of urban renaissance policies, see Lees, 2008). Despite this impetus, the lack of realistic political leverage with private developers, along with funding and planning issues, the plan delivered only five upgraded public spaces in a five-year period (Carmona and Wunderlich, 2012, p 42).

Following his election as Mayor of London in 2008, Boris Johnson published his *Manifesto for public spaces*, again reiterating the importance of public space, but identifying that:

> There is a growing trend towards the private management of publicly accessible space where this type of "corporatisation" occurs, especially in the larger commercial developments, Londoners can feel themselves excluded from parts of their own city. (Mayor of London, 2009, p 9)

The trend to privatise and commercialise public space had previously been highlighted by Anna Minton in her 2006 report for the Royal Institution of Chartered Surveyors (see Minton, 2006). This effective 'closing down' of parts of the city can only limit diverse encounters between members of the public, producing 'ghettoised' divisions within the city across class, ethnicity and other social divisions (Harvey, 2004, p 238; see also Minton, 2012).

In this chapter, largely through the frame of cultural diversity, I first look at the problems of associating sustainability with urban public space, in particular, issues surrounding the singular dimension of *a* public in such a multicultural global city as London. I then look at a contemporary example of shifting 'publics' and their spatiality, specifically in relation to the conflict between social and economic sustainability and other processes such as gentrification and sanitisation. I then focus in more depth on the Canary Wharf Estate in East London, the types of public spaces and publics produced within the estate, how these might reflect the future of urban public spaces in London and their prospects for social and cultural sustainability, followed by a brief review of public spaces currently in development and their potential for diversity.

Problematic publics and the importance of public space

An initial problem that must be addressed when investigating public space is the fact that there is no singular public (Warner, 2002), and therefore public spaces exist in what Shepard and Smithsimon (2011) refer to as a dialectical relationship of repression and resistance. In this conceptualisation, a specific group or public attempt to exert control over a public space, repressing accessibility and usage of the space to other publics. At the same time, other publics will attempt to resist the repression they are experiencing, either then repressing other publics or potentially resulting in conflict between the competing publics. This concept is demonstrated through the example in the next section, but first, it is useful to reflect on the importance of urban public space.

Public space has served as the principle civic forum of society in cities since at least the foundation of democracy in Ancient Greece (Geenens and Tinnevelt, 2008). In the contemporary city, urban public space, while still providing its civic and democratic functions, acts as a place where people can encounter others and experience the difference that exists within society (Merrifield, 2002). The Mayor has recognised the importance of public space in London, stating:

> Public spaces are part of what defines a city. They are the places where people come together to meet, talk, eat and drink, trade, debate or simply pass through. They shape the way communities and neighbourhoods mesh together. They inform the way everyone sees the city, and they contribute to the lives of its residents and the experiences of its visitors. Well designed and decently maintained public spaces can bring communities and people together and encourage physical and cultural activity, recreation and play. They can restore a sense of place, identity and pride in an area, and play a big part in attracting businesses and jobs. (Mayor of London, 2009, p 1)

Here, the Mayor emphasises both the social and economic benefits of urban public space in the contemporary city, and how the interaction of people in public space can develop and sustain communities. Importantly, he notes the use of space rather than its mere existence, as Merrifield (2013, p 131) also states when talking about encounters and interaction in public space:

> That is why they are public: because they enable public discourses, public conversations to talk to each other, to meet each other. They are public not because they are simply there, in the open, in a city center, but because these spaces are made public by people encountering one another in these spaces.

However, despite the social importance of encountering difference (see Sennett, 1970; Lofland, 1998), London is increasingly becoming polarised, driven in no small part by economic changes which are restructuring the city, through the reform of social housing and other forms of welfare and support, but also by multiple fear and insecurity complexes, leading to isolated lifestyles and securitised and insular spaces (Williams, 2004; Minton, 2012). Using Low et al's (2005) framework for social sustainability through cultural diversity, I now turn to examine a contemporary conflict over public space in London before looking towards the potential future of public space in the city.

Conflicting publics: Southbank Centre Undercroft skate park

The Southbank Centre complex covers 21 acres of development on the south bank of the River Thames. The Centre was commissioned by London County Council (LCC) and constructed in a series of phases between 1951 and 1964 (Carmona and Wunderlich, 2012, p 147). Since the 1970s, the Undercroft (see Figure 11.1) beneath the Queen Elizabeth Hall has been extensively used by skaters and skateboarders due to the concrete ramparts and protection from the elements (see Borden, 2001, 2013; Whitter, 2005). The skater Crispin Robinson (2013) recalls:

> Images of South Bank dominated the main UK magazine *Skateboard*. Bonafide US skate superstars passed through. In an era largely devoid of purpose-built skate spots, it was our home, our mecca. By the time some good commercial spots had been built, the bubble had burst, the money went elsewhere, and one by one they closed down until we were back where we started.

The use of the space has generally been tolerated, in part because it contains the skaters' activities in a specific space and away from the newly redeveloped areas of the Southbank Centre (Carmona and Wunderlich, 2012, p 161). A more cynical view might be that the use of the space is encouraged because it adds to the cultural capital of the Southbank Centre, especially given the permission of graffiti, attracting skaters who may use other facilities geared towards consumption, as well as additional visitors, such as tourists and the numerous photographers who are often gathered around the area.

On 6 March 2013 the Southbank Centre, a charity tasked with managing the complex by Arts Council England (a non-departmental public body of the Department of Culture, Media and Sport), formally launched a redevelopment plan that would see the removal of the skate park to make space for further retail units (for more information on the proposal, see www.thefestivalwing.com). The redevelopment plan set the Centre and their envisaged public against the existing public of skaters, their followers and supporters. The plan received extensive press coverage (see, for example, Escobales, 2013) and the launch of a petition that has received in excess of 60,000 signatures at the time of writing (2013). This is not the first displacement from the Centre – as part of an earlier redevelopment in

Figure 11.1: The Undercroft, Southbank Centre, London

© Rebecca Anderson

the 1990s, large numbers of homeless people were evicted from the site (Baeten, 2001), and although the Royal Festival Hall still maintains an 'open foyers' policy, allowing groups to meet inside the building, it is not uncommon to see *Big Issue* sellers or rough sleepers being removed from the area by the Centre's security staff.

The Southbank Centre replied initially to the skaters' contestation by launching a website along with their own petition, which they state will be used in support of their planning application (see www.southbankforall.org). The proposals were subsequently altered to offer an alternative space for the skate park; however, as professional skater Crispin Robinson (2013) argues:

> Moving the skaters to a purpose-built spot along the river misses the point. Reclaimed urban spaces are more than just bits of forgotten concrete. They have memories. They resonate with ghosts of the past. They contribute to the richness and diversity of our lives. Their value cannot be measured in material terms.

Consequently, the Southbank Centre offered to sell the Undercroft to the skaters for £17 million, which would cover the loss in retail space, with the artistic director of the Centre offering to assist in a fundraising campaign, but only giving the group potentially less than six months to raise the required capital (Rogers, 2013). This action resulted in counterclaims from both sides, with the Southbank Centre publishing a public letter stating that the skaters' group,

'Long Live Southbank', was acting in 'bad faith' (Southbank Centre, 2013). While the campaign to save the space has received significant support, there are still contestations over the continued use of the space, as a commenter on the Building Design architecture website states:

> Just because it has been there many years does not make it culturally significant. I cringed every time I passed by that space when taking a leisurely walk along the ever pleasant South Bank. They feel like squatters to me, selfishly hijacking a potentially nice public space for enjoyment of all, and impossible to get rid of. I am sure I am not the only one who feels this way. ('Jordan Duc', quoted in Rogers, 2013)

In addition to aesthetic claims, as above, especially as the surrounding area becomes more sanitised and commercialised, it is understandable that certain groups, such as older people or those with young children, may feel uncomfortable around such spaces, particularly when there are large groups of youths gathered (Sibley, 1995). However, diversity is not always comfortable, and conflict, even if purely as an affective response, is part of the process of learning to tolerate others in society (Shepard and Smithsimon, 2011, pp 4-5). It is also worth noting that there is a notable lack of criminal behaviour in the space, evidenced not just through the lack of press coverage, but also through the Southbank Centre's 'hands-off' approach to controlling the site, and therefore such fears appear unfounded (for more on the rationalisation of fear, see Minton, 2012). The sociologist Richard Sennett (1970, p 189), discussing the 'purified city', a place where diversity is hidden from view, calls for a city, and consequently urban public spaces, where the affluent are forced through the density of the urban form to encounter and engage with other classes, ethnicities, and so on. While Merrifield (1996, p 60) criticises Sennett for his 'naïve and voluntaristic understanding', arguing that he ignores the structural power and class relations in society, along with the empirical reality that people have already chosen to isolate themselves, he does, however, recognise the need for visible diversity in public space, stating that:

> ... [m]aintaining visible *presence* in public is ... vital for those unjustly stigmatized and marginalized groups struggling for *recognition*. (Merrifield, 1996, p 63; original emphasis)

The Southbank Centre and Lambeth Borough Council have already displaced homeless people from the complex; reducing the visible presence of difference, the displacement of the skaters to a more sanitised space further out of the way, can only limit the wider exposure of the public to difference. Crispin Robinson (2013) further argues that maintaining the Undercroft would allow:

> ... the South Bank complex [to] remain an exciting, multidimensional urban space that includes all aspects of culture, high and low, street and

salon, loose and structured. This is the sort of public space we need, not another glut of privately owned, heavily regulated opportunities to spend what little money we have left.

Returning to social sustainability and Low et al's (2005, pp 5-9) theoretical framework, the preservation of place at the Undercroft is lost as existing users are being displaced to a simulacra of their former space. Low et al argue that '[c]ultural ecosystems are located in time and space, for a cultural ecosystem to be maintained or conserved, its place(s) must be preserved'. In the above quote by Crispin Robinson, it is clear that the skaters have a cultural and historic attachment to the particular place, and relocating the skate park therefore disrupts these memories (see Pile, 2005, pp 137-40). The relocation of the skaters also has the potential to eradicate the established cultural ecosystem of the space as existing users move on and new users move in, replacing one public for another (Low, 2000; for a similar account of cultural ecosystem displacement in relation to skateboarding youth, see Lees, 2003).

In consideration of place preservation and the maintenance of cultural ecosystems alone, the Southbank Centre's redevelopment plans can be seen to be an example of social unsustainability. The third dimension, that of cultural diversity, is assumed to compound this as an organic, vibrant and convivial space is replaced by a managed, purpose-built space, to which the current users already feel resentment. In this instance, the Southbank Centre appears to be prioritising economic sustainability over a culturally diverse social sustainability, an act of 'vandalism of *our* cultural heritage' (Robinson, 2013; emphasis added). (For more on the debate, see Spensley and Holland, 2013.) I now turn to the Canary Wharf Estate, which has been argued to be symptomatic of the new development of public spaces in London (Minton, 2012).

Canary Wharf, a blueprint for the future of public space?

Canary Wharf, part of East London's Docklands, was once part of the busiest port in the world; however, the area suffered a dramatic decline from the late 1960s, due in part to a period of economic recession that saw world shipping rates fall, alongside technological innovation, in particular, the introduction of containerisation and larger ships than the docks were able to handle (Brownill, 1990). Through a series of complicated political and economic changes, the government instigated the regeneration of the area through the creation of the London Docklands Development Corporation (LDDC) in 1981 (Brownill, 1990). One outcome of the neoliberal-orientated redevelopment of the area was the creation of the Canary Wharf Estate (see Figure 11.2), which, over recent decades, has developed into a major global financial district with a host of integrated retail and leisure facilities. The Estate currently covers 97 acres, with plans to extend it through several stages and to double the working population of approximately 100,000 by 2025 (Canary Wharf Group, 2010a; Prynn, 2012).

The estate, often criticised for its heavy security, including extensive CCTV surveillance, security patrols with dogs, road barriers and vehicle searches, and insularity (see Williams, 2004), can be described as catering to a differentiated, yet homogeneous, public of finance and other related service sector workers. Strolling through the estate, which borders numerous economically deprived communities in Poplar and Wapping (Foster, 1999), one can immediately sense the homogeneity through the similarity of attire and purpose; the individual who stops to look at the direction markers is clearly an outsider. And yet, Canary Wharf contains a wealth of high-quality, well-maintained public spaces, albeit privately owned public spaces. From parks to piazzas, from shopping malls to riverside promenades, and not to mention one of the largest public art collections in the country (Canary Wharf Group, 2010b), the estate provides a wealth of spaces that are open to the public and easily accessible by public transportation or on foot from the neighbouring communities. The juxtaposition of Canary Wharf, a centre of high wealth, to areas such as Poplar, one of the most economically deprived areas in Britain (Institute for Sustainability, 2012), and their close proximity, should produce the opportunity for diverse encounters in the surrounding public spaces, if it were not for the Estate being produced as a space of transient workers, upmarket retail and sanitised and highly controlled public spaces.

One long-term resident of the Lansbury Estate, an adjacent council estate in Poplar, who I met at the Idea Store, a public library operated by the London Borough of Tower Hamlets in the eastern periphery of the Canary Wharf Estate, told me:

> 'I've lived in Poplar for long enough to remember the dock walls, now there is this. I was against the building [of the estate], I remember the posters "big money is moving in" … and a lot of us thought we'd get moved on. Nothing happened, but nothing has got better either. We have some new buildings, a new library, but I prefer to come here, it's a nice walk, not that I feel part of the place, the library is an island on an island, the whole place is just little islands, the rich island, the poor island.' (interview, April 2013)

However, this resident is one of a limited number of residents from the surrounding neighbourhoods to visit the estate, with the majority purely using the public library for internet access, or teenagers venturing into the shopping malls at the weekends when the executive working community is largely absent. The self-exclusion of visiting residents from surrounding neighbourhoods from the more central public spaces of Canary Wharf is somewhat at odds with user perceptions of those spaces. For example, Carmona and Wunderlich's (2012, p 109) survey of users of Canada Square, a piazza within the centre of the estate, demonstrated that 37 per cent of users thought that nobody would feel unwelcome and that 31 per cent thought 'beggars, homeless & alcoholics' would feel unwelcome (Carmona and Wunderlich, 2012, p 109). When the same question was raised during in-depth interviews, most participants admitted it was not something they had even considered. However, the label used by Carmona and Wunderlich, 'beggars, homeless & alcoholics', is telling in terms of the types of people one would never expect to find in such a sanitised and securitised space. As the estate manager states:

> If you wish to cause trouble you go elsewhere – part of that is about the feeling of the place, it's quality and upkeep, the lack of litter and graffiti, the fact that it is well lit and maintained, plus the knowledge that there is a security presence that will step in if necessary. (quoted in Carmona and Wunderlich, 2012, p 111)

While Canary Wharf employs a heavy security presence, including 1,600 CCTV cameras, programmatic urban design (see Figures 11.2 and 11.3), such as vast open spaces providing a form of 'natural surveillance', to highly prescribed routes through the estate, also make the space feel exclusionary to those who 'do not fit in' or do not know 'the rules' of movement, be they the homeless, beggars or even those not wearing the 'correct' attire (for more on security and sanitisation, see Williams, 2004; Lang, 2005). John Allen (2006) discusses what he terms the 'ambient power' of space which, in relation to the character of an urban setting,

Figure 11.2: Jubilee Park, Canary Wharf, London

© Rebecca Anderson

Figure 11.3: CCTV at the periphery of the Canary Wharf Estate, London

© Rebecca Anderson

produces 'a particular atmosphere, a specific mood, a certain feeling – that affects how we experience it and which, in turn, seeks to induce certain stances' (Allen, 2006, p 445). The deployment of urban design in this manner sees that power is:

Exercised through a seductive spatial arrangement, where the experience of being in the space is itself the expression of power. Choices are restricted, options are curtailed and possibilities are closed down by degree through the forum's ambient qualities. (Allen, 2006, p 454)

This affective power can be seen through the ways in which certain groups, namely, those from neighbouring communities (with the exception of those employed in security or cleaning positions with the estate) make use of the public spaces at the periphery of the estate, particularly the public library. One particular area local residents seemed more willing to visit was Churchill Place, a quiet corner at the edge of the estate, where the library, a prayer room, post office and a Starbucks cafe are located, along with a visibly lower security presence. This seemed preferable than venturing into the 'heartland', which is populated by more expensive shops and restaurants, and goes someway to explaining the homogeneity of users of the more central locations, such as the uniform attire and behaviours. The exception to this is teenagers, who particularly at the weekends, but also after school, make use of the central shopping malls, appearing ambivalent to their noticeable presence.

The sense of lack of belonging in the Canary Wharf Estate exhibited by the resident of Poplar quoted above reflects the 'it's not for us' psychology of those publics living next to upscale regeneration projects. Paul Watt (2013) found a similar situation at the London Olympic site in Stratford, only a short distance from Canary Wharf (for more on new build developments along the Thames in this area, see Davidson and Lees, 2005). How one increases a sense of belonging within spaces that have clearly been developed for specific publics and closely aligned to specific types and levels of consumption is a complex problem, and triggers debates over whether public space should even attempt to serve all publics (Carmona and Wunderlich, 2012). Such spaces, however, serve to raise resentment between the 'haves' and the 'have-nots' (Bauman, 2011). As the East London rapper Dizzee Rascal stated when looking back at the Canary Wharf Estate at the beginning of his rise to fame:

It's in your face. It takes the piss. There are rich people moving in now, people who work in the city. You can tell they're not living the same way as us. (Dizzee Rascal, quoted in Hancox, 2013)

Yet, as much as those from the neighbouring communities self-exclude themselves from the public spaces of the estate, those from within exhibit a tendency to insularity. Talking to a risk analyst who, unlike the majority of workers at Canary Wharf, lives with her family within the vicinity, this insular lifestyle was particularly apparent:

'I arrived here with my husband and daughter a month ago on placement from Hong Kong. I had been to London before, but not here ... we wonder if it is even in the city. With our work there is not time to travel too much, like into London, so we stay here, we can do everything needed for living, there is shopping, parks and we just found a cinema. It is nice ... but we could be anywhere. I worked in Battery Park [City] in New York in the past, it is similar, in the city but not in the city, you know?' (interview with a risk analyst at Canary Wharf, May 2013)

When discussing her household's daily routine, this interviewee said that the couple travel a short distance by Underground train from Canada Water to Canary Wharf, moving through the underground shopping malls at Canary Wharf, they drop their daughter at a nursery, before continuing to their office through the mall. At lunchtime, they dine in their office's canteen and after work, they pick up their daughter, do their grocery shopping at Canary Wharf before heading back to their apartment, a few minutes walk from their local Underground station. On an average day, they spend less than 20 minutes outdoors, in a similar way to that described by Boddy (1992) when examining the Calgary's Plus Fifteen network, where residents can move between their apartment, workplace and any retail and leisure facilities without ever stepping foot outside and thus without encountering anyone outside of their own social class (Davis, 1992, 2006; Kohn, 2004). This style of encapsulated living severely limits the potential for diverse encounters or even the observation of difference, and within such securitised spaces as Canary Wharf, can potentially 'feed' the fear that there is something dangerous about such encounters (Minton, 2012).

Another worker at Canary Wharf detailed his own insular existence on the estate:

'Now I come to London three to four times a week, most of the week really, it depends on the contract. I start with the 08:00 flight from Schiphol ... it takes just over an hour but I am actually in London at 08:10 ... I get a cab and can be in the office by 08:30 on a good day. Lunch is neither here nor there ... I can usually get the 7pm flight back to Amsterdam and be home by 10pm, it is a long day, but it is what I get paid for. (interview with a lawyer at Canary Wharf, May 2013)

In this case, the worker has even less chance for exposure to the local area, even opting for a taxi from the airport to the office to save time, but also limiting his potential for diverse encounters on public transport. In such a compact work schedule, every potential of losing time, such as going for lunch outside of the office or to outlets near the office, have been trimmed to ensure maximum efficiency but consequently also minimum exposure to society and diversity.

Through these examples, Canary Wharf can be seen to represent what Augé (1995) termed a 'non-place'. Within this conceptualisation, Augé defines a non-place as the binary opposite of place, such that:

> If place can be defined as relational, historical and concerned with identity, then a space which cannot be defined as relational, or historical, or concerned with identity will be a non-place. (Augé, 1995, p 63)

The non-place is a space of transition, a space to move through, 'where transit points and temporary abodes are proliferating … a world thus surrendered to solitary individuality, to the fleeting, the temporary and ephemeral' (Augé, 1995, p 63). These characteristics are evident in the public spaces at Canary Wharf for a variety of reasons. During the colder months, users rarely venture outdoors as there are few covered or sheltered spaces. At lunchtime this sees the underground shopping malls filled with employees and visitors queuing at the multitude of food outlets; however, a lack of seating means people either end up walking around eating or walking back to their offices. This constant mobility reinforces the ephemeral nature of the space (Sheller, 2008) and the somewhat solitary aspect of this. As one worker said, "grab lunch, by the time I've walked back to the office, I've eaten – there isn't really an option to 'have lunch' other than if we can bag a seat – it's either that or stay in the office" (interview with administrative worker, March 2013). This expediency of the lunch break is of little surprise given the dominate corporate culture, which requires lengthy time commitments to productive work, as was raised in multiple interviews, and reinforces the requirement to keeping moving. In the warmer months, workers flock to the outdoor spaces, but as a space predominately dominated by employees, working to schedules, the public spaces such as Jubilee Park quickly fill and at an equal speed, empty. However, conversations are dominated by work, or lunch is a solitary act, often mediated through a mobile phone, which serves in some way to create a private sphere in a public space. As Bauman (2004, p 27) states, '[s]witching on the mobile, we switch of the street.'

The urbanist Jane Jacobs (1961), in her own manifesto for public space, recognised the importance of diversity, particularly in the continual use of public spaces by multiple publics. When describing the 'ballet' of users' movements through Rittenhouse Square in Philadelphia, Jacobs quotes journalist Joseph Guess' observations:

> First, a few early-bird walkers who live beside the park take brisk strolls. They are shortly joined, and followed, by residents who cross the park on their way to work out of the district. Next come people from outside the district, crossing the park on their way to work within the neighbourhood. Soon after these people have left the square the errand-goers start to come through, many of them lingering, and in

> mid-morning mothers and small children come in, along with an increasing number of shoppers…. (Jacobs, 1961, p 96)

The 'ballet' continues on into the evening as different users replace each other. Jacobs attributes this continual usage to functional diversity:

> Rittenhouse Square is busy fairly continuously for the same basic reasons that a lively sidewalk is used continuously: because of functional diversity among adjacent uses, and hence diversity among users and their schedules. (Jacobs, 1961, p 97)

Contrasting this to the nearby Washington Square, Jacobs notes

> Its rim is dominated by huge office buildings, and both this rim and its immediate hinterland lack any equivalent to the diversity of Rittenhouse Square – services, restaurants, cultural facilities. The neighbourhood hinterland possess a low density of dwellings. Washington Square thus has had in recent decades only one significant reservoir of potential local users: the office workers. (Jacobs, 1961, p 97)

Going on to state that the temporality of uses of the square involve periods when the park is used by office workers, such as lunch times, and then when it becomes a vacuum, although unlike Canary Wharf, the vacuum here is filled with what Jacobs terms 'a form of blight' (Jacobs, 1961, p 97), at Canary Wharf, the spaces just remain largely empty. Sitting in a central cafe one Saturday afternoon for several hours, I saw four other patrons in a space that I wouldn't have been able to get a seat during a weekday; no long queues at food stalls – in fact, a fair proportion were closed. The security seem to keep the 'blight' out of the vacuum, but a vacuum still exists, and 'essential services', such as the Waitrose supermarket, still have a large number of visitors; it appears that the space simply serves consumerism and without the facilities to produce anything else, such as seating, non-consumer spaces to just sit and rest, it encourages constant movement (for more on resting and sleeping in public spaces, see Kingwell and Turmel, 2009).

With these factors in mind, an analysis of the social sustainability at Canary Wharf through a framework of cultural diversity is immediately problematic given the limited diversity found at the estate. As Marcuse (1998, p 105) argues, 'sustainability is not a goal; it is a constraint on the achievement of other goals.' As such, the framework should be inverted to look at how place can be created, how cultural ecosystems can be developed and how cultural diversity can be fostered, and then finally, once achieved, how these can be sustained.

The problem Canary Wharf faces in terms of creating place and sustaining diverse publics is in how to manage the transitory nature of the space, as people commute in and out, and as the provided facilities promote movement. The continuing development of the estate, including residential properties in the adjacent Wood Wharf (Virtue, 2013), may help sustain a certain local public; however, alongside this is the development of Crossrail, providing rapid transfers to London Heathrow Airport and the proposed expansion of London City Airport, giving the potential for more rapid transit both in but also out of the estate. The development plans also include the creation of further space for smaller companies, particularly technology firms, which the Canary Wharf Group has been successful in attracting to their 'Level 39' technology 'incubator', hosting 44,000ft² for technology start-ups, with increasing demand for more space (Shead, 2013). What impact such an influx of new people, not associated with the multinational banks and their corporate culture that currently dominates the space, will have on the diversity of the public using the estate is yet to be seen. The addition of diverse groups, against the background of the contrived urbanity that the estate attempts to create, can hopefully disrupt the dominant cultural logic, producing more convivial spaces and publics, and ultimately, a greater degree of cultural diversity and sense of place.

However, this operates alongside the fact that Canary Wharf can be seen as what Helbrecht and Dirksmeier (2012, p 1) term a 'new downtown', that is to say, a space that attempts to create a new, planned (and thus artificial) centrality within the city. New downtowns, they argue are spaces created through policies broadly associated with the 'urban renaissance' movement that are 'a completely new category of urban area in a globalised world' (Helbrecht and Dirksmeier, 2012, p 1). Such spaces are dominated by the development of a globally orientated milieu and the amenities and services to support this, as seen in the examples of the family from Hong Kong on secondment and the lawyer commuting from Amsterdam. This is further evidenced in the multicultural cuisine offered within restaurants and food stalls within the malls, multicurrency ATMs and the availability of print copies of the *New York Times* for the current day by 09:30am (04:30am EST). In her assessment of the HafenCity development in Hamburg, Lees (2012, p 24) examines how such new downtown developments attempt to plan urbanity, where urbanity is seen to be:

> ... an aesthetic experience, involving but moving beyond the urban built environment. It is to some extent intangible. Quite simply urbanity is the unexpected that is produced by, or comes out of, the urban.

Expanding on this, Lees states:

> For Lefebvre urbanity was about encounter – the meeting of difference, of strangers in the city, it was about everyday life and play, the sensuality of the city. (Lees, 2012, p 24; see also Merrifield, 2006, Chapter 4)

While Canary Wharf might produce the 'unexpected', such as a recent London incarnation of the Spanish tomato throwing La Tomatina festival, the reality is a contrived marketing event featuring 150 paid performers (Metro Hospitality, 2013). The truly unexpected, such as a flash mob protest against 'zombie' banks, featuring protestors dressed as public sector zombies, was met with an invoice from the French advertising agency JCDecaux for £4,375 for making use of an 'experiential advertising space' which they had exclusive marketing rights (Department of Corporate Sustenance, 2011), effectively demoting protest to a marketing event and commodifying it in the process.

The transient nature of encounter at Canary Wharf, coupled with the securitised and commercialised nature of its governance, further limits the potential for diverse encounters, and the unexpected. With the expansion of the estate into the adjacent Wood Wharf and the diversification of the industry sectors, it will be difficult for Canary Wharf to produce and sustain cultural diversity without a change in the way in which it governs its spaces.

Future of public space in London?

Despite the problems highlighted above, the Canary Wharf model has been adopted elsewhere in London as a blueprint of how to develop and manage public spaces, such as Paddington Basin (see Minton, 2012; see also Chapter Two, this volume). More often on brownfield land, luxury developments juxtaposed against economically deprived communities can now be seen across London, for example, Westfield London (Field, 2011), the Olympic developments in Stratford and Westfield Stratford City (Watt, 2013; see also Chapter Two, this volume), and the new build developments alongside the River Thames (Davidson and Lees, 2005). Such developments arguably serve a specific and wealthy public, displacing existing residents or users, either directly by removing their space, or indirectly by removing their association with a space (Marcuse, 1986).

Such developments destroy existing place, creating new places for new publics, shattering community ties and cultural ecosystems and creating less and less diverse spaces, where members of London's wealthy classes do not have to encounter anyone other than those from their own social class. As Merrifield (1996, p 57) argues:

> Engels suggested that the rich and powerful actually don't give a damn where the poor go so long as it is out of their sight.... Then the streets can be occupied solely by the well-heeled and by those who look and think the same and who play by the same rules, and where all is nice and dainty.

This was evident when Occupy London attempted to set up camp in Paternoster Square, a private development, the response being the immediate issuance of a High Court injunction banning them and effectively closing the square to the public, other than those who worked there or who wished to use the retail facilities (see Sennett, 2012). It is no surprise that other private estates in London, including Canary Wharf, also sought and were granted High Court injunctions against 'persons unknown' preventing the setting up of encampments on their land; copies of the injunction are taped to lampposts around the estate and displayed on wall mounts throughout the shopping malls.

While developers are now attempting to include seemingly more accessible public spaces into their developments, they still ignore the already existing reality of public space in London. For example, British Land's new skyscraper, the Leadenhall Building, a development more commonly known as 'The Cheesegrater', boasts that it will provide an:

> ... unprecedented allocation of public space – the lower levels are recessed on a raking diagonal to create a spectacular, sunlit seven-story-high space complete with shops, exhibition space, soft landscaping and trees ... [including] a half-acre extension to the adjacent piazza of St Helen's Square. Overlooking the space is a public bar and restaurant served by glazed lifts. This new public space will provide a rare oasis within the dense urban character of the City of London. (*ArchDaily*, 2013)

Land Securities' new skyscraper at 20 Fenchurch Street, also known as 'The Walkie-Talkie', will feature a 'sky garden' that will:

> ... span three floors and offer uninterrupted views across the City of London. Served by two express lifts, visitors arrive to a beautiful landscaped garden with a viewing area, terrace, cafe, bar and restaurant. The Sky Garden will be a truly unique space and has been designed to create an open and vibrant place of leisure offering visitors a rare chance to experience London from a different viewpoint. (Land Securities, 2012, p 31)

None of this is new – similar 'public' spaces already exist, for example, the roof garden at No 1 Poultry within the City of London, or the public art displays in the lobby of One Canada Square at Canary Wharf. But these public spaces are largely invisible to the general public, architecturally obscured. As with Trump Tower in Manhattan (see Miller, 2007), one must effectively enter what feels like a private space; at No 1 Poultry one must request a suited doorman to operate the elevator for you; at One Canada Square this involves walking into the expansive lobby of an office building and being faced with receptionists and security guards. While these spaces are open to the public, they exude Allen's (2006) ambient power, affecting exclusion. How the public spaces of the new skyscrapers mentioned above will pan out is yet to be seen, although if previous developments are anything to go by, they will also *feel* exclusionary, even if they are not actually exclusionary, further limiting diversity by enticing certain publics while deterring others.

Conclusion

As more urban public space in London becomes privately owned or managed, the tendency towards the production of transient and mono-functional spaces, such as those dedicated to work or consumerism, appears to be increasing throughout the city. While developments such as the Canary Wharf Estate are looking to diversify through mixed-use developments, broadly aligned with 'new downtown' principles (see Helbrecht and Dirksmeier, 2012), including residential, leisure and workplaces, such as at Wood Wharf, which potentially stands to diversify the publics of the estate, such developments are still largely exclusive, and cater to specific social and professional groups. Wood Wharf will be even further integrated into the already existing space, resulting in even less reason for residents to encounter diverse publics and difference elsewhere in the city.

Meanwhile, ironically, the new skyscraper developments within the City of London offer more potential to increase diversity, not least because of their centrality within London, but also through the range of public spaces that have been incorporated into their designs, which mix both commercialised spaces with expansions of existing public squares. Optimistically this may attract more diverse publics and thus encounters with difference, producing culturally diverse spaces where people of different backgrounds can *be* public alongside one another, reducing insularity and creating place, the key factors to socially sustainable public space. However, despite the Mayor of London's gushing praise for London's newest public space, King's Cross Square, part of the £550 million redevelopment of King's Cross, the development of properly socially sustainable public space in London has yet to materialise. Many public spaces in central London, especially around the City, remain largely mono-functional spaces of work and brief socialising after work, before becoming ghost towns, as is evident when strolling through them on the weekend. The assertions in the Mayor of London's (2009) *Manifesto for public space* are not being met:

> A successful public space is a well-used space. No matter how beautiful the design, or how costly the materials, if people do not use the space it is not fully contributing to city life. But public spaces can and should be used in all sorts of different ways, by the widest possible range of people ... London's diversity is one of its greatest assets, and its public spaces should be places which embody and celebrate this. (p 7)

Without a proper commitment to increased diversity, to accommodating and actively encouraging difference, and without individuals recognising the presence of difference rather than diverting their gaze (Merrifield, 1996), the prospects for socially sustainable, socially just, public space in London remains weak.

References

Allen, J. (2006) 'Ambient power: Berlin's Potsdamer Platz and the seductive logic of public spaces', *Urban Studies*, vol 43, no 2, pp 441-55.

ArchDaily (2013) 'In progress: the Leadenhall Building/Rogers Stirk Harbour & Partners' (www.archdaily.com/392494/in-progress-the-leadenhall-building-rogers-stirk-harbour-partners).

Augé, M. (1995) *Non-places: an introduction to supermodernity*, London: Verso.

Baeten, G.U.Y. (2001) 'Urban regeneration, social exclusion and shifting power geometries on the South Bank, London', *Geographische Zeitschrift*, vol 89, no 2/3, pp 104-13.

Bauman, Z. (2004) *Identity*, Cambridge: Polity.

Bauman, Z. (2011) 'Interview – Zygmunt Bauman on the UK riots', *Social Europe Journal* (www.social-europe.eu/2011/08/interview-zygmunt-bauman-on-the-uk-riots).

Boddy, T. (1992) 'Underground and overhead: building the analogous city', in M. Sorkin (ed) *Variations on a theme park: the new American city and the end of public space*, New York: Hill & Wang, pp 123-53.

Borden, I. (2001) *Skateboarding, space and the city: architecture and the body*, Oxford: Berg.

Borden, I. (2013) *Professor Iain Borden on the Festival Wing consultation*, London: Long Live South Bank (www.llsb.com/professor-iain-borden-on-the-festival-wing-consultation).

Brownill, S. (1990) *Developing London's Docklands: another great planning disaster?*, London: Paul Chapman.

Canary Wharf Group (2010a) *Future developments* (www.canarywharf.com/workwithus/Leasing/Leasing-Opportunities/Future-Developments).

Canary Wharf Group (2010b) *Visual arts at Canary Wharf* (www.canarywharf.com/visitus/public--art/public--art).

Carmona, M. and Wunderlich, F. (2012) *Capital spaces: the multiple complex public spaces of a global city*, London: Routledge.

Chiesura, A. (2004) 'The role of urban parks for the sustainable city', *Landscape and Urban Planning*, vol 68, no 1, pp 129-38.

Davidson, M. (2010) 'Social sustainability and the city', *Geography Compass*, vol 4, no 7, pp 872-80.

Davidson, M. and Lees, L. (2005) 'New-build "gentrification" and London's riverside renaissance', *Environment and Planning A*, vol 37, no 7, pp 1165-90.

Davis, M. (1992) 'Fortress Los Angeles: the militarisation of urban space', in M. Sorkin (ed) *Variations on a theme park: the new American city and the end of public space*, New York: Hill & Wang, pp 154-80.

Davis, M. (2006) *City of quartz: excavating the future in Los Angeles*, London: Verso.

Department of Corporate Sustenance (2011) 'Canary Wharf experiential space – fees to be paid' [Email] (Personal communication, 13 September).

Escobales, R. (2013) 'Skateboarding's South Bank home to be turned into retail units', *The Guardian* (www.theguardian.com/uk/2013/apr/12/skateboarding-south-bank).

Evans, J. and Jones, P. (2008) 'Rethinking sustainable urban regeneration: ambiguity, creativity, and the shared territory', *Environment and Planning A*, vol 40, no 6, pp 1416-34.

Field, J. (2011) 'Sorted? modalities of exclusion at a luxury shopping mall', Paper presented at the Annual RC21 Conference, 'The struggle to belong: dealing with diversity in 21st century urban settings', Amsterdam, Netherlands, 7-9 July.

Foster, J. (1999) *Docklands: cultures in conflict, worlds in collision*, London: UCL Press.

Geenens, R. and Tinnevelt, R. (2008) 'Truth and public space: setting out some signposts', in R. Geenens and R. Tinnevelt (eds) *Does truth matter? Democracy and public space*, Dordrecht: Springer, pp 1-14.

Hancox, D. (2013) 'Stand up tall: Dizzee Rascal and the birth of grime – extract', *The Guardian* (www.theguardian.com/music/2013/aug/19/stand-up-tall-dizzee-rascal-grime-extract).

Harvey, D. (2004) 'The right to the city', in L. Lees (ed) *The emancipatory city? Paradoxes and possibilites*, London: Sage, pp 236-9.

Helbrecht, I. and Dirksmeier, P. (2012) 'New downtowns: a new form of centrality and urbanity in a world society', in I. Helbrecht and P. Dirksmeier (eds) *New urbanism: life, work, and space in the new downtown*, Farnham: Ashgate, pp 1-21.

Institute for Sustainability (2012) *About the Institute for Sustainability – Poplar and Bow project* (www.communitieslivingsustainably.org.uk/project/institute-for-sustainabilty).

Jacobs, J. (1961) *The death and life of great American cities*, New York: Random House.

Kingwell, M. and Turmel, P. (2009) 'Introduction: rites of ways, paths of desire', in M. Kingwell and P. Turmel (eds) *Rites of way: the politics and poetics of public space*, Waterloo, ON: Wilfrid Laurier University Press, pp ix-xvii.

Kohn, M. (2004) *Brave new neighborhoods: the privatization of public space*, London: Routledge.

Land Securities (2012) *20 Fenchurch Street. The building with more up top* (www.landsecuritieslondon.com/websitefiles/20_fs_brochure.pdf).

Lang, J.T. (2005) *Urban design: a typology of procedures and products*, Oxford: Architectural Press.

Lees, L. (2003) 'The ambivalence of diversity and the politics of urban renaissance: the case of youth in downtown Portland, Maine', *International Journal of Urban and Regional Research*, vol 27, no 3, pp 613-34.

Lees, L. (2008) 'Gentrification and social mixing: towards an inclusive urban renaissance?', *Urban Studies*, vol 45, no 12, pp 2449-70.

Lees, L. (2012) 'Planning urbanity – a contradiction in terms?', in I. Helbrecht and P. Dirksmeier (eds) *New urbanism: life, work, and space in the new downtown*, Farnham: Ashgate, pp 23-37.

Lofland, L.H. (1998) *The public realm: exploring the City's quintessential social territory*, Hawthorne, NY: Aldine de Gruyter.

Low, S.M. (2000) *On the plaza: the politics of public space and culture*, Austin, TX: University of Texas Press.

Low, S.M., Taplin, D. and Scheld, S. (2005) *Rethinking urban parks: public space and cultural diversity*, Austin, TX: University of Texas Press.

Marcuse, P. (1986) 'Abandonment, gentrification, and displacement: the linkages in New York City', in N. Smith and P. Williams (eds) *Gentrification of the city*, London: Allen & Unwin, pp 153-77.

Marcuse, P. (1998) 'Sustainability is not enough', *Environment and Urbanization*, vol 10, vol 2, pp 103-12.

Mayor of London (2002) *Making space for Londoners*, London: Greater London Authority (http://legacy.london.gov.uk/mayor/auu/docs/making_space.pdf).

Mayor of London (2009) *A manifesto for public space: London's great outdoors* (www.london.gov.uk/sites/default/files/Manifesto%20for%20Public%20Space.pdf).

Merrifield, A. (1996) 'Public space: integration and exclusion in urban life', *CITY*, vol 1, no 5-6, pp 57-72.

Merrifield, A. (2002) *Dialectical urbanism: social struggles in the capitalist city*, New York: Monthly Review Press.

Merrifield, A. (2006) *Henri Lefebvre: a critical introduction*, New York: Routledge.

Merrifield, A. (2013) *The politics of encounter: urban theory and protest under planetary urbanization*, Athens, GA: University of Georgia Press.

Metro Hospitality (2013) *Amazing photo shoot today at Canary Wharf!* (https://twitter.com/MetroStaff/status/382902120451563520).

Miller, K.F. (2007) *Designs on the public: the private lives of New York's public spaces*, Minneapolis, MN: University of Minnesota Press.

Minton, A. (2006) *What kind of world are we building? The privatisation of public space*, London: The Royal Institution of Chartered Surveyors (http://annaminton.com/Privatepublicspace.pdf).

Minton, A. (2012) *Ground control: fear and happiness in the twenty-first-century city*, Harmondsworth: Penguin.

Mitchell, D. (2003) *The right to the city: social justice and the fight for public space*, New York: Guilford Press.

Pile, S. (2005) *Real cities: modernity, space and the phantasmagorias of city life*, London: Sage.

Project for Public Spaces (2012) *From government to governance: sustainable urban development and the World Urban Forum*, New York: Project for Public Spaces (www.pps.org/blog/from-government-to-governance-sustainable-urban-development-the-world-urban-forum).

Prynn, J. (2012) 'Canary Wharf banking on a bright future with £2bn plan for Shoreditch-style shops', *London Evening Standard* (www.standard.co.uk/news/london/canary-wharf-banking-on-bright-future-with-2bn-plan-for-shoreditchstyle-shops-8218296.html).

Robinson, C. (2013) 'Moving South Bank's skaters would be vandalism of our cultural heritage', *The Guardian* (www.theguardian.com/commentisfree/2013/may/13/south-bank-skaters-vandalism-cultural-heritage).

Rogers, D. (2013) '"£17m and the undercroft is yours," Southbank skaters told', *Building Design* (www.bdonline.co.uk/news/£17m-and-the-undercroft-is-yours-southbank-skaters-told/5060730.article).

Sennett, R. (1970) *The uses of disorder: personal identity and city life*, New Haven, CT: Yale University Press.

Sennett, R. (2012) *The Occupy movements have dramatised questions about public space: who owns it? And who can use it?*, London: British Politics and Policy at London School of Economics and Political Science (http://blogs.lse.ac.uk/politicsandpolicy/archives/27607).

Shead, S. (2013) *Level 39 opens start-up expansion space in London's Canary Wharf*, Techworld.com (http://news.techworld.com/sme/3467905/level-39-opens-start-up-expansion-space-in-londons-canary-wharf).

Sheller, M. (2008) 'Mobilities, freedom and public space', in S. Bergmann and T. Sager (eds) *The ethics of mobilities: rethinking place, exclusion, freedom and environment*, Farnham: Ashgate, pp 25-38.

Shepard, B. and Smithsimon, G. (2011) *The beach beneath the streets: contesting New York city's public spaces*, Albany, NY: State University of New York Press.

Sibley, D. (1995) *Geographies of exclusion: society and difference in the West*, London: Routledge.

Southbank Centre (2013) 'Public letter to long live Southbank' (www.southbankforall.org/downloads/01102013_AlanBishop-to-LLSB.pdf).

Spensley, A. and Holland, R. (2013) 'Should South Bank skateboarders welcome a new park?', *The Guardian* (www.theguardian.com/commentisfree/2013/sep/15/skateboard-south-bank-hungerford-bridge).

Throsby, D. (1995) 'Culture, economics and sustainability', *Journal of Cultural Economics*, vol 19, no 3, pp 199-206.

Virtue, R. (2013) *Canary Wharf's plans for future development*, London: The Wharf (www.wharf.co.uk/2013/02/canary-wharfs-plans-for-future.html).

Vitale, A. (2008) *City of disorder: how the quality of life campaign transformed New York politics*, New York: New York University Press.

Warner, M. (2002) *Publics and counterpublics*, New York: Zone Books.

Watt, P. (2013) '"It's not for us": regeneration, the 2012 Olympics and the gentrification of East London', *CITY*, vol 17, no 1, pp 99-118.

Whitter, W. (2005) *Rollin through the decades* [Film], directed by W. Whitter, London: Beaquarr Productions.

Williams, R. (2004) *The anxious city: British urbanism in the late 20th century*, London: Routledge.

Part 4

SUSTAINING LONDON'S ENVIRONMENTAL FUTURE

TWELVE

Rhetoric in transitioning to sustainable travel

Robin Hickman

Introduction

London is often viewed as a model for the development of sustainable transport planning, including the world's oldest Underground system (which celebrated 150 years in 2013); consistent enhancements to the public transport networks with a multi-modal nature; a compact and polycentric urban form (building on the original 'city of villages' on which contemporary London was developed); and even progressive policy measures such as congestion charging and streetscape designs that have proved difficult to implement in other urban areas. As a result, the city authorities – Transport for London (TfL) and the Greater London Authority (GLA) – have developed a reputation for developing broad-ranging and often innovative strategies to move towards greater sustainability in travel. The current policy approach is represented in the Mayor's Transport Strategy (TfL, 2010), and includes an ambitious overriding objective, in environmental terms, of a 60 per cent reduction in CO_2 emissions by 2025 on a 1990 base across all sectors. This is a globally leading policy position for a western industrialised country, perhaps the deepest reduction target relative to international practice.

The current levels of aggregate CO_2 emissions for London are at 48 $MtCO_2$ (million tonnes of CO_2), and transport accounts for 22 per cent of this, at around 10 $MtCO_2$ (TfL, 2011). A key question that remains – and is largely unanswered – is whether the extent of strategy development and, most importantly, implementation, is likely to deliver transport CO_2 emission reductions to anywhere near the target levels. Emissions have actually increased a little since 1990 (45.1 $MtCO_2$ in aggregate and 9.9 $MtCO_2$ in transport), suggesting that there is a long way to go before the aspirations are met. The target levels would require around 4 $MtCO_2$ in transport, assuming transport delivers its 'fair share' of the aggregate target. This chapter considers this key problem, commenting on the strategy development, the rhetoric, the progress being made and also the great scale of change required. It highlights the range of policy measures and interventions that are available in infrastructural, vehicle technology and built environmental terms, and attempts some quantification of likely impacts against CO_2 reductions targets. Some of the potentially important policy responses, such as cycling and public transport options in the suburbs, appear to be quite unprogressive relative to other international practice.

Travel behaviours are indeed difficult to change: at the individual level, travel patterns have a complex rationale, often with a deep socio-cultural 'embeddedness' of car-based travel within everyday life (Urry, 2007). This, among other things, means that there is much inertia in the system, with cultural values and norms often relatively fixed in nature, at least in the short term. Three arguments are developed in this chapter. First, using a case study of cycling in London, the rhetoric in policy making is compared to the actual mode shares of travel relative to international practice, leading us to understand how the framing of the debate seems to greatly influence what policy measures are pursued. Second, there is the governance framework and rhetoric in policy making and how these might be shaped to progress more effectively towards CO_2 reduction targets. There seems to be a large gap between policy aspirations, including the CO_2 reduction targets, and the likely achievement in transport, particularly given funding constraints for infrastructure investment and the 'governance at a distance' nature of contemporary governance structures (Lascoumes and Le Gales, 2007; Hickman and Banister, 2014). There are problems in the terms of the debate (Hajer, 1995), including the policy measures being considered (and not considered), and an important part of this is the language of the debate (Edelman, 1988; Rydin, 1998). Finally, reference is made to transition theory, concluding that the transition to sustainable travel behaviours needs to involve multi-level structures – including 'landscape', 'regime' and 'niche' aspects (Geels and Kemp, 2012). The ways of thinking, the framing of the debate and the problems and solutions, all are critical to the eventual outcomes. Yet we often tinker with limited policy tools, and then still seem surprised at the resulting incremental nature of change.

Potential low transport CO_2 futures

The VIBAT London study (Hickman et al, 2009a)[1] examined the potential for reducing transport CO_2 emissions in London. It looked over the long term to 2030, and developed a composite strategy with a series of policy packages covering technological and behavioural options. The strategy aimed to help encourage fewer trips, reduce trip lengths, develop mode shift towards public transport, walking and cycling, and increase vehicle efficiency – hence, to ultimately reduce transport CO_2 emissions. The policy packages include low emission vehicles, alternative fuels, pricing regimes, walking and cycling, urban planning, ICT (information and communication technologies), 'smarter choice' behavioural measures (travel planning and flexible working hours), ecological driving and slower speeds, and freight planning (see Figure 12.1). The approach to segmentation, estimating how much different policy areas might contribute to an overall target, is similar in approach to Pacala and Socolow's (2004) 'stabilisation wedges', although each policy area is assumed to give a different level of CO_2 reduction. Each package can be selected at a variety of levels of 'intensity' in

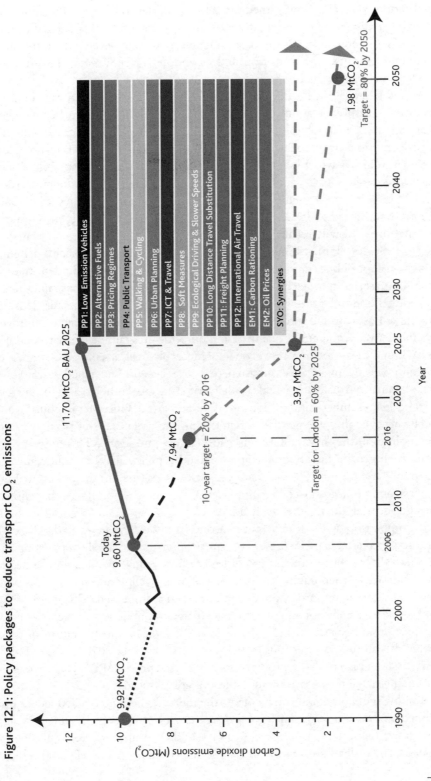

Figure 12.1: Policy packages to reduce transport CO$_2$ emissions

application, typically, 'low', 'medium' and 'high' levels, representing different levels of funding or policy initiative. Likely impacts are then modelled against levels of CO_2 reduction. Various data sources were used to develop the modelling, including commissioned runs from TfL's London Travel Survey (LTS) strategic model (Hickman et al, 2009b).

A key message is the need for an integrated and wide-ranging package of 'high intensity' measures if significant transport CO_2 reductions are to be achieved. Relying on the technological options – such as low emission vehicles – will only reduce emissions by up to 20-30 per cent. And this assumes a rapid take-up of low emission vehicles, which is not occurring to any degree in the London fleet. The packaging process itself is useful here, allowing an assessment of which measures need to be combined to achieve the deeper CO_2 reduction outcomes. The results demonstrate that the 60 per cent CO_2 reduction target is possible in transport, but that this is heavily reliant on developing a clean vehicle fleet (an average car fleet <100gCO_2/km); a London-wide emissions-based vehicle pricing scheme; a high level of public transport investment (beyond the current funded strategy, including a series of projects such as Crossrail2, and light rail and bus rapid transit in Outer London); greater use of urban planning to provide greater densities and mixed uses around interchanges, including in the suburbs; much improved cycling networks and public realm; a London-wide programme of smarter choice behavioural measures; and slower speeds and ecological driving across much of the network. Many of these infrastructure projects and wider policy initiatives are, of course, virtually impossible to deliver for the city authorities in the current context, either due to funding constraints or perceived difficulties in political and public acceptability. Hence the difficulties in implementing this strategy – and by implication the mayoral CO_2 emission target – are severe. This fundamental point seems to be hugely under-appreciated by policy makers, politicians and the public in London. The latter are very seldom engaged in the policy-making process, and this leads to a false complacency – even consciousness – that climate change issues are being effectively addressed.

A comparison with the current mayoral Transport Strategy (TfL, 2010) is instructive. The strategy focuses on two main approaches, namely, supporting and enabling the development and use of low carbon vehicles; and carbon-efficient mode choice – encouraging the use of walking, cycling and public transport. Within these, the important policy areas are seen as improved vehicle efficiency, biofuels, driver behavior and operational efficiency, public sector fleet efficiency, mode shift and smarter travel. The estimates are that implementation of these measures will reduce emissions to below 6 $MtCO_2$ (TfL, 2010, p.238). This is less than under a 'fair share' assumption, as discussed previously, relying on deeper cuts being made in the commercial and domestic sectors.

A number of comments can be made: the measures being modelled seem quite limited in range, and the major gains seem to be from vehicle efficiency and alternative fuels. This, again, seems to give undue reliance to the technological options, and really doesn't withstand any serious scrutiny. Around 70,000 vehicles a day enter the congestion charge zone, with 2,500 qualifying for TfL's greener vehicle discount because they emit less than $100gCO_2/km$ (representing less than 4 per cent of vehicles). Even this small proportion of vehicles is leading the Mayor to consider a tighter threshold for vehicles exempt from the congestion charge (*Evening Standard*, 2013). It seems a much wider range of policy measures needs to be developed. There can be much more potential in urban planning, use of public transport and walking and cycling – all of which act in a synergetic manner – particularly if masterplanning in the suburban areas can encourage local trip-making patterns by non-car means. The modelling available is weak at understanding the possibilities in mode shift, hence these impacts tend to be underestimated and a reliance on vehicle efficiencies results. This happens in most modelling studies considering the potential options for low CO_2 in transport. For London, the implications are a little perverse. The vast majority of CO_2 reductions seem to be reliant on other organisations delivering, such as European and national governments setting strict (preferably mandatory) standards for lowering vehicle emissions, the motor manufacturers delivering these to the market with attractive specifications and prices, and the public buying them. None of these are happening.

The development of policy in this way underplays the behavioural options to a very large degree, and this is where much more analysis is required to help the policy and decision makers. Traffic growth seems to have peaked in London which, if not a temporary phenomenon linked to the macro economy, will help in reducing transport CO_2 emissions. The trend break in vehicle kilometres travelled that is required is perhaps starting to occur (Le Vine and Jones, 2012), but of course, the changes are all too marginal as yet. This is likely to reflect a number of factors alongside economic factors – perhaps a policy approach aimed at reducing car usage, large investment in public transport, less favourable financial incentives for company car driving, less interest in attaining driving licenses in young people, and even greater use of overseas visits for holidays and business. The move away from high car usage may not be as difficult as envisaged – it may already be happening – and mode shift and reduced trip distances can make a larger contribution to reduced transport CO_2 emissions than currently projected.

Framing of the policy debate

There are some problems to be resolved. Much of the current practice and policy making, even much of the research, assumes that government interventions are effective and can have an impact on individual and societal travel behaviours to a significant degree. Unfortunately, this is far from certain. Governmental intervention may only have a limited impact on individual and societal behaviours, and effectiveness against long-term goals is dependent on the type of policy measures developed, the governmental framework and mechanisms employed, the levels of funding and application applied. Related here is the governance framework, the moves away from strategic planning towards deregulation in the transport environment, and the limited budget availability. All of these mean that effective intervention becomes less likely, and so, too, reduced transport CO_2 emissions. Although improving infrastructure and retrofitting the built form will be critical to reducing transport CO_2 emissions, it is unlikely to be sufficient in changing travel behaviours markedly. There also needs to be some emphasis on changing cultural practices, norms and beliefs (see, for example, Steg, 2005; Urry, 2007; Banister et al, 2011; Schwanen et al, 2012). This is likely to particularly apply in Outer London or the higher income Inner London areas where many people remain wedded to car use, often using large vehicles that are high in CO_2 emissions, and perceive car use as 'critical' to carrying out their everyday activities. But again, in the neoliberal governance landscape – where the interventionist state is discouraged – tackling these types of policy areas is often seen as reflective of 'excessive' state intervention, and that people should really be able to 'choose' their travel options as they wish.

However, if the current policy approach is unlikely to achieve the strategic CO_2 target as set, there is an urgent need to think through the framing of the transport debate in London. This includes the range of measures being used and the levels of application and investment. If many of the more radical measures are deemed as 'too difficult' to implement, then perhaps other policy measures need strengthening. There are also spatial dimensions, in that transport planning in London has conventionally focused on improving radial routes into central London, often ignoring orbital or tangential options. Investment is often (large) infrastructure-based, such as Crossrail (at a project cost of £16 billion), High Speed2, heavy rail and Underground capacity enhancements, including Thameslink (a project cost of £5.5 billion), all of which seek to improve linkages into central London. Schemes for Outer London are often missing, such as the very slow progress with tram schemes in the suburbs (beyond Croydon Tramlink). The private car is still by far the dominant mode for travel in the outer suburbs, and particularly for journeys that are orbital in nature or cross the Greater London boundary, yet the policy options available to limit the demand for these types of journeys are limited. The 'progressive' label for transport planning in London is primarily related to measures employed in Inner London and the central urban area in particular, the classic example being congestion charging.

The types of policies that are most easily delivered can be explored in terms of the degree of public intervention and authority required to implement them (Dunn and Perl, 2010). The level of 'coercion' is viewed as reflecting an element of 'forcing' another party to behave in a non–voluntary manner (through action or inaction). An increasingly 'weak state' position in terms of intervention means that policy tools are generally chosen from the least coercive part of the spectrum. In the transport sector, this means a reliance on voluntary emission standards, CO_2 emissions labelling schemes or limited media campaigns on 'travel awareness'. The more interventionist and coercive stance includes measures such as road pricing or carbon taxing on businesses and individuals, higher densities in suburban areas and higher levels of public transport funding where use of the car is high. Many of these types of measures result in hostile responses, intense lobbying and the 'watering down' of original proposals, particularly where there is a vocal public. There are also important issues of power and influence here, with the higher-income and educated groups tending to be more vocal and achieving greater influence (Dunn and Perl, 2010).

The language of the debate in sustainable transport is very important. Edelman (1988, p 103), for example, draws attention to: 'language games that construct alternative realities, grammars that transform the perceptible into non-obvious meanings, and language as a form of action that generates radiating chains of connotations.' Actors in the policy development process use language and argument to communicate and further their interests, and this is readily seen in transport, often with large, radial infrastructure investments or the economic instruments gaining most attention. The chosen argument can alter views on issues, define the focus of attention, promote particular agendas and shape differences or coalitions between actors (Rydin, 1998), for example, relegating the cycling and public realm improvements, and the investments in public transport in the suburbs, to the sidelines. The aspiration for increased development and growth is rarely questioned, with all development perceived in positive terms, and issues such as gentrification or social exclusion overlooked.

Much of this type of conflict is also hidden in the initial definition of the problem – in this case, the definition of 'sustainable mobility', the range of 'possible' policy measures considered, in the issues discussed and in those that remain largely undiscussed. A particular framing of the debate makes certain elements seem 'fixed' and 'inappropriate', some are viewed as 'problematic', while others are perceived as much easier to discuss and 'deliver'. Think, for example, of the potential to widen the congestion charge scheme into a London-wide road pricing scheme, perhaps even emissions-based; the possibilities to increase densities around some of the suburban rail and Underground stations; the gentrification of areas around new public transport investments (all ignored); the need to provide additional transport options to support economic growth; and support for increased air capacity in or around London (rarely questioned). These are seemingly 'technical' positions, but conceal, of course, a normative stance, supported by the institutional arrangements and knowledge employed (Hajer, 1995; Hickman and Banister, 2014).

Case study: cycling

The experience of cycling in London can be examined in these terms – a policy area that is very poorly developed and where cycling facilities are of a very low standard relative to practice in other European cities. The rhetoric is, of course, supportive, as can be seen in the current Transport Strategy (TfL, 2010), which seeks to: 'Excel among global cities – expanding opportunities for all its people and enterprises, achieving the highest environmental standards and quality of life and leading the world in its approach to tackling the urban challenges of the

21st century, particularly that of climate change' (p 31); as part of this, the city 'should also encourage a cycling revolution' (p 32); and 'mainstream cycling as a transport mode, making it more attractive to a wider range of people' (p 187).

This all reads well, but there is little below this. The state of cycling facilities on the street is another matter. There has been much recent pressure on the city authorities from lobby groups such as the London Cycle Campaign, including campaigns to 'Go Dutch' with much better cycling facilities. The recent Mayor's *Vision for cycling* (GLA, 2013) promises more funding, with an increase in the total cycling budget to almost £400 million over the next three years, almost the per capita levels found in the Netherlands. Some of the major highway junctions will be redesigned with a budget of £100 million (instead of the previous £19 million). There will be a 'signature 24km Crossrail cycle route' using the M40 Westway flyover and Embankment, and up to three 'mini-Holland' developments in outer London, the latter showcasing how suburban town centres can be redesigned around cycling. This is starting to sound more positive in terms of supporting cycling as a serious mode of transport, but it is critical to understand the context here, and the very low base that cycling is coming from in terms of mode share.

The overall number of trips[2] in London are forecast to increase from the current level of 24 million per day to more than 27 million by 2031, with the following mode share projection – cycling is to 'more than double', but this is simply to move from a base of 2 per cent of trips in 2006 to 5 per cent of trips in 2031 (see Table 12.1).

Table 12.1: Projected mode share for London (%)

Mode	2006	2031
Cycling	2	5
Walking	24	25
Public transport	31	34
Private motorised transport	43	37

Source: TfL (2010)

The 'globally leading' comparison to be made in international best practice is to be found in the Netherlands (Groningen, 40 per cent of trips by bicycle; Amsterdam, 27 per cent); in Denmark (Copenhagen, 35 per cent); or Germany (Münster, 38 per cent; Berlin, 15 per cent) (see Figure 12.2) (Pucher and Buehler, 2012). London, in comparison, seems to offer a minimal improvement on a very low base, similar only to experience in cities in North America or Australia, jurisdictions not known for their progressive approach to cycling. Although London has been developed as a 'public transport city', and a high public transport mode share is bound to take away from cycle usage, the 'cycling revolution' seems a little disingenuous on current aspirations. The historical fall in cycling (and walking) in the UK is also often overlooked. The data is a little unclear, but some estimates

Figure 12.2: Comparative cycling mode shares

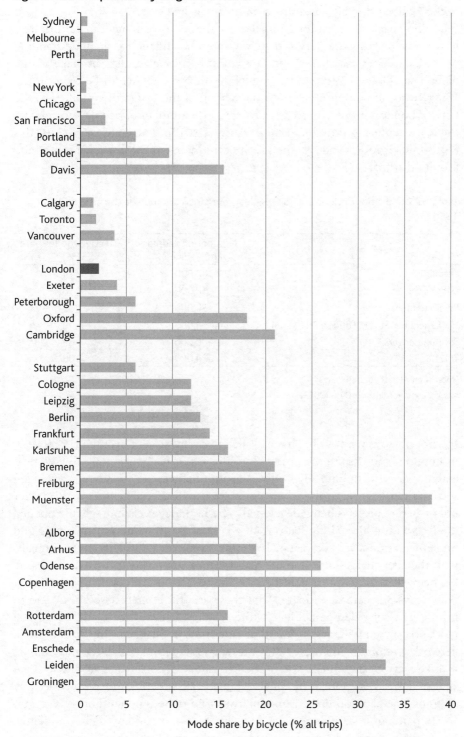

Mode share by bicycle (% all trips)

suggest cycle trip rates were at over 20 per cent in many urban centres in the UK in the 1950s and 1960s, meaning a dramatic decline since.

Looking back to the historic projections is, of course, difficult in comparative terms, but perhaps the very old surveys are also instructive in understanding how mode shares can change and how infrastructure planning can make a large difference. Table 12.2 shows the results of a survey by Charles Pearson, in the 1850s, who hired 'traffic-takers' to stand at all of the principal entrances to the City of London, from 8am to 8pm, to count the number of people and vehicles leaving or entering (London Transport Data, 2013). There are no cyclists, this is pre-Underground and also the private car – hence the dominance of walking is quite marked.

Table 12.2: Number of people and vehicles going into and out of the city, daily, in 1854*

Mode	Number of people and vehicles	Effective mode share (%)
Omnibus	88,000	14
Other vehicles	52,000	8
River steamers	30,000	5
Via Fenchurch St and London Bridge rail	54,000	9
Foot passengers	400,000	64
Total	624,000	100

Note: *Counting them both ways
Source: London Transport Data (2013)

It is not obvious why cycling has had such poor investment over the last 50 years in London, and despite the postulation, this is not really changing to any great extent. Many of the higher profile cycling initiatives are welcome, yet remain small initiatives, certainly when compared in financial terms to the larger infrastructure projects being developed. The London Cycle hire scheme opened in 2010 with 400 docking stations (at a cost of £140 million for planning and implementation over six years). It should eventually cover its costs annually, with the bike charges covering the maintenance and revenue costs. The scheme has been successful, but is confined to central London in coverage; there are a few extensions being considered, but these are still limited. Users also tend to from a particular demographic – white, young males. There could equally be residential-based schemes, as found in cities such as Shanghai. In terms of cycle networks in London, there are few routes segregated from traffic, and most simply involve a cycle lane on the side of the carriageway. Cycle lanes at junctions are almost always very poor. The much-lauded cycle superhighways are effectively strips of blue paint on the existing highway, and there is no level of segregation. Cycle parking at stations remains very limited, and parking at the residential end is often difficult in terraced housing and flats. Cycling remains a relatively dangerous activity in London – with 14 deaths in 2013 and hundreds of serious casualties. These levels are much too high – and require much more robust cycle facilities to be provided.

This desperate lack of provision seems in contrast to the potential benefits of increased cycling usage to the public realm, the development of attractive city design and the health benefits for individuals of active travel. The latter has been quantified to an extent, with improved air quality from reduced car use and daily physical activity helping protect against obesity, diabetes, cardiovascular diseases (including ischaemic heart disease), breast and colon cancers, dementia and depression (Woodcock et al, 2009). A cohort study in Copenhagen, for example, identified cycling to work as reducing all-cause mortality by 28 per cent, independent of other types of physical activity (Anderson et al, 2000). These seem to be very large benefits, and there are potentially many more that remain beyond quantification, such as general emotional wellbeing. All of these issues are largely overlooked in the development of transport strategies, and particularly investment programmes. If enhanced public transport networks are difficult in Outer London due to funding constraints and the public acceptability of widened pricing measures is questioned, then perhaps cycling should be front-staged, with a major effort made to provide state-of-the-art facilities. There seems to be a large latent demand.

In parallel, there is a concerning emphasis on increasing or at least maintaining road capacity in London in the Transport Strategy (TfL, 2010), seemingly assuming that increased capacity will lead to reduced congestion and improved economic growth: 'Congestion costs an estimated £2bn in lost economic productivity' (p 151) – a somewhat tenuous, but often repeated, argument, based on assumed lost time in congested road conditions and a supposed 'value of time', ignoring issues such as the actual use of time, and whether this release in time would be used productively (Metz, 2008).

Further, the Mayor aims to 'smooth traffic flow' to 'maximise the efficient and reliable operation of the existing road network' (TfL, 2010, p 154) – which is, of course, couched in very positive phraseology. This includes the use of 'intelligent traffic control systems' to improve the volume and speed of traffic throughput, and also 'Proposal 35' – the criteria for new highway capacity, that 'consideration [will be given] to new road schemes where there is an overall net benefit when judged against [...] the contribution to London's sustainable development/regeneration including improved connectivity and [...] the extent to which congestion (average vehicle delay, unreliable journey times and poor levels of network resilience) is reduced' (p 159). This is controversial position to take for TfL – out of step with the rest of the sustainable transport aspirations – and the resistance to reducing traffic capacity means that the space for cycle provision (and walking and public transport) is much less than might be expected. This policy position certainly needs to change if cycling provision, including segregated routes, is to be provided to any significant degree. A closer look at some of the headline measures in the *Vision for cycling* (GLA, 2013) might highlight the tension: the signature M40

Westway cycle flyover – although this may be segregated – for many cyclists this is not the welcoming cycle route, lined by active frontages, that is required. Perhaps it is the opportunity to develop cycle provision without taking away road space that has been the lead motivation?

A more comprehensive support for cycling would take the form of the concerted action found in cities in the Netherlands, Denmark and Germany. For example, Amsterdam (735,000 population) and Copenhagen (504,000 population) each have around 400km of completely separate bike paths and lanes. In 2004, Berlin (3.4 million population) had 860km of completely separate bike paths, 60km of bike lanes on the streets, 50km of bike lanes on pavements, 100km of mixed-use pedestrian/bike paths and 70km of combined bus/bike lanes on streets. Even many of the smaller cities, such as Münster in Germany, Odense in Denmark and Groningen in the Netherlands, have 400–500km of bike paths and lanes. This has involved 30 years of consistent effort in investing in the cycling environment from the 1970s onwards (Pucher and Buehler, 2008). Box 12.1 outlines the type of provision that is useful in developing high levels of cycling; it is striking to see how much of this remains undeveloped in London.

Towards a transition?

Achieving the Mayor's 60 per cent reduction in CO_2 emissions in transport will require a wide-ranging and well-integrated set of policy measures. This will involve major investment in public transport, walking and cycling facilities, urban planning, streetscape design, traffic demand management, new vehicle technologies and slower traffic speeds. It will also involve a different governmental framework, and a different articulation of the problems and the solutions. The contemporary form of governance has been shaped in a particular way in the UK, including in London, increasingly characterised by the neoliberalist mindset, championing individual freedoms and rights over the 'excessive intervention' of the state (Foucault, 1991; Lupton, 1999). This is unhelpful in transport and city planning, where the emphasis is on developing wide-ranging investments in infrastructure and designing new development in an integrative manner. This can only be 'interventionist' in nature, often requiring strategic and coordinated planning at different governmental scales. The end goal is to shape individual behaviours in a manner that is consistent with societal goals, such as reduced CO_2 emissions or improved social equity and wellbeing. Market-based strategies, such as limiting investment, reducing the amount of strategic planning and relaying on information provision or voluntary agreements, are unlikely to significantly alter travel behaviours or purchasing patterns, often because only the 'weak' measures are applied. The debate is often very subtly shaped – the role of the interventionist state is curtailed only in some areas, but not others. For example, investing in non-car based infrastructure (public transport, walking and cycling) or shaping the built environment (in strategic, city and neighbourhood planning, investment in the public realm) is framed as 'subsidy', 'unaffordable', 'only for a minority

Box 12.1: Policies and innovative measures used in Dutch, Danish and German cities

Extensive systems of separate cycling facilities
- Well-maintained, fully integrated paths, lanes and special bicycle streets in cities and surrounding regions
- Fully coordinated system of colour-coded directional signs for cyclists
- Off-street short-cuts, such as mid-block connections and passages through dead-ends for cars

Intersection modifications and priority traffic signals
- Advance green lights for cyclists at most junctions
- Advanced cyclist waiting positions (ahead of cars) fed by special bike lanes facilitating safer and quicker crossings and turns
- Cyclist short-cuts to make right-hand turns before intersections and exemption from red traffic signals at T-junctions, thus increasing cyclist speed and safety
- Brightly coloured bike lanes when crossing intersections
- Traffic signals are synchronised at cyclist speeds assuring consecutive green lights for cyclists (green wave)

Traffic calming
- Traffic calming of all residential neighbourhoods via speed limit (30 km/hr) and physical infrastructure deterrents for cars
- Bicycle streets, narrow roads where bikes have absolute priority over cars
- 'Home Zones' with 7 km/hr speed limit, where cars must yield to pedestrians and cyclists using the road

Bike parking
- Large supply of good bike parking throughout the city, including improved lighting, video surveillance, and priority parking for women

Coordination with public transport
- Extensive bike parking at all Metro, suburban and regional train stations
- 'Call a Bike' programmes: bikes can be rented by mobile phone at stations, paid for by the minute and left at any busy intersection in the city
- Bike rentals at most train stations
- Deluxe bike parking garages at key train stations, with video surveillance, special lighting, music, repair services and bike rentals
- Traffic education and training
- Comprehensive cycling training courses for virtually all school children with test by traffic police
- Special cycling training test tracks for children
- Stringent training of motorists to respect pedestrians and cyclists and avoid hitting them
- Traffic laws; motorists assumed by law to be responsible for almost all crashes with cyclists (including left turns across cycle pathway); special legal protection for children and elderly cyclists
- Strict enforcement of cyclist rights by police and courts

Source: Pucher and Buehler (2008)

or 'politically unacceptable', while new highway investment is seen as 'critical for business and freight', 'investment for the city' and 'helping the majority or important interests'. These are, of course, all social constructs, involving forms of control, guidance and exercise of sovereignty. These meanings do not emerge 'out of the blue', but are framed and put forward by a particular set of powerful actors, in a contested manner, where groups actively attempt to influence a particular issue (Hajer and Versteeg, 2005; Schwanen et al, 2011).

Although London is often cited as an example of a governance framework where integrated planning and transport is possible, there are also limits as to the reach and 'intensity' of interventions. Many of the policy targets, such as CO_2 reductions, are highly aspirational targets, which will need significantly more radical policy interventions than are currently under discussion. The socio-technical transition literature would advise that significant changes in (travel) behaviours will only occur if change is pursued at multiple levels, including those of 'landscape' (including city design, infrastructure, political ideology, the media, macro-economic trends, societal values and beliefs); 'regime' (activities of transport users, firms, transport planners, engineers, politicians, the motor industry, prevailing habits and norms); and 'niche' (emerging practices, technologies and policy measures) (Geels and Schot, 2007; Geels and Kemp, 2012). The range of intervention is hence beyond the usual focus of the transport planner. Added to this is the required focus on 'agency' (individual change, including the roles of advertising, marketing and lobbying). Perhaps it is here that London – at least in terms of cycling – has developed quite strongly in recent years, with increasingly effective support campaigns being developed.

The fairly sophisticated campaigns in support of better cycling networks and facilities seem to be leading to changed practices in the city authorities, and perhaps for the first time in years there are possibilities that much improved networks and wider facilities will emerge. Perhaps a 'transformation' will occur, where landscape developments exert pressure on the regime, so that 'reconfiguration' takes place, the niche innovations (including, perversely, an old means of travel in cycling) become well developed and exert pressure on the regime. The 'subjectification' (how the agents are to be understood, imagined, represented and governed) (Dean, 1999; Schwanen et al, 2011) to an extent reverses, or at least changes focus, from the individual to the governmental agencies and actors. There are, however, major difficulties in that the baseline levels of cycling remain very low, the current facilities are woeful, and the mainstream political beliefs, media, societal values and norms remain intransigently fixed, and are not hugely supportive of radical efforts to support sustainable mobility. Over the longer term, it is hoped that the cultural acceptance of, and support for, cycling can also change markedly.

Reflecting Hajer (1995) and Rydin (1998), it is contended that the rhetorical form of the debate is critical to any resulting changed behaviours, shaping the development of strategy and implementation, and the bounds of the discussion, as well reflecting them. Hence the nature of the language used is a critical layer to the technical discussion: 'a form of influence which backs up the exercise of power through control over resources' (Rydin, 1998, p 189). Perhaps we can turn this to our advantage, by talking up the benefits of sustainable mobility in general, and cycling in particular – but having real substance to the claims, by making the evidence abundantly clear in terms of the public realm, city design and health benefits, and disseminating the good practice that is developing in many cities. This can then lead to a well-funded and consistent strategy, applied over the long term. Perhaps then we can look forward to much greater progress towards sustainable travel.

Notes

[1] The VIBAT London study (Visioning and Backcasting for Transport) examined the potential for CO_2 reduction in London and whether the 60 per cent reduction could be achieved in the transport sector.

[2] A trip is a complete door-to-door movement, such as from home to employment. This can include several stages within it, such as a walk from home to the station, the journey on a train and then a further walk from the end station to the office (TfL, 2010).

References

Anderson, L., Schnohr, P., Schroll, M. and Hein, H. (2000) 'All-cause mortality associated with physical activity during leisure time, work, sports and cycling to work', *Archives of Internal Medicine*, vol 160, pp 1621-28.

Banister, D., Anderton, K., Bonilla, D., Givoni, M. and Schwanen, T. (2011) 'Transport and the environment', *The Annual Review of Environment and Resources*, vol 36, pp 247-70.

Dean, M. (1999) *Governmentality, power and rule in modern society*, London: Sage.

Dunn, J. and Perl, A. (2010) 'Launching a post carbon regime for American surface transportation: assessing the policy tools', World Conference on Transport Research, Lisbon, Portugal.

Edelman, M. (1988) *Constructing the political spectacle*, Chicago, IL: University of Chicago Press.

Evening Standard (2013) 'End of the free green run ... now hybrid cars will have to pay congestion charge too', 28 January (www.standard.co.uk/news/transport).

Foucault, M. (1991) 'Governmentality', in G. Burchell, C. Gordon and P. Miller (eds) *The Foucault effect: studies in governmentality*, Chicago, IL: Chicago University Press.

Geels, F.W. and Kemp (2012) 'The multi-level perspective as a new perspective for studying socio-technical transitions', in F.W. Geels, R. Kemp, G. Dudley and G. Lyons (eds) *Automobility in transition? A socio-technical analysis of sustainable transport*, London: Routledge, pp 49-79.

Geels, F.W. and Schot, J.W. (2007) 'Typology of sociotechnical transition pathways', *Research Policy*, vol 36, pp 399-417.

GLA (Greater London Authority) (2013) *Mayor's vision for cycling*, London: Mayor of London, GLA.

Hajer, M.A. (1995) *The politics of environmental discourse: ecological modernization and the policy process*, Oxford: Clarendon Press.

Hajer, M.A. and Versteeg, W. (2005) 'A decade of discourse analysis of environmental politics: achievements, challenges, perspectives', *Journal of Environmental Policy & Planning*, vol 7, pp 175-84.

Hickman, R. and Banister, D. (2014) *Transport, climate change and the city*, Abingdon: Routledge.

Hickman, R., Ashiru, O. and Banister, D. (2009a) *20% transport. Visioning and backcasting for transport in London. Executive summary*, London: Halcrow Group.

Hickman, R., Ashiru, O. and Banister, D. (2009b) *Visioning and backcasting for transport in London (VIBAT-London). Stages 1-4 background reports*, London: Halcrow Group.

Lascoumes, P. and Le Gales, P. (2007) 'Introduction: understanding public policy through its instruments – from the nature of instruments to the sociology of public policy instrumentation', *Governance*, vol 20, pp 1-21.

Le Vine, S. and Jones, P. (2012) *On the move. Making sense of car and train travel trends in Britain*, London: RAC Foundation.

London Transport Data (2013) *Long run trend in commuting into central London* (http://londontransportdata.wordpress.com/category/subject/modal-share).

Lupton, D. (1999) *Risk*, London: Routledge.

Metz, D. (2008) 'The myth of travel time saving', *Transport Reviews*, vol 28, pp 321-36.

Pacala, S. and Socolow, R. (2004) 'Stabilization wedges: solving the climate problem for the next 50 years with current technologies', *Science*, vol 305, pp 968-72.

Pucher, J. and Buehler, R. (2008) 'Making cycling irresistible: lessons from the Netherlands, Denmark and Germany', *Transport Reviews*, vol 28, pp 495-528.

Pucher, J. and Buehler, R. (2012) *City cycling*, Cambridge, MA: The MIT Press.

Rydin, Y. (1998) 'The enabling local state and urban development: resources, rhetoric and planning in East London', *Urban Studies*, vol 35, pp 175-91.

Schwanen, T., Banister, D. and Anable, J. (2011) 'Scientific research about climate change mitigation in transport: a critical review', *Transportation Research, Part A*, vol 45, pp 993-1006.

Schwanen, T., Banister, D. and Anable, J. (2012) 'Rethinking habits and their role in behaviour change: the case of low-carbon mobility', *Journal of Transport Geography*, vol 24, pp 522-32.

Steg, L. (2005) 'Car use: lust and must. Instrumental, symbolic and affective motives for car use', *Transportation Research Part A: Policy and Practice*, vol 39, pp 147-62.

TfL (Transport for London) (2010) *Mayor's transport strategy for London*, London: TfL, GLA.

TfL (2011) *Travel in London, Report 4*, London: TfL.

Urry, J. (2007) *Mobilities*, Cambridge: Polity.

Woodcock, J., Edwards, P., Tonne, C., Armstrong, B.G., Ashiru, O., Banister, D., Beevers, S., Chalabi, Z., Chowdhury, Z., Cohen, A., Franco, O.H., Haines, A., Hickman, R., Lindsay, G., Mittal, I., Mohan, D., Tiwari, G., Woodward, A. and Roberts, I. (2009) 'Public health benefits of strategies to reduce greenhouse-gas emissions: urban land transport', *The Lancet*, vol 374, pp 1930-43.

THIRTEEN

Building the 'healthy city' in London

Clare Herrick

Introduction

The 2010 election of the Coalition government ushered in a new era of economic austerity underpinned by a set of political ideologies designed, in large part, to justify it. In a now-(in)famous poster used as part of the Conservative Party campaign in the run-up to the General Election, David Cameron is pictured, delicately airbrushed, alongside the words 'We can't go on like this. I'll cut the deficit, not the NHS'. Soon after, the newly formed Coalition government announced that the NHS would have to find efficiency savings of £20 billion by 2014-15. This cut would be accompanied by a dramatic institutional recalibration of the organisation of the health service, with newly formed general practitioner (GP) consortia directly commissioning services, the dissolution of primary care trusts (PCTs) and their incorporation within local authorities as well as the establishment of a new agency, Public Health England (DH, 2010a, 2011). These changes have been accompanied by a powerful rhetoric of the importance of the local, expounded most powerfully in the Localism Act (2011) which makes provision for changes to housing, planning and council responsibilities. At the root of these governance shifts lies the belief that 'for too long, central government has hoarded and concentrated power' through, for example, targets, inspections and unnecessary bureaucracy (DCLG, 2011, p 3). Instead, the Localism Bill argues, power should be devolved to local government, democratically elected mayors and local communities. Together, these governance changes herald a new landscape of health provision, funding and political ideology in England, raising inescapable questions about the sustainability and future of the 'healthy' city at a time of austerity. As Barton and Grant (2008, p 131) argue, 'human wellbeing, now and in the future, is the "touchstone" of sustainability', and it is this contention and its significance for London that is the focus of this chapter.

Since 2010, very few areas of public service provision have been left untouched by austerity measures. Education, housing and social care are just a few of the domains undergoing high-profile organisational, ideological and economic restructuring, while simultaneously having their budgets cut by up to 40 per cent (DH, 2010a; DCLG, 2011). The emotive nature of the NHS, fears over privatisation and disparities in access to and quality of care has meant that the changes to the health system have been subjected to particularly sustained media and public scrutiny. The Coalition's ideology of health improvement has been largely drawn from Michael Marmot's celebrated, interdisciplinary 'Social determinants of health' work (Marmot, 2005, 2010; WHO, 2008). This highly influential body of work, which originated with the World Health Organization's (WHO) Commission on Social Determinants of Health (2005-08), argues for policy attention to the broad, upstream 'causes of the causes' of ill health, in which it is asserted that 'measures to improve health also have a direct relevance for sustainability' (Marmot, 2010, p 78). If we take sustainability to be 'the need to ensure a better quality of life for all, now and in the future, in a just and equitable manner while living within the limits of supporting ecosystems' (Agyeman and Evans, 2003, p 5), then this definition fits neatly with the approach to health proposed by Marmot. In brief, the social determinants perspective argues that 'avoidable health inequalities arise because of the circumstances in which people grow, live, work, and age, and the systems put in place to deal with illness. The conditions in which people live and die are, in turn, shaped by political, social, and economic forces' (WHO, 2008, preface). Furthermore, they contend that the existence of marked social gradients in health between and within places is a matter of gross social injustice where 'poor and unequal living conditions are the consequence of poor social policies and programmes, unfair economic arrangements, and bad politics' (WHO, 2008, p 1). This is of central importance to the urban sustainable development agenda if social and environmental justice (as markers of rights, equality and quality) are viewed as essential for health and, in turn, equitable health outcomes are a key indicator of an urban environment's sustainability. However, since the publication of Marmot's WHO report, the financial crisis threatens to widen inequalities, while fiscal austerity has lessened the appetite and capacity for redistributive policies in many countries (UCL Institute of Health Equity, 2012). Under austerity, Marmot's call to address the 'causes of the causes' through joined-up, cross-governmental working looks increasingly likely to undermine normative visions of what the 'Healthy City' should and could be.

Despite the centrality of Marmot's vision to current health policy, it sits somewhat uncomfortably with the claim that, 'we need a new approach that empowers individuals to make healthy choices and gives communities the tools to address their own, particular needs' (DH, 2010b, p 2). The White Paper aims to put 'local communities at the heart of public health' (DH, 2010b, p 2), but the work being undertaken by the Cabinet Office's Behavioural Insights Team highlights the centrality of *individual* behaviour change to the Coalition's broader governance logic. The notion that 'the lifestyle factors that impact upon people's health and wellbeing are often deeply entwined in the fabric of our everyday lives' leads the report to conclude that 'strong-armed regulation is not the answer' (Cabinet Office, 2010, p 6) to preventing future ill health, at odds with Marmot's advocation of greater regulation of employment (for example, the minimum wage), urban planning (for example, fast food outlet density) and utilities to reduce fuel poverty. The most appropriate use of regulation to create improved quality of life is particularly evident in the case of London, where aligning local authority priorities in such a way that the expectations laid down in the Mayor's *London Health Inequalities Strategy* (2010) and by London's Sustainable Development Commission are delivered is a complex problem. Despite the significant changes in health policy, it remains the case that the operational tension between where best to focus preventative efforts – the environment or individual behaviour – remains. Indeed, the focus on 'the local' has done little to clarify *where* and *how* efforts and resources should best be channelled and, moreover, over *whom*, with great significance for the holistic integration of economic, environmental and social agendas that urban sustainability requires (Agyeman et al, 2002, p 43; Agyeman and Evans, 2004; Wilkinson and Pickett, 2010). To explore these ideas, this chapter first sets out the recent shifts in policies relating to health (rather than merely health policies) at a range of spatial scales, and the ways in which these complement or complicate the sustainable development agenda. It then turns to a case study exploring the epidemiology and resurgence of tuberculosis (TB) in London, as both a challenge to sustainability and human evidence of the agenda's persistent failure to produce the kind of 'just and socially fulfilling society' (Wilkinson and Pickett, 2010, p 44) needed for its equitable realisation. London is exemplary in this regard as in 2012 the city had 40 per cent of England's 9,000 reported TB cases (HPA, 2012b), and this infectious, treatable respiratory disease exemplifies the extreme entwinements of social, economic, political and environmental risk factors that operate across multiple scales to challenge future urban sustainability agendas around health (Satterthwaite, 1997). Moreover, the case of TB in London clearly reveals the absolute importance of effective, planned, multi-scalar governance strategies that cross-cut departmental competencies to not just treat TB, but also ensure that the environmental, economic and social injustices that perpetuate vulnerabilities are viewed as crucial to the city's broader sustainability ambitions.

Changing landscape of health governance in England post-2010

In 2010, Andrew Lansley (then Secretary of State for Health) gave a speech to the UK Faculty of Public Health Conference succinctly conveying the Coalition's stance on health. In sum, the speech expounded the need for: (1) smaller government; (2) local initiatives to be driven by local needs rather than top-down diktat; and (3) that Whitehall would steer what outcomes were expected, but not how they should be achieved. Lansley criticised the Labour administration for encouraging 'Initiatives without evidence, without evaluation, without coordination and, most of all, without awareness of the cultural need to change behaviour' (Lansley, 2010). However, at the same time as he highlighted the need for behaviour change, he stressed that:

> Common factors like dysfunctional families, poverty, worklessness, weak family and community structures, lack of good parenting, or mental illness are all identifiable causes [of poor health]. But, most

of all ... the reason underlying all of this, especially amongst young people, is a lack of self-esteem.... The fact is, you can't legislate for self-esteem from Westminster. (Lansley, 2010)

The speech highlights the need to address the kind of deeply systemic risk factors for poor health, such as poverty, family problems, poor housing, worklessness and poor quality education identified in Marmot's report. Yet it also suggests that the cause of all such interwoven issues is 'a lack of self-esteem', itself sanctioning an approach to health that prioritises individual behaviour change. Layered on top of these two domains is a call for more evaluation and evidence, with the promise that, 'we must only support effective interventions that deliver proven benefits. We must be certain that every penny invested will achieve better health outcomes' (Lansley, 2010). The references to smaller government and the inefficacy of legislation to change behaviour are dotted throughout the speech and yet, some of the major systemic causes of poor health that are identified are rooted in the vulnerabilities and inequalities perpetuated by the same political, legal, economic and social structures and systems that are equally central to the achievement of sustainability. To state that you 'can't legislate for self-esteem from Westminster' is fallacious, given that you may be able to legislate for the improvement of the structural preconditions for self-esteem. Yet with additional legislation unpalatable, the speech instead challenges coherence by identifying a vision of devolving responsibility to the local level, locating causality in broader structural risks and also making it clear that the onus is on individuals to act responsibly. In reference to Thaler and Sunstein's highly influential 2008 book *Nudge*, it states that the government will be 'nudging' (individual responsibility) rather than 'nannying' (through regulation), but, importantly, details on tackling the systemic 'causes of the causes' remains vague at best.

The Coalition's new public health system rests on two new structures. First, local authority leadership on health promotion, prevention and service delivery. And second, the new Public Health England agency responsible for delivering public health information, behavioural insight, building the evidence base and appointing directors of public health with local authorities. Together they are responsible for the development of a Joint Strategic Needs Assessment (JSNA) and a Joint Health and Wellbeing Strategy. The NHS remains the chief care provider, the Chief Medical Officer still advises the Secretary of State for Health and the government and Department for Health set the national legal and regulatory framework. To cement this new structure, a series of outcomes are set out in the *Public Health Outcomes Framework for England 2013-2016* (DH, 2012), which rests on two core outcomes: (1) increasing *healthy* life expectancy and (2) reducing the differences in *life expectancy* and *healthy life expectancy* between communities. Thus, at root, the outcomes seek to reduce inequalities in mortality and morbidity within and between local areas. Achieving these outcomes is broken down into four domains: improving the wider determinants of health; health improvement (making healthy choices); health protection (from major incidents and threats);

and reducing the number of people living with preventable ill health and dying prematurely. These domains are delineated by a series of indicators, although the *Outcomes Framework* is quick to stress that 'the whole system will be refocused around achieving positive health outcomes for the population and reducing inequalities in health, rather than focussed on process targets, and will not be used to performance manage local areas' (DCLG, 2012, p 2). This is in stark contrast to Labour's approach to public health improvement, which was strongly orientated around short-term process target-setting (for example, waiting list times, hospital bed numbers and so on). Despite this aversion to targets, the new system still has a list of over 60 'outcome targets' against which to measure progress, including child poverty, domestic abuse, fuel poverty, homelessness, diet, alcohol-related hospital admissions, self-reported wellbeing and a range of mortality indicators. It is notable that these outcome targets are not direct measures of health, and instead reflect the 'causes of the causes' or social determinants identified as significant for the realisation of the goal of 'healthy and sustainable places and communities' (Marmot, 2010), in which 'sustainability' incorporates a number of aspirations: living within environmental limits; promoting wellbeing, social cohesion, inclusion and equal opportunities; good governance; a sustainable economy (in which people do not just have jobs, but quality employment); and the responsible use of 'sound science' (working with evidence, the precautionary principle, public attitudes and values). It is from these multiple arenas that 'the freedom to flourish' (Marmot, 2010, p 18) must no longer be 'graded' but rather a just expression of socially, economically and environmentally sustainable places and communities (Agyeman and Evans, 2003).

However, it should also be noted that running alongside the Outcomes Framework, the government has instigated a much-maligned set of public health 'Responsibility Deals'. These form part of its wider stance against excess regulation and over-zealous legislation for the modifiable risk factors of alcohol consumption, diets, physical activity and workplace health. The Deals aim to join non-governmental organisations (NGOs), industry, public health organisations and local government to 'pledge' their commitment to voluntary initiatives such as alcohol unit labelling, underage sales of alcohol, calorie information on food consumed out of home, salt reduction, trans-fats, promoting active travel and new occupational health standards. Together these fall under the rubric of 'nudging' people into making healthier choices (Jones et al, 2010, 2011; Whitehead et al, 2011), drawing heavily on Thaler and Sunstein's 2008 brand of libertarian paternalism that was taken up by the Cabinet Office's Behavioural Insight Unit in their 2010 *Applying behavioural insights to health* report. The Responsibility Deals work on the expectation of voluntary uptake of efforts to alter what Thaler and Sunstein term the 'choice architectures' that govern individual decision making and behaviours. Here, 'behavioural economists argue that decision making is rarely made in absolute, isolated contexts: it is normally positioned in relation to our surrounding sociocultural and physical environment' (Whitehead et al, 2011, p 2825). Therefore, libertarian paternalists argue, it is the environment (at a variety of scales, from the 'point of decision' prompt near lifts detailing the potential calories burnt by climbing the stairs, to the realignment of streetscapes along 'shared space' principles) that needs modification if the 'nudges' are to really have an effect. In turn, this commitment is matched by a reciprocal promise of 'proportionate' industry self-regulation on behalf of government.

The approach has, however, come in for great criticism from all fronts, with Geof Raynor – adviser to the Labour government's Foresight obesity project (Government Office for Science, 2007) – pointing out in the 'Health Matters' blog that 'The problem for public health is not what Nudge is able to achieve but which interventions are sidelined' (Raynor, 2012). Frustration with the clear omission of certain policy possibilities has meant that public health organisations have been outspoken in their opposition to the Responsibility Deals. Alcohol Concern, for example, has long argued for the need for greater industry regulation through legislation on the minimum pricing of alcohol. And while minimum pricing has been debated in Scotland and is now back on the table in England (Herrick, 2011a, 2011b), its progress through government has been stalled through industry lobbying and recourse to arguments concerning its illegality under current European Union (EU) competition laws (Baumberg and Anderson, 2008). It is worth remembering that Alcohol Concern actually withdrew from the alcohol Responsibility Deal in early 2011, citing their belief that the government's priority was ensuring the status quo of self-regulation rather than reducing alcohol-related harm. Moreover, the group argued that by having the Wine and Spirit Trade Association chairing the deal and by relying on a series of 'toothless' promises with no sanctions for failure to translate these into health outcomes, the system would be ineffectual. As Gilmore et al (2011, p 4) suggest, 'the core of these concerns is the apparent failure to acknowledge the essential conflicts of interest involved when corporations engage in activities and policies ostensibly aimed towards reducing the harmful behaviours on which their profitability depends.' In addition, the problem is that:

> The prominence of health discourses such as health promotion and social marketing for health run the risk of embedding a behavioural turn away from a focus upon wider social and environmental determinants of wellbeing. Further, they are indicative of a failure to implement coherent social policies capable of addressing structural inequality. (Crawshaw, 2012, p 207)

The multiple drivers of health risks are integral to the commercial functioning of urban space, but yet the negative externalities for health that result from 'the pernicious temptations that are increasingly etched into facets of everyday life' (Jones et al, 2011, p 487) – from the quality of food provision to the accessibility of safe green space – would seem to jeopardise urban sustainability as well as the social justices that Marmot's work argues are necessary for its achievement. This is further reinforced by the kind of short-termism that not only characterise risk behaviours such as smoking, drinking and eating unhealthily, but also current policy strategies. By contrast, true urban sustainability requires long-term, intergenerational thinking underpinned by a commitment to social and environmental justice. Yet, while great faith is being placed on nudging, 'evidence to support the effectiveness of nudging as a means to improve population health and reduce health inequalities is, however, weak. This reflects absence of evidence as well as evidence of little or no effect' (Marteau et al, 2011, p 265). Perhaps more importantly, nudge tends to be most effective on those people who may already be most amenable to behaviour change – not necessarily those who are most at risk or vulnerable (Salazar, 2012). Given the Secretary of State for Health's call for 'the use and collection of evidence so we build a stronger picture of what works' (Lansley, 2010), and the limited repertoire of nudges proven to change health behaviours, the question of 'what works' to make both people and places healthier is particularly uncertain.

The complexity of evaluating the short and long-term impact of the pledges made through the Responsibility Deals highlights the interconnections of health with a host of interlinked social, environmental and economic processes. As a result, Smith and Petticrew (2010) argue that better 'macro-evaluation' of the long-term sustained impact of interventions on societal and system effects on health, such as community empowerment, social capital and the economy, is essential. They further contend that when public health is reconfigured around Marmot's social justice aspirations, then health effects extend beyond the micro-scale, individual frame of evaluations that have long been used to measure the impact of interventions on infectious disease mortality, prevalence and incidence rates. Instead, they argue, multi-sector health interventions require interdisciplinary frames of evaluation and analysis that recognise that the determinants of health rest as much in the structural opportunities afforded by employment, housing, education and the affordability and availability of food, alcohol and tobacco as they do in healthcare processes and procedures. These systems are inherently complex and subject to ripple effects, spill-overs and externalities that challenge the existing methodologies and conceptual referents used in evaluations. In addition, the extent to which they are viable, liveable, convivial, equitable and prosperity-supporting as potential indicators of the Healthy City (Hancock, 1993) raises inevitable issues of subjectivity and measurement. Yet, without appropriate evaluation, few advances will be made in designing and implementing healthy and therefore sustainable urban futures, whether through the built environment or through behaviour change interventions. This is likely to be even more the case in a time of austerity when local authorities will have to justify the use of limited funds by reference to 'evidence of best practice', even though there is a 'dearth of evidence available on [for example] obesity prevention' (Swinburn et al, 2005, p 24), and what little exists is often geographically inconsistent. Experimentation and risk-taking are not the natural bedfellows of austerity, and yet, achieving the sustainable, healthy and socially just city may well require new levels of innovation or, what Swinburn et al (2005, p 25) term, 'practice-based evidence'. To explore these ideas in more detail, the chapter now turns to London and the example of TB in order to explore the ways in which the current health reforms intersect with the disease's structural and behavioural risk factors and, therefore, the potential consequences for urban sustainability and health.

Governing health and urban sustainability in London: the case of TB

London's rising rate of TB cannot be considered apart from its complex set of social, economic, ethnic, environmental and political risk factors and, as a result, the multiple governance systems and rationales that condition them. TB thus represents an instance of an infectious respiratory disease in which structural risk factors and resultant vulnerabilities usually far subsume individual behavioural risks. For this reason, TB is a particularly pertinent example through which to explore the intersections of urban sustainability and health agendas, principally as TB vulnerability touches on many of the same social, environmental and economic concerns that perpetuate inequality, derail social justice and therefore undermine London's sustainable development agenda. TB is notable for being included as one of the indicators in the public health Outcomes Framework, as well as featuring in the JSNAs of a number of London boroughs. In 2011, roughly 40 per cent of total TB cases in England were located in London, and the city now has the highest rates of any capital city in Western Europe (NHS London Health Programmes, 2012). From 2000-11, the number of active TB cases in London increased from 6,724 to 9,963, or by over 33 per cent. This climb has led TB to be identified as 'a major public health problem for the capital' (NHS London Health Programmes, 2011, p 5), and resulted in a draft strategy to help reduce the rate by 50 per cent over the next decade. The UK's TB profile is inextricable from the global processes of migration, urbanisation and economic restructuring that both relocate and compound risk and vulnerability. This is borne out in the demographic characteristics of TB cases shown in Figure 13.1, whereby rates among the non UK-born population in England stood at an average of 83.6 per 100,000 population in 2011, 20 times that of the UK-born population, at 4.1 per 100,000 (HPA, 2012a; see also Pareek et al, 2011a). This means that, as Figure 13.2 illustrates, from 2000-11, the number of cases among the non UK-born has increased by almost 82 per cent (from 3,458 to 6,287 per 100,000), while that of the UK-born population has risen by only 2 per cent (HPA, 2012a). Beyond the incidence rates, the TB burden has 'a strong socio-economic gradient between countries, within countries, and within communities and the poorest have the highest risk' (Lönnroth et al, 2009, p 2,243), which speaks profoundly to the issues raised by a social determinants of health perspective. This gradient is exhibited most profoundly by the difference in TB rates across London boroughs shown in Figure 13.3, which, in 2011, varied from 8.6 per 100,000 in Havering to 137 per 100,000 in Newham.

This data demonstrates that not only do high rates of TB incidence cluster in London, as shown in Figure 13.4, but that certain geographic locales are disproportionately burdened by the condition. In this case, the boroughs of

Figure 13.1: Tuberculosis rates in the UK, 2000-11

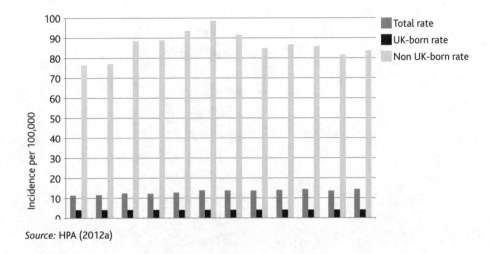

Source: HPA (2012a)

Figure 13.2: Total notified cases of tuberculosis in the UK, 2000-11

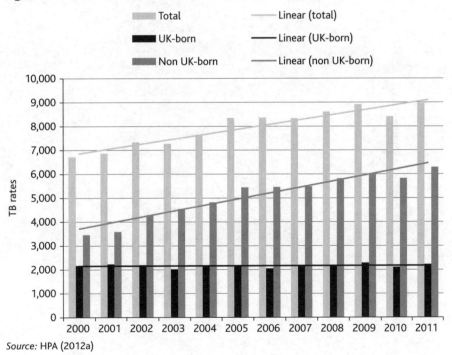

Source: HPA (2012a)

Newham and Brent (118 per 100,000) have rates that are triple the cut-off for 'high' levels of TB set by WHO (40 per 100,000), and equal or greater than average incidence rates in, for example, Ghana (86), the Russian Federation (97), Rwanda (106), Nigeria (118) and Thailand (127) (WHO, 2012). These international comparisons are important, not simply to illustrate the magnitude of TB incidence

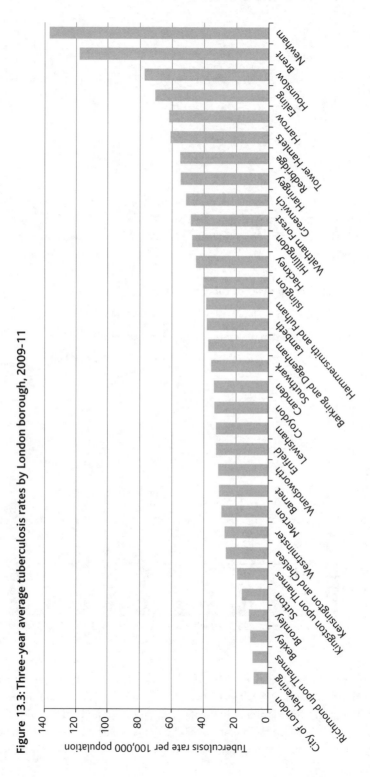

Figure 13.3: Three-year average tuberculosis rates by London borough, 2009-11

Source: HPA (2012a)

Figure 13.4: Three-year average tuberculosis rates by local area, 2009-11

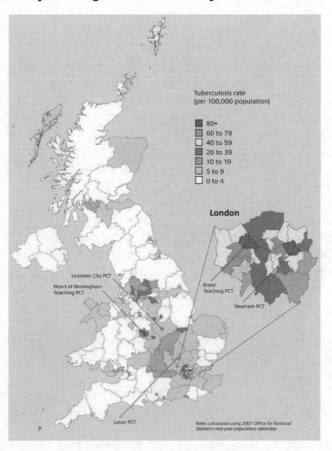

Source: HPA (2012b); Crown copyright

in Newham and Brent, but also to start to think through the ways in which the factors shaping vulnerability to TB are constituted in and through 'nested scales of causality and interdependence linking the dynamics of urban and regional change to processes of global economic restructuring' (Gandy and Zumla, 2002, p 390). As a result, and as Gandy and Zumla further argue (2002, p 390), there is a need to 'integrate the analysis of disease into the broader dynamics of social and political change.'More than anything this is because the burgeoning 'Healthy City' literature and the WHO movement of the same name (for an overview, see Herrick, 2013) often explores 'quality of life issues in a context which is divorced from the underlying dynamics of urban change' (Gandy and Zumla, 2002, p 390), despite a sustainable development perspective that highlights their inherent interconnectivity. This critique is particularly valid in the context of TB where, a decade on from the publication of Gandy and Zumla's paper, national guidance and policy on TB in England are still centred on treatment completion rates, debates over the efficacy and reform of migrant screening programmes and the need to actively seek out patients with TB rather than passively waiting for them to present to the healthcare system (NICE, 2011). However, the aetiology of TB represents a complex interplay between structural forces at work in the home countries of migrants and living conditions in the host/destination country that perpetuates either the transmission of TB or causes the reactivation of latent into active TB. The processes and practices of migration from low-income, high-incidence countries to high-income, low-incidence countries further exacerbates this (Blumberg et al, 2010), especially when migrants are most likely to settle in the most deprived areas of high-income countries. It is worth bearing in mind that among TB cases in the UK in 2011, 59 per cent were in people from South Asia and 24 per cent from sub-Saharan Africa. In the UK, the highest rate of TB were among those born in India (162 per 100,000), which is not that far removed from India's own incidence rate of 181 per 100,000 in 2011 (WHO, 2012). However, in Brent, rates of TB among the foreign-born exceed even this, with rates among Black Africans of 314, Pakistanis of 233, Indians of 224 and Bangladeshis of 131. With 58.6 per cent of Brent's population foreign-born and 10.3 per cent of those originally from India and 51.2 per cent of Newham's population foreign-born, with 8.5 per cent originally from India, the socio-spatial characteristics of TB infection in London start to become clearer.

At present, TB control measures in the UK are inconsistently deployed. In theory, migrants are selectively screened for *active* TB before entry visas are issued and chest x-rays are used at Heathrow and Gatwick for this purpose (Abubakar et al, 2011). This process is then supposed to feed into the primary healthcare system at the migrant's destination borough in order to follow up with treatment. However, a recent survey among PCTs demonstrated that those with the highest incidence of TB were among the least likely to screen migrants with normal chest x-rays for latent TB (Pareek et al, 2011a, 2011b). This is an important contributory factor to the extremely high rates of TB in Newham and Brent, given that the majority of TB infection in the UK results from conversion of latent TB on average two years after migration. Therefore, with no consistent process in place to systematically screen for latent TB, the multiple structural risk factors that converge to activate latent TB infection will continue to contribute to high rates in certain London boroughs. This situation therefore draws our attention to two strands of vulnerability. The first are the social risk factors understood by the Health Protection Agency (HPA) to contribute to TB: drug use, alcohol misuse, homelessness and imprisonment. The second are the broader environmental, economic and social conditions of vulnerability that increase the likelihood of TB transmission and reactivation, undermine quality of life and compromise social and environmental justice. Given that the HPA estimate that only 2.5 per cent of TB cases in 2011 correlated with a history of drug use, 3.5 per cent with alcohol misuse, 2.5 per cent with homelessness and 2.6 per cent with imprisonment (HPA, 2012b), there is scope to suggest that the broader conditions of vulnerability are far more significant, especially among high-risk migrant populations in London. In this case, the city functions as a 'biosocial' entity (Farmer, 1999; Keshavjee and Farmer, 2012) in which it may be the case that 'causal pathways linking poverty and low socio-economic status to increased risk of TB are not fully understood' (Lönnroth et al, 2009, p 2243), but there is nevertheless a great need to mitigate the social determinants of TB transmission and reactivation. These include overcrowding (Beckhurst et al, 2000), population density (Clark et al, 2002), indoor and outdoor air pollution, smoking, HIV, diet (Strachan et al, 1995), housing quality (Hyndman, 1990), as well as chronic conditions such as diabetes and stress that can compromise immunity. The Integrated Household Survey (HM Government, 2009), for example, shows that Newham had rates of overcrowding approaching 18 per cent and Brent of over 12 per cent in 2009. Notably, Satterthwaite's (1997) areas of action for sustainable cities include the control of infectious disease as well as achieving a high-quality urban environment for all inhabitants. The structural factors driving high TB rates in Newham and Brent thus demonstrate the limits to efforts to bring about sustainable urban environments, underscored by the pernicious effects of social, economic and environmental inequality. Moreover, 'the overriding issues linking all these [high risk] groups are poverty and social deprivation' (Abubakar et al, 2012, S294; see also Bhatti et al, 1995), with Beckhurst et al (2000) also finding that increasing unemployment was associated with rising TB rates in Newham between 1981-91.

Given this, an interesting question therefore emerges of the potential impact that the current austerity measures in local service and health provision will have on London's TB rates, given that many 'priority public conditions share many "upstream" social determinants. The further upstream the entry point for intervention, the more widespread the effect' (Lönnroth et al, 2009, p 2,245). In many respects therefore, the spatial and social distribution of London's TB prevalence is a barometer of the city's sustainability and, with rates among the non-UK-born population still rising, the future outlook for TB control looks bleak without the kind of centralised 'whole systems approach' that was undertaken in New York when the TB rate peaked in the early 1990s at 50 per 100,000 (Gandy and Zumla, 2003). This focused on improved surveillance, treatment completion rates (to minimise the chances of reactivation or conversion into multiple drug-resistant forms of TB, or MDR-TB), outreach activities to access hard-to-read cases as well as the establishment of a city-wide TB control board that incorporated a range of city services, from housing to prisons and social care (NHS London Health Programmes, 2011). At present, TB services in London are managed by five 'TB networks' across the city, but their commissioning and resource investment vary greatly, in part because they are 'the result of organic development rather than a planned response' to the rising rate of TB (NHS London Health Programmes, 2011, p 7). For example, the BCG vaccination is now universal as part of the childhood vaccination schedule only in the highest-risk boroughs (such as North West London) after national guidance issued in 2005 removed BCG from the list of compulsory immunisations due to uncertainties as to its long-term necessity given the low rates of TB outside the UK's urban centres. However, given the daily mobility of people *within* London and across national borders, the very notion of immunising according to spatial or individual social risk profiling alone seems lacking in logic. Moreover, even where BCG is part of a borough's immunisation schedule, uptake varies between 24 and 80 per cent, with knock-on effects for the risk of transmission.

The rates of TB in Brent and Newham are not only indicative of the high proportion of foreign-born residents, but should also draw our attention to their biosocial origins. Why, for example, are these two boroughs the kind of 'ecological niches' (Gandy and Zumla, 2002, p 391) in which TB is activated? Furthermore how do they reveal the kind of 'interconnections between tuberculosis and social injustice' (Gandy and Zumla, 2002, p 393) that a social determinants of health perspective on sustainable places seeks to break apart? In this line of investigation, it becomes important that Newham ranks 3rd in the UK's composite Index of Multiple Deprivation and Brent 35th, and that 41 per cent of children in Newham live in poverty and 23 per cent of residents of working age have a disability. Or that in Brent, almost 45 per cent of children live in poverty, 19 per cent of working-age residents claim unemployment benefits and average gross income is £27,000. While this exceeds Newham residents' average income of £26,000, it falls far short of that of residents in Kensington and Chelsea who, on average, enjoy £42,000 (a number that masks great inequalities within one of London's wealthiest boroughs). In the context of the present recession, it is worrying that in the Brent and Harrow Super Output Area 83 neighbourhoods out of the borough's 311 became significantly more deprived between 2004 and 2010. By contrast, in Camden and Barnet 97 out of 343 neighbourhoods became significantly less deprived over the same time period. It is therefore an important consideration for the broad sustainability of London boroughs that while TB threatens individual health, it also represents a significant potential cost to the NHS as well as the household and broader economy through lost earnings, long-term disability and absenteeism. The costs to the NHS are even more significant in the case of MDR-TB, which costs on average £18,500 to treat compared to £2,000 per patient for drug-susceptible TB (NHS London Health Programmes, 2011). The cost of treating cases of extreme drug-resistant TB (XDR-TB) can reach £100,000 per patient. Worryingly, cases of drug-resistant TB have risen from 8 per cent of all cases in 2008 to 10 per cent in 2010 (NHS London Health Programmes, 2011), further underlining the need for effective joined-up approaches to latent TB screening across London. And the underlying conditions of deprivation that provoke TB activation require attention to income inequality, quality of housing, access to healthcare services as well as addressing the stigma, marginalisation and processes of social exclusion of migrant populations that undermine both prevention and treatment strategies.

For this reason, TB control requires centralised, pan-London efforts that go beyond healthcare to incorporate housing, education, welfare, planning and employment that will enable action to identify and address the 'broader social and economic determinants of infection with tuberculosis' (Das and Horton,

2010, p 1756). This lays bare some of the inadequacies of a localised healthcare system which is the product of an ideological opposition to the kind of strong, centralised state needed to coordinate TB screening, prevention and treatment programmes. This is not to say that the local is unimportant, but rather that the kind of TB awareness-raising efforts currently being undertaken at a borough level are often a very inadequate dressing for the open wound of structural inequalities. For example, recent work by London-based charity Archive that promotes the importance of architectural solutions for health 'in vulnerable environments' (Archive UK, 2012) in Brent has concentrated on raising awareness of the prevalence of poor quality housing in the borough, and its importance as a risk factor for TB. They draw particular attention to the issue of overcrowding and the phenomenon of 'beds in sheds' where so-called rogue landlords rent out outhouses unfit for habitation, especially in the city's outer suburbs, and to illegal immigrants (Shapps, 2012). The threatened formation of 'suburban shanty towns' (Shapps, 2012) has clearly struck a chord given that it speaks to broader concerns over effective border control, rising disquiet over the lack of regulation of private landlords, spiralling rents in London as well as moral questions concerning the right to safe housing. TB is thus inextricable from the complex webs of urban processes that reproduce vulnerabilities and that may be exacerbated by the policy shifts emanating from austerity. In the case of housing quality, the changes to Housing Benefit may well result in greater overcrowding among the urban poor who wish to remain in London, especially given that it is estimated that only 35 per cent of the city's housing will be affordable once benefit allowances are changed compared to 75 per cent now (UCL Institute of Health Equity, 2012, p 11). It may also magnify existing overcrowding in boroughs that have lower rents. Given the importance of conquering TB stigma and social exclusion among high TB-risk immigrant populations to ensure that individuals access services, are properly diagnosed and that they complete treatment to avoid potential reactivation or development of MDR-TB, education and outreach will be essential. But at a time of cuts to funding for the voluntary sector that would otherwise undertake many of these activities, fears are mounting over their long-term sustainability. TB undermines the quality of life of patients as well as their dependants, compromising intergenerational equity of opportunity.

Conclusion

TB can be harnessed to a number of political causes that have great significance for the future of London's sustainability as a socially just, Healthy City. First, TB is a clear manifestation of the kinds of social, environmental and economic inequalities that impede London's capacity to be sustainable. Second, at a time of austerity and welfare reform, the rise in rates of TB among migrants has been taken up by anti-immigration campaigners such as the British National Party, stoking nationalist sentiment but also conveniently ignoring either the time-lag between entry to the UK and activation of latent TB or the role that the quality of London's urban environment plays in this process. On the flipside, 'the need to control TB has often been used as an argument for improving living conditions and reducing inequality' (Lönnroth et al, 2009, p 2240). Thus, if TB is a reflection of the gross structural inequalities that exist between countries, within countries and within London, then its rising rate and the greater incidence of deadly and costly MDR-TB and XDR-TB in London suggests that the turn to localism and soft governance through behaviour change measures will be ineffective in this instance. As Abubakar et al (2011, p 7) contend, 'devolving commissioning to local practitioners may have a negative effect on tuberculosis control. For example, tuberculosis outbreaks are likely to be very infrequent within each CCG's area or will cross several financial and administrative boundaries.' They suggest that TB control in the UK should be 'across a wider geographical area, especially in high burden urban conurbations' (Abukabar et al, 2011, p 7), corroborating the conclusions of NHS London's 2011 TB Services report that 'there is a significant risk that the separation of health protection, public health and commissioning responsibilities could result in a fragmented approach to TB control in London' (NHS London Health Programmes, 2011, p 40).

Talking and writing of the 'Healthy City' often provokes and invokes a consideration of social justice, even if political rhetoric is centred on a twin concern with healthcare provision and processes and individual behaviour change (Graham, 2012). It is therefore reasonable to assert that 'at the core of urban social sustainability ... [lie] social equity and the sustainability of community' (Dempsey et al, 2011, p 297), and, moreover, that health is both instrumental to the achievement of these as well as being the desirable product of their realisation. At a time of great financial uncertainty, the threats to sustainability, equity and, therefore, human health and wellbeing, are all too obvious. But assertions such as 'it is unlikely that the increasing incidence of tuberculosis in underprivileged areas can be reversed without first reversing the underlying decline in real income of the poorest sector of the population' (Bhatti et al, 1995) are likely to be politically unpalatable at a time of austerity. Understanding and addressing local needs is important, but the local is only constituted relative to the non-local. In London, the key drivers of poor health identified by a recent report on the potential impacts of the recession on inequality – sufficient incomes, decent housing and worthwhile employment – are constituted by forces often far removed from either individuals or local authorities (UCL Institute of Health Equity, 2012). The integration of PCTs and local authorities provides opportunities for cross-departmental action on health, but the sustainable, Healthy City really must have aspirations that go beyond this. For TB, this would mean ensuring not just that all migrants enter cities with habitable housing, but also that there is systematic screening for latent TB. The Mayor's promise to 'promote London as a healthy place for all – from homes to neighbourhoods and across the city as a whole' (Mayor of London, 2011, p 78) is far from the case for the city's rising number of TB patients. However, as Barton and Grant (2013, p 133) argue, 'ways of pursuing economic objectives without creating unhealthy settlements have to be found' if the long-term health of the population is to be assured. At a time of great economic, political and institutional change, the future of the Healthy City seems unclear. What is evident, however, is that both healthy places and people are crucial intergenerational social and environmental goods that require governance strategies extending far beyond the local, while still ensuring that the micro-scale drivers of poor health are identified, understood and acted on.

References

Abubakar, I., Lipman, M., Anderson, C., Davies, P. and Zumla, A. (2011) 'Tuberculosis in the UK – time to regain control', *British Medical Journal*, 29 July, vol 343, d4281.

Abubakar, I., Stagg, HR., Cohen, T., Mangtani, P., Rodrigues, L.C., Pimpin, L., Watson, J.M., Squire, S.B. and Zumla, A. (2012) 'Controversies and unresolved issues in tuberculosis prevention and control: a low-burden-country perspective', *Journal of Infectious Diseases*, vol 205, s293-S300.

Agyeman, J. and Evans, T. (2003) 'Toward just sustainability in urban communities: building equity rights with sustainable solutions', *The ANNALS of the American Academy of Political and Social Science*, vol 590, pp 35-53.

Agyeman, J. and Evans, B. (2004) 'Just sustainability: the emerging discourse of environmental justice in Britain?', *Geographical Journal*, vol 170, no 2, pp 155-64.

Agyeman, J., Bullard, R.D. and Evans, B. (2002) 'Exploring the nexus: bringing together sustainability, environmental justice and equity', *Space and Polity*, vol 6, no 1, pp 77-90.

Archive UK (2012) 'About us: overview' (www.archiveuk.org/about/overview).

Barton, H. and Grant, M. (2008) 'Testing time for sustainability and health: striving for inclusive rationality in project appraisal', *The Journal of the Royal Society for the Promotion of Health*, vol 128, pp 130-9.

Barton, H. and Grant, M., (2013) 'Urban planning for healthy cities', *Journal of Urban Health*, vol 90, no 1, pp 129-41.

Baumberg, B. and Anderson, P. (2008) 'Health, alcohol and EU law: understanding the impact of European single market law on alcohol policies', *The European Journal of Public Health*, vol 18, pp 392-8.

Beckhurst, C., Evans, S., Macfarlane, A. and Packe, G. (2000) 'Factors influencing the distribution of tuberculosis cases in an inner London borough', *Communicable Disease and Public Health*, vol 3, pp 28-31.

Bhatti, N., Law, M.R., Morris, J.K., Halliday, R. and Moore-Gillon, J. (1995) 'Increasing incidence of tuberculosis in England and Wales: a study of the likely causes', *British Medical Journal*, vol 310, pp 967-9.

Blumberg, H.M., Migliori, G.B., Ponomarenko, O. and Heldal, E. (2010) 'Tuberculosis on the move', *The Lancet*, vol 375, pp 2127-9.

Cabinet Office (2010) *Applying behavioural insight to health*, London: Behavioural Insights Team, Cabinet Office.

Clark, M., Riben, P. and Nowgesic, E. (2002) 'The association of housing density, isolation and tuberculosis in Canadian First Nations communities', *International Journal of Epidemiology*, vol 31, pp 940-5.

Crawshaw, P. (2012) 'Governing at a distance: social marketing and the (bio) politics of responsibility', *Social Science & Medicine*, vol 75, pp 200-7.

Das, P. and Horton, R. (2010) 'Tuberculosis- time to accelerate progress', *The Lancet*, vol 375, pp 1755-7.

DCLG (Department for Communities and Local Government) (2011) *A plain English guide to the Localism Bill*, London: CLG.

DCLG (2012) *National Planning Policy Framework*, London: DCLG.

Dempsey, N., Bramley, G., Power, S. and Brown, C. (2011) 'The social dimension of sustainable development: defining urban social sustainability', *Sustainable Development*, vol 19, pp 289-300.

DH (Department of Health) (2010a) *Equity and excellence: liberating the NHS*, London: DH.

DH (2010b) *Healthy lives, healthy people: our strategy for public health in England*, London: DH.

DH (2011) *The new public health system: summary*, London DH.

DH (2012) *The Public Health Outcomes Framework for England, 2013-2016*, London: DH.

Farmer, P. (1999) *Infections and inequalities: the modern plagues*, Berkeley, CA: University of California Press.

Gandy, M. and Zumla, A. (2002) 'The resurgence of disease: social and historical perspectives on the "new" tuberculosis', *Social Science & Medicine*, vol 55, pp 385-96.

Gandy, M. and Zumla, A. (2003) *The return of the white plague*, London: Verso.

Gilmore, A.B., Savell, E. and Collin, J., (2011) 'Public health, corporations and the new responsibility deal: promoting partnerships with vectors of disease?', *Journal of Public Health*, vol 33, no 1, pp 2-4.

Government Office for Science (2007) *Tackling obesities: Future Choices – project report*, London: Government Office for Science.

Graham, H. (2012) 'Ensuring the health of future populations', *British Medical Journal* (Clinical Research edn), vol 345, no 7885, e7573.

Hancock, T. (1993) 'Health, human development and the community ecosystem: three ecological models', *Health Promotion International*, vol 8, pp 41-7.

Herrick, C. (2011a) *Governing health and consumption: sensible citizens, behaviour and the city*, Bristol: Policy Press.

Herrick, C. (2011b) 'Why we need to think beyond the "industry" in alcohol research and policy studies', *Drugs: Education, Prevention, and Policy*, vol 18, pp 10-15.

Herrick, C. (2013) 'Healthy cities from/of the South', in S. Parnell and S. Oldfield (eds) *Routledge handbook on cities of the global south*, London: Routledge, pp 556-69.

HM Government (2009) *Integrated Household Survey* (http://data.gov.uk/dataset/integrated_household_survey).

HPA (Health Protection Agency) (2012a) *TB data by English local authority* (http://www.hpa.org.uk/webc/HPAwebFile/HPAweb_C/1317140127509).

HPA (2012b) *Tuberculosis in the UK: 2012 report*, London: HPA.

Hyndman, S.J. (1990) 'Housing dampness and health amongst British Bengalis in East London', *Social Science & Medicine*, vol 30, pp 131-41.

Jones, R., Pykett, J. and Whitehead, M. (2010) 'Big Society's little nudges: the changing politics of health care in an age of austerity', *Political Insight*, vol 1, pp 85-87.

Jones, R., Pykett, J. and Whitehead, M. (2011) 'Governing temptation: changing behaviour in an age of libertarian paternalism', *Progress in Human Geography*, vol 35, pp 483-501.

Keshavjee, S. and Farmer, P.E. (2012) 'Tuberculosis, drug resistance, and the history of modern medicine', *New England Journal of Medicine*, vol 367, pp 931-6.

Lansley, A. (2010) *A new approach to public health*, London: UK Faculty of Public Health Conference.

Lönnroth, K., Jaramillo, E., Williams, B.G., Dye, C. and Raviglione, M. (2009) 'Drivers of tuberculosis epidemics: the role of risk factors and social determinants', *Social Science & Medicine*, vol 68, pp 2240-6.

Marmot, M. (2005) 'Social determinants of health inequalities', *The Lancet*, vol 365, pp 1099-104.

Marmot, M. (2010) *Fair society, healthy lives*, London: The Marmot Review.

Marteau, T.M., Ogilvie, D., Roland, M., Suhrcke, M. and Kelly, M.P. (2011) 'Judging nudging: can nudging improve population health?', *British Medical Journal*, vol 342, pp 235-37.

Mayor of London, GLA (Greater London Authority) (2010) *The London Health Inequalities Strategy*, London: Mayor of London, GLA.

Mayor of London, GLA (2011) *The London Plan*, London: Mayor of London, GLA.

NHS London Health Programmes (2011) *Case for change: TB services in London*, London: NHS London Health Programmes.

NHS London Health Programmes (2012) *Tuberculosis* (www.londonhp.nhs.uk/services/tuberculosis).

NICE (National Institute for Health and Clinical Excellence) (2011) *NICE clinical guidelines for TB*, London: NICE.

Pareek, M., Abubakar, I., White, P.J., Garnett, G.P. and Lalvani, A. (2011a) 'Tuberculosis screening of migrants to low-burden nations: insights from evaluation of UK practice', *European Respiratory Journal*, vol 37, pp 1175-82.

Pareek, M., Abubakar, I., White, P.J., Garnett, G.P. and Lalvani, A. (2011b) 'UK immigrant screening is inversely related to regional tuberculosis burden', *Thorax,* vol 66, p 1010.

Raynor, G. (2012) *The Coalition approach to public health – a case of 'responsible' nudging?* (www.healthmatters.org.uk/?p=577).

Salazar, A. (2012) 'Libertarian paternalism and the danger of nudging consumers', *King's Law Journal* (http://ssrn.com/abstract=1973397 or http://dx.doi.org/10.2139/ssrn.1973397).

Satterthwaite, D. (1997) 'Sustainable cities or cities that contribute to sustainable development?', *Urban Studies*, vol 34, pp 1667-91.

Shapps, G. (2012) 'Major clampdown launched on "beds in sheds"' (www.gov.uk/government/news/major-clampdown-launched-on-beds-in-sheds).

Smith, R.D. and Petticrew, M. (2010) 'Public health evaluation in the twenty-first century: time to see the wood as well as the trees', *Journal of Public Health*, vol 32, no 1, pp 2-7.

Strachan, D.P., Powell, K.J., Thaker, A., Millard, F.J. and Maxwell, J.D. (1995) 'Vegetarian diet as a risk factor for tuberculosis in immigrant south London Asians', *Thorax*, vol 50, pp 175-80.

Swinburn, B., Gill, T. and Kumanyika, S. (2005) 'Obesity prevention: a proposed framework for translating evidence into action', *Obesity Reviews*, vol 6, pp 23-33.

Thaler, R. and Sunstein, C.R. (2008) *Nudge: improving decisions about health, wealth and happiness*, New Haven, CT: Yale University Press.

UCL (University College London) Institute of Health Equity (2012) *The impact of the economic downturn and policy changes on health inequalities in London*, London: UCL Institute of Health Equity.

Whitehead, M., Jones, R. and Pykett, J. (2011) 'Governing irrationality, or a more than rational government? Reflections on the rescientisation of decision making in British public policy', *Environment and Planning A*, vol 43, pp 2819-37.

WHO (World Health Organization) (2008) *Closing the gap in a generation: health equity through action on the social determinants of health*, Geneva: WHO.

WHO (2012) *Global tuberculosis report 2012*, Geneva: WHO.

Wilkinson, R. and Pickett, K. (2010) *The impact of income inequalities on sustainable development in London*, London: London Sustainable Development Commission.

FOURTEEN

Urban greening and sustaining urban natures in London

Franklin Ginn and Robert A. Francis

Introduction

How to value, govern and protect the non-human creatures that share our cities, and how to do so sustainably, is a question that is increasingly occupying ecologists, politicians and conservation groups. While green space may be broadly defined as 'open vegetated areas' within the urban environment, and although aquatic ecosystems are also often included, such a definition masks considerable variation (Francis and Chadwick, 2013). In London, green space can refer to everything from the Rainham marshes, an extensive area of wetlands in the Thames estuary, to small private gardens, to post-industrial brownfield sites. It is now widely recognised that the urban green often represents a crucial habitat for many species. Green space abundance is used as an indicator of both ecological health and quality of life in urban areas around the world, and London scores highly in such matrices (Environment Agency, 2010). At the same time, the field of urban conservation biology has grown steadily over the last two decades (Francis et al, 2012), and while urban nature lacks the political clout or romantic appeal of wilder lands, an energetic mix of non-governmental organisations (NGOs) and voluntary sector organisations now exists with the purpose of improving people's access to and connection with urban nature, as well as surveying, monitoring and advocating on behalf of non-human species that live in, or visit, London. The first reason we might care about sustaining London's urban green, then, is that the city is home to more than just human life, and that these other species deserve political consideration.

This chapter begins by considering the recent history of green space conservation in London, before exploring the emergence of new ecological policies, in particular, the idea of a 'green grid'. It then addresses how a move beyond connectivity to a model of 'saturation' may be necessary, discussing private space and conservation. While we understand that London's geographies of ecological responsibility extend well beyond the city's immediate territory, encompassing, for instance, networks of consumption and financial flows of virtual natures, we do not have the space to focus on those dimensions here. We take up the more modest task of exploring the challenge of sustaining the urban green within London's administrative area. In accounting for the politics of the urban green, it is important to address the ecological propensities and capacities of non-humans; hence this chapter is written collaboratively by an urban ecologist and a cultural geographer of nature. We have two aims: first, to offer a broad assessment of recent attempts at sustaining London's urban green; and second, to reflect on the ways that the recent history of the urban green in London reflects wider processes at work in conservation. We begin by outlining some of these processes.

Broadly speaking, a series of transformations have been turning conservation from a political enterprise into a neutral endeavour of responding to technical problems, problems often solved with market-based solutions, generally referred to as neoliberal conservation (Buscher et al, 2012). One seminal moment was the Millennium Ecosystem Assessment, in which the idea of 'ecosystem services' lurched into the policy mainstream (Redford and Adams, 2009). Ecosystem services, a concept imported from neoclassical economics, has fast become a dominant approach to re-conceptualising conservation and enhancing its policy relevance. Recently, for example, one of the key messages of the UK government's Natural Environment White Paper, *The natural choice* (not to be confused with the holistic health food shop of the same name in Rhos On Sea, North Wales), concluded that 'biodiversity and its constituent ecosystem services are critically important to our wellbeing and economic prosperity' (Defra, 2011a, p 9). Types of service include: regulating, such as run-off or carbon sequestration; supporting, such as air quality; provisioning, such as habitat for biodiversity; and cultural, aesthetic and amenity uses. Some 30 per cent of such services, the UK's National Ecosystem Assessment showed, are in decline. The reason for this decline, according to the government, is that ecosystem services have been 'consistently undervalued in conventional economic analyses and decision-making' (Defra, 2011a, p 9). The fault identified here is that nature has been *in*sufficiently integrated into conventional economic systems of production and valuation, and so the solution, according to this logic, is to translate nature's value into economic terms *more* systematically. Thus the degradation of nature is no longer due to too much economic activity, but rather the inverse: not enough market-based policy and procedure.

Of course, there are a whole range of processes of neoliberalisation and different types of nature being neoliberalised, as mapped by Karen Bakker (Bakker, 2010; see also Castree, 2008a, 2008b). There are three important dimensions of relevance to the urban green in London, which we introduce here. Each of these concerns not the direct marketisation of environmental processes or commodities, but rather the more subtle process of the governmentalisation of nature, by which we mean the way nature is circumscribed within rational, calculative and instrumental logics (Spash, 2008).

First, the 'new environmental governance' outlined above is post-political, that is, it leaves the liberal–capitalist order unchallenged and becomes merely an exercise in the efficient management of nature (Swyngedouw, 2011). It is well known that in terms of ecological energetics or metabolism, or the exchanges and fluxes of energy and environmental components that sustain a system, cities tend to be unsustainable: unlike natural systems, they cannot exist without heavy supplements of energy in the form of fossil fuels, and importation of resources from elsewhere (Folke et al, 1997). As the introduction to this volume suggests, cities are seeking to secure their own conditions of reproduction by enhancing their 'urban ecological security' (Hodson and Marvin, 2009). This includes better managing the way that urban nature enhances resilience to, in London's case, flooding, overheating and poor air quality, as well as amenity for a 'healthy' (and profitable) living space (GLA, 2011). Resilience is the capacity of a system – in this case, the socio-ecological networks of London – to absorb external shocks and return or reorganise within the boundaries of some baseline state or set of parameters. Resilience thus brings to the fore measures that promise a return to some set state, precluding any transformative or radical politics (Neocleous, 2013). In this manner resilience thinking suggests that nature's role is to sustain economic and social benefit. The environment no longer becomes a field of political contestation, but a valued and valuable, and hopefully pliant, source of labour in the ongoing constitution of the urban fabric.

The second key concern we raise here relates to the effectiveness of the new paradigm in environmental governance. As Redford and Adams point out, 'there is a danger that an economically driven focus on those "services" that are valuable to humans in their nature, scope and timing may lead to calls to "regulate" ecosystem services to times and flows that match human needs.' They continue, writing that 'such regulating may be highly detrimental to long-term survival of the non-human parts of the ecosystem' (2009, p 786). Such a danger can be seen in *The natural choice*. The crucial word in the title is *choice*: if we are concerned with securing resilient 'services', then nature becomes fungible and tradable, since there will be different ways of delivering any given service. This may involve choosing an engineered ecosystem that may be excellent at preventing flooding but is of little use to wildlife (as we explore below, in the case of front gardens). In this way the concept of ecosystem services emphasises the substitutability of nature (Yusoff, 2011). One central mechanism proposed by the White Paper is biodiversity offsetting, where the principle of 'net gain' in biodiversity means that negative impacts of developments can be 'offset' with improvement elsewhere (Defra, 2011b). Ecologists might, however, reasonably fear that a mantra of 'net gain' risks sliding all to easily into 'piecemeal loss' of biodiversity in the name of support for human activities with asymmetrical costs and benefits. As Karen Bakker argues, the 'reregulation of the environment under neoliberalism produces a shift in the "costs" and "benefits", and their allocation between different users – with some aspects of what we conventionally call "the environment" seeming to gain (while others lose) in the encounter' (2010, p 728). As such, *The natural choice* points to a new, fluid geography of nature conservation rather than a system of static defended spaces.

While in some ways this reflects new ecological understanding, a significant problem is that species assemblages (a collection of species occurring or making up a community of organisms in a given habitat) are not the same in one place as another – viewing nature as substitutable is problematic ecologically. The assumption that particular community or habitat typologies can be recreated as desired overlooks the past ecological dynamics of the site, wherein particular assemblages have formed through decades or centuries of localised adaptation to soil conditions, disturbance regimes and biotic interactions, and assemblage composition has been shaped by multiple cycles of (often stochastic) localised extinction and recolonisation. This leaves behind an 'ecological memory', held in the seed and spore banks, soil fauna and the genetics of plant and animal species present on a given site, which would ordinarily be important in shaping natural regeneration (Schaefer, 2009). Re-creation as substitution is problematic given the complexity of site history and the lack of suitable ecological memory at new sites – as many failed (or less successful) attempts at ecological restoration may attest (Hilderbrand et al, 2005).

Third, a growing reliance on 'services' thinking is likely to exclude intrinsic values in favour of valuing non-human life instrumentally. Our basic point is that there are other forms of human–nature relationships than those of measuring, counting and being 'served' by. For instance, the range of local networks of volunteers who look after small patches of land across London are not aiming to enhance the services that nature provides the city: they do so for a variety of reasons, from tradition, political or spiritual expression, aesthetic beauty, or connection to place. Nor are garden owners rational land managers who aim to enhance the 'provisioning' or 'supporting' functions of their domestic flora and fauna. Their activities cannot be adequately described as a 'cultural amenity' service – rather, domestic gardens are about craft, affective engagement with non-human creatures and 'living with', while more 'radical' forms of gardening can constitute and express transgressive political identities (McKay, 2011). The creatures that dwell with us in the urban fabric are not just a set of materials to be conserved or sustained: they are embedded in political processes of belonging and exclusion. Animal geography in particular has proposed re-thinking how we understand animals in the city, putting their biological, habitat and expressive requirements at the centre of urban environmental policy, re-placing the animal and combating its subjugation as an excluded constituency in urban space (Urbanik, 2012). Other geographers have explored the multi-sensory ways through which urban residents experience, care for and interact with non-human nature (Buller, 2013). Indeed, more than a decade's work in geography has shown that, in all sorts of ways, non-human agents matter as constitutive agents of social and economic life (Braun, 2008). Crucially, a fuller politics urban nature means not simply enhancing London's resilience or servicing our wellbeing, but recognising the imperative to 'live with' our non-human kin for their sake as well as our own. In what follows we therefore attempt to navigate between a critique of London's urban green policies and a more positive evaluation, acknowledging that there may be benefits, as well as costs, of recent shifts in managing the urban green.

We return to reflect on the challenges raised here in the conclusion at the end of this chapter.

Connectivity: sustaining species and ecological processes

Eco-historical context

London inherits a complex legacy of green space planning, development and conservation. The royal parks, possibly the most recognisable of inner London's green spaces, reflect a history of privilege and exclusion and, later, public amenity, with Hyde Park, for example, open to members of the public from the 17th century (Ackroyd, 2000). A Victorian and Edwardian concern with public hygiene and the moral geographies of the inner city led to greater provision of municipal green space. Postwar planning had comparatively little to say about urban conservation, as it drew a firm cartography in which nature resided in the countryside and Britain's wild spaces, not the city (Clapson, 1998). Where nature was preserved, this was often for social rather than environmental reasons, with the creation of green belts and internal green space being to prevent expansion and ensure healthy pleasant living environments rather than to preserve organisms or ecological processes (Amati and Yokohari, 2006). Arguably, London's great expansion between the world wars, during which the city grew by some 50 per cent in area, with only a 10 per cent growth in population, remains the most far-reaching shift in its urban nature. Agricultural land and private estates were converted into suburban housing estates, which overwrote vernacular ecologies and prompted much ecological outcry (Alexander, 2007). However, private and public suburban developments, which aimed to provide 'homes for heroes' to the lower and lower middle classes, were based in garden suburb ideals, which had a strong ideological commitment to providing domestic green space. This meant that leafy developments and the provision of private domestic space were the norm. The result is that, today, there are around two million dwellings with individual private garden plots, with gardens of much greater size in the city's outer boroughs (London Wildlife Trust, 2011).

As the result of fragmented but often determined local opposition to development, and the work of local conservation groups in caring for small patches of land, there remain over 2,500 individual local and publicly accessible gardens across London. For example, the country's first urban ecology park (William Curtis Ecological Park) was set up near Tower Bridge in 1976, by the Trust for Urban Ecology, while local action in the 1980s saved Gunnersbury Triangle in Chiswick from development, and Camley Street Natural Park was established at King's Cross, after a campaign run by local people and the London Wildlife Trust. Such spaces can be of greater biodiversity importance than manicured parks; indeed, there are over 1,500 specific spots of biodiversity significance, from Sites of Special Scientific Interest (SSSIs) to community-managed spaces, across London. Despite some observations that London has limited green space (Forman, 2008), there is probably over 100,000 hectares (ha) of green space in the city (approximately 63 per cent of a total area of 160,000 ha; see Environment Agency, 2010), although not all is publicly available (only 16 per cent of London's area, or 25,600 ha; see Environment Agency, 2010). Based on the 2007 population of 7.56 million, this equates to a crude estimate of around 1,300m² per capita, which is far higher than that recorded for many other cities (Jim and Chen, 2008), although this drops to 30m² per capita when public green space only is considered. This does not consider the quality of green space, however, and estimates of both quantity and quality vary depending on how green space is considered and classified in different studies (Fuller and Gaston, 2009).

In the decade following the 1992 Rio Earth Summit London's biodiversity policy focused on the need to protect rare species and habitats that were internationally, nationally or locally significant, with specific biodiversity and habitat 'action plans'. Procedures to curb biodiversity loss and retain natural or semi-natural ecosystems were included in detailed planning guidance issued by central government, which stipulated that spatial planning should protect, where possible, the urban green, including woodland, cemeteries, green corridors, open space and sites of significance (DETR, 2000). Of course, where this did not happen, protected species were enrolled, symbolically and materially, into local campaigns against roads, housing and other development. London has also been active in the arena of ecological restoration, especially with regards to improvements of its rivers and other aquatic infrastructure (see, for example, Eden and Tunstall, 2006; Shuker et al, 2012). Granted, ecological concerns have not always been at the forefront of these efforts, but both governmental and non-governmental organisations have been increasingly active in incorporating ecology and biodiversity into development or improvement work within the city. However, the limitations of these approaches are well established. Efforts are generally piecemeal, with insufficient funding, ill defined or conflicting objectives, under-planned methods and insufficient post-project monitoring (Gobster, 2001; Dufour and Piégay, 2009; Francis and Chadwick, 2013). In many circumstances critical urban ecologists dispute the ecological merits of some of the spaces created, particularly when vernacular and unofficial brownfield ecologies are tidied up under public–private partnership developments. In addition, borough council budget constraints have seen falling investment in green spaces, and a push for 'innovative funding models' that mean growing pressure on voluntary and charitable sector organisations.

From preservation to connectivity

In the last few years the national policy context has changed dramatically. Emphasis has shifted from preserving separate 'spaces for nature' to creating a 'coherent and resilient ecological network' (a phrase now widely repeated in policy documents from biodiversity action plans, to Wildlife Trust annual reports, to planning advice, to national strategies). One formulation that is growing in popularity suggests that girds or networks of 'green infrastructure' – that is, the diverse sets of spaces, from micro and macro, from street corner to cemetery to riverine ecosystem – are key to sustaining ecosystem services and enabling cities to protect and enhance biodiversity (GLA, 2012). Given the relatively limited options for expanding green space in London or restoring the built environment to high-quality green space, a diffuse 'green infrastructure' may offer new possibilities to ensure persistence of both species and ecological processes within the city. There is increasing recognition that understanding species interactions and biogeochemical processes at the landscape scale is particularly important for ensuring appropriate and ongoing functioning of ecosystems (Turner, 1989, 2005). Historically, the spatial management of ecosystems for biodiversity or species conservation has been shaped by the theory of island biogeography and more recently that of landscape ecology, both of which have demonstrated that the size of 'islands', or patches of ecosystems embedded in a matrix of different land use (such as green space within a city), is important for supporting species populations and biodiversity following well-established (although highly variable) species–area relationships (see, for example, Forman, 1996; Bender et al, 1998). Likewise, the relative isolation or distance between patches has an important influence on exchange of materials and biota that influences the capacity for individuals from different species populations (which together form a metapopulation) to interact. Spatially segregated populations have to be able to find each other to interact and reproduce in order for the species to persist as part of the regional ecosystem. Consequently, the size and proximity of habitat is crucial for allowing species to survive in the city in the long term.

There are two key aspects of green space that this influences: size and connectivity. Urban planning for ecology has more recently focused on these two aspects, with some good examples being found in Singapore (Tan, 2006), Beijing (Li et al, 2005) and Hanoi (Uy and Nakagoshi, 2008). London, as an old city that has developed piecemeal, has limited scope to increase the size of individual patches of green space. Understandably, more recent focus has been on connectivity of green space, creating linear landscape corridors or minimising distances between patches. Such approaches have been adopted in several planning and coordination efforts at varying spatial scales, with the most prevalent being the All London Green Grid (see Figure 14.1). Supplementary planning guidance is replete with references to the benefits of a connected green infrastructure, to be achieved by enhancing and linking existing pockets of green space with corridors of multifunctional green space or urban greenery (GLA, 2011, 2012). The term 'green grid' itself is a derivation of the common urban planning terms 'green network' or 'green web' (Francis and Chadwick, 2013), all terms describing a network designed to achieve maximum circuitry and flow of components. The intention is to move away from a city 'punctuated' by green space to one that has an infrastructural network of green space that is fundamental to the city's identity and environment, and which is multifunctional, reflective of local character, well planned and managed (GLA, 2012, p 17). The landscape linkages to be put

Figure 14.1: All-London Green Grid

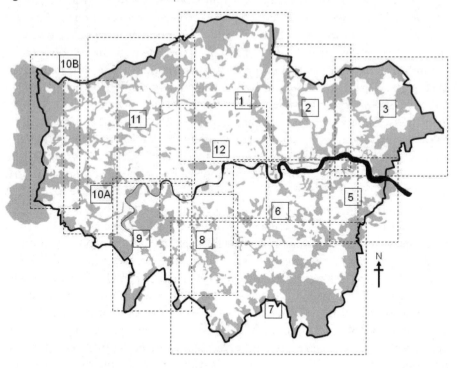

Source: Produced by Robert A Franklin, King's College London

in place are not necessarily contiguous, but are chains of green space or urban greenery placed in strategic areas, and can vary from street trees to living roofs and walls to off-road cycle routes and canal towpaths.

'Connectivity' is a theme that can be readily understood by a variety of actors and stakeholders, from ecologists to planners to the wider public. This focus on an All London Green Grid that ties together the human and non-human inhabitants of the city, as well as uniting the many different socio-ecological requirements of London's ecosystem, is laudable. It is, of course, more about technocratic planning than a politics of nature: palliatives, such as green roofs on new developments, are promoted to solutions; the desires and labours of local environmental groups are subordinated to private developers and government policy; and a geography of static spaces for nature is increasingly replaced by a fungible and fluid geography of flow and connection destined to deliver benefit to some over-aggregated, amorphous idea of 'London's citizens'. The green grid also emphasises the rational placement of green spaces to maximise 'win-wins', holding out the enticing vision where appropriate provision can be made for nature without disrupting – or even enhancing – the urban fabric. Connectivity, however, may not be the ecological panacea it at first appears.

Beyond connectivity: urban saturation and domestic space

Ecological limits of connectivity

In this section we discuss some of the ecological problems with connectivity, setting aside its political limitations momentarily. Essentially, the assumption of benefits to biodiversity, ecological processes and ecosystem services may be over-emphasised. There are two ecological problems that frequently occur when considering connectivity in any urban landscape. First, the connectivity is opportunistic, with linking habitat (whether infrastructural greenery or patches of green space) placed where convenient rather than where the most appropriate and effective place for a linkage may be for biodiversity. In particular, the linkages are often positioned in those areas that have been left behind following urban development, 'feral' spaces that are either given back to nature because they have low value for development or re-appropriated for human recreation. This is one particular problem of seeing green space as a landscape element within the city – that the 'grid' of green is something fundamentally 'other' than the 'matrix' of the built environment.

Second, perhaps the fundamental limitation of these efforts is that the connectivity is anthropocentric and focuses on structure rather than function, that a green network is connected because it *appears* connected to us, rather than because it actually connects flows of species and materials (Baguette and van Dyck, 2007; Ignatieva et al, 2011). Corridor function is affected by a range of characteristics that vary in their suitability for individual species, materials and processes, such as corridor width, length, internal composition, habitat type and dynamics (Forman, 1996, 2008). Even the fundamental process of species movement or dispersal, which corridors are supposed to facilitate, is highly complex, and different stages of dispersal will experience different efficacies within the same corridor (Baguette and van Dyck, 2007). Without substantial space it is difficult to create a corridor that will suit a wide range of species, particularly when other functions are also intended for the corridor. Basically, something like a green corridor along an abandoned railway or tramline may be an obvious planning 'solution', but does not necessarily benefit a diverse range of non-human species. This may account for why intentions are good, but remain vague. The All London Green Grid identifies 107 individual link corridors over 12 broad areas (Figure 14.1), but only gestures at what efforts will actually be implemented or how effective these are likely to be, usually referring to 'ecological improvements' or 'open space creation' without further elaboration. There is an assumption that provision will result in benefits; while this may be the case, the extent of benefits across different multifunctional demands is uncertain. This does not mean that corridors are a bad thing, but as a tool for ecological sustainability, there needs to be some caution. Although some benefits of green corridors have been demonstrated (Bryant, 2006; Ignatieva et al, 2011), Angold et al (2006) found that there was little evidence that corridors increased dispersal, community similarity or diversity of plants or invertebrates of the urban landscape in Birmingham (UK); their main value was as habitat, rather than as landscape linkages. Indeed, 27 per cent of plant species analysed had negative associations between their distributions and the presence of corridors, with only 2 per cent having positive associations. Small and medium-sized mammals were more likely to use urban green corridors, further illustrating that responses to corridors will vary according to which organisms are being considered, as well as corridor characteristics (Angold et al, 2006). In many cases, a connected green network is a preferential situation to a highly fragmented one, but its implementation follows the top-down desires of urban planners far more than the needs of London's non-human inhabitants.

Perhaps, then, a new spatial arrangement is necessary. There is an argument that *saturation* of the urban environment with green space or greenery is more important for biodiversity and its underpinning ecological processes, creating a permeable matrix across the city that a wide range of species can use. This would be a more fundamental change in our views on green infrastructure and the place of nature within cities – not as something running through the built environment, but found within its very fabric. London is beginning to embrace this form of urban greening, although in a more subtle way, and not at the crucial landscape scale. Small-scale, localised greening is being incorporated via ecological engineering techniques (see, for example, Figure 14.2); there is a certain level of excitement about the potential of roof and wall gardens, but these remain somewhat input-intensive, are accompanied by relatively high maintenance costs, and remain largely in the arena of corporate environmental responsibility bespoke projects (Francis and Lorimer, 2011). Planning guidance, does, however, emphasise how important these new forms of garden are to future private developments, although there are no statutory provisions (GLA, 2012). Other localised greening includes community gardening, urban farming and guerrilla gardening (see, for example, Figure 14.3), all of which often rely on voluntary labour and resources, or funding, by aiming to meet government policy objectives (see, for example, Dawe, 2010). This echoes trends in other global cities, and is central to the emerging concept of 'reconciliation ecology', wherein space is made available for a range of species directly within cities without losing the function of the landscape for society (Francis and Lorimer, 2011). Green space saturation offers the potential to subvert a narrow focus on ecological services and resilience, moving beyond top-down planning interventions and towards plural ways of relating to and nurturing nature. In this way we might not simply govern London's ecology, but allow ecology, and its non-human constituents, to have a fuller, more meaningful stake in the production and consumption of a global city.

Role of domestic green space in London's urban ecology

Notably, however, the green grid underplays the importance of domestic gardens, even though private green space comprises around 24 per cent of London's total

Figure 14.2: Top-down ecological engineering

© Jamie Lorimer

Figure 14.3: Bottom-up reconciliation ecology

© Franklin Ginn

land area, with 14 per cent being vegetated. A growing evidence base suggests that urban gardens provide significant local – rather than landscape-scale – spaces for a whole range of species, and tend to be hotspots of species richness (Davies et al, 2009). Amphibians, for example, are in decline in rural areas but doing well in urban gardens, as are bumblebees, while one longitudinal study recorded 25 per cent of Britain's native insect species present or passing through one typical suburban garden (www.bugs.group.shef.ac.uk), and birds in particular benefit from urban gardens (Chamberlain et al, 2009). One survey found that overall climate and location do not appear to be significant factors in predicting a garden's biodiversity; instead, garden management practices seem to be the determining influence in species richness, with some 60 per cent of respondents claiming to make some effort to attract wildlife, and 9 per cent focusing the majority of their gardening at wildlife (Loram et al, 2007). Indeed, domestic green space is now incorporated into many local Biodiversity Action Plans, including that of London (GLA, 2002). But overall, the ecology of garden habitats remains unclear. Some ecologists suggest that only more generalist, mobile and adaptive species benefit (Cameron et al, 2012); others argue that greater benefit can be realised by scaling up from individual gardens, which are too small individually to support viable populations (Goddard et al, 2010). Birds, for instance, forage widely, and interventions must take place beyond the individual garden scale; less mobile invertebrates, meanwhile, can benefit at the individual garden scale. It is clear, therefore, that interventions need to take place at various scales depending on taxa, according to body size, range, mobility, life cycle and so on, with no clear pattern overall (Cook et al, 2012).

Practically, some mixture of private and public space is probably necessary, particularly if the goal is 'saturation' rather than isolated green corridors to achieve an effective arrangement of patch size, connectivity and heterogeneity. The Greater London Authority (GLA) acknowledges that domestic gardens are particularly important, but that it is difficult to incorporate into conservation plans at the landscape scale – domestic green space would demand a bottom-up rather than top-down approach (Francis and Lorimer, 2011). Various NGOs do aim to foster biodiversity in domestic gardens across London, including the RSPB's encouragement of bird-friendly gardening practices, for example, to counter house sparrow decline (Whale and Ginn, 2014), and the RHS (Royal Horticultural Society) and the London Wildlife Trust's wildlife gardening campaigns. Moreover, there exists a range of citizen science programmes that aim to catalogue biodiversity, including the RSPB bird survey, and Greenspace Information for Greater London's (GiGL) 'What's in my backyard?' (WIMBY) online tool to help citizens take more of an interest in the species found in their gardens. These citizen science programmes are an example of post-normal biodiversity conservation science, in which legitimacy and authority are no longer limited to established bastions of expertise, but emerge from distributed networks. They also, although not unproblematically, show London residents relating to nature in meaningful ways that lie outside the instrumental, service-based mentality outlined earlier in this chapter.

Recent trends in domestic green space are, however, not encouraging. While there is a lack of reliable data, initial analysis suggests that a significant area of domestic garden space has turned from 'green to grey': vegetation cover decreased by 12 per cent between 1998 and 2008, an area equivalent to two-and-a-half times the size of Hyde Park every year (London Wildlife Trust, 2011). This was due to three processes, the first being front gardens paved over for parking and lower maintenance. This is likely to have had some impact on flooding – one study elsewhere in urban England experiencing similar trends suggested a 12 per cent increase in average annual run-off as a result of an increase of 138 per cent in paved front gardens (Perry and Nawaz, 2008). Planning regulations changed in 2008 so that planning permission was needed for new impermeable hard surfacing of front gardens, which dampened the trend somewhat, but permeable parking surfaces – while beneficial for flood risk – are no better for wildlife. Second, around 500 back gardens are being lost to development each year, with significant local impacts, particularly on tree canopy coverage. The decision to introduce a 'presumption against development' on back gardens was shunted from national to local government, such that the London Plan deems this a matter of 'local significance' (GLA, 2011, p 79). Of greater impact, third, is that back gardens, particularly lawns, have been replaced by decking, patio and other hard surfacing, which grew in area by 26 per cent between 1998 and 2008.

Additionally, gardening practices are also changing. The rise of 'lifestyle' gardening in the 1990s and early 2000s caused many commentators consternation at the hollowing out of 'authentic' gardening, as growing plants became less important than decking and barbeques to the gardening industry's economic health (Hitchings, 2007). However, since 2008, sales of garden furniture and 'leisure' products have fallen, while the emerging market of younger consumers, the previous generation of which drove the gardening boom, is in a much more precarious economic position, and much less likely to own their own homes (HTA, 2013). At the same time, sales of seeds and plant stock has increased as the popularity of 'grow your own' replaces the previous 'lifestyle' gardening, although the differences between the two are perhaps overstated (Ginn, 2012). Therefore, the trend of green to grey may not continue at the same rate as the previous decade. However, this demonstrates that gardening practices are socio-ecologically over-determined, subject to changing demands of status, domestic and leisure cultures, as well as the gardening industry.

When it comes to sustaining London's domestic green space, the trends outlined above show the dangers of relying on Londoners deciding to relate to nature rather than, say, investing in their property value. The loss of green space also shows the need for government intervention – as when new regulations dampened the trend to pave front gardens. On the other hand, moves to engage domestic gardeners are unlikely to make much headway if they invoke the language of ecosystem services, a term neither understood nor liked by the public (Metz and Weigel, 2010). There are also dangers in relying on private space to deliver public benefits. Spatial analysis by the London Wildlife Trust (2011) shows, predictably, that the greatest potential contribution of private space to biodiversity is the city's outer boroughs, but that – conversely – the inner boroughs contain more areas of 'nature deprivation', and those living in areas of deprivation are much less likely to have gardens (GLA, 2012). Any investment in domestic gardens must be mindful of the potentially regressive impacts of looking to private space – a lesson, in fact, well understood by third sector organisations working on urban greening (Gill, 2011). Overall, then, while attention to domestic green space broadens the range of nature–human relationships away from the purely instrumental, green saturation would need to integrate a range of gardens to avoid prioritising those – relatively privileged – Londoners in possession of significant outside space.

Conclusion: beyond sustaining nature

London has done a decent job of holding on to its green space, particularly public green space. It is now aiming to 'connect' its green space via the All London Green Grid and therefore applying the principles of landscape connectivity to conservation via the idea of landscape corridors. In this chapter we have suggested that while a focus on connectivity is essential, this must move beyond 'corridors' and perhaps even 'grid' designs, because these suit humans rather than other species. Despite the high transaction costs of any coordinated public intervention into private gardens, domestic space offers the possibility for 'green saturation' that might further benefit biodiversity, although there are practical political difficulties. Citizen science projects, enrolling local groups or domestic gardeners into understanding and caring for nature offers, on the one hand, a progressive, pluralist way of living with nature but, on the other hand, risks reproducing patterns of privilege, while 'privatising' or out-sourcing conservation to voluntary associations or relying on the goodwill of developers reflects a neoliberal credo that where nature does not pay for itself, it may not be sustained.

Ecological challenges remain. For instance, while connectivity and saturation are important, there is still a need to set aside land to create a functionally integral ecosystem. A healthy ecosystem will usually contain a mosaic of habitat types at different stages of succession, so that varying combinations of ecological niches are present in the landscape at any given time to support different species assemblages (Forman, 1996). This is sometimes referred to as a 'shifting habitat mosaic' (see, for example, Wimberly, 2006), and is particularly common in frequently disturbed ecosystems, where patches are created by disturbances that vary spatially in their intensity, frequency and duration. Kattwinkel et al (2011) proposed that biodiversity and ecological functioning in urban areas is best maintained by the same principles of disturbance, that it is best to have a mosaic of green space that is of different ages and disturbed in different ways so as to create a shifting habitat mosaic that is likely to support a wide variety of species and assemblages. London now needs to reinforce an acceptance of recombinant assemblages, or groups of species that would not occur naturally, and result from anthropogenic disturbances and human translocations of both native and non-native species, and the fostering of spontaneous (that is, independently colonising and therefore unplanned) species assemblages in green space. Of course, in urban governance such dynamism is not considered. Instead, it is largely assumed that the green space put in place or urban ecosystems will remain relatively 'fixed'. However, a much greater degree of dynamism is needed. This would mean a very different attitude to green space, a 'letting go', with some sites undisturbed, unmanaged or abandoned, alongside the green grid. In such spaces, new species assemblages could emerge and, crucially, this could happen in ways that exceed management or policy expectations.

We began this chapter by cautioning that, ecological merits aside, recent shifts in urban green policy have been increasingly inflected through a technocratic lens. This includes a reluctance to weigh ecological against economic good in favour of elusive win-wins; an emphasis on the services that nature provides rather than intrinsic value; and an underlying logic that sees the urban green as fungible, transferrable and mobile. If much of recent policy represents a shift from preserving valued spaces *for* nature to sustaining those natures that can be usefully inscribed as active labour in the procedures of production and consumption that sustain the city, two logical options follow. We can either decry the enclosure of nature within instrumental technocratic logics, or we can attend to the ways nature might subvert those logics. We conclude by suggesting that meeting the ecological challenges outlined above – namely, a looser organisation of green space with a habitat mosaic of managed, semi-managed and unmanaged, feral spaces at different scales and rates of disturbance – could perhaps be one route to problematising the post-political enclosure of nature in a narrow, instrumental vision wherein its only value is how it serves us. This is because that ecological vision of a shifting mosaic would need a shift in mentality, a move beyond 'sustaining' London's natures, and to ask what kind of natures we want, how they can be fairly shared among humans and other species and an openness to agencies other than those that currently drive governance regimes in London. Ultimately, we would like the effectiveness of ecological policy not to be measured by the resilience of 'ecosystem services', but by other less tangible benefits: the perseverance of some and the emergence of other, new, flourishing species assemblages. This would mean giving the role that ecosystems and their constituent processes and creatures play in the urban metabolism fuller political consideration, not as external limits or as passive resources to sustain 'us', but as active and – potentially – transformative agents.

References

Ackroyd, P. (2000) *London: the biography*, London: Chatto & Windus.

Alexander, S. (2007) 'A new civilization? London surveyed 1928-1940s', *History Workshop Journal*, vol 64, no 64, pp 296-320.

Amati, M. and Yokohari, M. (2006) 'Temporal changes and local variations in the functions of London's green belt', *Landscape and Urban Planning*, vol 75, pp 125-42.

Angold, P.G., Sadler, J.P., Hill, M.O., Pullin, A., Rushton, S., Austin, K., Small, E., Wood, B., Wadsworth, R., Sanderson, R. and Thompson, K. (2006) 'Biodiversity in urban habitat patches', *Science of the Total Environment*, vol 360, pp 196-204.

Baguette, M. and van Dyck, H. (2007) 'Landscape connectivity and animal behavior: functional grain as a key determinant for dispersal', *Landscape Ecology*, vol 22, pp 1117-29.

Bakker, K. (2010) 'The limits of "neoliberal natures": debating green neoliberalism', *Progress in Human Geography*, vol 34, no 6, pp 715-35.

Bender, D.J., Contreras, T.A. and Fahrig, L. (1998) 'Habitat loss and population decline: a meta-analysis of the patch size effect', *Ecology*, vol 79, pp 517-33.

Braun, B. (2008) 'Environmental issues: inventive life', *Progress in Human Geography*, vol 32, no 5, pp 667-79.

Bryant, M.M. (2006) 'Urban landscape conservation and the role of ecological greenways at local and metropolitan scales', *Landscape and Urban Planning*, vol 76, pp 23-44.

Buller, H. (2013) 'Animal geographies I', *Progress in Human Geography*.

Buscher, B., Sullivan, S., Neves, K., Igoe, J. and Brockington, D. (2012) 'Towards a synthesized critique of neoliberal biodiversity conservation', *Capitalism Nature Socialism*, vol 23, no 2, pp 4-30.

Cameron, R.W.F., Blanusa, T., Taylor, J.E., Salisbury, A., Halstead, A.J., Henricot, B. and Thompson, K. (2012) 'The domestic garden – its contribution to urban green infrastructure', *Urban Forestry & Urban Greening*, vol 11, no 2, pp 129-37.

Castree, N. (2008a) 'Neoliberalising nature: processes, effects, and evaluations', *Environment and Planning A*, vol 40, no 1, pp 153-73.

Castree, N. (2008b) 'Neoliberalising nature: the logics of deregulation and reregulation', *Environment and Planning A*, vol 40, no 1, pp 131-52.

Chamberlain, D.E., Cannon, A.R., Toms, M.P., Leech, D.I., Hatchwell, B.J. and Gaston, K.J. (2009) 'Avian productivity in urban landscapes: a review and meta-analysis', *Ibis*, vol 151, no 1, pp 1-18.

Clapson, M. (1998) *Invincible green suburbs: social change and urban dispersal in post-war England*, Manchester: Manchester University Press.

Cook, E.M., Hall, S.J. and Larson, K.L. (2012) 'Residential landscapes as socio-ecological systems: a synthesis of multi-scalar interactions between people and their home environment', *Urban Ecosystems*, vol 15, no 1, pp 19-52.

Davies, Z.G., Fuller, R.A., Loram, A., Irvine, K.N., Sims, V. and Gaston, K.J. (2009) 'A national scale inventory of resource provision for biodiversity within domestic gardens', *Biological Conservation*, vol 142, pp 761-71.

Dawe, G.F.M. (2010) 'Street trees and the urban environment', in I. Douglas, D. Goode, M. Houck and R. Wang (eds) *The Routledge handbook of urban ecology*, London: Routledge, pp 424-49.

Defra (Department for Environment, Food and Rural Affairs) (2011a) *Biodiversity 2020: a strategy for England's wildlife and ecosystem services*, London: The Stationery Office.

Defra (2011b) *The natural choice: securing the value of nature*, London: The Stationery Office.

DETR (Department of the Environment, Transport and the Regions) (2000) *By design: urban design in the planning system: towards better practice*, London: DETR.

Dufour, S. and Piégay, H. (2009) 'From the myth of a lost paradise to targeted river restoration: forget natural references and focus on human benefits', *River Research and Applications*, vol 25, pp 568-81.

Eden, S. and Tunstall, S. (2006) 'Ecological versus social restoration? How urban river restoration challenges but also fails to challenge the science – policy nexus in the United Kingdom', *Environment and Planning C: Government and Policy*, vol 24, no 5, pp 661-80.

Environment Agency (2010) *State of the environment of London for 2010*, London: Greater London Authority, Environment Agency, Natural England and Forestry Commission.

Folke, C., Jansson, A., Larsson, J. and Costanza, R. (1997) 'Ecosystem appropriation by cities', *Ambio*, vol 26, pp 167-72.

Forman, R.T.T. (1996) *Land mosaics: the ecology of landscapes and regions*, Cambridge: Cambridge University Press.

Forman, R.T.T. (2008) *Urban regions: ecology and planning beyond the city*, Cambridge: Cambridge University Press.

Francis, R.A. and Chadwick, M.A. (2013) *Urban ecosystems: understanding the human environment*, Abingdon,: Earthscan from Routledge.

Francis, R.A. and Lorimer, J. (2011) 'Urban reconciliation ecology: the potential of living roofs and walls', *Journal of Environmental Management*, vol 92, no 6, pp 1429-37.

Francis, R.A., Lorimer, J. and Raco, M. (2012) 'Urban ecosystems as "natural" homes for biogeographical boundary crossings', *Transactions of the Institute of British Geographers*, vol 37, pp 183-90.

Fuller, R.A. and Gaston, K.J. (2009) 'The scaling of green space coverage in European cities', *Biology Letters*, vol 5, pp 352-5.

Gill, T. (2011) *Sowing the seeds: re-connecting London's children with nature*, London: London Sustainable Development Commission.

Ginn, F. (2012) 'Dig for victory! New histories of wartime gardening in Britain', *Journal of Historical Geography*, vol 38, no 3, pp 294-305.

GLA (Greater London Authority) (2002) *Connecting with London's nature: the mayor's biodiversity strategy*, London: GLA.

GLA (2011) *The London Plan: Spatial Development Strategy for Greater London*, London: GLA.

GLA (2012) *Green infrastructure and open environments: the All London Green Grid: supplementary planning guidance*, London: GLA.

Gobster, P.H. (2001) 'Visions of nature: conflict and compatibility in urban park restoration', *Landscape and Urban Planning*, vol 56, no 1-2, pp 35-51.

Goddard, M.A., Dougill, A.J. and Benton, T.G. (2010) 'Scaling up from gardens: biodiversity conservation in urban environments', *Trends in Ecology and Evolution*, vol 25, no 2, pp 90-8.

Heynen, N., McCarthy, J., Prudham, S. and Robbins, P. (eds) (2007) *Neoliberal environments: false promises and unnatural consequences*, London and New York: Routledge.

Hilderbrand, R.H., Watts, A.C. and Randle, A.M. (2005) 'The myths of restoration ecology', *Ecology and Society*, vol 10, no 1, art 19.

Hitchings, R. (2007) 'Approaching life in the London garden centre: acquiring entities and providing products', *Environment and Planning A*, vol 39, pp 242-59.

Hodson, M. and Marvin, S (2009) '"Urban ecological security": a new urban paradigm?', *International Journal of Urban and Regional Research*, vol 33, pp 1193-215.

HTA (Horticultural Trades Association) (2013) *Garden retail market analysis 2013*, Reading: HTA.

Ignatieva, M., Stewart, G.H. and Meurk, C. (2011) 'Planning and design of ecological networks in urban areas', *Landscape and Ecological Engineering*, vol 7, pp 17-25.

Jim, C.Y. and Chen, W.Y. (2008) 'Pattern and divergence of tree communities in Taipei's main urban green spaces', *Landscape and Urban Planning*, vol 84, pp 312-23.

Kattwinkel, M., Biedermann, R. and Kleyer, M. (2011) 'Temporary conservation for urban biodiversity', *Biological Conservation*, vol 144, pp 2335-43.

Li, F., Wang, R., Paulussen, J. and Liu, X. (2005) 'Comprehensive concept planning of urban greening based on ecological principles: a case study in Beijing, China', *Landscape and Urban Planning*, vol 72, pp 325-36.

London Wildlife Trust (2011) *London: garden city? From green to grey: observed changes in garden vegetation structure in London, 1998-2008*, London: London Wildlife Trust, Greenspace Information Centre for Greater London, Greater London Authority.

Loram, A., Tratalos, J., Warren, P. and Gaston, K. (2007) 'Urban domestic gardens (X): the extent and structure of the resource in five major cities', *Landscape Ecology*, vol 22, no 4, pp 601-15.

McKay, G. (2011) *Radical gardening: politics, idealism and rebellion in the garden*, London: Frances Lincoln.

Metz, D. and Weigel, L. (2010) *Key findings from recent national opinion research on 'ecosystem services'*, Arlington, VA: The Nature Conservancy.

Neocleous, M. (2013) 'Resisting resilience', *Radical Philosophy*, vol 178, no March/April, pp 2-7.

Perry, T. and Nawaz, R. (2008) 'An investigation into the extent and impacts of hard surfacing of domestic gardens in an area of Leeds, United Kingdom', *Landscape and Urban Planning*, vol 86, no 1, pp 1-13.

Redford, K.H. and Adams, W.M. (2009) 'Payment for ecosystem services and the challenge of saving nature', *Conservation Biology*, vol 23, no 4, pp 785-7.

Schaefer, V. (2009) 'Alien invasions, ecological restoration in cities and the loss of ecological memory', *Restoration Ecology*, vol 17, no 2, pp 171-6.

Shuker, L., Gurnell, A.M. and Raco, M. (2012) 'Some simple tools for communicating the biophysical condition of urban rivers to support decision making in relation to river restoration', *Urban Ecosystems*, vol 15, no 2, pp 389-408.

Spash, C. (2008) 'How much is that ecosystem in the window? The one with the bio-diverse tail', *Environmental Values*, vol, pp 259-84.

Swyngedouw, E. (2011) 'Depoliticized environments: the end of nature, climate change and the post-political condition', *Royal Institute of Philosophy Supplements*, vol 69, pp 253-74.

Tan, K.W. (2006) 'A greenway network for Singapore', *Landscape and Urban Planning*, vol 76, pp 45-66.

Turner, M.G. (1989) 'Landscape ecology: the effect of pattern on process', *Annual Review of Ecology and Systematics*, vol 20, pp 171-97.

Turner, M.G. (2005) 'Landscape ecology: what is the state of the science?', *Annual Review of Ecology, Evolution and Systematics*, vol 36, pp 319-44.

Urbanik, J. (2012) *Placing animals: an introduction to the geography of human-animal relations*, Plymouth: Rowman & Littlefield.

Uy, P.D. and Nakagoshi, N. (2008) 'Application of land suitability analysis and landscape ecology to urban greenspace planning in Hanoi, Vietnam', *Urban Forestry and Urban Greening*, vol 7, pp 25-40.

Whale, H. and Ginn, F. (2014) 'In the absence of sparrows: the decline and conservation of a species', in K. Landman and A. Consulo (eds) *Environment and/as mourning*, Montreal and Kingston: McGill-Queen's University Press.

Wimberly, W.C. (2006) 'Species dynamics in disturbed landscapes: When does a shifting habitat mosaic enhance connectivity?', *Landscape Ecology*, vol 21, no 1, pp 35-46.

Yusoff, K. (2011) 'The valuation of nature: *The natural choice* White Paper', *Radical Philosophy*, vol 170, pp 2-7.

Part 5

POSTSCRIPT

Beyond urban sustainability and urban resilience: towards a socially just future for London

Loretta Lees and Rob Imrie

With risks ranging from severe weather and flooding, to industrial action, pandemic flu and terrorism, there is never a dull day in the London Resilience Team! The best part of our job? Knowing we're doing our bit to help make London a safer, and more resilient city. (London Resilience Team, 2012, p 1)

The reason London is so resilient is because it adapts. It innovates. It invests. It stays modern. It remains at the top of its game. It treats the changing shape of the world economy as an opportunity, not a threat. Let us rejoice in that fact and challenge the doomsters who keep predicting the end of everything. (Fraser, 2012, p 1)

In the same way that the term 'urban renaissance' became overshadowed by the catchword 'urban sustainability', it now seems that urban sustainability is going out of fashion and 'urban resilience' is the new buzzword for cities around the world, including London (see Cochrane, 2006, p 689). We are in the midst of a resilience turn, and urban sustainability may rapidly be reaching the end of its shelf life, because it is being challenged, from without, and from within. A growing number of academics, social innovators, community leaders, policy makers, non-governmental organisations (NGOs), philanthropists and governments are touting a supposedly new idea, resilience – how to help vulnerable people, organisations and systems persist amidst unforeseeable disruptions. Ash Amin (2012) describes urban resilience as a new culture of risk management that is accompanied by a return to public narratives about apocalyptic futures.[1] The Mayor of London (GLA, 2011, p 5) has suggested that creating a resilient London is the way forward:

We have all seen the disaster movies, in which a sprawling modern metropolis is brought to its knees by a global-warming induced deluge of Biblical proportions, or plunged into a glacial Ice Age of permanent winter. However, Hollywood hyperbole aside, London's climate is changing. We must take steps now to ensure the city is prepared for the future. Not just to avert environmental disaster but also to preserve and enhance our quality of life and prosperity for generations to come.

Resilience is not only a new buzzword in government, policy and academic circles, but also in the business world. For example, the City of London has a Resilience Forum that plans resilience for businesses in the Square Mile. Likewise, KPMG, a major investment and financial service corporation, has, like many global companies, a 'business reliance' team that covers four categories relating to business activity, technology, crisis management and financial resilience.[2]

Whereas urban sustainability aims to put the city back into balance, urban resilience looks for ways to manage an unbalanced city. Urban resilience is often limited to natural hazards, risk reduction, climate change and developing more effective responses to them, but it also includes strategies to prevent and recover from urban decline, and to cope with new social and economic challenges. It is viewed, by many policy makers, as more dynamic than urban sustainability, and to be better able to cope with new challenges. The term 'resilience' is attractive because it refers to something positive and active: to be able to withstand hardship and disturbance, to recover from disaster and destruction, to be able to prepare for the unforeseen and to deal with risks in an appropriate way. But it is our contention that urban resilience is just another term for urban sustainability, and that neither is helping London move towards being the kind of city that we, and the contributors in this book, would like it to be.

Resilience has a long history in engineering science, but its most influential origin is ecology (see Holling, 2001). Resilience suggests that humans and nature are strongly interrelated and should be conceived of as one 'social-ecological' system, and that complex systems, like cities, are in constant flux, with feedback loops across time and space (Holling, 2001; Alberti et al, 2003). A key feature of complex adaptive systems is that they can settle into stability, for example, a financial market can sit on a housing bubble or sink into a basin of recession. But at the scale of the city, resilience is merely an approach to meeting the challenges of sustainable development. Like sustainability, resilience is a conservative concept; both are about keeping systems as they are, avoiding change and transformation, returning to (protecting and reinforcing) the status quo or merely treading water. It is our contention that we need different concepts to work with. We need a new label to attach to the future of cities like London, one that encompasses a transformative social justice agenda that moves things well beyond the status quo. We do not want London to bounce back (resilience is from the Latin *resilire*, 'to leap back'), but to bounce forwards.

As such we need a change of narrative, we need to move away from the modernist ideas of social-ecological theory. We need urban transformation, not sustainability, as it exists in neoliberal urban policies about urban renaissance, or resilience, for it is our contention that the status quo is not working for London, and that we need policy and action that will change the system itself, creating something fundamentally new. 'Resilience thinking' is starting to shape how urban planners in big cities like London think about updating antiquated infrastructures to withstand unanticipated shocks such as flooding, pandemics, terrorism or energy shortages. But the focus on these significant, in the future, possibly one-off, shocks or disasters, is to the detriment of a focus on the everyday quality of life and social justice for Londoners. London will soon be a 'majority rich city', the first in the UK; it is already approaching 'an embarras de richesses in her central area', as Ruth Glass (1964, p 141) predicted.

The map of gentrification in *The Economist* (2013), developed by a real estate analyst at Savills, shows that London is turning inside out, with affluent young professionals staying in the inner city and people who cannot afford inner London property prices being pushed to the outer suburbs. While house prices and rents in the inner city have soared, places that have gone downmarket include the old Metroland suburbs from the 1920s and 1930s, stretching west of Acton and Willesden, and east around Ilford and environs. Statistically, let alone socially, this is not a good thing. What is worrying is that the moral and ethical arguments about social diversity have all but disappeared in policy discourses about London, as 'resilience' has overtaken 'sustainability' (see Lees et al, 2011). Indeed, these tensions surfaced in the Examination in Public (EiP) of the 2009 draft London Plan, now the 2011 London Plan, when hearings from those affected, and evidence from those researching, was received on the adverse effects of property-led regeneration on London's communities, from displacement to social immobility.[3]

Like urban sustainability, urban resilience is an ambiguous, even ambivalent, term that is useful for politicians because it allows for ideological flexibility (that is, it fits with both the Left and the Right and in-between). In fact, because it can mean all things to all people, pinning down its actual meaning is difficult. In many ways it is a new brand, 'free-floating signifier', disconnected from a fixed meaning and thus capable of attaching itself to any relevant agenda. It is the perfect neoliberal concept (Peck, 2010). The emerging urban resilience discourse supposedly offers a new lexicon, a new repertoire of tools, to make sense of, and attend to, the challenges affecting urban areas like London. It is an inherently geographical metaphor that refers to resilience *in* cities, for example, London, and the resilience *of* cities – at the scale of a system of cities tied to each other through trade, migration and flows of resources, that sustain the flow of energy, matter and information among the cities (see Batty, 2008). Resilience *in* cities has been the main preoccupation of urban ecologists, and the focus is on urban form and land use patterns on the one hand, and local and spatial ecological processes on the other (Francis et al, 2013). The stakeholders are urban planners, housing organisations and urban social movements. Resilience *of* cities tends to focus on technical infrastructures such as water, electricity, sewage, waste disposal and telecommunications.

The glocal linkages between the scale of the city and the scale of systems of cities are complex, and to understand them requires extensive conceptual and empirical research. Such research, and, subsequently, how we come to know the city, is increasingly through 'big data', especially digital data. These data have real-time availability, providing a wide range of information about cities, their physical infrastructure, services and interactions between people. Those with a techno-optimism are shaping digital 'big data' gathering, a process influenced, largely, by corporations. This makes it difficult to challenge the process from a progressive urbanist standpoint. What we know about urban life is becoming increasingly controlled and politicised by corporate data providers. This is worrying, and the move towards 'urban resilience' is escalating this – resilience theorists argue that we need smarter cities that use 'big data' to improve infrastructure, planning, management and human services.[4] The goal is to make cities more sustainable, desirable and liveable. For example, the Greater London Authority (GLA) is working with the European Union (EU) to develop the London Datastore to help facilitate the building of a 'smarter' London. The argument is that because there was not enough information in the past, we were not able to build cities that were adapted to the needs of their citizens. But as any good social scientist can tell you, more data are not 'better data', and 'big data' are not necessarily more reliable, or insightful, than 'small data'.

Moreover, as Davoudi (2012, p 306) has argued with respect to urban resilience: 'in applying an ecologically rooted concept to the social setting, we need to tread carefully and ensure that in trying to understand society through the lens of ecology, we do not lose the insights from critical social science.' Resilience thinking assumes that 'socio–ecological' categories exist naturally when in fact, many are socially constructed. Porter and Davoudi (2012, p 333) develop this insight in noting that resilience thinking:

> … normalises phenomena as if they are inevitable, and depoliticise(s) the value choices underpinning courses of human intervention (which) should strike a highly cautionary note. As the reframing of planning through a resilience lens gains currency, it is paramount that we continue asking critical questions about its potential depoliticisation of the planning field.

London, like other cities worldwide, needs much more debate exploring the meaning of sustainability and resilience in its urban context, and how it might contribute to glocal sustainability and resilience through transformative actions that redefine its role as a major world city, both inside and outside its city boundaries. Some of the most obvious ways to become more resilient are not sustainable. As Fry (2011, p 23) states, the dominance of an economic paradigm means that unsustainable practices are intrinsic to the 'modernised human being'. From an urban resilience perspective, urban governance can be thought of as purposeful collective action among state, private and civil society stakeholders, either to sustain or improve a certain regime. Any attempt to trigger a transition to a more preferable regime is referred to as transformative capacity. It is our contention that the urban governance of London needs to build transformative capacity in order to change. It can only do this by recognising that planning and governance are always entangled in politics.

Sustainability discourse has more to offer than resilience discourse, but in reality, sustainable development is not easily attainable, and, as critical civil society organisations in London point out, it has not lived up to its promises. The case of what Southwark Notes Archive Group (SNAG) has called 'Stratagate' demonstrates the symbolic failure of sustainability in London, or what sustainability means in reality beyond the rhetoric.[5] 'Stratagate' refers to the redevelopment of the Heygate Estate and Strata Tower in Elephant & Castle, Southwark (see Chapter Eight, this volume). In October 2013 the Heygate Estate developer, Lend Lease, was awarded participant status in Bill Clinton's Global Climate Initiative for reducing operational emissions, in other words, reducing day-to-day C02 emissions from homes and businesses.[6] In fact, Bill Clinton had selected the Elephant & Castle regeneration programme back in 2009 to be part of the Climate Positive Development Program of the Clinton Climate Initiative. In 2012 he praised the environmental credentials of the Elephant & Castle regeneration in a fundraising speech for the Clinton Foundation at the Old Vic Tunnels in Waterloo:

> Here in Southwark we have a project that we are working on with the city of London that will be a zero-emission or carbon-positive development – one of two in London.... If it happens, people will come from all over the UK to see how it happened and whether they could do it.... They won't be paying utility bills – they will be making money which will put more people to work. (London Community website, 2012)

The Clinton Climate Initiative recognises the Elephant & Castle regeneration as one of 16 founding projects of the Climate Positive Development Program that will support the development of large-scale urban projects that demonstrate cities can grow in ways that are 'climate positive'. It is a model of urban sustainability to be copied around the world. But such praise is deeply problematic in the face of alternative evidence, and the reality of what has happened in the building of the Strata Tower and is likely to happen in the regeneration of the Heygate Estate. At the Public Inquiry into the Compulsory Purchase Orders on the Heygate Estate, in February 2013, testimonies showed that if Lend Lease's redevelopment of the Heygate Estate was to go ahead, it would remove 450 large and thriving trees, mostly London plane trees, and disrupt wildlife habitat for birds. It also pointed out that the zero carbon development of the Heygate Estate, with a zero increase in carbon emissions, was a fallacy because its calculations were based on operative carbon emission forecasts alone, and ignored the 40,000–45,000 tonnes of embodied CO_2 in the existing buildings (see Heygate Leaseholders Group, 2012). It was noted that:

> The carbon debt incurred by the original demolition and rebuild of the Heygate area 35 years ago, will remain in the atmosphere for a further 65 years. The huge carbon debt proposed for yet another comprehensive demolition and rebuild will remain in the atmosphere for another 100 years. This seriously compromises both the Government's CO_2 reduction targets and Bill Clinton's praise for the scheme as "carbon positive sustainable growth". (http://betterelephant.org/Environmental)

What has also become apparent is that Lend Lease has pulled back significantly from their sustainable plan – the plan that attracted Clinton's attention included a multi-utilities services company that would have produced 100 per cent renewable energy on site, with zero carbon emissions, and possibly more than was needed, making it carbon positive. This has been dropped in the new plans for the redevelopment, and Lend Lease is planning to buy in bio-methane gas from off-site producers instead. Is this an example of greenwashing, perhaps?

These developments have not fulfilled their environmental sustainability commitments, nor have they addressed significant concerns about creating stable, socially sustainable communities (see Imrie, 2007). Sustainability discourses rarely do what they say they will. The regeneration of the Heygate Estate has displaced a significant community of council tenants and leaseholders (see the displacement maps in Lees et al, 2013). As commentators warn: '… if the future involves the redevelopment of London's long-protected social housing, then the politics of gentrification in London could eventually become quite tetchy' (*The Economist*, 2013, p 1). The idea of the Strata Tower was also sold to the local community, especially Heygate council tenants and leaseholders, as mixed income – a third of the flats were to be affordable (see Chapter Eight, this volume). Construction has now started on another new residential tower on the site of the old Elephant & Castle leisure centre, One the Elephant. This has no affordable housing, and many of its luxury flats have been sold off-plan to foreign investors, or a new cadre of super-rich, primarily from Russia, China and Middle Eastern countries, who have pushed up London property values and are displacing longer-standing communities.

This is not just, fair or humane, and it can be argued that property in the capital has become a global reserve currency for the new super-rich, while contributing to the opening up of new socio-spatial inequalities. The socially unjust developments at Elephant & Castle, and indeed those yet to come, also follow the Mayor of London's idea about creating small-scale, highly local and interpersonal ways of living. As Mayor Boris Johnson (GLA, 2011, p 5) has said: 'My ambition is to put the village back into the city. What I mean by this is that we can improve the quality of life for Londoners by ensuring that we focus our efforts on delivering a cleaner and greener city with stronger and safer communities through our work to make the city more sustainable and preserving its prosperity for decades to come.' In many ways this is an extension of the 'gentrifiers charter'; it is gentrification with a green or environmental spin, a new take on the rustic desires of middle-class gentrifiers to live in leafy villages in the inner city (Lees, 2003).

In London, discourses of environmental (zero carbon) and social sustainability (mixed communities) are linked to economic, health and even educational sustainability. But the fact is that the entwining of these sustainability discourses with market capitalism may mean the displacement of traditional systems of reciprocity and collective welfare. There is no guarantee that the wellbeing of individual Londoners will be ensured; only that the 'productive utility' of the majority will be maximised. Sustainable London, as it stands, is a market-oriented worldview that cannot be separated from the consumerist lifestyle that accompanies it. Most disturbingly, from a sustainability standpoint, it has instigated a cycle of increasing material wealth that is premised on the escalation of consumption and the creation of an increasingly unequal city (Norgaard, 1994; Sachs, 1999). The fact is that both sustainability and resilience discourses in London, like elsewhere, are uncritically modern. Through them, the state acts as an agent for the normalisation and repression of minority groups (Latouche, 1993; Luke, 2005). In addition, sustainability and resilience discourses extend the reach of the 'patriarchal project' of techno-science and industrialism (Shiva, 1989). It is time to move beyond these modernist ideas about the future of London.

This critique of urban resilience and urban sustainability suggests that the political questions of power, institutions and the deeply unequal distribution of resources in London should be taken seriously in any reframing of a new plan for London. It makes the case for a materialist analysis of urbanism to be (re)centred within academic and policy debates. It underlines the need to link academic knowledges, especially critical urban theory, to real practical knowledges of urbanism as part of social action. In so doing, we should draw on social justice concepts in our support for rights to the city (Marcuse, 2009; Minton, 2012). Such concepts revolve around notions of care and inclusion, recognition of one's dependence within the world, and, in Sayer's (2011, p 226) terms, requiring one 'to accept and honour responsibilities of care and for the public good.' These ideas are embedded in Fell's (2012) persuasive outline of an alternative, progressive way of reconceiving London's future, based, in part, on a context of care, in which a flourishing and inclusive society depends on significantly different, dematerialised relationships emerging to those shaping contemporary social and political agendas (see Box 15.1).

For Fell (2102), a sustainable future for London means structural economic change and questioning the logics of development and modernisation. It should not mean business-as-usual development, which is not able to respond to, or even recognise as part of its modus operandum, the complexities of creating a caring, and nurturing, place for all to live. Instead, appropriate, people-sensitised approaches to London's sustainability ought to include guarantees of individuals' welfare, the provision of good quality social housing, public transport, education and health and the development of a caring, collective future for Londoners rather than one mired in so-called preparedness and individualism. But this is

Box 15.1: A sustainable future for London

'I want to suggest that there is available to us a much more sustainable London in 2062: and a much less sustainable one; and which one we end up with will be, in large part, a function of the way in which a variety of norms pan out and interact. Here are three examples:

- **Masculine/feminine** – London is presently a macho city, characterised by needlessly tall buildings, aggressive corporate behaviour, narcissistic decision-making and damagingly ruthless individualism. Left unchecked, these behaviours will continue to generate extreme levels of social inequality, the unrestrained consumption of finite physical resources and an environment of profound psychological stress for the majority of London's citizens. A more feminine city – attending to notions of care, concern, inclusion, small-scale production and consumption – would, by contrast, inherently counter such trends. A more sustainable London in 2062 would come about not through direct measures to – say – reduce CO_2 emissions but, instead, indirectly and more powerfully through the development of a greater ethic of care.

- **Walled/open** – a great deal of London's economic life currently happens behind walls. Corporate decision-making is opaque: wealthy citizens immunise themselves from their 'neighbours' by living in gated communities; political processes are dominated by lobbyists and careerists conversing in inaccessible settings. A London of 2062 in which these barriers persist would probably function as a city, but it could not possibly be described as sustainable. A sustainable London would be one in which inclusion and participation was ordinary, in which openness and transparency was normal. The inevitable consequence of a more open London would be reduced injustice, greater environmental sensitivity and a more balanced economy. Such outcomes would emerge organically from the change in an underlying logic and would not need to be 'engineered' through interventions from 'the top'.

- **Material/de-material** – the London of 2012 remains a citadel to consumer-led capitalism, even in the teeth of recession. Londoners, and the tens of thousands of tourists that visit the city, go shopping as if the world is going to end (!) and spend stupendous amounts of money on largely pointless products. It is conceivable that this could continue and that a London of 2062 will be wealthy enough to protect itself from the reality that will by then have come about, in which the effects of climate change will have become severe and in which a great many natural resources are either seriously depleted or have already vanished. But better, surely, to begin the process of weaning ourselves off our addictions, and to de-materialise our economy and our lifestyles. Let's learn rather than spend; let's sing rather than fly; let's stop with all the stuff'.

Source: Fell (2012)

not a return to the tried remedies of the postwar welfare state settlement (see Hall et al, 2013, p 18). It necessitates a different social contract for London – one which is socially distributive in nature, and based on an acceptance of higher taxes (council, business, wealth) to nurture and enhance the lives of *all* Londoners, promoting a city for the many, not just the few (Amin et al, 2000).

Such observations are usually met with cynicism and scepticism by those who say that nothing much can be done to change the prevalent political cultures and times that we live in. We would argue, however, like most authors in this book, that there is much to be lost by not recognising, and seeking to challenge, the market developmental logics that dominate the shaping of sustainable development, a term that is, like that of the emergent notion of resilience, constitutive, broadly, of a socio-political culture that is anathema to progressive social change. Here, the political-culture frustrates alternative opportunities and directions for social and political action, such as stymieing the decentralisation of social and economic activity, and it reduces the scope for people in local communities to create contexts for mutual self-determination. Lefebvre's (1991) call for the 'right to the city', for social justice and a caring, humane culture, is more appropriate than ever, and it provides a challenge to London's government to change the modernist logic shaping contemporary discourses of sustainability to something else that can make the city a more equal and just place.

We recognise that Lefebvre wrote about the 'right to the city' more than 40 years ago, and that the socio-spatial processes shaping cities, everywhere, have changed significantly in a context of 'planetary urbanisation' (Merrifield, 2013). Many individuals and groups, such as some of London's council tenants, are sceptical about the 'right to the city' movement as led by a middle-class intelligentsia and not for them. Some are critical of the 'right to the city' in that its call for the socio-institutionalisation of rights has led to little more than the assimilation of citizens into a rights and responsibilities agenda, and the propagation of new ways of marketising urban development (see Mayer, 2009; de Souza, 2010). There is also the sense that whatever one would hope for, that it cannot be achieved outside of the capitalist system, or that there is no real alternative to the status quo. Human history shows this to be false, and the major challenge to assure London's sustainable future is the politicisation of sustainable development discourse, and resistance to the (re)capitalisation of land and property.

Notes

[1] This is not a new argument. See Harvey (1999) on crisis management as a restructured scalar architecture of the state.

[2] KMPG describe the four areas of company resilience as: 'Business Continuity – Allowing people to carry on during disruption, getting on with their work; Technology Resilience – Protecting critical IT services, keeping services running when it matters; Crisis Management – Knowing how to cope when the unexpected happens; and Financial Resilience – Stress testing your financial preparedness' (www.kpmg.com/uk/en/services/advisory/management-consulting/pages/business-resilience.aspx).

[3] Some examples of the problematic impacts of property-led regeneration can be heard by listening to sound recording at http://ucljustspace.wordpress.com/eip-recordings; see also Chapter Three, this volume.

[4] See, for example, www.meetup.com/big-data-london

[5] For further details on 'Stratagate', see http://southwarknotes.wordpress.com/our-longer-writings/a-different-strata

[6] See also www.35percent.org

References

Alberti, M., Marzluff, J., Shulenberger, E., Bradley, G., Ryan, C. and Zumbrunnen, C. (2003) 'Integrating humans into ecology: opportunities and challenges for studying urban ecosystems', *BioScience*, vol 53, pp 1169-79.

Amin, A. (2012) *Land of strangers*, Chichester: John Wiley & Sons.

Amin, A., Massey, D. and Thrift, N. (2000) *Cities for the many, not the few*, Bristol: Policy Press.

Batty, M. (2008) 'How tall can we go? How compact can we get? The real questions of urban sustainability', *Environment and Planning B*, vol 35, no 1, pp 1-2.

Cochrane, A. (2006) 'Devolving the heartland: making up a new social policy for the "South East"', *Critical Social Policy*, vol 26, no 3, pp 685-96.

Davoudi, S. (2012) 'Resilience: a bridging concept or a dead end?', *Planning Theory & Practice*, vol 13, no 2, pp 299-333.

de Souza, M. (2010) 'Which right to which city? In defence of political-strategic clarity', *Interface*, vol 2, no 1, pp 315-33.

Economist, The (2013), 'Mapping gentrification, the great inversion', 9 September (www.economist.com/blogs/blighty/2013/09/mapping-gentrification).

Fell, D. (2012) 'London 2062: an economist dreams of a sustainable city' (www.futureoflondon.org.uk/2012/08/30/london-2062-an-economist-dreams-of-a-sustainable-city).

Francis, R., Lorimer, J. and Raco, M. (2013) 'What is special about urban ecologies?', *Transactions of the Institute of British Geographers*, vol 38, no 4, pp 682-4.

Fraser, S. (2012) 'Resilient London stays at the top by adapting', *City A.M.* (www.cityam.com/article/resilient-london-stays-top-adapting).

Fry, T. (2011) *Design as politics*, Oxford: Berg.

Glass, R. (1964) 'Introduction: aspects of change', in Centre for Urban Studies (ed) *London: aspects of change*, London: MacKibbon & Kee, pp xiii-xlii.

GLA (Greater London Authority) (2011) *Managing risk and increasing resilience: the Mayor's climate change adaptation strategy*, London: GLA.

Hall, S., Massey, D. and Rustin, M. (2013) 'After neo-liberalism: analysing the present', in S. Hall, D. Massey and M. Rustin (eds) 'After neoliberalism? The Kilburn manifesto', *Soundings: A Journal of Politics and Culture*, pp 3-19.

Harvey, D. (1999) *The limits to capital*, London: Verso.

Heygate Leaseholders Group (2012) *Compulsory Purchase Order, statement of case* (http://betterelephant.org/images/HeygateCPOStatementOfCaseFinal.pdf).

Holling, C.S. (2001) 'Understanding the complexity of economic, ecological, and social systems', *Ecosystems*, vol 4, pp 390–405.

Imrie, R. (2007) 'Olympiad dreams of the urban renaissance', *Publication of the Modern Language Association of America*, vol 122, no 1, pp 310-15.

Latouche, S. (1993) *In the wake of the affluent society: an exploration of post-development*, London: Zed Books.

Lees, L. (2003) 'Visions of "urban renaissance": the Urban Task Force report and the Urban White Paper', in R. Imrie and M. Raco (eds) *Urban renaissance? New Labour, community and urban policy*, Bristol: Policy Press, pp 61–82.

Lees, L., Butler, T, and Bridge, G. (2011) 'Introduction: gentrification, social mix/ing and mixed communities', in G. Bridge, T. Butler and L. Lees (eds) *Mixed communities: gentrification by stealth?*, Bristol: Policy Press, pp 1–16.

Lees, L., Just Space, LTF (London Tenants Federation) and SNAG (Southwark Notes Archive Group) (2013) 'The social cleansing of council estates in London', in B. Campkin and L. Hirst (eds) *Urban Pamphleteer #2, 'London: regeneration realities'*, London: UCL Urban Lab, pp 6–10.

Lefebvre, H. (1991) *The production of space*, Chichester: Wiley.

London Community Website (2012) 'Bill Clinton hails Elephant & Castle regeneration in Old Vic Tunnels' (www.london-se1.co.uk/news/view/6032).

London Resilience Team (2012) 'Introducing … the London Resilience Team' (www.london.gov.uk/mayor-assembly/mayor/london-resilience/london-prepared-blog/2012/10/introducingthe-london-resilience-team).

Luke, T. (2005) 'Neither sustainable nor development: reconsidering sustainability in development', *Sustainable Development*, vol 13, pp 228-38.

Marcuse, P. (2009) 'From critical urban theory to the right to the city', *CITY*, vol 13, pp 2-3.

Mayer, M. (2009) 'The "right to the city" in the context of shifting motos of urban social movements', *City*, vol 13, no 2-3, pp 362-74.

Merrifield, A. (2013) *The politics of encounter: urban theory and protest under planetary urbanization*, Athens, GA: The University of Georgia Press.

Minton, A. (2012) *Ground control: fear and happiness in the twenty-first-century city* (2nd edn), Harmondsworth: Penguin.

Norgaard, R. (1994) *Development betrayed – the end of progress and a co-evolutionary revisioning of the future*, New York: Routledge.

Peck, J. (2010) *Constructions of neoliberal reason*, Oxford: Oxford University Press.

Porter, L. and Davoudi, S. (2012) 'The politics of resilience for planning: a cautionary note', *Planning Theory & Practice*, vol 13, no 2, pp 299-333.

Sachs, W. (1999) *Planet dialectics: explorations in environment and development*, London: Zed Books.

Sayer, A. (2011) *Why things matter to people*, Cambridge: Cambridge University Press.

Shiva, V. (1989) *Staying alive: women, ecology, and development*, London: Zed Books.

Index

Page references for tables and figures are in *italics*; those for notes are followed by n